BORN TRANSLATED

Literature Now

LITERATURE NOW

Matthew Hart, David James,
and Rebecca L. Walkowitz, Series Editors

Literature Now offers a distinct vision of late twentieth-
and early twenty-first-century literary culture. Addressing
contemporary literature and the ways we understand its
meaning, the series includes books that are comparative
and transnational in scope as well as those that focus on
national and regional literary cultures.

Caren Irr, *Toward the Geopolitical Novel: U.S. Fiction in the
     Twenty-First Century*
Heather Houser, *Ecosickness in Contemporary U.S. Fiction:
     Environment and Affect*
Mrinalini Chakravorty, *In Stereotype: South Asia in the Global
     Literary Imaginary*
Héctor Hoyos, *Beyond Bolaño: The Global Latin American Novel*

Rebecca L. Walkowitz

BORN TRANSLATED

The Contemporary Novel
in an Age of
World Literature

COLUMBIA UNIVERSITY PRESS

NEW YORK

Columbia University Press
Publishers Since 1893
New York   Chichester, West Sussex
Copyright © 2015 Columbia University Press
Paperback edition, 2017

Portions of the Introduction and chapter 1 previously appeared under the title "Comparison Literature," in *New Literary History* 40, no. 3, pp. 567–82. Copyright 2009, *New Literary History*; reprinted by permission of Johns Hopkins University Press. An earlier version of chapter 2 previously appeared under the title of "Unimaginable Largeness: Kazuo Ishiguro, Translation, and the New World Literature," in *Novel* 40, no. 3, pp. 216–39. Copyright 2007, *Novel*; reprinted by permission of Duke University Press. A portion of chapter 3 previously appeared under the title "The Location of Literature: The Transnational Book and the Migrant Writer," in *Contemporary Literature* 47, no. 4, pp. 527–45. Copyright 2007, *Contemporary Literature*; reprinted by permission of the University of Wisconsin Press. Chapter 3 also includes material that appeared under the title "Building Character," in the online review *Public Books* (March 2012). An earlier version of chapter 5 previously appeared under the title of "Close Reading in an Age of Global Writing," in *Modern Language Quarterly* 74, no. 2, pp. 171–95. Copyright 2013, *Modern Language Quarterly*; reprinted by permission of Duke University Press.

Library of Congress Cataloging-in-Publication Data
Walkowitz, Rebecca L., 1970–
Born translated : the contemporary novel in an age of world literature /
Rebecca L. Walkowitz.
pages   cm. — (Literature now)
Includes bibliographical references and index.
ISBN 978-0-231-16594-5 (cloth : alk. paper)—ISBN 978-0-231-16595-2 (pbk. : alk. paper)—ISBN 978-0-231-53945-6 (e-book)
1. Literature—Translations—History and criticism. 2. Fiction—Translations—History and criticism. 3. Translating and interpreting. I. Title.

PN241.W35 2015
418'.04—dc23   2014036138

COVER DESIGN: Diane Luger

For Henry and Lucy

CONTENTS

Acknowledgments   *ix*

INTRODUCTION: THEORY OF WORLD LITERATURE NOW   1

1   CLOSE READING AT A DISTANCE   49

2   THE SERIES, THE LIST, AND THE CLONE   93

3   SAMPLING, COLLATING, AND COUNTING   121

4   THIS IS NOT YOUR LANGUAGE   163

5   BORN TRANSLATED AND BORN DIGITAL   203

EPILOGUE: MULTIPLES   235

Notes   *247*

Bibliography   *291*

Index   *309*

ACKNOWLEDGMENTS

I **AM DELIGHTED** to be able to thank the many individuals and collectives that helped me research and write this book. Funding from the Center for European Studies, the Graduate School, and the Vilas Trust at the University of Wisconsin–Madison was vital to the development of the project. Most of the chapters were written with the generous support of the National Humanities Center, where I held the Hurford Family Fellowship in 2010–2011, and the Radcliffe Institute for Advanced Study at Harvard, where I held the Walter Jackson Bate Fellowship in World Literature in 2012–2013. I am also grateful for a year-long sabbatical awarded by Rutgers University, which allowed me to complete the manuscript in 2013–2014.

I want to acknowledge, with profound thanks, my colleagues at Wisconsin and Rutgers, who have supported my work on campus and my work away from campus in equal measure. I am also very grateful to the staff and administration of the National Humanities Center and the Radcliffe Institute for nourishing academic research in the humanities, and for creating such stimulating and warm environments for thinking and writing. My sincere thanks to my fellow fellows on both occasions, especially Daisy Hay, Katherine Ibbett, Margot Livesey, Feryal Özel, Renée Poznanski, Eliza Richards, Douglas Rogers, and Hilary

Schor, whose rare accomplishments and good cheer made me want to think harder and write better.

An enormous number of readers and listeners have enriched this project in small and large ways. Several dear friends and colleagues were willing to talk to me about translation and world literature on many, many occasions, and their readings of multiple chapters and parts of chapters have been invaluable. It gives me great pleasure to thank Amanda Claybaugh, Lee Edelman, Susan Stanford Friedman, Eric Hayot, Caroline Levine, Joseph Litvak, Sharon Marcus, Martin Puchner, Gayle Rogers, and Henry Turner. I am deeply grateful for their friendship and their intellectual generosity. Jed Esty, John Marx, and Paul Saint-Amour have been loyal comrades in the fields of contemporary literature, modernism, and the anglophone novel. At conferences and colloquia far and wide, they have asked probing as well as practical questions. My thanks to them for reminding me to think about the delivery of the argument as well as the argument.

Timely suggestions have also come from Nancy Armstrong, Timothy Bewes, Christopher Bush, Sarah Cole, Guillermina De Ferrari, Marianne DeKoven, Vinay Dharwadker, Rita Felski, Lynn Festa, Lisa Fluet, Marjorie Garber, Jane Gallop, Sara Guyer, Matthew Hart, Gil Harris, Nico Israel, John Kucich, David Kurnick, David James, Priya Joshi, Michael LeMahieu, Jacques Lezra, Pericles Lewis, Cliff Mak, Venkat Mani, Jeffrey Masten, Meredith McGill, Madhavi Menon, D. A. Miller, Monica Miller, Mario Ortiz-Robles, Andrew Parker, Jessica Pressman, Leah Price, Eileen Reeves, Effie Rentzou, Kelly Rich, Bruce Robbins, Victoria Rosner, Dianne Sadoff, Jonah Siegel, Scott Straus, Philip Tsang, Stephen Twilley, Aarthi Vadde, Judith Vichniac, Christy Wampole, Susanne Wofford, and Carolyn Williams. For enriching and testing my examples, my thanks to everyone, and also to the readers, hosts, and audiences at the institutions at which I presented my work in progress. I also want to thank the two anonymous readers solicited by Columbia University Press. Many aspects of the book's argument were improved and refined substantially in response to their exceptionally detailed reports.

Special thanks is due to my coeditors at Literature Now, Matthew Hart and David James, who have been great collaborators and keen supporters of this project. Philip Leventhal at Columbia University

Press has expertly and warmly led the project through every stage, and I am very grateful to him for his support of my work. I am also very glad to thank Whitney Johnson for helping me navigate the world of copyright permissions, and Patti Bower and Marisa Pagano for editing and marketing my book on behalf of the Press. Several research assistants and former students have located books, gathered statistics, and translated editions over the years, including Thom Dancer, Octavio Gonzalez, Taryn Okuma, Tarina Quarishi, Jennifer Raterman, and Nami Shin. My sincere thanks to them for their hard work, their suggestions, and their patience.

I am grateful, as always, to my parents, Daniel and Judith Walkowitz, for their love and intellectual example, and to my extended family, Robert Oaks, Sarah Turner, Harriet Turner, Jamie Zelermyer, Karen Zelermyer, and Sarah Zelermyer-Diaz. This book is dedicated to Henry, with whom it is a joy to share so many projects, and to our daughter Lucy, who is a pleasure to acknowledge at every opportunity.

BORN TRANSLATED

INTRODUCTION

Theory of World Literature Now

*Theresa would read the originals and I would read
the translations and the translations would
become the originals as we read.*

—Ben Lerner, *Leaving the Atocha Station*

THE LOCATION OF LITERATURE

There is nothing easier and nothing more contemporary than translation. Nothing easier because all you have to do is press that *translate* button at the top of your Internet browser. *Go ahead. Appuyez dès maintenant.* There's nothing more contemporary because Google and Google Translate seem to go hand in hand. It's hard to imagine the immediate gratifications of the digital age without the immediate gratifications of digital translation: new words, in a new language, at your service. Translation saturates our everyday culture of reading, writing, and viewing. Whether you're searching the Internet or streaming a video on Netflix, languages seem to be readily available and more or less interchangeable. Films and books, too, are saturated by translation, and indeed the lines between established and emergent media are not so clear. Consider that many books are released—or as we say, delivered—not only in print, as clothbound or paperback editions, but also in electronic files as DVD, MP3, or Kindle editions.[1] Pages can be heard or swiped as well as turned, and expanding formats redouble the impression of proliferating originals, even in a single language.[2]

But many books do not appear at first only in a single language. Instead, they appear simultaneously or nearly simultaneously in multiple languages. They start as world literature. Of course, long before the twenty-first century there were literary works that traveled from their first language into multiple languages, geographies, and national editions. Yet these travels were relatively slow and initially confined to regional distribution. Take several well-known examples. The international bestseller *Don Quixote*, famous for its exceptionally fast absorption into many language systems, took fifty-one years, from 1605 to 1656, to find its way from Spanish into five national languages; and it was only in 1769 that the novel was published outside of Western Europe.[3] *The Pilgrim's Progress*, first published in 1678, has been translated from English into more than two hundred languages, including eighty African languages, but it began its migration beyond Europe and the North Atlantic in 1835.[4] *The Communist Manifesto*'s Swedish, English, Russian, Serbian, and French editions followed the 1848 German edition within a speedy twenty-four years; yet the first edition printed in a non-European language was the Japanese translation, published in 1904.[5] Many of the most popular novels of the eighteenth and nineteenth centuries, published before the era of robust international copyright, were translated within a few weeks or months, sometimes appearing in competing editions in the same language.[6] However, those novels generally circulated within Europe. Daniel Defoe's *Robinson Crusoe*, one of the most successful novels of the early eighteenth century, was published in English in 1719 and by the end of 1720 had appeared in German, French, and Dutch.[7] But it arrived in Japanese, translated through a Dutch edition, in 1857.[8]

The translation and circulation of literature today is historically unprecedented once we consider how quickly books enter various national markets, small and large, across several continents. While I discuss the translation of several genres of literature, including poetry and digital art, my account of translation focuses on the novel because the novel is the most international genre, measured by worldwide translation, and because the novel today solicits as well as incorporates translation, in substantial ways.[9] Contemporary novels enter new markets with exceptional speed. By "enter," I mean that they are published in different editions in the same language (Australian, U.K., U.S., British, and South African English; or, Argentinean and Iberian Spanish) and in different editions in different languages

(French, Mandarin, and Hebrew). Examples from the past decade are telling. Between July and December of 2005, the phenomenally successful sixth installment of the Harry Potter series, *Harry Potter and the Half-Blood Prince*, appeared in fifteen languages, including Vietnamese, Afrikaans, and Estonian.[10] And even more recently: between February and December 2013, J. M. Coetzee's *Childhood of Jesus* was published on five continents in nine languages, including Chinese, Polish, and two versions of Portuguese.[11] To be sure, the circulation and reception of Coetzee's book has been different from the circulation and reception of Rowling's, and that's to be expected. Rowling's character-rich fantasy, marketed through films, merchandise, and worldwide distribution events, sold a record number of copies; Coetzee's slow-moving allegory prompted speculation about a third Booker Prize.[12]

Yet there are two surprises. First, *Childhood* appeared in translation faster than *Harry Potter* did. In fact, Coetzee's novel initially appeared in Dutch, though Coetzee, born in South Africa and now living in Australia, composes his works in English. Piracy concerns delayed the initial translation of Rowling's novel by two months, whereas Coetzee's novel could be translated, as it were, before it was published in the original.[13] Global demand for the Harry Potter novels—fans were clamoring to produce their own unofficial (and illegal) translations—actually slowed global distribution. The second surprise: global demand drives translation only up to a point. The language of Coetzee's first edition can be explained personally as well as commercially. Coetzee has an ongoing relationship with his Dutch translator; he was raised speaking Afrikaans (closely related to Dutch), and he has translated several works of Dutch poetry and prose into English.[14] And as the story of *Robinson Crusoe*'s circulation reminds us, there is a long and distinguished history of English-language novels traveling the world as Dutch books.[15]

Paying homage to the past, many novels do not simply appear in translation. They have been written for translation from the start. Adapting a phrase for artworks produced for the computer ("born digital"), I call these novels *born translated*.[16] Like born-digital literature, which is made on or for the computer, born-translated literature approaches translation as medium and origin rather than as afterthought.[17] Translation is not secondary or incidental to these works. It is a condition of their production. Globalization bears on all writers working in English today. However, it bears on them differently. Some works of fiction are sure to be translated. Others hope to achieve it. Some novelists are closely tied to the mass market, some to prestige cultures, and others to avant-garde communities. But even those novelists who don't plan on translation participate in a literary system attuned to multiple formats, media, and languages. Born-translated novels approach this system opportunistically.

How does translation shape the narrative structure of the contemporary novel?[18] To begin, we can observe that Coetzee's *Childhood* is born translated in at least two ways: it appeared first in Dutch, and it pretends to take place in Spanish.[19] For its principal characters, Simón and David, English is a foreign language. David, a young boy, recites a stanza from a German song, but both he and Simón mistake the source of the lyrics. "What does it mean, *Wer reitet so?*" David asks.[20] "I don't know. I don't speak English," Simón replies. He doesn't speak German either.[21] It turns out that you need to have at least a passing acquaintance with a language in order to recognize it as the one you are missing. Simón lacks even that little bit, and thus Coetzee imagines a world in which English is so distant, or so insignificant, that it can be confused with a neighboring tongue.

In born-translated novels, translation functions as a thematic, structural, conceptual, and sometimes even typographical device. These works are *written for translation*, in the hope of being translated, but they are also often *written as translations*, pretending to take place in a language other than the one in which they have, in fact, been composed. Sometimes they present themselves as fake or fictional editions: subsequent versions (in English) of an original text (in some other language), which doesn't really exist. They are also frequently *written from translation*. Pointing backward as well as forward, they present translation as a spur to literary innovation, including their own. Coetzee makes this point by incorporating a novel whose actual translation was crucial to the development of anglophone fiction. Simón is reading a version of *Don Quixote*. Cervantes's work is itself a fake translation, from Arabic into Spanish, whose four-hundred-year absorption into many languages has shaped the writing of subsequent novels throughout the world. By adopting some of the thematic features of *Don Quixote*, *Childhood of Jesus* imitates its content and structure—as well as its reception.

In Coetzee's imitation of *Don Quixote*, he attributes authorship not to Cervantes but to "Señor Benengeli," the fictional author of the fictional Arabic original. He thus also imitates Jorge Luis Borges's story, "Pierre Menard, Author of the *Quixote*" (1939). According to Borges's fiction, presented as a posthumous appreciation, Menard was an underappreciated French writer who created new chapters of *Don Quixote* by producing words that "coincide" perfectly with the words in Cervantes's novel.[22] Claiming that Menard's chapters were "verbally identical" but nevertheless unique, the story's narrator presents repetition as a strategy of invention and celebrates the creative energies of foreign readers.[23] With tongue-in-cheek, Borges seems to applaud the anachronism of Menard's project, producing a seventeenth-century Spanish novel in twentieth-century France, and seems to suggest that changing the context, placing the same words in a new time and place, can be a way of changing the work. Embracing this tradition, Coetzee animates the rich conceptual history of translation. Moreover, he shows that his Australian novel is indebted, fictionally as well as literally, to translation's past and to the literatures of Argentina and Spain. And of course this is not Coetzee's debt alone, since Spanish literature of the Golden Age was exported internationally before its English counterpart. Shakespeare probably read Cervantes, but Cervantes is unlikely to have read Shakespeare.[24] Coetzee uses Spanish to remind us that English has not always been the principal medium of literary circulation and that Spanish remains today, in the wake of its own empire, a source of many national literatures. Coetzee's English-language novel activates the histories of Spanish, which has functioned variously and sometimes antagonistically as a language of colonialism, utopian aspiration, exile, migration, and European lingua franca.[25]

As Coetzee's novel shows, then, there is nothing older than translation. Translation is the engine rather than the caboose of literary history. Considering for a moment only the history of literature in English, there would be no *Hamlet*, no *Pilgrim's Progress*, no *Absalom, Absalom!*, and no *Mrs. Dalloway* without it.[26] Yet translation is contemporary because it allows us to consider that the work we are reading includes subsequent editions as well as previous ones. Encountered on the page, translation announces that the work is still arriving: we have before us a language on its way from somewhere else—literature produced for other readers. That is translation's paradox: it is contemporary, above all, because it is historical. In translation, literature has a past as well as a future. While many books produced today seek to entice or accommodate translation, aiming to increase their audiences and the market-share of their publishers, born-translated works are notable because they highlight the effects of circulation on production. Not only are they quickly and widely translated, they are also engaged in thinking about that process. They increase translation's visibility, both historically and proleptically: they are trying to be translated, but in important ways they are also trying to keep being translated. They find ways to register their debts to translation even as they travel into additional languages. Most of all, whether or not they manage to circulate globally, today's born-translated works block readers from being "native readers," those who assume that the book they are holding was written for them or that the language they are encountering is, in some proprietary or intrinsic way, theirs.[27] Refusing to match language to geography, many contemporary works will seem to occupy more than one place, to be produced in more than one language, or to address multiple audiences at the same time. They build translation into their form.

Whereas Coetzee's literary fictions approach translation explicitly, asking readers to imagine English-language novels that began in Spanish, Portuguese, Afrikaans, and German, other writers approach translation conceptually and sometimes fantastically. Continuing with English-language examples for the moment, we can observe the enormous range of approaches by looking at the genre fiction of British novelist China Miéville and the visual writing of U.S. novelist Walter Mosley. Miéville is unusual because he uses the stock devices of science fiction, fantasy, and police procedural to raise complex questions about the politics of language.[28] His most substantial engagement with translation is *The City, The City* (2009), in which two nations share the same territorial space, and citizenship is a matter of cultural rather than corporeal topography. Where you are legally, in the book's logic, depends on how you walk, what you wear, how you speak, what you acknowledge, and what passport you hold. Every place is thus two places, both "the city" and "the city," though most of the inhabitants have learned to live as if there were only one. The novel suggests that political disavowal is managed in part by linguistic disavowal, and thus the fiction of homogeneity is expressed through heterogeneous syntax. Instead of altering the novel's diction to incorporate the sounds or even the vocabulary of two languages, a more typical way to represent multilingualism, Miéville represents a binational society by creating a bifurcated sentence structure. Accidentally seeing a woman who is not a citizen of his country, the narrator "looked carefully *instead of at her in her foreign street* at the façades of the nearby and local GunterStrász. . . ."[29] Later he describes the experience of "standing in a near-deserted part [of his own city] . . . surrounded by a busy *unheard* throng."[30] Only unhearing and unseeing, Miéville suggests, allows the city to appear as one. Making foreignness audible and visible, the novel generates alternatives to the experience of native reading.

Walter Mosley, best known as the author of the hugely successful and widely translated Easy Rawlins mysteries, launched by *Devil in a Blue Dress* in 1990, has produced more than thirty-seven books in several genres, including memoir and science fiction in addition to detective fiction. *Devil in a Blue Dress* does not reflect on translation and in fact incorporates variations in diction and vernacular dialogue, which can make translation difficult. But in an ongoing series of drawings that is also a series of writings, subsumed under the heading of *Alien Script*, Mosley has extended his exploration of subterranean and counterfactual worlds to the exploration of subterranean and counterfactual languages. The images can be understood both as pictures and as words (figures 0.1 and 0.2).

The works are not individually titled. All are part of the collective, *Alien Script*. A script can be a writing system, as in Roman or Cyrillic script, and it can also refer to cinematic or theatrical instructions, as in a film or play script. Mosley has produced dozens of these sheets, and continues to produce them, and thus the work is an open series. The colors, shapes, and patterns vary, but all of them are made on

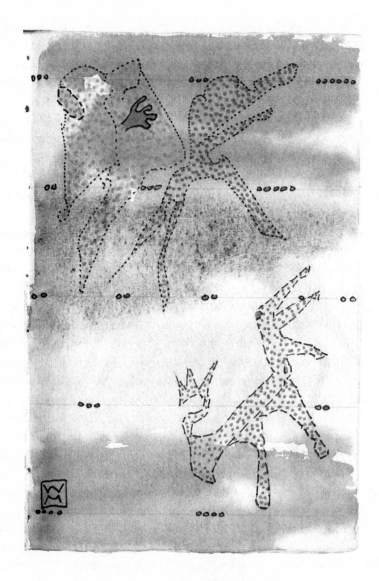

FIGURE 0.1 Image from Walter Mosley, *Alien Script*.

Reprinted by permission of Walter Mosley and the
Watkins/Loomis Agency.

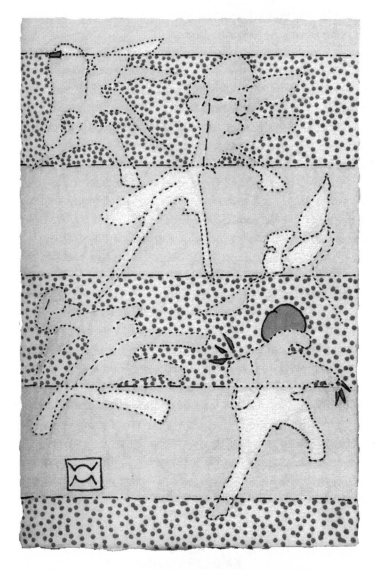

FIGURE 0.2 Image from Walter Mosley, *Alien Script*.

Reprinted by permission of Walter Mosley and the
Watkins/Loomis Agency.

lined notebook paper. The lines create the structure and retain the impression of writing generated by hand.

Mosley's scripts seem "alien" in a variety of ways: the kinetic forms are uncanny; they are almost but not quite human bodies, which seem to be wearing something like human clothing. They are also alien because they are, literally, outside the bounds: under, over, and on top of the lines. Finally, they are alien because they thwart our ability to read them, or even to isolate their constituent parts. Are we looking at letters? Hieroglyphs? Characters? What is the alphabet from which this writing has been made? This sense of alien extends beyond Mosley's work: illegible and unrecognizable, writing becomes alien when readers project their own estrangement onto the pages. Unknown marks or letters will seem to block expressivity. Yet Mosley's *Script* also affirms an infinite expressivity: there is always another pattern, another color, and another shape. The work's futurity is suggested by a recent exhibit of the drawings, in which curator Lydie Diakhaté placed eighteen of the *Alien Script* pages next to nine iterations, in different languages, of the first paragraph of *Devil in a Blue Dress*.[31] For most viewers, at least one of those languages was "alien," and thus the scripts could serve as allegories or illustrations for the texts. But the scripts also assert their difference from the texts: while the paragraphs register a world system of literatures and the commercial logic of international publishing, the alien scripts—hand-made and irreducible to place or territory—aspire to new systems. While the pages evoke various traditions in dance, fabric, typography, and painting, their insouciant forms, at once overflowing and extracted, retro and sci-fi, hint at moorings to come.

ENGLISH LAST

Embracing fake translation, genre fiction, and visual media, Coetzee, Miéville, and Mosley are deploying aesthetic strategies that are used by writers in many other languages. It is not only—or even primarily—English-language novels that address themselves to multiple audiences. In fact, in the invention of born-translated fiction, anglophone writers are the followers, not the leaders. This makes sense when we consider that anglophone works can succeed without being translated. English is the dominant language of commerce and technology, at least for the moment, and it has the greatest number of readers, once we include second- and third- as well as first-language users throughout the world.[32] Those who write in English can therefore expect their works to be published in the original and to reach many audiences in English-language editions. But writers in smaller languages, meaning languages for which there are fewer readers and publishers, have had to depend on translation for survival. Translation into English and into other major languages such as French and Spanish has been for some a condition of publication and for many a path to translation into subsequent national editions. Those who publish in major languages also have better access to lucrative international prizes.[33]

Some writers have tried to mitigate the need for translation by choosing to write in a dominant language, if they can. We could call this strategy preemptive translation. This is in some ways an old strategy. Late Medieval and early modern European writers often circulated their work both in Latin and in vernacular languages in order to reach secular as well as clerical audiences. A language of commerce and international exchange, read and sometimes spoken across many geographies, Latin allowed merchants and scholars to communicate without having to manage local idioms.[34] Eleventh-century Iranian philosophers wrote not in Persian but in Arabic, while Chinese, Japanese, and Korean intellectuals used Chinese for nearly one thousand years.[35] From the perspective of the past, it is in some ways a misnomer to call this practice translation or even preemptive translation since it is a relatively recent assumption that one's writing language and one's speaking language would naturally be the same. Put another way, writing in Latin while speaking French is only a species of translation, or second-language use, if writing in French is the norm.

For most of literary history, written languages such as Greek, Latin, and Arabic have diverged from spoken languages, which were used for other purposes. People who could write—very few people—would have had a first language for writing and a first language for speaking. Periodically, it has seemed important for writers to align these two uses of language. Dante was unusual in his time because he chose to write an epic in Italian rather than Latin. Preemptive translation, or the division of writing and speaking languages, was the expectation until the late eighteenth century, which inaugurates the era of national languages and literary traditions. We are still part of that era. The expectation that the language of writing will match the language of speech remains dominant. We can tell that this is so because writing in a second language has its own special name, "translingual writing."[36] This distinction between first- and second-language writing is continuous with the Romantic distinction between native and foreign languages. Early-nineteenth-century German philosopher Friedrich Schleiermacher famously referred to writing in a second language as a species of translation because he believed that writing in the original could take place only in one's own tongue.[37]

We can find many examples of preemptive translation in the twenty-first century. In 2004, contemporary novelist Elif Shafak, who lives in both Istanbul and London, shifted from writing novels in her first language, Turkish, to writing them in her second language, English. Shafak follows a path—and a rationale—traveled by mid-twentieth-century writer Vladimir Nabokov, who composed his early novels in Russian but began producing novels in English, starting with *Lolita*, so he could publish in New York.[38] Novelist and poet Jaime Manrique, who was born in Colombia but has lived in the United States since 1980, publishes his novels in English and his poetry in Spanish. He calls English his "public language."[39] English is the language in which he feels comfortable writing for and about public "conversation," whereas Spanish is his language of "intimacy." Spanish is hardly a minor tongue, but dominance is relative. Consider the case of Albanian writer and journalist Gazmend Kapllani, who composes his books in Greek, a language he learned only as an adult. Kapllani's works have subsequently appeared in Danish, English, French, and Polish. Long based in Athens but now living in Boston, Kapllani has said that he may start writing in English.[40] Manrique's and Kapllani's choices reflect a mix of political exigency, aesthetic preference, and economic opportunity. Publishing in two languages concurrently, Manrique's practice is reminiscent of the strategies developed by the early-twentieth-century Indian writer Premchand (the pseudonym of

Dhanpat Rai Srivastava), who sought to evade British colonial censors by producing each of his works in two original languages, Hindi and Urdu.[41]

Sometimes, preemptive translation takes place at the moment of publication rather than at the moment of composition. Milan Kundera, who wrote many of his best-known novels in Czech, published them first in French and has in recent years claimed that he is in fact a "French writer."[42] The translations have come to shape the compositions: Kundera has used the French editions to update the Czech originals.[43] Elena Botchorichvili, a Georgian writer who lives in Montreal, also publishes her novels in French even though she writes them in Russian. Six of Botchorichvili's books appeared in French and several other languages before they appeared in their original language.[44] Bernardo Atxaga writes his novels in Basque and self-translates them into Spanish; most of the subsequent translations are based on the Spanish editions.

Anglophone writers who are located outside of the largest centers of publishing, New York and London, have had to translate too. Kenyan writer Ngũgĩ wa Thiong'o famously chose to publish his novels first in Gikuyu, but he has also published them, self-translated, in English. Chinua Achebe's *Things Fall Apart*, which features a smattering of Igbo terms, required a glossary when it was published in the London-based Heinemann series in 1962, while several paragraphs of Coetzee's *In the Heart of the Country*, first published in South Africa in 1977, were translated from Afrikaans into English for the U.K. edition.[45] Non-anglophone languages that are well known or at least familiar to anglophone readers in regional contexts—consider the use of many Spanish, Yiddish, and French words in U.S. writing, for example—often require translation or explication when they appear in anglophone books published outside those regions. And it is not only words from other languages but also words from regional or colonial versions of languages that travel uneasily within dominant languages. The title of Ferdinand Oyono's francophone African novel *Une vie de boy*, first published in 1956, makes use of an English word (boy) that operates differently in French than it does in English.[46] In English editions of the book, the so-called English word has had to be translated.[47]

While some novelists expand their audiences by publishing their books in second languages or by standardizing their vocabulary, others have found ways to accommodate translation within global languages such as Spanish and French and also within regional languages such as Turkish and Japanese. Like Coetzee, Miéville, and Mosley, many build translation into the form of their works, emphasizing translation's history and ongoing relevance while insisting that a novel can belong to more than one language. They are not preempting translation so much as courting it. Sometimes they do a bit of both. For example, Nancy Huston, a Calgary-born writer who has lived in Paris for the past forty years, writes novels and essays in French and then writes them in English. She publishes her works in both languages, and others have translated her work into many additional languages. Like Kundera, Huston uses her own translations to revise the originals, and, like Samuel Beckett, who produced many of his own works in English and French, she regards both versions as original texts. In 1993 she won an award for fiction in French for a novel she wrote first in English. Huston thus preempts translation because she operates both as author and as translator. But she also treats translation as a species of production, as when she argues that her award-winning book should be understood as an original creation.[48] In addition, some of Huston's works take translation as a principal concern. The English version of the nonfiction book *Losing North* (2002), for example, includes an essay about the difficulty of translating idioms such as the one that constitutes the book's title.[49]

The Japanese novelist Haruki Murakami, whose work has been widely translated and who is also an accomplished translator of U.S. fiction, has taken a somewhat different tack: using his second language to create a new kind of first language. To be clear: Murakami submits his manuscripts to his publisher in Japanese, and his novels first appear in that language. But from the start of his career he has deployed translation as a method of composition, in a variety of ways. First, the most literal way: he has claimed that he found his style in Japanese by writing pages first in English and then translating them into Japanese.[50] By starting in English, he sought to avoid the conventional diction and syntax of Japanese literature. In this sense, Murakami's project is similar to Huston's and indeed to Beckett's, except that Murakami uses his adopted language, English, not to depart from his first language, Japanese, but to create a less natural version of it. Murakami's later novels have involved self-translation of another kind: incorporating cuts made for the U.S. editions in subsequent Japanese editions.[51] The later works thus involve a kind of triple translation: from English into Japanese into English, and then back into Japanese.

The second way that Murakami deploys translation in the service of composition is in his liberal use of generic devices, historical references, and even words culled from anglophone popular culture. Invoking English, he reflects on the translated sources of contemporary Japan and generates works that can appeal to multiple audiences, who recognize both theme and terminology.[52] This is not to say that Murakami's novels appeal to each audience in the same way. Indeed, his blockbuster, *1Q84*, published in Japan in 2009, has been marketed as romantic fiction in one place and as a futuristic thriller in another.[53] And, paradoxically, the references to anglophone culture, while they may help the books travel into additional languages, do not always help the books travel into English, where those words no longer serve the same function.[54] Murakami also incorporates translation—this is the third way—by emphasizing the difference among Japanese writing systems, the character-based kanji and the syllabic hiragana and katakana, to create the impression of multilingualism on the page. Most notably, he uses katakana, the script in which foreign or "loan" words typically appear, to signal a much broader range of nonnormative or eccentric speech.[55] This practice has proved challenging to his translators, since they have had to find analogues in single-script writing systems such as English, Danish, Norwegian, Polish, and many other European languages.

Murakami's longstanding effort to incorporate histories of literary circulation into the production of his Japanese novels can be understood as an effort to insist on the comparative origins of contemporary Japan. For his Japanese readers, he is trying to make his language less accessible, and thus to interfere with the distinction between native and nonnative readers. This is not a gesture of exile, or an embrace of the global in lieu of the local, so much as an affirmation of translation's place within Japanese history. Murakami's inventive use of multiple writing systems, counterfactual worlds, and popular genres creates an internal climate of traveling narratives that operates in tension with the external movement of his novels from one language to another.[56] Murakami's texts may be "suited to translation," as he has said, but they are also saturated by translation.[57]

Two additional examples are instructive: one, the Nobel Prize–winner Orhan Pamuk, who writes in Turkish; the other, the (late) celebrated novelist Roberto Bolaño, who wrote in Spanish.[58] Pamuk's novels have moved from Turkish into sixty other languages, including—just to name the Ks—Kannada, Korean, and two varieties of Kurdish. His works began to receive international recognition in 1991 after the French translation of *The Silent House* received the Prix de la découverte européenne. Readers of Pamuk's novels in Turkish have argued that his later works solicit translation by emphasizing international lineage, postmodern devices, and "Istanbul cosmopolitanism," whereas the earlier works engaged more substantially with the Turkish literary tradition and social realism.[59] Yet, through various narrative strategies, Pamuk's later works also reflect on global circulation: they accommodate translation and also identify translation as a source of local production. Published in Turkey in 2002 and in the United States in 2004, *Snow* features characters who, like many readers, lack information about regional histories; it considers Turkey's debts both to European and to Ottoman influences; and it presents social and cultural differences through dialogue rather than through idiolect. Strangers are useful because they allow Pamuk to make the description of regional history part of the novel's story: something a character learns rather than a feature of omniscient narration. Registering multiple sources is useful because Pamuk can show that Turkish literature is, at least in part, embedded in other literatures and cultural traditions. Dialogue is useful, as Gloria Fisk notes, because characters point at differences in ways that can be understood by readers unfamiliar with regional contexts or variations in diction.[60] Pamuk presents his readers with details about Turkey's past, and he raises questions about the historical reliability of those details and their interpretation by various characters. Readers are thus asked to engage directly with the phenomenon of world literature: its tendency to make guidebooks or cultural primers out of literary works from representative spaces. The process of overgeneralization has a special resonance for Pamuk's writing, which returns often to the complex geopolitical history of Turkey and especially of Istanbul, a city literally divided between Europe and Asia. The translated quality of Pamuk's writing can thus be understood both as an effort to reach audiences beyond Turkey and as an effort to insist on multiple audiences within Turkey.[61]

I want to pause somewhat more deliberately over Roberto Bolaño's fiction, which has been enormously successful in multiple languages. It would be difficult to say that the extensive circulation of Bolaño's work animated his strategies of production since he wrote his major novels in a very compressed period, between 1993 and his death in 2003.[62] Like many of the English-language writers I have discussed so far, his address to multiple audiences seems to reflect a mixture of literary, political, personal, and commercial impulses. Among these are his attunement to the multilingualism of his first language, Spanish; his effort to consider geopolitical relationships of various scales, such as those between Mexico and other Latin American countries, Europe, and the United States; and his engagement with transnational literary movements whose poets, critics, and writers appear as fictional characters in many of his works. Bolaño was born in Chile, lived for many years in Mexico City, and produced his novels in Spain. Readers of his Spanish-language editions have noted that his diction is not reducible to Chilean, Mexican, or Iberian Spanish. His novels seem translated, in part because they combine several regional idioms and seem to have no one native tongue.

However, Bolaño also manages to communicate multilingualism spatially, visually, and narratively.[63] The Savage Detectives, the novel that brought Bolaño to worldwide attention when it captured two prestigious Spanish prizes in 1998, moves across several continents while placing its action in locations that function at the very smallest scale: the park bench, the lawn, the perambulated street, the hotel room, the mental health clinic, and the bar, to take only a few examples.[64] There may be many nations in the text, but the text doesn't treat the nation as the most important or most coherent unit of belonging. Several of the novel's places, for all their smallness, are also vague. They don't really fit the logic of civic nomenclature.

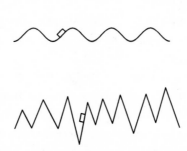

FIGURE 0.3 Renderings of figures from Roberto Bolaño,
The Savage Detectives, translated by Natasha Wimmer

(New York: Picador, 2007), 398.

Where is a park bench? Where is a lawn? What language do their
denizens speak? Bolaño turns the global novel on its head by replacing the principle of expansion (a larger whole) with the principle
of extraction (unclassifiable parts). This is one of the ways that his
work, for all its attention to Mexico City, appears to resist the idea of
a unique regional audience.

In addition, *Savage Detectives* involves for several hundred pages
what appear to be interview transcripts, whose first audience, the
person asking the questions, is not represented. Readers of this long
section are second readers, always overhearing rather than hearing.[65]
This creates the impression of a narrative that is taking place in at
least two locations: the location of the interview and the location of
the transcription. And then there are the translations built into the
novel's conversations. The interviewer is searching for information
about two poet-heroes, but the poet-heroes are searching for information about an older poet, Cesárea Tinajero, whom they honor as
their inspiration. When they find one of her poems, it consists of an
apparently multilingual title, "Sión," and a series of graphic lines,
which Bolaño reproduces on the page (figure 0.3).

The Savage Detectives offers some possible meanings for the
poem's heading, in Spanish, German, French, Hebrew, and English,

FIGURE 0.4 Renderings of figures from Roberto Bolaño,
The Savage Detectives, translated by Natasha Wimmer

(New York: Picador, 2007), 648.

but the possibilities are open-ended, like "Zion" itself, proverbially a place that has not yet come. The lines, according to the young poets, tell several possible stories.[66] They are translatable because they consist of visual images; they also seem to dramatize translation insofar as they represent a ship or a mathematical vector on its way somewhere else. The lines of the poem, as literal lines on the page, deflate poetry's usual emphasis on words while at the same time drawing attention to metaphor (graphic and poetic lines/*líneas*, for example). In the title's invocation of various languages and spaces of the future, the poem appears to be born translated: not so much a work for all readers as a work for other readers.

Finally, in the very last section of the novel, Bolaño returns to several themes of translation, one in which he pits popular knowledge of Mexico City's slang against recondite knowledge of poetic terminology; and another in which characters amuse themselves by translating pictures into stories, much as they did with the earlier poem. In both cases we are asked to consider that translation operates within languages and literary histories as well as between them. The final words of the novel are an image that can be understood in several ways (figure 0.4). It is a box made of dashed lines; a window with a broken or unfinished frame; and a container whose outside permeates its inside. Translatable, this image is also a symbol of translation. It resembles the book we are holding.

Bolaño's emphasis on "the border"—the book's border, the border between plot and form, and the border between the United States and Mexico—reminds us that born-translated novels are not produced from nowhere for everywhere. In fact, they are often very local in their approaches to translation and the politics of translation. The text may engage with the regional history of languages even as the book circulates into many editions.[67] There is an enormous and growing critical literature on each of the four novelists I've discussed in this section, and I won't do justice to that here. Instead, my brief and telescopic account of non-anglophone writing is meant to demonstrate the various strategies of born-translated fiction in other languages; to explore some of the reasons for those strategies; and, finally, to suggest by contrast how born-translated fiction in English both follows and diverges from its neighbors.

ENGLISH NOW

Anglophone novels are more likely than novels in other languages to appear in translation: more works are translated out of English than out of any other language.[68] However, many English-language works encounter multiple audiences—and are produced in multiple national editions—before they even leave English. This will be true of other global languages, such as Portuguese and especially Spanish, which are also often published in more than one place and involve multiple national versions. But the English language is dispersed like no other: it is a first, second, or third language used in the largest number of countries. As Pascale Casanova has persuasively argued, this is what it means to be the world's dominant language. It is not a matter of counting first-language or "native" speakers. Rather, it is a matter of counting both first-language speakers and all of the "plurilingual speakers who 'choose' it."[69] To write in English for global audiences, therefore, is to write for a heterogeneous group of readers: those who are proficient in several languages, those who may be less-than-proficient in English, and those who may be proficient in one version of English but not proficient in another. This diversity creates an enormous range of English-language geographies, writers, and audiences. It also means that readers of English-language texts are likely to have very different experiences: the work will be foreign, strange, or difficult to some; it will be familiar to others. Anglophone novelists are thus managing comparative beginnings from the start and must find ways to register internal multilingualism (within English) even as their works travel out into additional national languages (beyond English).[70] In addition, English is not only a source of translations, the language from which translations often begin, it is also the most frequent medium of translations, the language through which texts in other languages move into yet additional languages. In this sense, English-language writing is, like writing in other languages, an object of globalization; but it is also, unlike writing in other languages, crucial to globalization's machinery, both because of its role in digital media and commerce and because of its role as a mediator, within publishing, between other literary cultures.[71]

In fact, while anglophone writers in New York and London may have thought about or even criticized the conditions of literary globalization, only recently have they begun to think of themselves as subject to those conditions. Today English-language writers in the United States and Britain are faced with the unprecedented commodification and "global networking" of intellectual spaces such as universities, and the consolidation of publishing into a smaller number of international units. Not even English-language writers, it turns out, can imagine audiences only in one language. This has led to a new emphasis, within the anglophone novel, on the histories and institutions of literary circulation, from the uneven distribution of literacy (Jamaica Kincaid), to the production of anthologies (Caryl Phillips), to international art competitions in the present (Amy Waldman) and Pacific trade routes of the early eighteenth century (David Mitchell). As I've suggested, English-language writers who operate furthest from the centers of publishing have had to address multiple audiences for some time. This is true as well for many migrant writers, who may compose in several languages and whose political and literary affiliations often diverge. Indeed, affiliation complicates composition since writers addressing many places are less likely to believe that language confers belonging, or that belonging limits language. They are more likely to assume that the language of writing and the language of speaking do not necessarily overlap. The increasing use of English by writers for whom English is not a first or only language has exerted new pressure on longstanding assumptions about "native" competency, the Romantic belief that those who are born into a language, as it were, are the rightful or natural users of that language.

Born-translated novels in English often focus on geographies in which English is not the principal tongue. These works purposefully break with the unique assignment of languages, geographies, and states in which one place is imagined to correspond to one language and one people, who are the users of that language. Born-translated works articulate this break by extending, sometimes radically, the practice of self-translation, a term that translation specialists have often limited to authors who produce both an original work and the translation of that original work. Self-translation has opened up in two directions. First, it now includes works that pretend to be translated.[72] Coetzee's *Childhood* is "self-translated" from the perspective of narration because it seems to be taking place in Spanish; and it is also self-translated from the perspective of book history because it was published first in Dutch. The English edition appears to be a tributary to the Spanish and the Dutch. Second, self-translation now includes works that contain translation within them by incorporating multiple editions or multiple versions. These works are not translated in the sense of combining or moving between separate national literatures. Instead, they ask readers to consider that literatures, as we have known them, are already combined.[73]

In the novels I discuss in this project, self-translation involves pretending to write fiction in another tongue (Coetzee and Miéville); presenting English-language works as translations of some other language, some other version of language, or some other medium (Kincaid and Mohsin Hamid); reflecting on English literature's debts to other languages and literary traditions (Mitchell and Waldman); and inviting translators to regard themselves as authors and collaborators (Kazuo Ishiguro; Young-Hae Chang Heavy Industries; and Adam Thirlwell). Many English-language writers draw attention to the unevenness of the global marketplace—and sometimes try to remediate that unevenness—by welcoming translation, by devising strategies of multilingualism that can survive global circulation, and by emphasizing translation's crucial role in the development of the English-language novel.[74] Reflecting on circulation at a global scale, born-translated novels introduce new ontologies of the work. They imply new understandings of literature's place and emphasize new objects of analysis such as the chapter, the page, the edition, the illustration, the script, and the medium.

Novels have always reflected on their own languages, and it shouldn't be surprising that the surge in translation would lead novels to reflect on future and past languages too. However, an acknowledgment of translation's central role—as spur, problem, and opportunity—has to change what the anglophone novel is. Literature in dominant languages tends to "forget" that it has benefitted from literary works in other languages.[75] Born-translated fiction, therefore, engages in a project of unforgetting. Fiction is not alone in that project. *Asymptote*, a digital journal launched in 2011, has followed this path by seeking out translations from smaller languages into dominant languages—English, but not only English—and by publishing both original and translation so that first and subsequent languages are readily available to the reader.[76] The emphasis is not on the foreignization of the word, in which a single-language edition tries to retain the impression or the quality of a prior language.[77] Instead it is on the foreignization of the form, in which the history of translation is preserved through the presence of two or more texts. For scholars, unforgetting translation means that, instead of organizing literary histories according to the citizenship of authors, as the Library of Congress does, we might organize literary histories according to the languages and versions of language in which a work is read, whether as original, translation, edition, adaptation, or collaboration. A work would thus appear several times, in each of the histories in which it has a presence, and some of those histories would extend well beyond literary fiction and the medium of print. To be sure, fields will seem to get bigger, but we will have to imagine our frames, after Bolaño, as windows made of dashed rather than solid lines.

Allowing books to count as part of several traditions and media has the salutary effect of tipping the balance of literary history from writers to readers, from a language's natives to its users, and from single to multiple chronologies. The tip toward circulation also tips back: thinking about overlapping literary histories allows us to consider how reception alters the work, and what it is that readers read. Literature produced in dominant languages becomes part of literary histories in other languages. Literature produced in smaller languages continues to have a place in those histories, but its uptake by other literatures also has to be registered. Some works will not travel into new languages, and the history of translation will have to include both works that reach multiple audiences and works that do not. Like *Asymptote*'s effort to make English-language readers aware of a much greater number of works from many nondominant languages, literary histories that include adaptation, rewriting, and translation make room for unheralded traditions while also creating the conditions for more expansive heralding.

To approach the future of classification from the history of multilingual circulation is to recognize that anglophone writing operates in many languages, even when it appears to be operating only in English. The novel theorist M. M. Bakhtin made this point long ago, when he argued that the "unity of a literary language is not a unity of a single, closed language system, but is rather a highly specific unity of several 'languages' that have established contact and mutual recognition with each other."[78] Writing of the modern European novel (pre-1900), Bakhtin means that what we take to be the distinctive national voice of any one tradition in Europe in fact involves the explicit and implicit negotiation of several different regional languages as well as versions of language (poetic, ordinary, official). In the early twenty-first century, when contact among languages is not only generic and regional but also multiregional, continental, and planetary, multilingualism within a single language operates at an even greater scale. For Bakhtin, internal multilingualism does not undercut the possibility of national languages because national language–users who live in a relatively contained geographic area can be expected to achieve some fluency with the significant contact languages. However, when so-called national languages operate at great distances, as they do in English, and when they operate alongside other strong literary traditions, as they do in India, the Caribbean, and the United States, the expectation of common fluency both across versions of the national language and with neighboring languages has to change. In addition, viewed from the perspective of migration, the concept of literary belonging may have outlived its usefulness. European novels of the nineteenth century belonged to their national languages, or often thought they did. But at earlier moments, Bakhtin argues, literary consciousness has been constitutively "bilingual," inspired by a relationship between languages even if those languages did not appear, simultaneously or literally, on the page. The Latin word in Ancient Rome, Bakhtin asserts, "viewed itself in the light of the Greek word," which produced an "exteriorizing" style.[79] Today's born-translated novel, rather than expand belonging, strives to keep belonging in play. It does this by implying that the book we are holding begins in several languages.

IMAGINED COMMUNITIES IN TRANSLATION

The notion that a book could begin in several languages complicates traditional models of literary history and political community. Literary critics have to ask how the multilingualism of the book changes the national singularity of the work. Philosophers of the nation have to ask how the translation of literary texts into more languages and faster than ever before establishes networks of affiliation that are less exclusive and less bounded than the nation's "community of fate." Generally speaking, we can identify two paradigms that shape the way we talk about the effect of books on political communities: the paradigm of "possessive collectivism," which has a long history in philosophy, anthropology, and legal theory, and the paradigm of "imagined communities," which Benedict Anderson introduced in 1983 and which has become so influential in history, literary studies, and many other fields that it operates almost tacitly.[80] Where have these theories brought us, and where might we now go in thinking about literature's engagement with conceptions of the collective?

"Possessive collectivism" extends the idea of possessive individualism to nations and ethnic groups.[81] In Quebecois ideology, anthropologist Richard Handler explains in a well-known study, the nation was understood as both a "collection of individuals and a collective individual," possessing unique, permanent qualities such as a "soul, spirit, and personality" and having the capacity to exercise sovereignty, free will, and choice.[82] Rosemary Coombe has used Handler's work on nationalist ideology to describe the effects and underlying assumptions of international copyright. In copyright law, Coombe argues, "Each nation or group is perceived as an author who originates a culture from resources that come from within and can thus lay claim to exclusive possession of the expressive works that embody its personality."[83] Literary works belong to the nation because they are the embodiment of its internal spirit or genius, and we know the nation has a spirit or genius because it has literary works to show for it. This is a feedback loop: nationhood owes its identity to authorship, but there is no authorship without nationhood since expressivity belongs to unique individuals who in turn belong to unique groups. Among minorities and colonized subjects, possessive collectivism has had the positive effect of validating intellectual labor and justifying political sovereignty. For our purposes, possessive collectivism is notable because it helps to explain why emphasizing the original production of artworks tends to affirm national literary histories: original art and original nations grow up together. We could speculate, however, that a theory of artworks that understands acts of editing and translating as acts of making might affirm a different norm of literary history and a different conception of the community that literary history helps to justify.

Before I push this speculation further, consider Benedict Anderson's idea of "imagined communities." Rather than rehearse Anderson's now-classic theory, I would like to mark an important difference between his account of literary nation making and the possessive collectivism model. It was Anderson's innovation to argue that the rise of print culture, especially the rise of novels and newspapers, contributed to the possibility of imagining a nation as a shared, exclusive collectivity among strangers. Print culture contributed to this possibility in two structural ways: by creating the impression of simultaneous reading across space, and by creating the impression, within the novel, of simultaneity among people who never meet—an impression that Anderson memorably calls the experience of "meanwhile."[84] The second impression strengthens the first: if we can perceive the novel as a container for strangers who act together without knowing it, then we can imagine the nation as a container for us, the readers of that novel, who act together in just the same way—simultaneously, collectively, and invisibly. As Jonathan Culler has observed in an essay on Anderson's work, it is not the novel's content or theme but its form, its way of being a container for simultaneity among strangers, that creates "a political distinction between friend and foe."[85] Anderson's model does not imply that the artwork is expressing a repertoire of national characteristics that could be owned; rather, it argues that the novel represents—and generates—a community based on the imagined concurrence of action. If there is a residue of possessive collectivism in Anderson's materialism, it is in his assumption that a text has an original language and that the text's language will coincide with the language of its readers. What happens, we need to ask, when these languages are not the same? Or when there is no original language to speak of?

We can address these questions by returning to Anderson's project. But instead of approaching *Imagined Communities* as an argument, as others have done so well, I want to treat it as an example since it is as an example of world literature that Anderson's book coincides, historically and formally, with today's born-translated novel.[86] Like many contemporary novels, *Imagined Communities* stages an encounter between literary history and political theory. And like those novels, the study functions as a work of world literature both because of its circulation and because of its production. As a text, *Imagined Communities* takes as its subject the effects of print culture on the development of nation-states throughout the world. Individual chapters are devoted to case studies of small countries such as Hungary, Thailand, Switzerland, and the Philippines. As a book, *Imagined Communities* has circulated among many of these small countries, and among many large ones too. It was first published in English in 1983 and has been translated over the past thirty-some years into at least twenty-seven languages, including Japanese, German, Portuguese, Serbo-Croat, and Catalan. Yet the phenomenal success of Anderson's project has led not only to translation and retranslation but also to new production. In 1991 and 2006, respectively, Anderson issued second and third English editions, each of which includes new material that responds to criticism of the work and analyzes the transnational communities that the book's circulation has helped to create.

The third edition adds to the book's subject matter—how print culture contributes to the imagination of community—an account of how the translation and reception of the book we are reading has contributed to the imagination of communities to which the book now belongs. In this account we learn that the transnational and multilingual circulation of *Imagined Communities* has led Anderson to consider that the global appeal of his argument may have been spurred by its own transnational beginnings—that is, by origins understood not simply as London or the Anglo-American academy but as a transnational conglomerate, the United Kingdom, in which devolution and multiculturalism offer conflicting models of political history and collective fate. Anderson acknowledges in the 2006 edition that the original rhetoric of the book was borrowed in part from debates about postcolonial migration and the decline of empire that had become especially urgent in the United Kingdom of the late seventies and early eighties. From the perspective of later editions, we see that Anderson's text is rather more transnational than we had at first perceived. Yet what I am calling transnational, the narrative's attunement to histories of devolution and multiculturalism, also remains local in an important sense. Regional, semi-metropolitan, Anderson's work shows us that global disarticulation—belonging to nowhere—is not the only alternative to national simultaneity. Moreover, it suggests that the repression of translation may be tied, as it is in Anderson's text, to the repression of transnational impulses within national projects.

There is no chapter in *Imagined Communities* that presents itself as an analysis of the novel today, but the afterword to the third edition is suggestive about translation's effects on literary history. Readers become part of the book's story about how print culture structures imagined communities, and thus the community of the book is shown to exceed the community of the text. In this way *Imagined Communities* shares its narrative structure with many other contemporary transnational works and resembles edited and translated works from earlier eras.[87] As Anderson argues, translation can contribute to the imagination of national communities. But as Anderson demonstrates, translation puts pressure on the conceptual boundaries between one community and another and may spur the perception of new communities altogether.

This insight can be useful for our understanding of world literature. In books published since 2000, scholars of world literature have focused on what happens to literary works when they travel into new literary systems. The emphasis on travel has sought to replace two older definitions: the one that designated literary masterpieces, those books everyone in the world should read; and the one that designated literary underdogs, those books produced outside of Western Europe and the United States. Whereas world literature once referred to a group of "works," it now refers to a "network," a "system," a "republic," or a "problem."[88] The movement from a specific bookshelf of classic or marginalized literary works to the relationship among many different bookshelves has drawn attention to the ways bookshelves come to be organized, and to the ways and reasons that works move—or do not move—among them. Yet the focus on travel, while tracing uptake and renovation and therefore also new emergence, has also tended to emphasize the distinction between literature's beginnings and its afterlives.[89] Translation appears as part of literature's second act.

This understanding of translation is one of Emily Apter's principal concerns in *Against World Literature* and in her earlier study, *The Translation Zone*. She calls for greater engagement with translation in the calculation of literary histories at a global scale.[90] Title notwithstanding, in the later book Apter is not really against world literature, or even World Literature.[91] She is interested in "when and where translation happens," expanding the corpus of literary works geographically and linguistically, and rethinking foundational concepts from the perspective of literary histories beyond Europe.[92] But she is against the organization of literature from the perspective of national languages and literary histories. And she is against the expansion of ownership, preferring instead "deowned literature," whose paradigmatic example is the translated book.[93] Of course, as Apter acknowledges, literary ownership is not a creature of world literature studies. The rise of national languages in the early nineteenth century made it seem natural and necessary for literature to begin—even to be "born"—in one language. When theories of literary circulation take nineteenth-century European fiction as their examples, as they often do, it makes sense that the national model would rule the day.[94] But what happens when we turn to new examples?[95] Instead of asking about the contemporary novel from the perspective of world literature, we might ask about world literature from the perspective of the contemporary novel.

In this book, I suggest that what literature is now has to alter what world literature is now. Once literary works begin in several languages and several places, they no longer conform to the logic of national representation. Many born-translated novels signal this departure by blocking original languages, invoking multiple scales of geography, and decoupling birthplace from collectivity. New objects change the shape as well as the content of world literature. When world literature seems to be a container for various national literatures, it privileges source: distinct geographies, countable languages, individual genius, designated readers, and the principle of possessive collectivism. When world literature seems instead to be a series of emerging works, not a product but a process, it privileges target: the analysis of convergences and divergences across literary histories.[96] The analysis of target languages and literatures involves, paradoxically, an analysis of the past. Literary scholarship has to approach operations that once seemed secondary or external (not only reading but also translating) as sources of production.[97] Taking production and circulation together, it is impossible to isolate the novel today from the other genres in which its authors regularly participate. Many novelists are also reviewers, translators, anthologists, poets, editors, publishers, graphic designers, journalists, visual artists, intellectual impresarios, and essayists.[98] This has always been so—the novel is the genre of many genres—but today novels and novel-like fictions have found new ways to dramatize the relationship among these activities, in which writing, reading, adapting, and translating all take part.[99]

In contemporary fiction, we see many originals that are also translations. Readers are asked to experience the text as a delayed or detoured object: a book that began somewhere else. Instead of identification, these texts offer readers partial fluency, approximation, and virtual understanding, from the syntactical translations of Miéville's

The City, the City and the diegetic translations of Coetzee's *Childhood* to the intermedial, collaborative, and serial translations of Mosley's *Alien Script*, Young-Hae Chang Heavy Industries' digital narratives, and Adam Thirlwell's "Multiples."[100] If world literature is to involve asking "where a particular text starts, how it moves, and who ends up reading it," as Caroline Levine has recently suggested, we will need to know more about how *starting* has changed, when *movement* takes place, and what kinds of practices and chronologies *reading* has involved.[101] Because a work may be produced several times, through adaptation, rewriting, and translation, we can no longer assume that its language will always precede its composition and that its audience will always follow it. By challenging dominant models of literary sequencing, in which circulation always trails production, literary histories that incorporate translation recalculate the meanings of author and translator, original and derivation, native and foreign, just to name a few of the foundational distinctions that have shaped world literature as we've known it.[102] Born-translated works, because they value the history and future of translation, its conduits as well as its blockages, bring circulation into view. Rather than dodging translation, they try to keep being translated.

NON-TRANSLATION STUDIES

This commitment—to keep being translated—doesn't fit our usual ways of thinking about the portability of literary works. It is conventional to distinguish between works that impede translation ("untranslatable") and those that invite it ("translatable"). But what would it mean for a work both to impede and to invite at the same time? The work that is difficult to translate is celebrated for its engagement with a specific national language and for its refusal to enter, or enter easily, into the pipeline of multinational publishing. The portable work, for its part, is vilified for having surrendered to that pipeline, exchanging aesthetic innovation for commercial success, eschewing the idiosyncrasy of the local for the interchangeability of the global.[103] "In the global literary market there will be no place for any Barbara Pyms and Natalia Ginzburgs," Tim Parks has warned. "Shakespeare would have eased off the puns. A new Jane Austen can forget the Nobel."[104] Global circulation, we are told, breeds literary decline and political lassitude. Literature is thus never worse than when it is "eminently translatable."[105] And it is never better than when it can't be translated at all.[106]

But translation, like world literature, needs to be approached comparatively: the concept has a history and a present, and it operates differently across languages and literary cultures. For example, the celebration of the untranslatable is in some ways a recent phenomenon in the United States. Spurred by the explosion in world literature studies and by new conditions of global literary production, its advocates are trying to halt the absorption of many literatures into a super-sized English-language curriculum. For many scholars, the obstruction of circulation is a necessary strategy of minority self-expression. By using nonstandard versions of a national language, a work opposes political and cultural homogenization, both the kind imposed by other speakers of that language and the kind imposed by translators and publishers. Brian Lennon, one of the more radical advocates for this position, has called for "a renewed emphasis . . . on idiolectic incommensurability" and what he calls "non-translation studies."[107] Lennon values books that refuse to participate in standards of linguistic, typographical, or semiotic accessibility. The most original books, he argues, will be unpublishable or barely publishable or perhaps only publishable by independent publishing houses. He suggests, in addition, that a "strong" version of non-translation scholarship would eschew its own monolingualism by producing "pluralingual" works: scholarship in languages other than English as well as individual works of scholarship that incorporate into English "significant quantities of a language or languages other than English."[108]

In truth, this turn away from translation is something of a return. The notion that important literary texts have a distinctive language and that they are intended for a specific group of competent readers has been the reigning intellectual paradigm for at least the past century. The exemplary works of non-translation studies tend to feature idiosyncratic diction, portmanteau words, or phrases that gather several national languages into a single sentence. Doris Sommer calls these works "particularist," by which she means that they are directed to a relatively small group of readers who can operate in two or even three languages.[109] Particularist writers, Sommer emphasizes, know their readers, or think they do.[110] Additionally, she argues, they know whom they are excluding: monolingual readers who lack access to multilingual puns that operate at the level of the word or the phrase. Particularist works are not meant to circulate globally. Rather, they are meant to be regional and to comment on the specific relationship among languages in that region. They are born untranslatable in the sense that they do not travel well and in fact often resist it.[111]

At this point it seems important to acknowledge that the concept of the untranslatable, its meanings as well as its political consequences, is not one. I mean by this that it functions differently across various languages and that those differences have been largely invisible. These differences are important for our understanding of what the born-translated novel is trying to do. In English, as it has been used recently by Emily Apter, untranslatable texts or concepts involve "semantic units that are irreducible."[112] They cannot circulate in another language, and in fact, as Apter puts it, they declare a "ban on passing from one language to another."[113] Untranslatable words, Apter argues, are often bilingual and denote "shared zones of non-national belonging."[114] They resist travel because their meaning is tied to the arrangement of phonemes or to the historical relationship among specific languages. This definition of the untranslatable fits well with the project of non-translation studies in the United States and with the idiolect-driven novels on which it has focused.

In French, as it has been used recently by Barbara Cassin, whose *Vocabulaire européen des philosophies* (2004) Apter helped to translate and adapt for anglophone audiences, "untranslatable" means "what one doesn't stop (not) translating."[115] The double negative is significant. It allows the statement to imply both "what one keeps translating" and "what one never finishes translating, or never manages to translate." These two ideas together produce something like, "what one doesn't stop translating even though one cannot finish translating." Cassin's is not a principle of repeated accomplishment (translating over and over) so much as a principle of ongoing failure (not translating, still). She writes in her introduction to the *Vocabulaire*: "To speak of *untranslatables* in no way implies that the terms in question, or expressions, the syntactical or grammatical turns, are not and cannot be translated: the untranslatable is rather what one keeps on (not) translating."[116] Cassin's untranslatable means something like, "un-translated-able": that is, unable to be finished being translated.[117]

If we follow the logic of Cassin's thinking, translatable terms would be words or concepts for which translation can come to an end, and in which translation has not yet appeared to begin.[118] These words may have circulated, as all words have, but they do not register the trace of that circulation. Untranslatable words, on the other hand, are those for which translation is interminable. They express not the refusal of translation but the persistence of it. These words are translated from the start; they find ways to dramatize that history; and they carry that history into the future, requiring readers to engage in translation rather than to imagine that the work, as if from a later vantage, has been translated. Instead of a distinction between translation invited or banned, incorporated or alienated, Cassin points us toward a distinction between translation terminable or interminable, socialized or dramatized, managed or ongoing. Cassin's "untranslatables" seem to be not simply born translated but virtually translated. They halt before the actual; they are solicitous of additional translation.

Literary works may be untranslatable, then, because they are difficult to translate (Apter's sense) or because they are difficult not to translate (Cassin's sense). The first version of untranslatable, as I have suggested, has a long history within postcolonial and minority writing of the past century. It also has close ties with literary modernism. In some ways the association between non-translation and modernism is odd since so many modernist writers served as translators and created new works out of the translation and collage of other works. But the project of collage and the turn to the lyric in fiction emphasized the development of a particular language in relation to other languages and other versions of language. Promoting a sense of intimacy through sound and voice, many of the signal works of modernist fiction have to be heard as well as read. Scholars have called these works untranslatable not because they haven't been translated but because they seem committed to the history and structure of their original language. Beckett's famous aphorism about *Finnegans Wake*, that the "writing is not *about* something; *it is that something itself*," helped to produce what is now the standard account of Joycean fiction.[119] And of course James Joyce's *Portrait of the Artist as a Young Man* makes this point on its own behalf when it presents a story about the revitalization of a paralyzed idiom. Stephen forges the uncreated conscience of his race by teaching the English how to speak their language, and by outdoing the English in a language that has never been theirs. By the time we get to *Ulysses*, we are offered the opportunity to learn a new vernacular, and indeed that acquisition is crucial to the plot.

Thinking about Joyce, we can locate two ways of engaging with translation within anglophone writing.[120] One, which involves the *description* of languages, corresponds to Apter's emphasis on phonemes and irreducible parts. And the other, which involves the *narration* of languages, corresponds to Cassin's emphasis on interminable process.[121] In Joyce, these versions of translation lead in two directions. The first generates a new, oppositional fluency, whereas the second seeks to neutralize fluency as a principle of aggregation. These two goals get their start in modernism, and in this sense they have the same history. But they do not share the same future, having spawned two largely divergent paths in contemporary fiction. The path of description can be traced from *Ulysses* to G. V. Desani's *All about H. Hatterr* (1948) and Anthony Burgess's *A Clockwork Orange* (1962) to Theresa Hak Kyung Cha's *Dictée* (1982), Ken Saro-Wiwa's *Sozaboy: A Novel in Rotten English* (1985), and Junot Díaz's *This Is How You Lose Her* (2012). We could easily choose other points in the trajectory—Salman Rushdie's *Midnight's Children* (1980) and Zadie Smith's *White Teeth* (2000) come immediately to mind—but the ones I've selected trace a striking ninety-year route from 1922 to 2012.

In *Clockwork Orange*, a made-up amalgam of Russian and English is meant to convey the unconscious totalitarianism of the supposedly liberal English state. The relationship between the two languages, condensed in the narrator's argot ("there were three devotchkas sitting at the counter all together, but there were four of us malchicks . . ."), tells a story about Cold War Britain, and it does so in ways that are difficult to replicate in other languages.[122] In many other twentieth-century works, multilingualism has served to record the political history of language imposition and language use; generate a new language;

and give shape to an audience whose distinctiveness is affirmed by the work. Díaz's stories are exemplary since they demonstrate some important continuities and divergences from the Joycean model. Take this passage about the narrator's brother's girlfriend, Pura:

> Pura was her name. Pura Adames.
>
> Pura Mierda was what Mami called her.
>
> OK, for the record, I didn't think Pura was so bad; she was a hell of a lot better than most of the ho's my brother had brought around. Guapísima as hell: tall and indiecita, with huge feet and an incredibly soulful face, but unlike your average hood hottie Pura seemed not to know what do with her fineness, was sincerely lost in all the pulchritude. A total campesina, from the way she held herself down to the way she talked, which was so demotic I couldn't understand half of what she said—she used words like *deguabinao* and *estribao* on the regular. She'd talk your ear off if you let her, and was way too honest: within a week she'd told us her whole life story. How her father had died when she was young; how for an undisclosed sum her mother had married her off at thirteen to a stingy fifty-year-old (which was how she got her first son, Nestor); how after a couple of years of that terribleness she got the chance to jump from Las Matas de Farfán to Newark, brought over by a tía who wanted her to take care of her retarded son and bedridden husband; how she had run away from her, too, because she hadn't come to Nueba Yol to be a slave to anyone, not anymore; how she had spent the next four years more or less being blown along on the winds of necessity, passing through Newark, Elizabeth, Paterson, Union City, Perth Amboy (where some crazy cubano knocked her up with her second son, Adrian), everybody taking advantage of her good nature. . . . [123]

Three characteristics stand out: First, the bilingual puns, which are accessible only to some readers. Second, the way that bilingualism, or code-switching, is associated not only with a single character but with the narrator, and thus with the work as a whole. And third, the use of italics for some but not all of the Spanish words.

Díaz's story performs a kind of reverse assimilation. Instead of translating Dominican speech into a standardized version of the

English language, Díaz asks readers comfortable with standard-ized English to acquire Dominican.[124] But he does more than this. He makes a new standard. He presents Spanish words as part of New Jersey's native language. In this gesture, his writing stands out from the multilingualism of most U.S. fiction. Joshua Miller has used the term "accented" to describe works that register, through nonstandard English spelling, the voices of their immigrant char-acters.[125] Accented novels such as Henry Roth's *Call It Sleep* (1934) and Monique Truong's *Book of Salt* (2003) incorporate the sounds of migrant speech and occasionally words from languages other than English. When non-English words appear, however, they appear in dialogue. The words seem to belong to some of the characters, but they do not belong to the novel. Roth and Truong use what appears to be unaccented English—often called Standard English—as the principal language of their texts. In Díaz's work, by contrast, Span-ish and English are internal to the work. The originality of Spanish, its presence as part of the novel's primary idiom, is emphasized by selective italicization (the slang words, *deguabinao* and *estribao*, in the passage above). Neither italicized nor footnoted, words such as "tía" and "indiecita" are local. They are not foreign. Indeed, when the story was published in the *New Yorker*, Díaz rejected house style (requiring italicization) and helped to bring about a new policy at the magazine in which foreign words are no longer distinguished typographically from so-called English ones.[126] Díaz's use of Span-ish and English together is very difficult to render in new languages, and indeed the text would prove difficult, too, for readers of the orig-inal who are not acquainted with Spanish—or who can't recognize Spanish at all.

Díaz creates a distinction between those who can read the lan-guage—those who are in on the multilingual joke about Pura, for example, which in Dominican pronunciation sounds like *puta*, mean-ing whore—and those who are not. But more to the point: his vocab-ulary is ephemeral. (Those familiar with modernist literature might think of Joyce's short story "The Boarding House.") Díaz records words of the moment, "on the regular"; as well as words on their way out, "the winds of necessity"; "taking advantage of her good nature." Called "The Pura Principle," the story captures a single moment, in a regional environment, among a small group of friends, whom the narrator calls his "boys." In all of these ways, Díaz's work fits the first path of non-translation.

However, the actual translation of Díaz's work offers an interesting coda and points toward the second path. If Díaz writes by describing languages, he translates by narrating them, and indeed one might argue that there is some narration built into his description. Díaz helped to produce the Spanish version of his award-winning novel, *The Brief and Wondrous Life of Oscar Wao*.[127] Instead of replicating the English version's puns at the scale of each individual word, he replicates what the puns do at the scale of the work. The novel in translation retains the relationship between English and Spanish but does not always preserve the specificity of Dominican-American phrases. Díaz explains in an interview that he began by translating the entire book into Spanish and then replaced some of those words with Spanish-functioning English terms, preserving "that sort of multilingual madness," as he puts it, but not the original lexicon.[128] In this translation practice, Díaz is suggesting that the relationship between English and Spanish can be reproduced structurally if not locally. The relationship, that is, is formal and thematic as well as semantic.

In the Spanish version of *This Is How You Lose Her*, Díaz's strategy is most readily apparent in the translation of the phrase "not anymore," as in, "she hadn't come to Nueba Yol to a be a slave to anyone, not anymore." *Así es como la pierdes* inserts the English-sounding phrase, "ya no" ("you know" / "no longer"): "porque ella no había venido a Nueba Yol a ser esclava de nadie, ya no."[129] The Spanish edition gains a bilingual phrase in one place while losing it in many others. For example, the phrase "Nuebo Yol" appears more familiar in the Spanish edition than it does in the English. In the French version, translated as *Guide du loser amoureux*, the title displays Díaz's structural technique, since the American word "loser" has some currency, as American, in colloquial French.[130] That phrase also retains part of original's pun ("lose her" / "loser"). However, the French stories add back italicization. Spanish terms such as "guapísima," "indiecita," and "tía," which are distinguished from "deguabinao" and "estribao" in the English version, appear imported (italicized) in the French edition.[131] The translation has difficulty retaining the reader's encounter with words that operate in two languages (English and Spanish, or English and French) instead of one. Compare the following with the passage from the U.S. edition:

> Pura, elle s'appelait. Pura Adames.
>
> Pura Mierda, comme l'appelait Mami.
>
> Bon, je précise que je ne la trouvais pas si mal; elle valait cent fois mieux que la plupart des traînées que mon frère avait ramenées. *Guapísima* en diable: grande et *indiecita*, des pieds immenses et un visage incroyablement expressif, mais contrairement aux autres beautés du quartier, Pura semblait ne pas savoir quoi faire de ses atouts, sincèrement perdue devant tant de charmes. Une *campesina* pur jus, de sa façon de se tenir à sa façon de parler, si péquenaude que je ne pigeais pas la moitié de ce qu'elle disait—elle utilisait régulièrement des mots comme *deguabino* et *estribao*. Elle bavassait à n'en plus finir si on la laissait faire, et elle était beaucoup trop spontanée: en moins d'une semaine elle nous avait raconté l'histoire de sa vie. Que son père était mort quand elle était petite; que sa mère l'avait donnée en mariage quand elle avait treize ans, en échange d'une somme inconnue, à un radin de cinquante piges (avec qui elle avait eu son premier fils, Nestor); qu'après quelques années de cette atrocité elle avait eu l'occasion de quitter Las Matas de Farfán pour Newark, invitée par une *tía* qui voulait qu'elle s'occupe de son fils attardé et de son mari grabataire; qu'elle s'était aussi enfuie de chez elle, parce qu'elle n'était pas venue à Nueba Yol pour être l'esclave de quiconque, plus jamais. . . .[132]

The story depends on the idea that some of the Spanish words also function in English: they are native to New Jersey. This is important to the English edition because the story is not, in fact, about foreignness. Just as children expand their vocabularies by reading more widely and adding new terms to their lexicon, readers of Díaz's fiction are meant to *learn* words rather than to *translate* them. This is one reason why Díaz's work might be best understood as regional rather than global. It is written in one language.

NARRATING LANGUAGES

Where does a text's multilingualism reside? When Coetzee's Simón mentions in the English text that "the alphabet" has twenty-seven letters, as it does in Spanish, the novel is narrating rather than describing languages. Or, when China Miéville dramatically interrupts a statement that signals one nation with a clause that signals another, he is registering the presence of foreign languages without representing them directly. Yasemin Yildiz has proposed that Kafka's multilingualism has more to do with his "writing *on* Yiddish" than with the so-called Yiddish features of his German language.[133] And Theodor Adorno, in an essay that has been foundational to theories of accented writing, acknowledges that it may be foreign ideas or unusual syntax, rather than foreign diction itself, that create the impression of nonnative expression.[134] In subsequent chapters I present other examples, including David Mitchell's references to a writing system of "characters" in a novel produced in Roman script; Jamaica Kincaid's and Mohsin Hamid's second-person narration; and the collation of editions in Young-Hae Chang Heavy Industries' digital narrative "Bust Down the Doors!" The example I pursue here comes from Ben Lerner's novel *Leaving the Atocha Station*, published in 2011. Lerner's novel has been enormously successful and has appeared in several languages, including German, Spanish, French, Dutch, and Italian. Raised in Kansas and now based in Brooklyn, Lerner won international awards as a poet before publishing his first work of fiction, whose title is taken from a poem by John Ashbery. His background in poetry is notable since Lerner's fiction strives to keep language at a distance.

Like Díaz, Lerner is concerned with the relationship between Spanish and English, and for that reason alone his novel offers a useful comparison. But there are other reasons too. *Leaving the Atocha Station* tells the story of a young American, Adam Gordon, who spends a year in Madrid on a fellowship.[135] He's supposed to be writing an epic poem about the Spanish Civil War, and it is part of the novel's irony that Adam thinks the world needs a U.S. poem about Iberian militarism while the United States is busy invading Iraq. At least initially, Adam appears to have minimal command of Spanish, and much of the plot involves his efforts, first, to fake proficiency and, later, to fake ignorance. The novel filters every conversation through the medium of the character's competence. The impression of multilingualism is achieved not through idiolect, as in Burgess and Díaz, but through the dilation of possible translations. Multilingualism in the novel is not a matter of *voice*, the literary quality that critics from Roland Barthes to Franco Moretti have deemed most sensitive to place.[136] It is instead a matter of *form*.[137] To pick up on the distinction between description and narration I've been using, Lerner's novel tells us about translation—how it works, how it doesn't work, and many of the meanings it might, theoretically, produce—but it doesn't represent either an original phrase or an accomplished translation at all.

Approached by a sympathetic young woman after he has been punched in the face for inadvertently saying something inappropriate, the narrator reports:

> She began to say something either about the moon, the effect of the moon on the water, or was using the full moon to excuse Miguel or the evening's general drama, though the moon wasn't full. Her hair was long, maybe longer than the guard's. Then she might have described swimming in the lake as a child, or said that lakes reminded her of being a child, or asked me if I'd enjoyed swimming as a child, or said that what she'd said about the moon was childish.[138]

The novel doesn't choose among the narrator's linguistic suppositions. It asks us to encounter the effort rather than the achievement of translation. The conjunction "or" and subjunctive syntax ("she might have described") appear frequently throughout the text. Whereas Díaz writes in a language we might call "native New Jersey," Lerner makes English into a foreign language. Both Díaz and Lerner are interested in two kinds of multilingualism: *internal multilingualism*, the varieties of expression within English or within Spanish, and *external multilingualism*, the movement between English and Spanish. They find different ways to put these two kinds of multilingualism into conversation. Díaz does this by introducing Spanish words that are foreign to New Jersey while also pointing at Spanish words that are local. Lerner does this by asking us to think about English versions of Spanish while he asks us to consider English versions of English, mediated in the novel by instant messaging, poetry, literary criticism, and free indirect discourse. Díaz's emphasis on description—all those Spanish and English words on the page—means that his novels are largely untranslatable, in Apter's sense. Lerner's are untranslatable in Cassin's sense: they approach translation from the perspective of reception.

Lerner is interested in the phenomenon of art's consumption, and indeed his novel begins with the narrator watching someone behold a painting in the Prado. The painting is reproduced in the novel so that readers too behold what Adam sees someone else behold. In this sense, readers are asked to think of themselves as the objects of the novel's attention, or at least as objects of Adam's attention. The novel stages various scenes of reception, which Lerner has described as a strategy of "recontextualization."[139] What the narrator and the reader encounter is someone else's encounter. This is one of the ways that Lerner promotes secondary, or mediated, experience. In his prose, Lerner is interested in the operations of language but not in what he calls the "surface effects of language," which he reserves for poetry.[140] Instead, he is focused on larger scales, deploying a collage of genres and circulating materials from one genre into another. There is no direct presentation of voice in the novel, apart from a short exchange involving instant messaging. Lerner's novel offers "a blueprint" for translation rather than the product of translation.[141] Hewing to the blueprint, Lerner keeps his novel from (not) being translated.

Both Lerner and Díaz are trying to produce works that provincialize English.[142] They force readers to grapple with partial fluency, register the arrogance of U.S. monolingualism, and invent strategies for incorporating the several languages, geographies, and audiences in which they get their start. Díaz's novel allows readers to learn the diegetic language, whereas Lerner's does not. Lerner's novel is less sanguine about creating new originals and about soliciting the reader's intimacy with the text. To be schematic for a moment, we might say that Lerner's novel welcomes translations into new languages by translating the original, whereas Díaz's stories themselves alter English but resist absorption by new languages. Díaz's texts are asserting their place in the world. Lerner is trying to retract that place. To put it in Casanova's terms, Lerner's novel tries to *unforget* its dominance. *Leaving the Atocha Station* reflects on the politics of language by dramatizing reception and by extolling the virtual. Partial fluency becomes in the novel a resource for self-expression and a basis for civic participation. Because Adam is not a knowing operator, he has to depend on what might be thought about him rather than on what he believes himself to be.

One could say that Lerner's novel accommodates translation because it avoids the "surface effects" of language. That accommodation is born out in the novel's Spanish edition, which has no trouble retaining the subjunctive quality of Adam's English-translated Spanish: "She began to say something either about the moon, the effect of the moon on the water, or was using the full moon to excuse Miguel" becomes simply "Empezó a contarme algo de la luna, del efecto de la luna sobre el agua, o utilizaba la luna llena para excusar a Miguel."[143] However, by recording the distance between "the actual words" in Spanish and "the claims made on their behalf," as Adam puts it in the U.S. edition, the novel keeps (not) being translated.[144] Lerner's text asks readers to confront the history and future of translation, and it invites translators into the literary history of the work within the work. At the end of the novel, Adam proposes to his translator that they "swap parts" for a public reading of his poems.[145] This means, he explains, that "Teresa would read the originals and I would read the translations and the translations would become the originals as we read."[146] The transformation is an effect of reading: the "translations" become the "originals" because they are presented first. There are now two originals, the ones made by the narrator and the ones made, as it were, by the audience. Originality, Adam implies, is produced by listening rather than (only) by writing or speaking. The status of the original, Lerner suggests, depends not on the artist but on the beholder.

In some ways the narration of languages retreats from the local since vernacular speech is often diminished. But narration also involves new ways of representing the local. We see this in the emphasis on the history and practice of translation, the distribution of literacy, the geopolitical institutions of literature, and the experience of partial fluency. The local now involves thinking about the origin of audiences and the mechanisms through which audiences add meaning to books. If we approach untranslatability as the dramatization of translation, then the most untranslatable texts become those that find ways to keep translation from stopping. They are those that invite translation rather than prohibit it. The engagement with idiolect is a distinctive trait of experimental fiction in the twentieth century.[147] But experimental fiction in the twenty-first century often withdraws from that engagement. Written for multiple audiences, contemporary novels have developed strategies of multilingualism designed for the foreign, nonfluent, and semifluent readers who will encounter them.

NEW VOCABULARIES

Approaching world literature from the perspective of translation means confronting the idea that languages are not really countable: they do not separate easily into discrete units, "like an apple and an orange," as one scholar has put it, and they are not equivalent units, as we notice when we compare the literatures of global languages such as English and Spanish with those of somewhat more localized languages such as Japanese and German or with those of even more localized languages such as Turkish and Swedish.[148] Literature scholars have generally relied on the distinctness of languages. That is how we organize our literary histories and how we construct world literature anthologies and syllabi. A focus on translation and contact among languages, however, implies new scales of literary history and new principles of literary belonging. By emphasizing the afterlives of individual works, the uptake of aesthetic strategies across regions, and generic developments, for example, Wai Chee Dimock, Martin Puchner, and Jahan Ramazani have established literary traditions based on formal and political affinity rather than simultaneity of language or historical period.[149] In this book, I gather anglophone works that address themselves to multiple audiences, invite reading as a source of making, and appear to be—and to be derived from—translated editions. These works point backward to the multilingual histories of the novel, including the history of writing in nonnative languages, and forward to its many possible futures.

The distinguished translator Edith Grossman has suggested recently that we need a new vocabulary for talking about the relationship between original works and works in translation.[150] This seems right to me. For literary historians, thinking about the several editions in which a work appears would involve devoting much more substantial attention to the reading of translations. Instead of asking about fidelity, whether the subsequent editions match the original, one might ask about innovation and about the various institutional and aesthetic frameworks that shape the work's ongoing production. Examining all of the translations that appear in a single year, for example, would allow scholars to consider as part of a literary culture all of those works that began as part of other literary cultures. Or one could track the translation of a single work as it moves out into new spaces.[151] These are important strategies for recovering the histories of translation and reception, and for thinking about how, where, and when translations have mattered. While I will have occasion to discuss the translations of some works, especially in chapters 1, 2, and 5, this book is devoted to a different question: how contemporary novels have incorporated translation into production, and what this development does—what it needs to do—to our analytic categories and procedures. It's not that we need a new vocabulary for reading works in translation. We need a new vocabulary for reading works. Instead of choosing between a literary history of originals and a literary history of translations, I approach these projects together. We have to do this because translation seeds production and is a crucial part of the literary ecosystem. We have to do this because many novels today address themselves to comparative audiences. There is no literary history without translation. Never has been. But today's novels have expanded the register of self-translation and multilingualism in unprecedented ways.

The chapters of *Born Translated* are organized conceptually, asking what happens to the signal categories of author, reader, original, translation, nation, world, native, and foreign when works appear to begin in many places and many languages. The chapters are also organized chronologically. Chapters 1 and 2 focus on Coetzee and

Ishiguro, whose longstanding engagement with translation can be traced to works published in the 1970s and 1980s. Later chapters focus on writers such as Mitchell, Phillips, Waldman, Hamid, Kincaid, Young-Hae Chang Heavy Industries, and Thirlwell, whose works featuring global circulation and multiple audiences emerge dramatically in the 1990s and after. Yet concepts drive this story. Chapter 1 shows that born-translated fiction, because it emphasizes ongoing production and multilingual reception, interferes with the novel's traditional role as an instrument of monolingual collectivity. It also interferes with traditional practices of close reading, which privilege fluency when they emphasize the text's smallest possible units: words. However, instead of proposing that born-translated works negate close reading or make it obsolete, I suggest that they direct close reading toward multiple editions of the work, larger units of the text, and units of the text that are also units of the book. Chapter 1 shows how the project of close reading and the usual objects of its attention ("details") are altered by the production of works intended for multiple audiences.

Chapter 2 turns from the question of how we read to the question of what we are reading. What is the object we hold in our hands? Book historians have asked: Is it the work, or is it simply one version of the work? Extending that question, this chapter asks: How many books constitute the work? Does the work consist of an edition in one language? Or does it consist of all editions, including those that may be produced in the future? The conceit of translation allows contemporary writers to approach their novels as series or lists of comparative versions. To invoke a distinction made by philosophers of art, novels that incorporate translation function more like performances than like site-specific sculptures. Acknowledging collaboration with translators, contemporary writers distance themselves from Romantic models of individuality and uniqueness. Born-translated works do not give up on uniqueness. Not exactly. Instead of assigning uniqueness to an object's internal characteristics, they assign uniqueness to the object's social properties: the way it relates to different objects in the same language, the same object in different languages, or objects of the same color or size or location. Beginning, in this sense, takes place over and over again.

Chapters 3 and 4 address the relationship between the character of books and the character of readers. In the first case, I look at novels in which readers seem to constitute texts; in the second case, I look at novels in which texts seem to constitute readers. Chapter 3 introduces the idea of the "world-shaped novel," a work of fiction that attributes its aesthetic and spatial origins to planetary circulation rather than to national, regional, or urban geographies associated with one language. All collectives depend on strategies of sampling, collating, and counting. World-shaped novels ask how those strategies are altered by migration and other histories of circulation. Whereas chapter 3 asks how audiences contribute to the meanings of aesthetic objects, chapter 4 asks how aesthetic objects make—or classify—audiences. In the latter chapter, I ask what it means, today, to be a "native reader," when many books appear in translation from the start and when many readers operate in languages that are different from those that they speak. I consider, first, the concept of native reading, and, second, how and why contemporary novels might choose to reject that concept. The chapter examines novels that dramatize the practical conditions of being—or not being—an audience. Deploying the second-person voice ("you"), these novels suggest that the most competent readers in the original will need to approach the works as translations. At the end of the chapter, I consider the generalization of this practice: reading all originals as if they are or will be translations.

The final chapter considers the irreducible collectivity of the born-translated novel as a paradigm for literary history and political belonging. I take as my examples several born-digital works because, self-published and irregularly updated, they appear in multiple languages and multiple versions of language at the same time. Operating as series (many editions, each in a different language) and as objects (one edition, consisting of different languages), these works reflect on the relationship between language and citizenship, testing common definitions of monolingual and multilingual, national and international, domestic and foreign. At the end of the chapter I turn to examples of born-translated literature in print that have integrated digital practices. These post-digital works draw attention to the embodiment of the book and to the institutional, technological, and geopolitical histories of circulation.

My epilogue introduces Adam Thirlwell's collaborative project "Multiples," published in 2013. Like many of the born-digital works discussed in the previous chapter, Thirlwell's edition can be understood both as an anthology of individual objects in different languages and as an anthology of individual translations of the same object. Eighteen languages appear on its pages. While Thirlwell seems to present two kinds of serial individuality, individual works and individual translations, in fact his project is profoundly social in a variety of ways, hearkening back to the multilanguage periodicals of the modernist era and indebted to the coterie publishing of today.[152] Thirlwell celebrates his translators' creativity but also dramatizes profound disagreements about translation's political meanings and normative procedures. The translations included in the book run from paraphrase, collaboration, and adaptation to homage, imitation, scrupulous transposition, and replacement. As a template for literary history, "Multiples" testifies to contemporary fiction's robust uncountability in an age of world literature. Yet, through paratextual essays and visual images that emphasize translation practices, it also makes world literature accountable. The born-translated novel strives to embrace this paradox: accountability without countability; a literature of global circulation from the perspective of ongoing production.

1

CLOSE READING AT A DISTANCE

Yet where in the world can one hide where one will not feel soiled? Would he feel any cleaner in the snows of Sweden, reading at a distance about his people and their latest pranks?

—J. M. Coetzee, *Summertime*

MAKING WORLD LITERATURE

Literary works that begin in translation require a new understanding both of what we read and of how much. Pointing at past and future versions, works may appear as unfinished collectives: not as one monolingual edition but as many editions in languages as varied as Korean, Dutch, French, English, Greek, and Urdu.[1] Readers will be able analyze only some parts closely because few will possess the necessary combination of languages and because the quantity of languages one would need to know continues to grow as subsequent translations appear. In this sense, born-translated writing repels attention and impedes the reader's mastery or knowledge of the work. But it also redirects attention. There is certainly no consensus about what close reading involves, whether the microscopic analysis of a text's very smallest units (words) or the macroscopic analysis of its thematic clusters, structural elements, and narrative devices. Yet born-translated writing modifies both kinds of closeness by expanding the notion of what an individual text is. Our interpretive energies shift rather than dissipate. The objects of closeness now include a narrative's visual as well as verbal qualities, paratextual materials such as typography and illustration, and aspects of the work that

06. On guidance systems

There were times during the Cold War when the Russians fell so far behind the Americans in weapons technology that, if it had come to all-out nuclear warfare, they would have been annihilated without achieving much in the way of retaliation. During such periods, the *mutual* in Mutual Assured Destruction was in effect a fiction.

These interruptions in equilibrium came about because the Americans from time to time made leaps ahead in telemetry, navigation, and guidance systems. The Russians might possess powerful rockets and numerous warheads, but their capacity to deliver them accurately to their targets was always much inferior to that of the Americans.

As a typist pure and simple, Anya from upstairs is a bit of a disappointment. She meets her daily quota, no problem about that, but the rapport I had hoped for, the feel for the sort of thing I write, is hardly there. There are times when I stare in dismay at the text she turns in. According to Daniel Defoe, I read, the true-born Englishman hates "papers and papery." Brezhnev's generals sit "somewhere in the urinals."

As I pass him, carrying the laundry basket, I make sure I waggle my behind, my delicious behind, sheathed in tight denim. If I were a man I would not be able to keep my eyes off me. Alan says there are as many different bums in the world as there are faces. Mirror, mirror on the wall, I say to Alan, whose is the fairest of them all? Yours, my princess, my queen, yours without a doubt.

FIGURE 1.1 Text from J. M. Coetzee, *Diary of a Bad Year* (London: Harvill Secker, 2007), 25.

Reprinted by permission of the publisher.

exceed the single monolingual version. What I call "close reading at a distance" differs from traditional "close reading" in two principal ways:[2] it demotes the analysis of idiolect, the privileged object of close reading's attention, in favor of larger narrative units and even units that seem to exceed the narrative; and it adds circulation to the study of production by asking what constitutes the languages, boundaries, and media of the work.[3]

We combine these two gestures when we approach literature that seems to be both an object and a collection of objects. As soon as a work appears as a group, we have to toggle between literary history and literary work. J. M. Coetzee's 2007 novel *Diary of a Bad Year* solicits this procedure by imitating the visual format of interlineal and facing-page translation (figure 1.1).[4] Whereas translation in 2013's *Childhood of Jesus* is principally a matter of story and literary precedent, in *Diary* Coetzee has built translation into the physical layout of almost every page. Pointing at the embodiment of the text in this dramatic way, Coetzee asks us to consider how circulation shapes production. More than this, he suggests that understanding circulation as an agent of production alters our most basic principles of literary and political collectivity: exclusive beginnings, the completeness of novels and nations, and a developmental narrative that sequences—and separates—composition, publication, and reception.

Diary of a Bad Year is born translated because it was published in multiple languages almost simultaneously and premiered in Dutch rather than in English (figure 1.2).[5] It does not belong to any one national, ethnic, or linguistic tradition. It is also born translated because it displays, both fictionally and formally, its own multilingual start. Formally, the novel experiments with comparative inventories such as lists and catalogues; typographically, it invokes visual practices of comparison associated with the print culture of translation; and thematically, it reflects on gestures of ethical, national, and generic comparison. Because of the novel's architecture, we have to follow individual strands of narrative while comparing across those strands. We are led to compare visually as well as verbally: to consider how a word's appearance in a philosophical essay at the top of the page relates to its appearance in one of the two diaries printed below, and how the meaning of an idea changes as it moves among the novel's many discursive

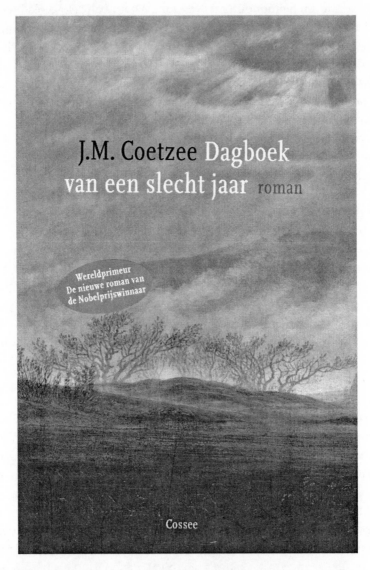

FIGURE 1.2 Front cover of the Dutch translation of *Diary of a Bad Year*, J. M. Coetzee, *Dagboek van een slecht jaar*, translated by Peter Bergsma (Amsterdam: Cossee, 2007).

Reprinted by permission of the publisher.

registers. Those registers include academic and popular; public and private; the geopolitical and the neighborhood; oral, written, analog, and digital; standard and vernacular. Comparison functions, too, as one of the novel's abiding ethical concerns. The text asks whether transnational enlargement in fact enhances or ultimately thwarts our capacity for social responsibility and political agency.

The global expansion and increased speed of translation have led many novelists to ask whether it remains useful or even accurate to associate their works with original languages. What does it mean to refer to *the text* when the work exists from the start in several editions? How does the multilingualism of the book change the way we understand the literary and political culture to which the work belongs? These are political as well as aesthetic questions. For his part, Coetzee has been reluctant to distinguish between original and translated editions. In a 1977 analysis of Gerrit Achterberg's poem "Ballade van de gasfitter," Coetzee refuses to say whether his interpretation relies on the Dutch version of the poem or on his translation of the Dutch version into English. He claims that the distinction is irrelevant because "all reading is translation, just as all translation is criticism."[6] We could understand this quip to mean that the process of analyzing the poem in Dutch is analogous to the process of translating the Dutch poem into English. And we could associate Coetzee with the belief that all translation, from any language into any other language, is historically, intellectually, and politically equivalent. But in fact in his novels and criticism, Coetzee has explored the history and politics of translation practices. He has associated translation, variously, with projects of colonialism, nationalism, and transnational solidarity. In his 1988 study of nineteenth-century South African literature in English, *White Writing*, Coetzee examines in scrupulous detail how writers produced "convincing imitations in English" of speech patterns from other languages such as Afrikaans. He argues that the representation of language "transfer" from Afrikaans into English had the effect of assigning a simplified consciousness to Afrikaans-speaking characters.[7]

Coetzee often represents non-English speech or writing, but he generally avoids stylistic marking such as grammatical inversion or broken diction that would remind readers of a specific foreign language.[8]

There are at least three consequences to this choice. Coetzee's texts can be more easily translated, since there is little dialect or accent to be reproduced in another language. He does not associate the consciousness of a kind of character, where "kind" refers to ethnic community or national origin, with specific features of language. And he creates a text in which even English readers are blocked from imagining a direct, simultaneous encounter with a language that is their own. This last point is crucial: for Coetzee, it has always seemed inappropriate, both ethically and historically, to suggest that his writing is part of a distinct national-language tradition that emerges from a coherent national community. For this reason, one could say that all of Coetzee's fiction, not only those works that approach translation thematically or graphically, aspires to comparative beginnings. Because Coetzee associates linguistic and cultural homogeneity with apartheid nationalism, his fiction is in some ways most South African—most attentive, that is, to the history and politics of apartheid—when it appears most translated.

We can find Coetzee's ambivalence about national traditions stated more or less explicitly throughout his interviews, criticism, and fiction. "Perhaps—is this possible?—I have no mother tongue," *Diary*'s essayist considers (195). The protagonist implies that his sense of discomfort in any one language, his sense that in his voice "some other person (but who?) is being imitated, followed, even mimicked" (195), can be attributed to the history of colonialism. He imagines that middle-class Indians might experience something similar:

> There must be many who have done their schooling in English, who routinely speak English in the workplace and at home (throwing in the odd local locution for colouring), who command other languages only imperfectly, yet who, as they listen to themselves speak or as they read what they have written, have the uneasy feeling that there is something false going on. (197)

The falseness that Coetzee hears in his own voice and imagines in the voices of postcolonial readers and writers elsewhere does not represent a failure to use English successfully. To the contrary: it represents the difficulty of registering, as one speaks or writes flawlessly, the history of other languages. As both a colonial and a postcolonial nation, to use Andrew van der Vlies helpful formulation, South Africa has continued to struggle over whether national belonging should ever be associated with a single tongue.[9] Coetzee engages with this struggle by creating works that appear in multiple-language editions while also emphasizing the dynamics of translation within those editions. In the remainder of this chapter, I consider how Coetzee's recent novels reflect on the relationship between literary history and political belonging, and how they refine and in some ways resist paradigms of possessive collectivism and simultaneous community. Finally, I suggest why new approaches to collectivity require new approaches to reading.

READERS, NOT WRITERS:
ELIZABETH COSTELLO AND SLOW MAN

Fluent from childhood in Afrikaans and English, Coetzee often writes about communities in which people speak different languages and sometimes speak more than one language. Now a resident of Australia, where he has become yet another kind of migrant-settler and where the characters of his recent novels make their homes, Coetzee emphasizes the differences within language, such as the English of Cape Town and the English of Adelaide. However, he almost always handles these moments diegetically: he tells us about words in addition to describing or citing them on the page. Coetzee also writes book reviews, which he collects in volumes whose tally now rivals the number of his fictional works. It is remarkable how many of the reviews published since 2002 focus on the histories, difficulties, and opportunities of translation. In those essays, published in 2007 as a volume called *Inner Workings*—a suggestive title for a book focused largely on translation—Coetzee considers the difficulty of translating texts that are written either in a regional version of a national language or in multiple languages.[10]

Not only the translation of other people's books but also the translation of his own books has filtered into Coetzee's production. In a 2005 essay he tells a story about helping his French translator choose among the several equivalents for the English word "darkness."[11] To find the word that would best convey the meaning of his original text, Coetzee reports, he sent the translator to French versions of D. H. Lawrence. Since he meant his use of "darkness" to evoke the tone of Lawrence's fiction, he explains, the French translation of his novel should above all sound like the French translation of Lawrence's novels. Translation, in this case, becomes both a localizing and a globalizing procedure: localizing because Coetzee's Lawrentian tone is preserved; globalizing because Coetzee's Lawrentian tone is preserved—but only by conforming to a tradition of francophone translations. Past translations have established the conditions for the future of Coetzee's originals.

We see this explicitly in *Diary of a Bad Year*; in 2005's *Slow Man*, whose principal characters treat English as a second language; and in 2003's *Elizabeth Costello*, named for the fictional writer whose experiences on the international lecture circuit are described in many of the chapters. We see it also in 2009's *Summertime*, a fictional memoir that consists of five transcribed and edited interviews, of which at least two and possibly three have been translated into English. Critics are sometimes reluctant to describe Coetzee's works as novels since he has made resisting the historical and cultural meanings of the novel a persistent feature of his literary career.[12] Yet, paradoxically, Coetzee's resistance to the novel may be the best reason to retain it as both context and classification for his work. Coetzee does not relinquish novelistic concepts such as agency, collectivity, individuality, development, and action. Instead, he approaches them as if they no longer function or as if they need new functions. The generic oddness of Coetzee's works, their existence as novels that no longer underwrite novel-concepts, may help to explain why so many of Coetzee's texts—those that look like memoirs, those that look like essays, and those that look like novels—are marketed as "fictions," as if Coetzee or his publishers are trying to thwart classification altogether.[13] In this chapter, I refer to all of Coetzee's narrative fictions as "novels," emphasizing Coetzee's focus on the novel's elasticity as a genre, its history as a medium of national collectivity, and its function, in translation, as a source of collectivities both smaller and larger than the nation.

Slow Man and *Diary* ask how new technologies of reproduction and prosthesis transform our sense of the enclosed national community. They are testing two of Benedict Anderson's central claims: first, that "the book . . . is a distinct, self-contained object, exactly reproduced on a large scale"; and second, that the book's self-containment imitates and even stimulates the imagination of a contained, simultaneous collectivity.[14] Coetzee asks how a translated edition or a spare leg might alter our conceptions of the individual. As readers will know, the appearance in Coetzee's fiction of nonfiction genres, self-referential characters, and even novelists is not an innovation of the late style. His third-person autobiographies, which began with *Boyhood* in 1997, offer striking, inventive contributions to the tradition of fictional memoir. And there is Coetzee's very first novel, *Dusklands* from 1974, one of whose short narratives contains what is presented as an English translation of a Dutch document attributed to an eighteenth-century explorer named Jacobus Coetzee. So, translation, metafiction, and biography have been there together in Coetzee's work for more than forty years.[15] But in the recent work there has been a decided turn to technologies of writing, to the making of world literature, and to the relationship between production and circulation.

Elizabeth Costello is a classic example of world literature in both the older and the newer senses of the term: it is at once a literary masterpiece, a book produced by a Nobel laureate; and it is a literary underdog, a book produced by a native of South Africa who now lives in Australia. It is also a book produced within many literary networks: it began in at least four countries—Australia, South Africa, Great Britain, and the United States—and has now appeared in at least nineteen languages and twenty-one editions. As a text, *Elizabeth Costello* builds on several traditions of world fiction while also describing the institutions of making, evaluating, and promoting that constitute world literature today. There are references throughout to world masterpieces such as Joyce's *Ulysses*, Kafka's "Report to an Academy" and "Before the Law," and the writings of Edgar Allan Poe and Harriet Beecher Stowe. There are references to real African novels such as *The Palm Wine Drinkard* and to made-up Australian ones such as *The House on Eccles Street*, a rewriting of *Ulysses* that constitutes Elizabeth Costello's best-known work. Coetzee's protagonist is described as a "major world writer" (2).

And there is the transnational literary marketplace, what we might call the guts of world literature, represented in brutal anecdotes about the exigencies of book publishing, classifying, reviewing, interviewing, prize-receiving, and lecture-giving. These anecdotes are matched to a range of venues, including the lecture hall, the banquet room, the seminar table, the academic conference, the cruise ship, and the radio station. The venues correspond to a range of geographic locations, including college towns in Pennsylvania and Massachusetts, a hotel in Amsterdam, a university in Johannesburg, and the shores of Antarctica. Because many of the chapters of Coetzee's book were first presented as public talks, the text's anecdotes constitute both the real and the fictional occasions of Coetzee's book. Without its audiences, Coetzee seems to say, *Elizabeth Costello* would never have been made.

Elizabeth Costello is everywhere interested in the difference between the inside of literary works—their verbal content—and what appears to us as the outside: the bodies of writers, editions, reviewers, critics, and audiences. At many points Coetzee will suggest that a book's outside is continuous with its inside, or that a book's inside exists only because its outside was there to contain it. In this vein, Elizabeth Costello, the character, will assert that a literary tradition succeeds because it has a "readership, not a writership" (53) and elsewhere that we should value literature and animals as well as people not by what they seem to be in themselves but by our "engagement" with them (95–96). Committed to the embeddedness of books among communities of readers, Elizabeth tells a large audience, "The book we are reading isn't the book he thought he was writing" (82). Later, she tells a class, "Writers teach us more than they are aware of" (97). These may sound like pronouncements about the metaphorical nature of all language—the way it is always meaning something else—but they are also arguments for the history and geography of books. Writers teach us more than they are aware of because they cannot possibly account for all of the communities, editions, languages, and literary histories into which a book will travel. A novel's inside, Coetzee suggests, is inseparable from its embodiment in the world. In this sense, a book might be said to have several insides or to produce its own inside multiple times.

Of course, when one thinks of *Elizabeth Costello*'s treatment of interiority, it is not the inside of books that first comes to mind. The two most infamous chapters, which Coetzee presented as the Tanner Lectures at Princeton University, feature lectures and post-lecture dinners in which Elizabeth Costello, the honored guest at a sumptuous meal, denounces what she calls the "holocaust" of animal slaughter (80). Ventriloquizing Plutarch on the subject of eating meat, Elizabeth tells her hosts that she is "astonished that you can put in your mouth the corpse of a dead animal, astonished that you do not find it nasty to chew hacked flesh and swallow the juices of death wounds" (83). Elsewhere, she will say that she is not going to remind her audience—and then she does remind them—about "what is being done to animals at this moment in production facilities, . . . in abattoirs, in trawlers, in laboratories, all over the world" (63). She will argue while visiting an undergraduate seminar that the relationship between the systematic slaughter of Jews and the systematic slaughter of animals is not simply rhetorical: "the Nazis learned how to process bodies," she asserts, by imitating the production methods of the Chicago stockyards (97). Coetzee asks us to think about the world systems that produce both dinner and novel, and he will suggest that such expansion—from the novel to the book, and from the dinner to the stockyards—both intensifies one's attention and in some ways limits it. Coetzee points readers to the mechanisms (abattoirs and trawlers) that transform animals into meat, to the quotidian and visceral details of the transformed object, to the total process by which "corpse" is mystified as "dinner," and to the complex geographies of production that link one kind of slaughter to another. To take ethical action, the novel suggests, we need to know that our lunch comes from the slaughterhouse, but ethical action is stalled—the character of Elizabeth Costello is physically overcome—when every intimacy is tainted by the process of enlargement, and by the inevitable connection of animal slaughter to endless other unseen slaughters such as Nazi genocide. In the novel's final chapter, a letter-writer who goes by "Elizabeth C." finds she can no longer think because she is consumed by metaphors: everything feeds into to everything else.[16]

Even before its final chapter, *Elizabeth Costello* offers several images of self-consuming consumption: the Moebius strip—one character is named Susan Moebius—in which every end also serves as a beginning (15); the traveler's jetlagged watch that is three and also fifteen hours out (27); the sexual encounter remembered as one person's knee fitted into another's armpit (24). And there is also the writer's voice, about which Elizabeth Costello muses, "Only by an ingenious economy . . . does the organ of ingestion sometimes get to be used for song" (54). Each of these images points away from possessive collectivism: the notion, as one character proposes, that African novels emanate from African bodies, or that literary texts are expressive of a permanent, shared past. Instead, Coetzee suggests, novels are collaborative insofar as writers are always addressing their books to future readers as well as to prior writers. But Coetzee is also trying to say something different about bodies and texts: instead of treating them as containers for a unique and coherent interiority (a kind of person or literary work), he presents them as containers of fragile and often repulsive matter (a kind of animal). At the end of the novel's first chapter, titled "Realism," Elizabeth's son is horrified to consider that what is inside his mother is not her consciousness but her "gullet, pink and ugly, contracting as it swallows, like a python, drawing things down to the pear-shaped belly-sac" (34). He balks at having to think about the body's mechanisms. "That is not where I come from," he tells himself. The son wants to "come from" a person or a nation of sovereign agency, whereas Elizabeth associates individuality with nonhuman systems and social relations ("you in me, I in you" [32]). *Elizabeth Costello* reminds its readers persistently that texts, like people, have physical substance. The folding of speech into digestion, voice into stomach, production into consumption, can lead to futility, as in Elizabeth C.'s letter. But digestion can also create opportunities for new inspiration, allowing individuals to "act out of character" and to enter the lives of other characters (149, 155).

In order to act out of character, it is helpful to have a character, or a sense of one, in the first place. Not being sure of one's "situation" can lead simply to vertigo: what appears in the novel as a misfit between rhetoric and context (224). There can be no writing, the novel suggests, without at least some provisional situation. Yet the novel continually asks what a situation is, and how many situations count, for writers whose works start in several places and in conversation with writers from other traditions. By focusing on consumption, Coetzee's novel resists the logic of unique origin that governs most accounts of world literary history. In *Elizabeth Costello*, various kinds of consumption intersect, consumption feeds production, and knowing where things come from has to be established multiple times. Coetzee asks readers to consider that national literary histories, like animal slaughter and the Holocaust, are made possible by a theory of collectivity that privileges the simultaneity of consciousness over the solidarity of social contact. In the possessive-collectivism and imagined-community paradigms, the uniqueness and coherence of a text's inside leads to a nation-based model of literary history.[17] Coetzee suggests an alternative model by emphasizing the multiple contexts—and multiple scales—of aesthetic production. Building circulation into his novels, Coetzee registers the unsettling effects of the global marketplace, but he registers, too, the several beginnings that circulation makes possible. For readers of *Elizabeth Costello*, collectivity is always out of joint. Like a jetlagged watch or a Moebius strip, the novel places readers both after and before the narrative action. A grammatical stutter on the novel's second page takes us from the rhetoric of fiction ("Elizabeth Costello travelled . . .") to the rhetoric of fiction-making (" . . . or travels [present tense henceforth]") (2). By suggesting that readers have prompted the text's alteration, Coetzee makes them agents as well as objects of the novel's community.

Elizabeth Costello reflects on translation by emphasizing the global itinerary of novels and novelists and by dramatizing the transnational origins of world literature. *Slow Man*, which also asks "where we come from" (52), approaches translation not through the migration of books but through the migration of people. The novel's main characters, the injured Paul Rayment and his nurse, Marijana Jokić, live in Australia but began somewhere else. Paul came from France when he was a small child; Marijana arrived much more recently from Croatia. Marijana speaks an accented English: her unusual choice of words indicates that she is translating ideas from Croatian. Paul, whose thoughts are often part of the novel's discourse, is constantly selecting English words or invoking words from other languages. His English seems fluent, but he claims that the language feels unnatural to him. Is it because he is a character in one of Elizabeth Costello's novels, as she tells him when she appears on the scene? Or is it, as he tells her, because he is using a language that belong to someone, or someplace, else?

> As for language, English has never been mine in the way it is yours. Nothing to do with fluency. I am perfectly fluent, as you can hear. But English came to me too late. It did not come with my mother's milk. In fact it did not come at all. Privately I have always felt myself to be a kind of ventriloquist's dummy. It is not I who speak the language, it is the language that is spoken through me. It does not come from my core, *mon coeur*. (197–98).

Paul's comments are in some ways untranslatable, since they involve both the consonance and the dissymmetry between the English "core" (interior) and the French "*coeur*" (interior, but also heart). Yet Paul's explicit translation of English into French should draw our attention to his implicit translations of French into English and of one kind of English into another. The appearance of a French phrase serves as a reminder that English, at least for the speaker, is a foreign language too. We are reading an anglophone novel, Coetzee suggests, but its characters are speaking and thinking in translation.

Describing languages, as I argue in the introduction, some contemporary novels use slang, local references, foreign words, and accent to exclude uninitiated readers and to welcome those who know, or who can master, the text's idiom. Mastery is possible: some have it, and some don't. Coetzee's novel leans in another direction. It uses words in French, Spanish, Croatian, and other tongues—there are at least seven besides English—to create a general sense of partial fluency. There is no original text to know, and no single vernacular community that could know all of it. Paul is always translating, both in the sense of testing the resources of different national languages and in the sense of trying to speak to a target audience without any source to call his own.

Like a good translator, Paul is obsessed with accents, double meanings, and clichés. His attention to idiolect may seem counterproductive for a novel interested in global circulation since it is difficult to move clichés from one language to another. But this is exactly the point. The novel doesn't just repeat clichés (*"Like a cat he tells himself"* [1]; *"full of beans!* he thinks" [6]; and so on); it flags them emphatically. Paul's overzealous selection of words—the way he "picks up the primly disapproving word of the day, weighs it, tests it," or the way he dubs one character "Mrs. Putts or Putz" and another "Wayne something-or-other, Bright or Blight" (180, 16, 20)—isolates him by emphasizing fluency at the expense of sociability.[18] And in truth, for all his weighing and testing, Paul's words are worn rather than expressive. The more the novel asks us to notice that Paul speaks "like a book," as Elizabeth Costello puts it, the more we sense that Paul is trying to control language rather than deploy it (230–31). Paradoxically, the logic of fluency underwrites the logic of exclusion. "You speak English like a foreigner," Elizabeth tells Paul (231). Paul embraces his foreignness, insisting, "if there were no foreigners there would be no natives." But Elizabeth means something else. She isn't telling him to speak better. She is telling him to "speak from the heart," and thus she counters his clichés with one of her own (231). If we return for a moment to *Elizabeth Costello*, we find that speaking from the heart corresponds to an ethics of hospitality: we are supposed to live with nonhuman animals, or other people, not because we know what they are thinking but despite the fact that we don't. Community cannot be premised on common language or on unique expressivity, Coetzee suggests; instead, it has to be attempted on the basis of partial understanding and even misunderstanding.

Because Paul values fluency, he is relentlessly fixing or lamenting someone else's diction. At one point Marijana asks him in her English-translated Croatian if he is a "book saver," and he responds almost immediately that he is a "book collector" (47). But as he suspects and as the novel implies, Paul is in fact more interested in conservation than collection. He is committed to natural languages, even though what passes for natural language often involves unrecognized translation and the appropriation of other languages. For example, Paul lights on "unstrung" as the perfect term to describe his fragile emotional state. The term appears several times in the novel, and Paul says he has taken it from Homer's *Iliad* (27). However, he has in fact taken it from an English translation of Homer's *Iliad*. The perfect English word is a Greek word. Paul is unstrung not because he has lost his resolve but because his accommodations have become visible. He has managed thus far by passing as an Australian, which means he did what was necessary to fit with everyone else: "'That, as far as I am concerned, is all there is to it, to the national-identity business: where one passes and where one does not, where on the contrary one stands out. Like a sore thumb, as the English say; or like a stain, as the French say, a stain on the spotless domestic linen'" (197). Paul's invocation of national idiom, "as the English say" and "as the French say," reminds us that fitting requires fluency, and here Coetzee seems to share Paul's disdain for political collectivities defined by the appearance—and the sounds—of similarity. It is precisely by reminding us that "the English" have a way of speaking that the novel registers its own multilingualism. Coetzee uses these moments to emphasize circulation as a source of production: Paul is not English, and he is addressing himself to readers who might not be English either.

Slow Man associates passing—a kind of invisible translation—with unmindfulness. The problem, the novel suggests, is not one's success or failure to pass but forgetting the demand for invisibility to which one has tacitly acceded. While passing can sometimes function as a tactic of appropriation or subversion, here it seems to register capitulation: the idea that everyone should look or sound the same. Sounding the same requires a natural language. Looking the same requires a natural body. Paul registers his desire for naturalness most intensively when he states his reasons for refusing a prosthesis. After losing part of his leg in a bicycle accident, he says he wants to "feel natural" rather than "look natural" (59). He means by this that he doesn't want to think about his body at all. "Did he feel natural before the occurrence on Magill Road? He has no idea. But perhaps that is what it means to feel natural: to have no idea" (59). Coetzee associates Paul's desire to be disembodied, to be a self without a body, with his desire for continuity with the past. He wants to be remembered "As I used to be"; he wants his bookshelves to be dusted but everything to remain "in the same order" (50). He collects nineteenth-century photographs depicting Australia's first waves of English and Irish migration because he wants to preserve "the last survivors," by which he means not only "the men and women and children" whose images are captured but also "the photographs themselves, the photographic prints" (65). In some ways, Coetzee seems to support Paul's "fidelity" to these photographs (65), which display not only the history of Australia's several migrations but also the history of the technology that recorded them. In other ways, however, Paul's instinct for *preservation* seems to obstruct Marjiana's and the novel's projects of *restoration*.

In the novel, "restoration" refers to the process of animating objects, people, or artworks that have ceased to function. Marijana, a day nurse and former refurbisher of paintings, has made two careers out of reviving damaged goods. Her son, Drago, updates Paul's photographs of Australian history by scanning them and adding in his own Croatian ancestors; later he turns Paul's broken bicycle into a recumbent suitable to Paul's damaged leg. Paul is absolutely set against restoration, ostensibly because he wants the real thing or nothing at all, but really because he doesn't want to think about utility. "A recumbent. He has never ridden one before, but he dislikes recumbents instinctively, as he dislike prostheses, as he dislikes all fakes" (255). Paul is repulsed by the idea that a bicycle or a self or a work of art could be transformed by use, or by the material that serves as its container. But in order to be mindful, as Elizabeth Costello demands of him, Paul has to acknowledge embodiment. Like people, it turns out, words have function rather than character: they can be restored, and they can develop new functions. This is true for communities too. Speaking of the nation, Paul seems to understand that Australian history cannot be as "fixed, immutable" as he wants his photographs to be (64). He wonders to Marijana, "Don't immigrants have a history of their own? Do you cease to have a history when you move from one point on the globe to another?" (49). The nation's history, the novel suggests, is always in need of restoration. Because immigrants keep arriving, there can be no concurrence of action and language, and there can be no finished or completed nation. To a simultaneous past, Coetzee prefers a translated present in which histories of circulation remain ongoing and formative.

WRITING IN TRANSLATION:
DIARY AND *SUMMERTIME*

Elizabeth Costello and *Slow Man* approach translation thematically by focusing on technologies and experiences of global circulation, including the global circulation of people. In its treatment of English as a foreign language, *Slow Man* recalls modernist works such as *Ulysses* and *Lolita*. Yet, emphasizing the role of audiences in the ongoing production of the work and reflecting on the limits of individuality as a model for expressivity, it fits well with Coetzee's other recent novels. *Diary of a Bad Year* and *Summertime* approach these concerns formally, asking readers to analyze the physical properties of the text and to consider what constitutes the work before them. Both novels resist the principle of fluency, or what is often valorized as "reading in the original," by suggesting that only part of the work, or an unfinished work, is held in the reader's hands. They obstruct access to a unique language and reject the association between simultaneity and collectivity by insisting on comparison: in *Diary*, we encounter paragraphs in different genres; in *Summertime*, we encounter interviews in translation.

Diary presents its essays—this is the fiction—as the work of a famous South African writer who has been asked to compose a series of "strong opinions" for publication, first in German and later in French. The writer is called "J. C." and sometimes "Señor C.," so again we are in the presence of autobiographical fiction. The publication history of the novel increases the autobiographical effect. An excerpt was first published in a July 2007 issue of the *New York Review of Books* (*NYRB*), where Coetzee more often appears as a reviewer or commentator than as a novelist.[19] In the *NYRB*, one finds bracing short essays titled "on the origins of the state," "on anarchism," "on democracy," "on Machiavelli," and "on terrorism." Aphoristic in length and style, the essays are interrupted every few paragraphs by a single paragraph, printed in boldface, in which a narrator describes his encounter with a shapely woman in a short red dress, whom he has met in his building's laundry room. The narrator's crass reflections on the shortness of the dress, the shapeliness of the woman, and his own comparative decrepitude provide an odd but welcome contrast to the dour seriousness of the political compositions. As the excerpt ends, it becomes clear that the diary writer is the essay writer, and the shapely woman in the short red dress will be his typist.

The July teaser gives the impression that the longer book will consist of two voices: one impersonal, political, and a little stilted; the other intimate, solipsistic, and a little coarse. But in the novel, there is a third voice—the typist's account of her interactions with the writer—and on almost every page at least two and usually three of these voices appear. Each is separated from the others by a thin horizontal line (figure 1.1). At the top, we find the essays; in the middle we find the author's account of his interactions with the typist; and at the bottom there is the typist's account of those same encounters. What seems in the *NYRB* excerpt to be a series of political and philosophical essays interrupted by the occasional paragraph of personal diary comes in the novel as a much more balanced structure, or even a rivalry, in which the essays and the two diaries vie for our attention and indeed require us to organize our attention at every turn. A Victorian novel might have organized these internal texts into serial form—essays followed by diary followed by second diary—but Coetzee's novel presents them synchronically, at least on the page. Because most pages are separated into three sections, our attention is drawn to the paragraphs, which function as parts of different narratives organized by genre and as parts of the same narrative organized by the book. Individual words may be of interest to us, but it is the paragraph and the grouping of paragraphs that appear as the fundamental units of attention and that remind us of a language circulating alongside other languages.

While the *NYRB* excerpt implies that the diary exists as light background for the strong opinions, the novel gives greater emphasis to the diary's subject matter: the dictating, the typing, and the conversation between author and typist. The novel suggests that those processes inform, both structurally and thematically, the essays' models of sovereignty and political action. For example, Señor C. does not write the essays—at least not in any traditional sense. Rather, he scrawls a few illegible notes onto a sheaf of papers, dictates into a tape recorder, and then hands both notes and tape to his typist, who transfers his words onto computer disks, though not before fixing

FIGURE 1.3 Front cover of *Diary of a Bad Year,* J. M. Coetzee
(Melbourne: Text Publishing, 2007).

Reprinted by permission of the publisher.

them up, as she puts it, "where they lack a certain something" (29). The essays are thus born electronic, both in the analog (audiotape recording) and the digital sense (microchip). I'll have more to say about the relationship between translation and technology later on, but for now let's simply note that Coetzee's novel asks us to think from the start about its status as a reproduced artifact, about the ways that narratives are shaped by contemporary and near-contemporary writing technologies, and about what happens to accounts of the enclosed nation-state—the subject of many of the novelist's essays—when they are played back, invisibly altered, and mechanically blended with other genres.

It is important to Coetzee's project that the personal essay and the diary are two of the genres we associate most closely with individual voice. *Diary*'s first English edition encourages this association by displaying a bound notebook and words in typewriter font on its cover, even though neither self-contained notebook nor typewriter appears in the narrative (figure 1.3). Both of these technologies promise what Shakespeareans call "character": the character of handwriting, the character of a typewriter's unique impression, and the character of an author's unique expression. But the novel obstructs generic promises of self-revelation by introducing multiple diaries and by making the diaries part of the novel's action. Additionally, the fact that the author's essays have been dictated and then transferred to a computer makes it impossible to establish whether the essays we are reading are the author's words or the author's words altered by the typist's purposeful editing and the computer's automatic corrections. The novel confirms that the essays are collaborative in at least minor ways: for example, the fourth essay begins with a reference to "talkback radio" (17), and many pages later we find out from one of the diaries that the South African Australian author incorporated this Adelaide idiom at the suggestion of his Filipina-Australian secretary (51). This recursive correction makes us wonder whose feelings, language, and tone are represented in each section of the novel, and tells us that the apparently distinct voices of personal essay and diary are in important ways collective.

We should note that idiomatic distinctions such as "talkback radio" are treated diegetically, allowing the problem of idiom, if not the precise example, to survive translation. And it can be no accident that talkback radio is itself an example of vernacular culture: it is a species of popular media in which hosts and listeners talk and talk back in colloquial, often colorful language. The theme of idiom is addressed by the novel's comparative structure, which asks us to consider that there are several ways to speak, as it were, on any one page, and by the proliferation of diaries, whose addition and revision suggest the social nature of the essayist's individualism. The relationship between language and community is thus treated through words, to be sure, but it is also treated through the physical layout of the book and through a thematic engagement with topics such as interiority, migration, embeddedness, and solidarity.

Apart from representing a collaborative interiority, the proliferation of diaries in the novel has an important generic effect. It shifts the text's emphasis from matters of political theory such as global economy, genocide, and ethical abstraction to matters of social realism such as private economy, jealousy, and sentiment. At the same time, it suggests that social realism, insofar as it emphasizes the embeddedness of social agents, exerts a strong, collective—we might even say, national—pull on the novel's anti-national theories. We encounter those anti-national theories in both explicit and implicit ways. Implicitly, *Diary* approaches the problem of national containment by invoking the problem of scale: How do we determine the boundaries of a person or a nation? The only pages in the novel that feature a single narrative—the only pages, that is, that display what appears as an individual voice—are those assigned to the essay "On the Afterlife," which focuses on the question of the individual soul. Unsurprisingly, the essayist finds "the notion of an individual afterlife" unconvincing (154). Central to his critique is the changeability of the self and the self's transformation through its encounters with other selves. Which version of the individual, the essayist asks, will the afterlife recognize? These observations about the limitations of individuality as a concept are immediately followed by the second part of the novel, in which the essayist tries to revise not only his opinions but also his relationship with the typist. We learn from these later pages that the earlier essays, including the one on the afterlife, were influenced by the author's conversations with the typist, which were in turn influenced by the typist's conversations with her boy-friend, which were in turn influenced by the boyfriend's surreptitious reading of the author's essays and of the author's computer-born diary. This is all to say that even the pages that seem to feature a single voice and focus on an univocal conception of the self are made to function polyvocally: they are not self-contained. If the essays do not support the uniqueness of the individual, either as a concept or as a narrative device, neither do they support the uniqueness of the nation. The writer treats with irony and distaste the assumption "that each person on earth must belong to one nation or another and operate within one or another national economy" (78). His complaint is in part directed at the so-called naturalness of the assumption, and in part it is directed at the exclusivity and competition that follow.

Yet, for all its rejection of uniqueness in individuals and nations, the text finds room for uniqueness in collectivities such as those formed by the novel's paragraphs and those generated between author and typist by the circulation of those paragraphs. Additionally, Coetzee's affection for social realism—references to Tolstoy and Dostoevsky appear throughout the novel—competes with his suspicion of caricature and national containers. The persistence of collectivity becomes increasingly notable in the latter part of the novel, where the essayist is no longer committed to the version of enlargement he had espoused in his initial writings and where he embraces the sentiment and intimacy of realism even though he often disapproves of realism's approach to enclosed community.

Diary begins with sweeping transnational and transhistorical comparisons: the essayist considers together the U.S. torture of prisoners, South Africa's violent preservation of apartheid, and Britain's imposition of colonial rule (39–45); elsewhere, he moves from the suppression of indigenous populations in Australia to histories of genocide in South Africa and the United States (107–9). But the novel ends with the sense that large-scale comparisons, while ethically necessary, are socially paralyzing. "Moral theory," the essayist opines, "has never quite known what to do with quantity, with numbers. Is killing two people worse than killing one person, for example? If so, how much worse?" (204). He then queries comparisons of quality: "Which is worse, the death of a bird or the death of a human child?"

(205). The problem implicit in these questions, a problem that concerns Coetzee in all of his recent world fictions, is not only how to order narratives of violence but whether there is a single conceptual scale that can comprehend each and every example. Instead of comparison as a measure of quantity (which is more?) or quality (which is worse?), Coetzee suggests that comparison might function better—more effectively, more sympathetically—as a practice of irreducible translation in which the heterogeneity among terms leads to overlapping collectives rather than to no collective at all. In this he does not evade or even trump the national container. Not really. Aspiring to solidarity without exclusion, agency without possessiveness, Coetzee's born-translated works make groups of various kinds. For Coetzee, the principle of comparison guarantees only that those groups will have to be generated over and over again. By creating a novel in which individual voices are modified by circulation, Coetzee suggests that transnational communities—like transnational novels—operate at several scales at once.

Summertime, which follows *Diary* by two years, also solicits comparisons. Formally, Coetzee presents a divided book: a collation of fragments, transcriptions, translations, and redactions. Instead of the paragraph, *Summertime* isolates the chapter, each of which appears either as an interview in which characters reflect on past encounters with the deceased John Coetzee, or as a collection of notebook entries in which John, writing in the third-person voice, reflects on his encounters with his father, with neighbors, with the news, and with popular culture of the 1970s. If *Diary* is a novel that takes the shape of a memoir, *Summertime* is a memoir that takes the shape of novel. The book is based very loosely on Coetzee's early adulthood, and in this sense it resembles and fits with the fictional memoirs *Boyhood* and *Youth*. But several major life events have been substantially altered or even made up, including the principal conceit: the fact of Coetzee's death and the existence of an English biographer who has traveled the world conducting interviews with the dead author's acquaintances, friends, and former colleagues. Apart from its outright fictions, *Summertime* dramatizes the minor fictions of recounting, editing, projecting, framing, and embellishing that have been crucial to a long tradition of novelistic biographies.

We might think here of Conrad's *Heart of Darkness*, with its reports inside reports, or Nabokov's *Pale Fire*, with its eager and bumbling interpreter. Like those works and like many of Coetzee's earlier novels and novelistic memoirs, *Summertime* presents genres of individual voice—diary, interview, letter, autobiography—only to suggest that what seems unique, self-contained, and personal is in fact collaborative, social, and shaped by other voices. What differentiates *Summertime* from other novelistic biographies, however, is its effort to align the collaborative interiority of the self with the collaborative interiority of the state.

Even the interview, that genre of direct discourse and unmediated quotation, comes to us altered by transcription, translation, abbreviation, addition, and in one case paraphrase and dramatization. To be sure, all interviews are shaped by questions asked and not-asked, but Coetzee emphasizes that condition by including the voice of the English biographer, known to us only as Mr. Vincent, and the interviewees' queries about the nature and scope of the conversation. The transcripts include unanswered questions and questions the interviewees decline to answer. Because *Summertime*'s interviews are organized by name—the table of contents reads "Julia," "Margot," "Adriana," "Martin," "Sophie"[20]—we are encouraged to think of each chapter as a monologue: a memoir narrated by a single character (Julia), in the service of a memoir about a single character (John). But in various ways Coetzee implies that every monologue is in fact a dialogue, even when there is only one voice on the page. We are reminded, often indirectly, that the interviews have been transcribed and edited and that most have been translated in part or in whole from a language unknown to the biographer. Sometimes the words attributed to individual characters have been adjusted or abridged. Each chapter presents, therefore, not only a response to the biographer's questions but also an implicit interpretation of that response. The notebook fragments, too, are dialogues since each fragment is followed by a brief, italicized paragraph in which John reflects on the episode and considers how it might be used effectively in a future memoir. Throughout the book individual voices have been and are always about to be modified by others voices.

Given all of the editing, commenting, and other incursions, very little in the text can pass for direct discourse: sometimes we are reading what seems like a transcription of a character's voice, but later we find that words have been excluded, added, or altered for effect. We are in the presence of born-translated fiction. There is no first edition because the final object—the biography of Coetzee—has not yet been produced, and there is also no original archive because even the interviews have been edited, translated, and "fixed up" (87). Patrick Denman Flanery has called *Summertime* "a fictional biography in the process of becoming," and this seems right.[21] Flanery's comment conveys effectively Coetzee's effort to display—and halt at midstream—the process of reducing social relations to a unique and coherent person. We encounter a collection of different voices, including the biographer's voice, but there is no omniscient narrator or framing mechanism to unify them.

In addition, most of the chapters begin in a foreign language. At the end of the interview with Adriana, we find out that the entire exchange has taken place in Portuguese, in São Paulo, Brazil, and in the company of a translator, Senhora Gross, who never speaks and is never described (199). She will "transcribe our conversation and tidy up the translation," Mr. Vincent explains. Apart from these direct statements, there are some earlier hints that the chapter's English words may not have originated with the speaker. Adriana refers at one point to the interviewer's "colleague . . . [who] must be exhausted"; "Yes, I know how it is, being a translator" (173). She refers elsewhere to her "bad English" and to her sense that "how we speak in Portuguese" will be different than "how you speak in English" (164–65). Adriana's interview is the only one that seems to have been translated in its entirety, but Sophie's and Margot's remind us too that, at least for them, English is a foreign tongue. A former colleague in French literature who now lives in Paris, Sophie interrupts herself to ask, "can you say that in English?" (231). Margot, John's cousin, often speaks in Afrikaans phrases that are then immediately translated into English. Afrikaans words she and her sister "throw around rather easily" (115), the biographer tells us, but English words have to be dredged up, selected, and used: "He was—the English word occurs to her—a *go-getter* in a land with few go-getters, a man with plenty of—another English word—*spunk*, more spunk probably than all his children put together" (106, emphasis in original). Italicizing English as well as Portuguese, French, and Afrikaans, Coetzee presents readers with an anglophone book that begins in several languages. There is no single idiom and no single community of speakers to which the text belongs. In Coetzee's novel, undoing the repression of the transnational within the national is a linguistic as well as a political project. It is a linguistic project because we are meant to see that it is only the invisibility of translation within literary histories and the literary marketplace that makes global fictions appear to be English. It is a political project because Coetzee shows that South African governance is accomplished through agents who operate both inside and outside the state's geography. The history of the state involves many cycles of migration, colonization, and violence.

By emphasizing translation as a source, a structure, and an outcome of his fiction, Coetzee demotes English as the language of South Africa and as the language of access to South Africa while at the same time acknowledging that English is the language of economic and literary circulation. At one point John insists to Adriana, "There is nothing special about English. It is just one language among many" (161). Coetzee seems to support this claim, insofar as his text decouples concurrence from collectivity: you don't have to be English to teach it; and the history of South Africa can't be all in one language. But Coetzee also modifies this claim and in some ways rejects it: what's special about English is its function as a language of colonialism, a language of upward mobility for migrants such as Adriana and her children, and a language of world literature such as the book we are reading. The dominance of English is a diegetic as well as a grammatical feature of the text. All of the interviews have been translated into English, and the biographer himself is English. These facts serve to demonstrate that the language remains historically if not characteristically "special." However, Coetzee is not suggesting that the biographer's parochialism can be attributed simply to his monolingualism. It is not fluency but modesty that the biographer lacks: he is quick to assume that "changing the form should have no effect on the content" (91).[22] The point for Coetzee is not to protect and reify the form. The point is to recognize that translation is both unavoidable and generative: it creates something new.

Chronologically as well as linguistically, *Summertime* has no single beginning. The order of the narrative does not correspond to the order of the plot. Put another way, the itinerary presented in the table of contents and offered to the reader differs from the biographer's actual journey.[23] The fifth chapter, the interview with Martin, draws our attention to this discrepancy by including an exchange in which Mr. Vincent announces his future plans to interview the four other subjects, three of whom we have already met (216–17). After Martin, the biographer says he plans to visit Margot, Adriana, Julia, and Sophie. But in fact, according to the dates given at the end of each transcription, he visits Sophie before he visits Julia, and then returns to South Africa to visit Margot once again. And of course, for us, he has already visited Julia, Margot, and Adriana. By presenting a book made up of several interviews rather than one narrative, Coetzee allows the parts to operate both independently and collectively: independently because the inconsistencies are allowed to stand; and collectively because we can assemble competing versions or editions of the text. Narrative and plot diverge in other ways as well. The order of the episodes recounted in the interviews does not correspond neatly to the order of John's life, and the notebook fragments, which focus on and at first seem to have been written in the early 1970s, later seem to have been written in 1999 or 2000, the years in which John is said to have added his commentary.[24]

And then there are the seasons. The book's title promises "summertime," and in some ways it delivers. Julia met John in the "summer of 1972" (20); Margot's account begins with a summer gathering at the family farm; and all of the pieces focus on what the biographer seems to regard as the "summer" of John's life, the period in which he ripens as a novelist.[25] But most of the interviews and both of the notebook entries take place in another season, usually winter, and one would hardly call "summery" either John's disposition or that of any of the characters. Summertime is one of those designations that seems natural—surely, there is nothing more natural than a season?—but turns out to be contextual, located, and historical. The French edition of the work, *L'été de la vie*, seems to know this espe-

FIGURE 1.4 Front cover of *Summertime*, J. M. Coetzee
(London: Harvill Secker, 2009).

Reprinted by permission of the publisher.

cially well: the title evokes Proustian associations between self and nature, while the cover—like Proust's novel—suggests that both self and nature are subject to art (compare figures 1.4 and 1.5). In this light, we need to understand the work's title, both in English and in French, as part of the biographer's discourse: what he would call it, rather than a denotative classification. It's hard to imagine Coetzee embracing the kind of developmental narrative that we associate with the progression of seasons and the season-like progression of a life. But more than this, "summertime" suggests something about geography, about the planet, and the relationship among one part of the planet and another. If a South African novel can't be all in one language, Coetzee seems to say, it can't be all in one season either. Comparison is thus required by the ordering and reordering of the chapters, and it is also required within the chapters. For example, the interview with Margot takes place in June 2008, but Mr. Vincent is reading aloud from a narrative version of a previous interview he conducted with her some seven months earlier. It is not only that there is a discrepancy between the text's many seasons and the one declared confidently by the title. It is more fundamental. For a born-translated work, there can be no simultaneity across space. It is never the same season everywhere.

The geography of *Summertime* is complex and difficult to describe, and here we encounter what I take to be the chief purpose of the work's born-translated structure. Coetzee asks readers to think differently about place, about the collectivities attached to place, and about the limits and opportunities of "reading at a distance" (4). Measured by characters and principal subject matter, the memoir's ambit is small: including John, we hear about nine or ten people, at the most, and we learn about only a very narrow slice of those lives. The interviews focus on encounters that took place in rural South Africa and Cape Town. Yet, if we consider the biographer's itinerary, the circle grows somewhat larger. Each interview ends not only with a date but also with a location, and thus we are invited to reconstruct the biographer's path. The reader travels from Canada to South Africa, Brazil, Britain, and then finally to France, but Mr. Vincent has traveled from Britain to South Africa, then to Brazil, France, Canada, and back to South Africa. In this literal way,

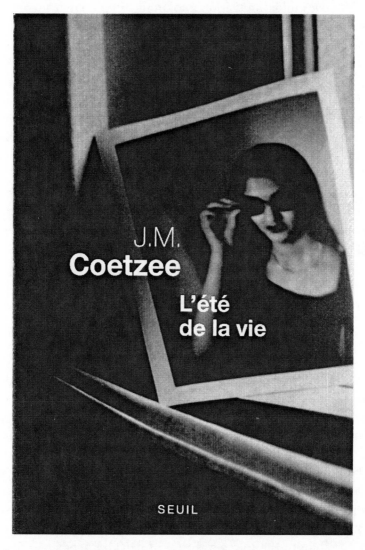

FIGURE 1.5 Front cover of *L'été de la vie*, French translation of *Summertime*, J. M. Coetzee, translated by Catherine Lauga du Plessis (Paris: Seuil, 2010).

Summertime builds circulation into production: there is no original place of composition or collation.

Summertime is about South Africa, if we understand this to mean that it is about the local, regional, transnational, and global actors that have generated the nation's history. We should note, however, that it is not nations but towns, suburbs, and cities that the biographer identifies at the end of each interview: "Kingston, Ontario," "Paris," "Somerset West, South Africa," and so on. By emphasizing small units of geography and civic space, Coetzee seems to be hewing to his subject's preferences. We're told that John finds national and even transnational collectivities much less meaningful and much less appealing than collectivities that operate within nations or at scales smaller than the state. He was "sympathetic" to the novelist and political organizer Alex La Guma, Sophie explains, "because La Guma was from Cape Town, not because he was a communist" (228). Part of the appeal of the city or town seems to be its intimacy. But another part is its relative detachment from the historical trajectories and linguistic uniformity that Coetzee associates with the imagined community of the nation. As it unfolds in the memoir, Coetzee's life in Cape Town consists of friends and acquaintances who live in South Africa but who are also Brazilian, French, Afrikaans, English, and Jewish/Hungarian. Coetzee presents Cape Town as a city not only of educated cosmopolitans like himself and perhaps Sophie but also of migrants, exiles, prisoners, workers, and settlers. *Summertime*'s subtitle, at least in the U.K. edition, promises "scenes from a provincial life." Placing his cosmopolitan roster beneath the flag of provincialism, Coetzee suggests that South Africa's history is both more global and more local than apartheid nationalism could possibly comprehend. Narrowing and varying classifications, Coetzee draws our attention to the micro-histories of neighborhoods and to intimate relations that are not reducible to geopolitical arrangements. At the same time we are asked to notice that geopolitical arrangements inform the work and its sense of place from the very start.

To take the most dramatic and immediate example: the text begins in South Africa by beginning in the neighboring country of Botswana. Here, in August 1972, several Afrikaans-speaking men, probably members of the South African Defense Force, have killed a family of

South African refugees. The men, John's notebook reports, arrived in a "white American model" car (3). Even before we know the language of the killers, the white Americanness of the car implicates the South African government, which has drawn support, rhetorically and economically, from the United States. We're asked to understand that the violence of apartheid takes place—that is, begins, finds financial and political backing, and shows itself most explicitly—both inside and outside South Africa. At some point, John imagines, the leaders of South Africa will "pack their bags, shred any incriminating evidence, and fly off to Zurich or Monaco or San Diego," where they have bought houses and established businesses with obscure names (5–6). With Switzerland in the future and Botswana in the past, *Summertime* sets its South African scene well beyond the geography of a single state.

This is why, for John, there is no possibility of hiding "in the snows of Sweden," and no comfort in "reading at a distance about his people and their latest pranks" (4). Distance brings neither affective nor ethical detachment. South Africa's leaders remain "his people," whether he lives with them or believes in their project. Living in Sweden would not change this. Of course, Sweden functions symbolically as well as spatially. It calls to mind a contrasting hemisphere, topography, and climate. But it also evokes an ideal of neutrality: think here of that country's official status during the Second World War as well as its continuing function as host of the Nobel committee, whose conferral of global prestige can create the conditions for local amnesty. Coetzee rejects both the ideal and the promise: he may be writing for translation, but he is not writing from nowhere. He can't because he associates global invisibility ("Zurich or Monaco or San Diego") with the very forces he wishes he could disavow.

The initial pages of *Summertime* tell us that National Party leaders justify the rule of apartheid by narrowing their view geographically and historically, and by evaluating action only in terms of self-interest. By way of contrast, we are presented with John's approach to current events. He thinks comparatively, as we have seen, and he refuses to embrace self-interest—that central tenet of liberal individualism—as a motor either for action or for collectivity. Like Stephen Dedalus at the start of *Ulysses*, John has returned to his provincial city feeling "soiled" by personal and collective guilt (4).[26] We don't yet know of his personal guilt but of his collective guilt—as one who has benefitted, even indirectly, from the apartheid system—we are immediately aware. *Summertime*'s opening, then, offers two models of "reading at a distance." The first model, which John discards, associates geographical remoteness with ethical and emotional detachment. "Reading at a distance" allows one to imagine that someone else—not you!—is soiled.[27] The second model, which corresponds to the structure of John's analysis, suggests that there is no neutrality and that those spaces that seem to us distinct or contrasting—winter to our summer—may be integral to actions at home. Instead of developing some Sweden-like sense of impartiality, John has to be attentive to the many ways that inside and outside are established. It is therefore important to read at a distance but not in the way that John at first imagines.

Summertime begins and ends by suggesting that collectivity cannot depend on affinity. In fact, Coetzee proposes, it has to depend on and is most substantially tested by the lack of affinity. John is South African not because he shares the government's values but despite the fact that he doesn't. Similarly, the book's final notebook entry suggests that John can have a relationship with his ailing father only if he is willing to sacrifice his own pleasures: "He is going to have to abandon some of his personal projects and be a nurse. Alternatively, if he will not be a nurse, he must announce to his father: *I cannot face the prospect of ministering to you day and night. I am going to abandon you. Goodbye.* One or the other: there is no third way" (265–66, emphasis in original). We see here Coetzee's strenuous conception of ethical duty, in which it is not ideas or outcomes that justify care but the obligation to respond to someone else's suffering. *Diary* ends on a similar note, with the essayist confessing that fictional characters move him by the "accents of anguish" rather than the "substance of . . . argument" (175–76). And this fits with his sentiments in *Elizabeth Costello* and *Slow Man*, in which collectivity is based on contact instead of consciousness. By building translation into its form, *Summertime* calls on readers to participate in a world in which no one is altogether fluent. This is not an argument for exile, for feeling distant while others feel close. Rather, it is an argument for participation without affinity and for a kind of mindfulness about the distances that exist within any collectivity.

WORLDS ON THE PAGE

Coetzee's comparative approach, in which we are asked to see how the logic of transnational circulation places characters, episodes, and even paragraphs within multiple containers, suggests new directions for literary critical methodology. Historians of the novel will need to analyze how a work participates not only in one literary system, the literary system of the language in which it was composed, but also in the other literary systems in which it has a presence. Because a text may begin in several places and because it may continue to travel to numerous regions and languages, its location and culture will be dynamic and unpredictable. It is no longer simply a matter of determining, once and for all, the literary culture to which a work belongs. Born-translated literature such as Coetzee's implies the intersection of several major methodologies: close reading, book history, and translation studies. Benedict Anderson has helped to show us that the history of the novel requires the history of the book. The history of the born-translated novel requires the history of many books.

Thinking about the history of many books can lead in several directions. We might investigate the publishing conglomerates, regional markets, and advertising strategies that manage and differentiate the circulation of works throughout the world. But the history of many books also leads to a practice I have called close reading at a distance because it challenges the distinction between intrinsic and extrinsic properties of the work, draws our attention to the role of global audiences in the production of literary fiction, and asks us to consider how literature written for the world establishes new paradigms of uniqueness. The originality of the born-translated work, no longer expressive of a single language or national territory, now refers to the work's appearance as editions and translations that function within several literary geographies. Put another away, the history of many books will need to account for a text's multiple beginnings, and for the ways that it participates in and cuts across various collectivities. In "The Ethics of Reading and the Question of the Novel," Peter McDonald has argued that the history of many books should not be seen as one approach among many but rather as "an essential precondition" for understanding the aesthetic strategies of works such as *Diary of a Bad Year* (493). Yet this approach, McDonald acknowledges, "obliges us to begin much farther back from Coetzee's project in *Diary* than many 'close readers' would find comfortable." (492). McDonald is advocating a kind of close reading that involves some alternative to close reading, or at least some alternative to the close reading performed and approved by most "close readers."

As examples of beginning "farther back," McDonald points to the contrast between Coetzee's ambivalence about generic categories within *Diary* and the various affirmations of genre one finds on the front and inside covers of the different editions; to the analysis of the books' several formats and typographies; and to the conceit of a novel about a novelist who shares the same initials as the work's author (494–95). McDonald's approach involves acknowledging that what is putatively outside the text—its covers, its typography and pagination, its author's name—informs the inside. Historians of the book have been calling for this acknowledgment for some time. However, thinking about books instead of "the book" leads us to notice in addition that many outsides lead to many insides, and that not all of these insides will be legible to any one critic. For his part, McDonald seems uncertain about whether the turn to the geopolitics of readers and publishers—the study of "who reads and who publishes" (492)— negates, alters, or simply supplements traditional reading practices. First, echoing generations of book historians, he says, "particular readers find themselves face to face not with the 'words on the page' but with a richly coded artifact that bears witness to multiple intersecting histories" (490). But later he insists, "The point, however, is not to privilege the book above the words on the page" (492). Like many contemporary critics, McDonald finds himself repeating a familiar opposition between the book and the word, between the broad analysis of literature's economic, political, and physical histories and the deep analysis of a single work's rhetorical properties.[28]

Instead of asking whether books occlude words, what if we were to ask whether books lead us to privilege, analyze, or value something in the text other than words? We might have to pay greater attention to typography, layout, and illustration as well as to many things that are not strictly speaking "on the page" or on the page we have before us. Close reading may involve attention to "details," as Jonathan Culler and Jane Gallop have argued, but what are details?[29] How large are they? How do we know when we have attended to them intensively, substantially, or, as we say, deeply? How would our reading practices change, what more or what less would we learn, if we focused our attention on larger units such as the chapter or the edition or on elements of the physical book such as lines moving across the page? Finally, what if we defined close reading, as John Guillory has proposed, less by its objects than by its practice, where it is not the deep attention to words but the deep attention itself that matters most?

As I suggested in the preceding pages, born-translated works often proceed from the fiction, sometimes the fact, that readers are encountering an original translation: a work that has begun in several languages or a work that has been composed in one language and then published in a foreign tongue. These works can't expect us to read and to master the words on the page since, on some level, attending to all of the words and all of the pages would involve reading many more editions than we could hold in our hands or would involve reading an edition that doesn't really exist. Instead they ask us to focus on the text's resistance to mastery—or what I call fluency—by pointing at versions and editions beyond our reach. Foreignness in these works operates diegetically, narratively, and physically much more than it does semantically. To be sure, many novels emphasize narrative structure and theme rather than idiolect and metaphor, and close readers of those works may find themselves analyzing the former rather than the latter qualities. But it is nevertheless unexpected and unprecedented to find literary fiction veering away from idiolect in order to veer toward multilingualism. In *Diary of a Bad Year*, fluency is impeded not by portmanteau words or invented diction but by a misfit between story and physical structure. Only by thinking carefully about "the book"—the way the words are organized on the page, and on different pages—can we analyze "the words" at all. In *Summertime*, the location of the text is irreducible to any one beginning or geography; and in fact we are asked to think about the geopolitical, topographic, historical, linguistic, and meteorological relations that govern the meaning of place. Because the text starts in circulation—it literally begins by reflecting on South African violence in Botswana and the way that violence in Botswana tells us something about the true boundaries of South Africa—we have to conceive of its community as something we discover rather than as a linguistic, territorial, or political entity concurrent with either author or reader.

As an intellectual strategy, close reading at a distance overlaps with two major developments in transnational literary studies: first the turn toward books in the study of texts, and, second, the effort to challenge, historicize, transform, and in some cases reject dominant practices of close reading.[30] To be sure, these are separate developments, since some of the critics who call for new reading strategies are not especially interested in book history or in the history of translation implied by global circulation, and some of those interested in book history are not principally interested in reading at all. But in the field of world literature, a new attentiveness to books has changed the approach to texts. Perhaps the most influential critic in this regard is Franco Moretti, whose model of "distant reading" involves tracking the way groups of literary works travel from their national origin into new spaces and languages. Distant reading calls for new objects of attention, and it imagines collaborations among scholars rather than one person's knowledge of every relevant language. However, distant reading presupposes someone else's traditional close reading of individual works. The synthetic calculations at the heart of distant reading are based on other readers' analyses of voice and idiom, on the comparison of national literary histories, and on the assumption that all literary texts begin in a unique language.

If Moretti's project separates the analysis of literary circulation from the analysis of literary production, Daniel Hack's related approach suggests that transnational book history can coexist with close reading if we hew to linguistic rather than national frameworks.[31] He shows, for example, how a nineteenth-century British work such as *Bleak House* developed new cultural meanings—new emphases, new ironies, and new political uses—when it was serialized in U.S. antislavery periodicals. A text that promoted British localism through the exclusion of Africans became, in the hands

of some African American readers, a text that could be used to promote U.S. localism and the abolitionist cause (731). Through commentary, dramatization, and rewriting, Hack argues, the "African-
Americanization" of *Bleak House* created "new *Bleak Houses*" (729).
Hack calls his methodology "close reading at a distance," but his
procedure involves something more like distant reading up close
since he is interested above all in the dynamics of reception: how an
original text with "intrinsic features" travels from one political context to another, and how it is deployed in each of those contexts (730).
Hack's method diverges from Moretti's since Hack does not begin
from the presumption of a self-contained work moving through time
and space. Instead he analyzes several anglophone versions: serialized parts of the novel, rewritings that appear as completely different
novels, and discussions of the novel in essays and letters. Yet Hack
shares Moretti's emphasis on beginnings and dispersals. Comparing "afterlife" with original, new U.S. versions with the version that
Dickens published in Britain, Hack follows Moretti's general model
in which texts start in one place and then move out to others (730).
What Moretti and Hack share most of all, of course, is a focus on
nineteenth-century fiction. A novel such as *Bleak House* was designed
to support the logic of national literary history. That is, Dickens may
have read Frederick Douglass, and Douglass may have read Dickens,
as Hack details, but the novel provides an argument for—and seems
to solicit—serial nationalism. Hack calls this feature "the portability
of the novel's localism."[32] Because they affirm national literary histories in order to compare them, distant reading and even distant reading up close might be best understood as methodologies both suited
and indebted to specific literary works and kinds of literary works—
namely, those that affirm localism and a sharp distinction among literary geographies.

For our purposes, the key innovation in Hack's work is the principle that readers may have to think of any text as one version among
many and of literary analysis as a dynamic process shaped by place,
contexts of publication, and political climate—as well as method. It
is here that the turn to books in transnational literary studies most
overlaps with new theories of reading. These theories have called
for alternatives to "critical distance" and "mastery," both of which

conceive of the reader as a disinterested authority who stands outside of the text, comprehends it, and speaks its language. Stephen Best and Sharon Marcus have argued that the dominance of "symptomatic reading" has led critics to miss what happens on the "surfaces" of texts or to look always and only for what texts do not seem to be saying.[33] They propose instead "surface reading," while Timothy Bewes in a related essay suggests "reading with the grain."[34] Best, Marcus, and Bewes are developing alternatives to "suspicious" reading.[35] Yet even those critics who seek to preserve the general tenor of suspicion have tried to uncouple the identification of puzzles in the text from the notion that one could possibly solve them. Jonathan Culler emphasizes above all attention to the "stubbornness" of texts.[36] Among the list of "conflicts" to which the reader should be attentive, Culler points not only to words but also to syntax, grammar, rhetoric, figure, and example.[37]

Jane Gallop, one of the most distinguished practitioners of close reading, argues that being "aware of the words chosen" is the best line of defense against generalization, projection, and other ways of mis- or not-reading.[38] Her principle of regarding each word as if it were "unfamiliar" or in some way inaccessible suggests that the reader should imagine herself not as a master interpreter but as a translator even when she is reading in a native tongue. Because Gallop seeks to keep herself and her students from comprehending too quickly and from identifying the "sort of book" they have before them, she associates the function of closeness with the disruption of groups and classifications.[39] Best, Marcus, Bewes, Culler, and Gallop, for all their differences, agree that readers need to pay attention to the details of the literary work and to resist the impulse to master it.

How might born-translated novels change this calculus? First of all, they ask us to think about the history and practice of translation in which the dominance of some languages and the relative absence of others contributes to the generalizations we make as readers. Instead of suggesting that all texts are equally foreign or unfamiliar, Coetzee suggests that English has a special status as a language of imperialism, as a mediator of other languages, and as the language of composition for most translated works. Second, born-translated fictions are designed to obstruct the traditional alignment among language, territory, and nation, and they often do so by thwarting our expectations about the physical boundaries of the work. They test our confidence about groups and classifications not only through estranging or puzzling words within the text but also through details that operate narratively, thematically, structurally, and paratextually. Because they shift the locus of stubbornness and puzzlement from the smallest units of the text to units of various scales, they ask us to analyze closely and deeply a greater range of details than most programmatic versions of close reading have required. And because they feature narratives that seem to have begun in many different languages, they ask us to think about the political dynamics of foreignness and especially about the foreignness that is internal to any multilingual collectivity.

Naomi Schor's important study of "reading in detail," first published more than twenty years ago, points out that the analysis of details has not always been central to literary criticism and that what counts as a detail is not self-evident but often hotly debated, not only across periods but also within them.[40] Schor shows that the turn to details such as words, which she traces from Realist fiction and painting onward, was an important correction to the longstanding emphasis on idealization and abstraction. Schor suggests that the denigration of what seemed to be intellectually and textually "ornamental," not only words but also themes such as domesticity and women's lives, was rooted in the exclusion of a whole range of social, sexual, and philosophical dispositions.[41] To speak for details, then, was also to speak for the idiosyncratic, the everyday, the feminine, and the inessential. When critics today speak of a literary text's "small details," they almost certainly mean individual words, perhaps especially words that seem ordinary rather than determinative: articles and conjunctions, or even punctuation marks. But Schor suggests that the emphasis on everyday words is just one aspect of the detail's rise. In the late twentieth century, the detail often meant, as it did for Jacques Derrida, paratext rather than text: "notes, epigraphs, postscriptums and all manner of *parerga*."[42] And the details of nineteenth-century fiction are often diegetic, Schor explains. They are undernoticed not because they are graphically or syntactically small—like a word—but because they are rhetorically and socially small: ordinary, common, and appearing with too much frequency.[43]

If we continue to assume that the most significant details of any text are its individual words, we may simply reproduce the logic of the ornamental, excluding from our attention any aspect of the text that is not reducible to "words," now coded as important. Instead, born-translated novels ask us to conceive of details more broadly and more variously as those parts of the text, of potentially any scale or size, that seem prosaic, beneath notice, or simply mechanical. If we follow this lead, we attune our reading strategies to the strategies of our literary texts, and we acknowledge that reading strategies can, in effect, produce texts, insofar as, say, reading for the plot will tend to single out for praise or for notice those works in which plot is emphasized. Understanding details broadly also has the benefit of acknowledging the intellectual history of details in which expectations about thematic and semantic meaningfulness have changed and continue to change. Because it emphasizes details that have seemed too large, too functional, or too irrelevant to justify sustained analysis, close reading at a distance participates in the long recovery of the ornamental, but it does so by deemphasizing the kinds of details we have associated with the closest practices of close reading. The ornamental is not inherent to the text. It is an historical feature of reading. If we want to preserve the idea that close reading means analyzing details meticulously so as to avoid generalization and misapprehension, we need to direct our meticulousness to all aspects of the literary work, and we will need to understand details to include all of those elements that have gone without saying, or without seeing.

We should pay attention to small details, Gallop has proposed, not to understand the text better but to find in the text new aspects of its incomprehensibility. To read closely, for Gallop, is to acknowledge and cultivate our incomplete understanding. In *Summertime*, Coetzee yokes the ethics of incomprehensibility to the politics of translation. We have to regard the chapters "as if" they are foreign—full of anecdotes that are partial, inaccessible, and in need of careful interpretation—but we also have to regard them as actually foreign: part of the regional, global, and micronational histories of South Africa. By dividing the work into unfinished interviews and diary fragments, Coetzee keeps readers from assembling any kind of coherent "big picture," to use Gallop's phrase: a biography of John Coetzee or a history of South Africa in the 1970s.[44] We have to be close readers because we need to notice that the text doesn't fit one period, one nation, or one language. But it also doesn't fit one object, and in this sense we need to read at a distance. We have to think about the many insides and outsides produced by the narrative structure, the seasons, and the traveling biographer. The closest of readers, Coetzee suggests, are the South African leaders who restrict their attention solely to events in South Africa. Instead, Coetzee proposes, the novel takes place among a network of peripheries that are irreducible both to nation and to globe. We have to consider how that network changes what we know of South Africa and how it changes the way we think about South African, Australian, and world fiction in English. We need to add the history of translation to the history of reading and thus to think about how novels that begin in several places are changing the ways that communities are imagined. But we will also need to think about how born-translated works understand the relationship between individuals and groups. In the next chapter, we turn to works that gauge various models of uniqueness, including the list, the series, and the clone.

2

THE SERIES, THE LIST, AND THE CLONE

---

*To an ever greater degree the work of art reproduced becomes
the work of art designed for reproducibility.*

—Walter Benjamin, *Illuminations*

UNIMAGINABLE LARGENESS

THINKING ABOUT world literature, we often assume that translation leads to cultural as well as political homogenization.[1]
Translation leads to cultural homogenization, the argument
goes, because readers will learn fewer languages, and texts written
for translation will tend to avoid vernacular references and linguistic complexity.[2] It leads to political homogenization because the
world market requires stories that everyone can share, which means
fewer distinctions among political antagonists and social agents.[3]
The concern is this: translation is bad for what it does to books
(presents them apart from their original language and context); but
it is worse for what it does to authors (encourages them to ignore
that language and context). In truth, the effects of translation will
depend on what is being translated, who translates, and what happens when translated books are read. Moreover, the meaning of
these effects will depend on how we evaluate sameness and difference. Do we assume, for example, that homogenization is always a
negative outcome? To answer this question, we have to consider not

only the global production and circulation of texts but also our ways of thinking about cultural and political uniqueness.

As we saw in the last chapter, the idea of novels as bounded containers has been important to the idea of communities as bounded containers. Yet many contemporary novels present themselves not as autonomous objects but as copies, grafts, versions, or clones. They are thus not only containers; they are also contained. They are distinctive in some ways, but they are conjoined in others. This chapter argues that the conceit of linguistic and geographic unoriginality creates new paradigms for collectivity in the novel. Comparative beginnings change the kind of community that authors and readers are able to imagine. I take up these concerns by turning to the work of Kazuo Ishiguro, whose novels have been translated from English into more than forty languages and who has written throughout his career about problems of authenticity, comparison, and adequacy.[4] More than any other writer of anglophone literary fiction, Ishiguro has reflected on and largely affirmed translatability. Beginning in the late 1980s and continuing through the present decade, Ishiguro has approached his writing from the perspective of multilingual reading, in early interviews worrying that addressing many groups diminishes literary fiction and in later interviews embracing the challenge of having audiences in Denver, Oslo, and Kuala Lumpur.[5] In an interview from 2001, Ishiguro explains, "I have to really ask myself, 'Does the line have substance? It's not just a clever line, is it? Does its value survive translation?'"[6]

Ishiguro's fiction can be understood as born translated in a number of different ways. First, he writes in English while thinking about readers in other languages.[7] Second, as a migrant to England from Japan at the age of five, he is in fact writing in a second language, though he speaks and writes English fluently, and speaks only rudimentary Japanese. From the perspective of early nineteenth-century theorists of translation, Ishiguro's language of composition is foreign since it is not the (official) language of his native country. Third, Ishiguro has spoken of his effort to create works in English that appear to be translated from another language, and this dynamic is legible at different registers throughout his oeuvre.[8] Sometimes this is presented literally: in two of his novels and several of his short stories, the characters appear to be speaking Japanese.[9] But sometimes this is a matter of tone: the first-person narrators in many of his other works often speak in a vague or convoluted diction that can seem like translatese. Finally, in a sense that is most distinctive of contemporary fiction, Ishiguro's novels are born translated because they emphasize the influence of global circulation on histories of art's production, because they decouple the meaning of artworks from the expression of intrinsic cultures, and because they test the value of aesthetic originality as a baseline for political agency. From *The Artist of the Floating World* (1986) and *The Unconsoled* (1995) to *Never Let Me Go* (2005) and the short story collection *Nocturnes* (2009), the transnational circulation of art and artists has been a persistent theme. Questions about the relationship between agency and geographic scale have been crucial in all of the novels to date, perhaps most famously in *The Remains of the Day* (1989), for which Ishiguro won the Booker Prize.

This chapter brings together an analysis of that celebrated, widely discussed book with an analysis of Ishiguro's most well-known book about originality, *Never Let Me Go*.[10] Translation is crucial to both novels since it allows Ishiguro to consider how the logic of individuality has shaped both the politics of imperialism and the politics of art, and indeed also to think about how claims for art's uniqueness have served, rather than blocked, imperialism.[11] Ishiguro suggests in these novels that the commitment to intrinsic characteristics, whether of nations, persons, or artworks, recapitulates global inequality. It does so, first, by extending democracy only to the edges of the nation, and, second, by limiting the value of aesthetic production to the expression of its interiority. Ishiguro explores instead other values and other models of collectivity.

In *The Remains of the Day*, scalar thinking is invoked most explicitly through the conceit of "unimaginable largeness," which refers to the notion that any small action, including the polishing of household silver, needs to assume the same ethical and political significance as the more expansive system of actions in which it participates.[12] For Ishiguro's narrator, who invokes the phrase as a dramatic intensifier, *largeness* refers both to geographic extension (beyond the local) and to social consequence (beyond the individual). Most readers of the novel find it difficult to hear in this phrase anything other than Ishiguro's ironic commentary about the failings of his ambitious butler. But I argue that *The Remains of the Day* uses this concept to emphasize the transformation of international, collective events by local, individual decisions. "Unimaginable largeness" has a multilocal application since it suggests not only looking outward, how my actions affect many other unseen people, but also looking inward, how the actions of many unseen people affect my actions. In Ishiguro's novel, it is difficult to tell whether understanding actions globally leads to greater knowledge or even to greater fairness. But by encouraging readers to notice both proximate and distant contexts, Ishiguro registers the multiple containers of literary culture and mediates between interpretive strategies that abjure political and geographic distinctions and those that try to preserve them.

In the study of world literature, thinking about unimaginable largeness has its uses. It allows us to consider how the way we understand the uniqueness of books relates to the way we understand the uniqueness of communities, and how our models of literary culture shape what we need to know about the nature and scale of social lives. In turn, we need to allow new ways of thinking about the nature and scale of social lives to change fundamentally our models of literary culture. Since the disciplinary protocols of English literary studies are rooted "in a particular national ethos and ethnos," as Simon Gikandi has suggested, scholars are likely to analyze even born-translated anglophone texts according to national principles and objectives. Gikandi asks: "What are we going to do with these older categories—nation, culture, and English—which function as the absent structure that shapes and yet haunts global culture and the idea of literature itself?"[13] I do not suggest that Ishiguro's writing eludes this kind of "absent structure"; on the contrary, it invokes absent structures over and over again. Yet, by imagining a largeness constituted by books rather than by texts, by copies rather than by originals, Ishiguro forces categories such as "nation, culture, and English" to operate comparatively. He challenges us to see that a new conception of "global culture," if it is to be something other than an enlargement of national culture, will require a new idea of literature.

THE GEOGRAPHY OF THE BOOK

Kazuo Ishiguro's novels function as world literature in two principal ways.[14] As objects, they are written, printed, translated, circulated, and read in several places. As narratives, they distribute anecdotes into multiple systems and then consider the ethical consequences of that process. Thinking about how and where his books will be read, Ishiguro explains, has led him to emphasize "shape, structure, and vision," or what he calls "architecture," rather than "sentences" and "phrases."[15] Ishiguro knows that the books he is producing will circulate beyond a single nation and in near-immediate translation into many languages. Like Coetzee, Ishiguro has acknowledged the long history of collaboration in which his novels take part and from which he has benefited, and he seems to accept and to appreciate that his novels will exist in several languages and become part of several literary traditions.[16] In an essay about translation, Coetzee tells of helping his Chinese translator with a reference to "the Summer Palace," which appears in his novel *Waiting for the Barbarians*.[17] The translator had asked whether the phrase alludes to "the Old Summer Palace in Beijing" (144). Coetzee suggests that this question may be understood in two ways: as a question about intention (did he produce that allusion on purpose?) or as a question about effect (do the words generate that allusion?). Ultimately, he reflects, "As for whether the words in question do refer to the palace in Beijing, as an author I am powerless to say. The words are written; I cannot control the associations they awaken" (145).

One may assume that Coetzee is simply invoking the "death of the author," acknowledging, pace Barthes, that the meanings of his words will proliferate willy-nilly in the minds of readers.[18] But Coetzee is proposing something more specific and, indeed, more limited: the readers he is thinking about are translators and those who read translated works, and the future "associations" he imagines for those works are not entirely arbitrary. Translators, he explains, have the power to "nudge" readers (his word) toward one allusion or another, and phrases will have more resonance in some cultures than in others. This attitude about translation, with its patent equanimity about variation and collaboration, is quite different from worries about a single "world literature" or about source languages infiltrating or overwhelming target languages. Instead, Coetzee imagines—and invites—a network of traditions.[19]

The collaboration between writers and translators that Coetzee imagines in his essay appears as an extension of literary production, in which collaboration is there from the start. World literature may require a special kind of collaboration so that scholars can see how a text circulates in many languages and so that writers can produce books in many languages, but all scholarship relies on social process since we approach literary texts through established traditions and classifications. This is true for literature as well, which depends on collaboration that is both visible (editing, publishing, printing, distributing) and less visible (building on previous representations, uses of language).[20] This is not to subtract from the strenuous, often global collaborations that translation may require but rather to note that translation makes literature's status as a collaborative, often global enterprise more difficult to miss.

Ishiguro has made a similar point about translation's networks: in an interview with Polish journalists at the end of 2005, he acknowledges the influence on his work not only of Fyodor Dostoyevsky, Anton Chekhov, and Leo Tolstoy but also of the translator of Dostoyevsky, Chekhov, and Tolstoy. He claims, "I often think I've been greatly influenced by the translator, David Magarshack, who was the favourite translator of Russian writers in the 1970s. And often when people ask me who my big influences are, I feel I should say David Magarshack, because I think the rhythm of my own prose is very much like those Russian translations that I read."[21]

Ishiguro values not just any Dostoyevsky, but Magarshack's Dostoyevsky, and he seems to appreciate the idea that his own novels are imitating translations. We generally assume that some works of art such as plays, films, or novels have multiple iterations (to own a book is to own a "copy"), while others such as paintings or site-specific sculptures are unique objects. But, as Ishiguro's comments suggest, a book can be a unique object, too, both because translations create several versions of a text and because reception distinguishes the social itinerary of one version from another. In the last volume of Marcel Proust's novel, the narrator tells us that he values above all "the first edition of a work," by which he means not one of many copies from the publisher's first imprint but the single version of the book in which he read the text for the first time.[22] In making this distinction, Marcel (the narrator) emphasizes what he calls the history of his own life rather than "the past in general." The book Marcel read in his youth is a unique object, of which there are not even copies in the same language. And yet his experience is in some ways universal since every other reader of that work will also have his or her own first edition. Today each person can have his or her own first edition of a work, but it may not be an edition first printed by the publisher or an edition whose language corresponds to the one in which the work was originally composed. Indeed, it may be more correct to say that a work of world literature exists in many original languages, especially if we don't want to say that it exists originally in none.[23]

The distinction between "tokens" and "types" that Peter McDonald uses in his discussion of literary editions can be useful here.[24] In McDonald's account, tokens refer to instances of a work (my own copy of a book) while types refer to the intellectual content of the work (Ishiguro's *Never Let Me Go*). Building on Noël Carroll's theory of artworks in mass culture, McDonald compares book editions to two other kinds of "multiple instance or type artworks": film and theater.[25] Carroll groups books with films because their circulation relies on a "template" (the print), but McDonald groups books with plays because their circulation depends on much more than a template (on the decisions of directors and actors, in the case of plays; on the decisions of editors, cover designers, and typesetters, in the case of books). McDonald regards book editions as "separate artworks" because they are produced by "a creative process, involving interpretive decisions that effect and constrain meaning."[26] Editions in translation, while they surely depend on a printer's template and on the creative acts of designers and typesetters, further complicate the type-token dynamic: translations are tokens of a single type (the work), however mediated by the printer's template, as well as tokens of different types (the work in different languages). If we allow that the creative process includes the "social, political, critical, and institutional histories" of a book's publication, as McDonald claims, as well as the personal histories of readers like Marcel, as Proust,

Barthes, and Ishiguro claim, then the distinction between "multiple instance or type artworks" and "singular artworks" begins to disappear.[27] Legally, of course, translations are one more instance of the author's type; practically they can operate as originals and as copies at the same time.[28]

Ishiguro has made the literary conditions of uniqueness and comparison a principal concern in his work, but let's return for a moment to the case of J. K. Rowling. Her "Harry Potter" novels, which appear in more than sixty-five languages, have prompted a range of consumer practices and have been translated not only into hardy, living languages such as French and Chinese but also into so-called dead languages such as Latin and Ancient Greek. In this respect they contribute to linguistic diversity even if this was not their author's chief intention. Of course, the value and consequence of linguistic diversity should not be taken for granted. Variation is not in itself democratic or liberal if the demand for authenticity and distinctiveness restricts freedom rather facilitates it. Homogenization, the process of creating sameness or similarity, fits the project of uniqueness as well as the project of comparison.

Ishiguro well understands this forked potential. Whereas his interviews show him thinking about the production and circulation of world literature, his novels display a more indirect approach: they present global comparison as story and discourse, as something that characters do to assess the value and consequence of their actions, and as something that readers do—or need to do—to reflect on those assessments and to consider the ways that value and consequence can be determined. I have written elsewhere about the trope of the echo in Ishiguro's work: the way that later scenes or phrases will sound like, or almost repeat, earlier scenes or phrases, and the way that these repetitions will in retrospect seem to have preceded or motivated what appeared to be the originals.[29] Ishiguro uses comparative devices like the echo to introduce complex patterns of world circulation. His comparisons create new groups of themes, persons, and objects, but they also prompt us to examine the shape and scale of that variety.

For this reason above all, I associate Ishiguro's work with the project of born-translated writing. The novels register the tension between the writing of world literature and the reading protocols we bring to those texts. In literary studies, we generally distinguish between the disciplines of national literature, which typically refer to what books are, who wrote them, or where they were produced, and the discipline of comparative literature, which typically refers to what we do with books. Ishiguro's novels incorporate comparison. They can't—and do not try to—predict their future as translated works. That would be impossible, as Stefan Helgesson has persuasively shown.[30] But the novels acknowledge the multiple contexts of their making and remaking. They ask to be read across several national and political scenes. They trump an ignoble "translatability" not by resisting translation but by demanding it.[31]

THE COPY, THE CLONE

Never Let Me Go, published in 2005 in Spanish, Danish, Polish, English, German, and several other languages, is a book about the value of unoriginal expression. Set in some kind of alternative England at the end of the twentieth century, the novel offers us a collection of bad copies and eccentric interpretations: there is a cassette tape that plays a monotonous pop song called "Never Let Me Go" whose lyrics the narrator adapts to her own story;[32] there is a mediocre television program whose sitcom relationships the adolescent characters take as role models for adult behavior (120); there is the magazine insert whose glossy image and cheerful rhetoric ("Are you the dynamic, go-ahead type?") the narrator's friend appropriates for her ideal future (144); there are the drawings of metallic animals, which are said to look "laboured, almost like they'd been copied" (241); and there is of course the narrator and her friends, all of whom are human clones brought up to be organ donors for—what shall we call them?—non-cloned, original humans.

The narrator, Kathy H., recounts her experiences as a child and adolescent in a special school she attended before she understood the role she would play in society, and she tells of her experience as "a carer," one who takes care of other clones (her former school-mates, including Tommy and Ruth) after their vital organs have been

FIGURE 2.1 Front cover of the Japanese translation of *Never Let Me Go*,
Kazuo Ishiguro, *Watashi o hanasanaide*, translated by Tsuchiya Masao
(Tokyo: Hayakawa Publishing, 2006).

Reprinted by permission
of the publisher.

harvested and before they die, usually in their late twenties or early thirties. Three non-clone adults feature in the story: Miss Emily, the school's headmistress; Madame, a visitor to the school who carries away the best examples of the children's art; and Miss Lucy, who tells the clones, called "students," that they should know more than they do about the future that is planned for them, though she does not ultimately provide that information. The novel is disturbing because of its premise, to be sure, but it is all the more disturbing because our knowledge of Kathy's role, her existence as a future organ donor and as an accomplice to the organ donation system (as a carer, she tells us, she's good at keeping other clones "calm"), is obscured by the aleatory style and vague diction of her narration (3). That narration, which encompasses the entire novel, seems to be one of the unoriginal expressions that Ishiguro wants us to value. In Kathy's speech there is a kind of doubling between the novel's story and the novel's discourse. And insofar as one critic, no less than Frank Kermode, has faulted the novel's discourse for its "familiar, chatty style," Kathy H.'s unoriginality seems to be Ishiguro's too.[33]

It is arguable that Ishiguro wrote *Never Let Me Go* as a critique of anthrocentrism, the idea that it is ethical or acceptable to sacrifice nonhuman animals to the needs and desires of human life. At many points in the text we are asked to notice that an unquestioned hierarchy in which humans are distinguished from animals makes the donation system possible. Tommy's drawings are telling about how that distinction is preserved. They suggest that strategies of abstraction allow us to see some bodies as mechanisms and others as individuals. Looking closely at Tommy's pictures, Kathy is unable to see "animals" at all: "The first impression was like one you'd see if you took the back off a radio set: tiny canals, weaving tendons, miniature screws and wheels were all drawn with obsessive precision, and only when you held the page away could you see it was some kind of armadillo, say, or a bird" (187). The donation system functions because the humans see the clones as non-individuated organisms, like radios or spiders (35), and because the humans fail to see themselves, too, as radios or spiders. The failure to see is a failure to compare: the humans think that individuality is the highest value, and they convince themselves that they are "not like" the clones—

FIGURE 2.2 Front cover of *Never Let Me Go*, Kazuo Ishiguro
(New York: Knopf, 2005).

Reprinted by permission
of the publisher.

"not like" because as a group they possess a quality that they believe the clones do not have (individuality), and "not like" because they believe they are incomparable (only a clone is "like" someone else) (263). From the beginning of the novel, likeness is both the apex and the nadir of value: while it is "natural," Kathy H. claims, to establish and prefer "your own kind" (like some and not like others), it is also "natural" and desirable, she argues, not to be the same as other people (exactly alike) (4, 122–24). For Kathy, to be human is to be a type rather than a token.

The donor program continues because the humans believe that the clones lack interiority, which is measured, according to all of the characters, by the capacity for genuine love, authentic expressivity, and artistic originality. The disdain for things that are "copied"—the novel is studded with this word—is ubiquitous: if the children admire a friend's poem, they are not happy to "copy it down" but want instead to possess the manuscript (14); Kathy criticizes Ruth for "the way you copy everything they [the older clones] do" (124); the clones think of themselves as having been "copied at some point from a normal person" (139); and so on. In contrast, Kathy and Tommy think that if they are "really, properly in love," they will have earned the right to have their donations deferred by a couple of years (153); Kathy thinks that the clones, to be more like "normal" humans, should aim for social mannerisms that are spontaneous rather than imitated (120); and Miss Emily believes that, by producing works of art, the clones will show that they are "as sensitive and intelligent as any ordinary human being" (261).

Clones and non-clones declare the importance of spontaneity, sincerity, and creative talent. Yet, in the novel, most of the clones do seem to lack intellectual complexity, exceptional artistic abilities, and ideas of love that depart from sitcom banality. In addition, the case for the clones' originality is made most strenuously by Miss Emily, whose methods—she tries to rally sympathy for her clone-students by organizing public art exhibitions—seem comic and on some level unconvincing. When Kathy and Tommy visit Miss Emily late in the novel, she explains: "We took away your art because we thought it would reveal your souls. Or to put it more finely, we did it to *prove you had souls at all*" (260, original emphasis). Miss Emily's efforts, like her

FIGURE 2.3 Front cover of the Dutch translation of *Never Let Me Go*, Kazuo Ishiguro, *Laat me nooit alleen*, translated by Bartho Krieck (Amsterdam: Eldorado, 2006).

Reprinted by permission
of the publisher.

argument, only go so far: while they do improve conditions for the clone children, by creating schools like the one Kathy and Tommy attended, they do not alter or really aim to alter the donation system.

But the novel's critique does not focus on the limits or hypocrisy of Miss Emily's improvements. Rather, it focuses on the logic of originality and Romantic genius that undergirds the beliefs of Miss Emily, of those who control the donor system she tentatively opposes, and of the clones themselves. Kathy H. seems naïve in her insistence that people "in normal life" don't derive their mannerisms from popular culture (124). Seeing clones as humans is not the point. Instead we are urged to see humans as clones. That is, we are urged to see that even humans produced through biological reproduction are in some ways copies, and that human culture, full of cassette tapes and television programs and rumors and paperbacks of *Daniel Deronda*, is also unoriginal. It is by seeing the likeness between human originality and the novel's unoriginal objects—Kathy H., the cassette, the song, the television program, the narration—that we recognize the large networks of approximation and comparison in which individuality functions.

One of the novel's final episodes involves a discussion about the eponymous song, "Never Let Me Go." Kathy and Madame recall an episode in Kathy's childhood, in which Madame had seen Kathy holding a pillow to her breast and swaying to the music of a tape recording. At the time Madame had imagined that the lyrics ("Never let me go. Oh, baby, baby. Never let me go . . .") express the fear of losing an "old kind world" to the advance of new technologies (272). For her part, Kathy had imagined that she was singing to a baby whom she held in her arms (70, 271). Neither "version," as Kathy calls her interpretation, seems to correspond to the song's "cocktail-bar" genre, but Kathy doesn't mind (271, 70). She explains, "Even at the time, I realized that this couldn't be right, that this interpretation didn't fit with the rest of the lyrics. But that wasn't an issue with me. The song was about what I said, and I used to listen to it again and again, on my own, whenever I got the chance" (70). Madame makes much the same point in her conversation with Kathy: while she knew her interpretation "wasn't really you, what you were doing," it was what she "saw" nevertheless (272). For Ishiguro, the point is

FIGURE 2.4
Front cover of the Spanish translation of *Never Let Me Go*,
Kazuo Ishiguro, *Nunca me abandones*, translated by
Jesús Zulaika Goicoechea (Barcelona: Editorial Anagrama, 2005).

not simply that art can mean anything—that it is what you say or see—but rather that the content of art will be transformed by expansive circulation and by the local interpretations that readers impose. Like Kathy H., Ishiguro seems to prefer phenomenology to ontology. He suggests that works of art, like people, should be valued for the social life they help to establish.

For this reason, we need to understand the title of the novel not simply as the name of a song or as the expression of a sentiment that characters interpret but as a reference to a material object: the cassette-tape recording, which is also one of the novel's preeminent "copies." Early in her story, Kathy distinguishes between two different tapes of the song: "the actual cassette, the one I had back then at Hailsham," and the "copy of that tape . . . the one Tommy and I found in Norfolk years afterwards" (64). Later she acknowledges that there might be two tapes or even "thousands of these [copies] knocking about" (172). In truth, Kathy does not know whether the Hailsham and Norfolk tapes are different objects or the same object: whether they are different because the found tape is not "the first edition" that she possessed at Hailsham, or whether they are the same because both tapes are "tokens" of a single album or perhaps even the same token (the Norfolk tape may be the Hailsham tape). It depends, to be sure, whether it is the cassette or the album that Kathy most values. It would seem that she, too, is uncertain. She recalls that, after the Norfolk trip, "I really appreciated having the tape—and that song—back again. Even then, it was mainly a nostalgia thing, and today, if I happen to get the tape out and look at it, it brings back memories of that afternoon in Norfolk every bit as much as it does our Hailsham days" (173). The tape can bring back memories of Norfolk because it is a singular object, and it can bring back memories of Hailsham because it is a clone of the edition she possessed as a child. She has the tape "back again" and also has a new tape. As a token, a cassette is one of many copies, perhaps one of thousands. And it is a copy of a copy: the cassette was "originally an LP" (67), and the LP was originally a "recording" of the performer Judy Bridgewater's voice, and the voice is an interpretation of the song "Never Let Me Go."

Instead of thinking about the novel's comparison between humans and clones, we could think about its comparison between

Kazuo Ishiguro
Ole luonani aina

FIGURE 2.5 Front cover of the Finnish edition of *Never Let Me Go*,
Kazuo Ishiguro, *Ole luonani aina*, translated by Helene Bützow
(Helsinki: Kustannusosakeyhtiö Tammi, 2005).

Reprinted by permission
of the publisher.

humans and cassette tapes. The novel introduces two different ways of thinking about uniqueness: one that is attributed to people and sometimes to works of art such as poems and drawings, and one that is attributed to objects such as cassette tapes and desk lamps. The first model assumes that uniqueness depends on sincerity and consistency. According to Kathy H., the clones believe that "when you saw the person you were copied from, you'd get *some* insight into who you were deep down, and maybe too, you'd see something of what your life held in store" (140, original emphasis). In this model, individuals have an ontological existence that defines what they are and what they will be; copies simply inherit that existence. The second model attributes uniqueness not to a prior existence but to social embeddedness and unpredictable futurity. Consider the "four desk-lamps, each of a different colour, but all the same design" that Kathy keeps in her bedsit, and how she enjoys herself in new towns by "looking for a shop with another lamp like that in its window—not to buy, but just to compare with my ones at home" (208). Kathy doesn't value the desk lamps for what each one normally does (shed light). Instead she values them because they constitute a group, because they allow her to contemplate similarities and differences, and because they provide an occasion for new comparisons. Kathy's desk lamps are part of group, but that group is incomplete, and each desk lamp has the potential to join other groups—those defined by, say, color rather than design. Consider, also, Kathy's cassette tape from Norfolk, which has become one of her "most precious possessions" not because she listens to it but because it reminds her of at least two occasions: the afternoon she spent with Tommy, when they found the tape in a second-hand store, and her childhood at Hailsham, where she was absorbed in a song-inspired fantasy (64). She values the Norfolk tape in much the same way as she values another cassette tape, the one of dance tunes given to her by Ruth to replace the lost tape of "Never Let Me Go." Because "the music has nothing to do with anything," Ruth's gift is more important to Kathy as "an object" than as a token (a recording); it is one of Kathy's "most precious possessions," a term she repeats twice in the same chapter to refer to two separate tapes (76). In the novel the preciousness of both tapes is an effect of the social relationships they have helped to establish.

If there were any doubt that the novel privileges the second model of uniqueness, we might consider the Japanese edition, which features a book-sized image of a cassette on its cover (figure 2.1). That cover stands out from the covers of all of the other early editions of the novel, most of which display an image of humans or what appear to be parts of humans (figures 2.2, 2.3, 2.4, and 2.5).[34] The Japanese cover, in its apparent singularity, raises several questions, including this one: why might one wish to privilege, as an icon for the novel, the image of a cassette tape over the image of a person? To begin, we might return to Miss Emily's logic, her idea that the work of art conveys the soul of its creator and moreover affirms that its creator has a soul or, as Kathy would put it, some quality "deep down" (140). In Ishiguro's novel, the work of art has no "deep down": its meanings are collaborative and comparative, and thus affirm, instead of a soul, various networks of production and consumption. Ishiguro suggests that a song or a novel or a person can be a singular object as well as a multiple-type object. In so doing, he proposes that uniqueness depends not an absolute quality or a predetermined future but on the potential for comparison and likeness: all art is a cassette tape, for better or for worse. Only by appreciating the unoriginality of art, Ishiguro suggests, can we change the idea of literature itself.

THE SERIES, THE LIST

I want now to bring *Never Let Me Go*'s emphasis on replication and circulation to bear on Ishiguro's most familiar text, *The Remains of the Day*, which asks readers to consider not only networks but also scale. *The Remains of the Day* is usually discussed as an allegory about one of several world-political themes: the shrinking of Britain into England, the commodification of English heritage for American tourists, and the hypocrisy of English liberalism in the face of colonial exploitation abroad and anti-Semitism at home. Initially I bracket these themes and focus instead on the ways that the novel arranges them. *The Remains of the Day* approaches the project of uniqueness by establishing the relationship between individual anecdotes or actions and what the voluble narrator, Stevens, calls "unimaginable largeness." This phrase and the ideal of uniqueness it represents will occupy me for the remainder of the chapter. At the end, I return to the question of whether translation leads to homogenization, and I try to suggest what cultural and political homogenization might look like in the context of Ishiguro's work.

By presenting individual anecdotes as versions or explanations of more dramatic, collective events, such as colonialism and the Holocaust, *The Remains of the Day* invokes the principle of enlarged thinking—and in many ways supports it. Stevens promotes a Benjaminian analysis of history: his stories show how unnoticed, almost invisible labors facilitate well-known achievements, and they display the past actions and processes that have led to present-day situations.[35] The ideal of enlarged thinking also matches Benjamin's sense of translation: his belief that a work of art will have an "afterlife" in another language, which its author can neither predict nor realize; and his conceit that translation preserves the original by helping it to mature.[36]

Stevens introduces enlarged thinking as the enrichment, rather than the abstraction, of ordinary actions. Preparing for the arrival of German, British, American, and French statesmen in March 1923, Stevens says he was "only too aware of the possibility that if any guest were to find his stay at Darlington Hall less than comfortable, this might have repercussions of unimaginable largeness" (76–77). This idea, that ordinary actions could have extraordinary consequences, is articulated in the text on at least two prior occasions: once when the housekeeper, Miss Kenton, reminds Stevens that household errors "may be trivial in themselves" but still possess "larger significance" (59); and once when Stevens's employer, Lord Darlington, asks Stevens to remove his ailing father (Stevens senior) from public duties because an accidental fall during the dinner service "might jeopardize the success of our forthcoming conference" (63). Stevens at first attributes the concern about "larger significance" to Miss Kenton, but he later acknowledges that it may have been Lord Darlington's phrase (60). However it begins, this way of thinking structures all of the anecdotes that Stevens presents, in which we are asked to see individuated actions in the context of pervasive consequences. The model here is the scale rather than the network: serving a well-orchestrated dinner contributes directly and uniquely to negotiating peace.

Some of the time Ishiguro's novel takes enlarged thinking seriously and seems to admire its critical impulse. We learn that the meeting organized by Lord Darlington aims to convince the British and especially the French to relax the terms of the Versailles treaty. For readers, who know that this fictional visit will soon be followed by the Second World War, Stevens's worry about failed hospitality and unhappy guests intimates two chief "repercussions": Darlington's efforts to bring economic stability to Germany could be compromised, and the subsequent effect, which Stevens is not imagining here but which some would say should have been imagined by him and others, that a failure to modify the Versailles treaty could lead to German unrest and later to militarism and finally to the Holocaust, an unimagined largeness signaled in the novel by an anti-Semitic incident that imposes its ethical and emotional weight on many other incidents in the text. Given this history, the novel does in fact ask us to see both analogy and contiguity between the act of polishing silver and the act of negotiating peace treaties. In a general way, welcoming guests is important because it triggers subsequent social interactions; in a more specific way, welcoming guests to talks about international peace takes on the ethical significance of alleviating poverty, preventing war, and extending sympathy across national borders. The stakes of alleviation, prevention, and sympathy are large, and Stevens transfers this quality onto the functioning of his employer's household.

The novel is especially persuasive in its support of enlarged thinking when it offers examples that reflect poorly on Stevens and when Stevens seems least aware of that outcome. Good household service may lead to peace treaties, but it may also lead to military aggression or political appeasement. While Stevens's early conversation with Lord Darlington about the "larger significance" of the dinner service precedes the 1923 meeting, a later conversation about polishing silver refers to a meeting between Lord Halifax and Herr Ribbentrop (eventually, Hitler's ambassador to Britain) in the middle of the 1930s (135–36). Lord Darlington tells Stevens, "By the way, Stevens, Lord Halifax was jolly impressed with the silver the other night. Put him into a quite a different frame of mind" (135). From this, Stevens concludes, "the state of the silver had made a small, but significant contribution towards the easing of relations between Lord Halifax and Herr Ribbentrop that evening" (136). Enlarged thinking is vital, Ishiguro seems to suggest, because it allows us to see that Stevens's actions were in part responsible for the friendship between Hitler's agent and the British foreign minister. Stevens knew at the time that this was a significant occasion, but only in retrospect can he (and we) know what that significance would be.

Moreover, when Stevens claims that some actions, including his dismissal of two Jewish maids in the early 1930s, are simply "trivial"—that they have no "larger significance"—readers know to think otherwise. Recalling the circumstances that caused him to fire the maids, Stevens refers to a "brief, entirely insignificant few weeks" when Lord Darlington was influenced by British fascists and acknowledges "one very minor episode . . . which has been blown up out of all proportion" (145, 137). Of course, blowing things up out of all proportion is just what enlarged thinking requires, and it is Stevens who has taught readers how to do so. Stevens fires the Jewish maids because he thinks he is acting in the service of Lord Darlington's larger European project. He fails to see or even really to evaluate the quality of that project, and he fails to see that his action has its own significance, especially for the maids and for his relationship with Miss Kenton. Finally, he fails to see that this episode sheds light on the significance of several previous anecdotes about model butlers who ignore or placate offensive masters. With the story about the Jewish maids, Ishiguro seems to imply—I am overstating only slightly—that self-abnegation and incuriosity lay the groundwork for genocide.

And yet it is important to notice that Stevens's call for enlarged thinking is not to be taken seriously or to be admired all of the time, and thus the ironic reading of Stevens's phrase is in some ways correct. Ishiguro is making fun of his character's overblown rhetoric and absurd formality while he is nevertheless constructing a novel that seems to follow the logic of Stevens's grammatical claim. Put another way, the novel takes "unimaginable largeness" seriously by valuing in Stevens's anecdotes both the sublime and the ridiculous. It is ultimately the ridiculous, Ishiguro suggests, that allows for new networks of responsibility to emerge. In the novel, the ridiculous is represented by the practice of "bantering," an activity and style of activity that generates inconsistency, playfulness, and surprise. Importantly, bantering appears not as the opposite of Benjaminian historicism but rather as its supplement: by recognizing paradox, absurdity, and metaphor in the structure of Ishiguro's novel, readers can see the several large networks in which each of Stevens's anecdotes takes part. For example, in Stevens's mind, firing the Jewish maids is exactly like polishing the silver: both acts are meant to facilitate Lord Darlington's political maneuverings; Stevens sees them as equivalent parts of that largeness. For us, however, these acts are also parts of other kinds of largeness: a climate of anti-Semitism, or a national strategy of political appeasement. Just as a single text can operate in several literary cultures, polishing silver can be part of several political histories. It is not a matter of choosing between scale and network but of recognizing the networks of varying scales in which a single action may participate.

Bantering introduces several networks of meaning, but it also focuses attention on the process of communication. At the end of the novel, Stevens considers that "in bantering lies the key to human warmth," though this is not because of what people say but because of how they say it (245). Stevens notes earlier that bantering requires a kind of speech that is not "safely inoffensive" (15–16). In fact, the success of one's banter is measured by its ability to cause surprise; for this reason, there has to be something inconsistent and unpredictable in bantering's style. Like Kathy H. in her interpretation of "Never Let Me Go," those who banter refuse to be constrained by the consciousness of larger meanings or by the sense that there is only one larger meaning.

From beginning to end, *The Remains of the Day* is structured by a parade of anecdotes. Sometimes this parade seems to constitute a series, and sometimes it seems to be a list. It is a series insofar as the novel follows the chronology of the narrator's four-day travelogue and the story he tells about the meaning of his anecdotes. It is a list, however, insofar it contains the potential for many different series, chronologically as well as thematically arranged; insofar as it gestures to future comparisons that have not yet been imagined; and insofar as it allows each anecdote to have its own momentary life. Understood formally, the plot of Ishiguro's novel emerges in the difference between the professional largeness that Stevens sees and the many qualities of largeness—personal relationships, anti-Semitism, colonialism, political appeasement, the death of a family member—that we see but that he does not even apprehend.

Stevens applies to his anecdotes a theory of comparison that is somewhat different from the one that the novel asks us to adopt. The first theory, articulated by Stevens and reaffirmed at the end of the novel by the nativist liberal Mr. Harry Smith, proposes that every person must imagine his or her actions as part of a larger, unified whole. This theory allows Stevens to assert that his willingness to tolerate slights and ignore his personal feelings contributed to the forging of international alliances. It allows Harry Smith to assert, conversely, that his willingness to speak plainly contributes to a more democratic, egalitarian England. Both of these assertions are valued in the novel, but they are also criticized for their rigidity and for their singularity of scale. Stevens fails to notice that his professional restraint contributes not only to international alliances but also to anti-Semitism, political appeasement, and emotional isolation. Harry Smith fails to notice that his speech is premised on the silence of Britain's colonial subjects, whose independence he wishes to suppress while advocating his own. The largeness that Harry Smith can recognize ends at the borders of Britain. He claims repeatedly to have "done his part" (fought in the war, made his opinions known, urged others to participate in democracy), but it is in his commitment to a whole that extends only as far as the nation that his conception of largeness matches the single-minded scale that Stevens promotes (189). The novel thus articulates a theory of comparison that emphasizes the largeness to which each incident contributes but also refuses the wholeness in which each incident might be contained.

Harry Smith's comments at the end of the text recall an anecdote that Stevens tells at the beginning about a butler serving in colonial India. According to Stevens, the butler displays professional dignity by protecting his employer's guests from the knowledge that a tiger has entered the dining room. The butler is able to alert his employer, kill the tiger, and report his success with such discretion that the guests never learn of the tiger's removal, or even of its presence. Stevens is especially pleased by the butler's unflappable manner and by his command of euphemism, which allow him to report blandly in the earshot of his employer's guests that "dinner will be served at the usual time" and without "discernible trace of the recent occurrence" (36). Surely, we can see—it's almost a cliché—that there is something strongly allegorical about Stevens's story: the British ruling classes used servants and other subalterns to separate their lives from the proverbial tiger in the dining room that had to be killed, but softly, so that afternoon tea could continue uninterrupted in the parlor. Stevens offers this anecdote as an example of what we might call professional formalism: an ideal of grace under pressure, which means maintaining one's role under any condition, no matter how alarming or dangerous. And while the repercussions of this ideal will become increasingly visible over the course of the novel, we learn right away about the butler's small role in the largeness that was colonialism. It is a key aspect of the novel's theory of largeness that Stevens will only ever recognize one context for his anecdotes, whereas the novel will always intimate several. The problem with Stevens's ethos of enlarged thinking, Ishiguro suggests, is not that he translates every action and every story but that he fails to translate enough.

In the novel Stevens calls this kind of persistent translation "forever reappraising," and it is an activity he resists because it seems to him impossible to follow a path and evaluate its direction at the same time. It seems "misguided," he explains, for "a butler with serious aspirations . . . to be forever reappraising his employer—scrutinizing the latter's motives, analyzing the implications of his views," testing whether "one's skills were being employed to a desirable end" (200). But this is what the novel's structure requires from its readers: a movement between inside and outside, or between text and book, if you will. On the one hand, we read with Stevens, enlarging his anecdotes into more expansive systems; on the other hand, the more we read as Stevens reads, the more we encounter systems whose meanings are obscured by the strategy of symptomatic interpretation. Largeness, which usually promises depth or latent content, appears in this novel as a perennial surface. Sharon Marcus has suggested that all symptomatic reading, because it emphasizes what is absent or invisible, tends to devalue or often simply miss what is present.[37] This is certainly the problem that Stevens often faces, or indeed does not face, as when he identifies his father's housekeeping mistakes as signs of a peace treaty that might be ruined rather than as signs of ailing health. Stevens thinks of his life as a series, whereas we have to see it as a list. A series privileges one context over another and situates each action in terms of an outcome or referent. The list, like a group of clones, implies equivalent objects, even if the arrangement and circulation of those objects generates distinctions and new objects. Ishiguro forces us to compare several outcomes (the Holocaust, Americanization, imperialism) by treating each anecdote as part of a list that can be arranged in several ways and whose meanings will change according to future arrangements.

The novel's structure invites readers to think about the relationship between text and book, as I've suggested, because it proposes that enlarged reading—reading globally—changes not simply the meaning but what I have been calling, after Benjamin, the life of a novel. Texts, as they exist in the world, are many different books; they are, like Stevens's anecdotes and Kathy H.'s cassette tape, part of several series—originals not simply in their own culture but in several cultures. If thinking about largeness can promote acts of comparison, as it does for the reader of Ishiguro's novels, it can also prompt (less retrospectively) acts of production, as it does for Ishiguro and other novelists working today. Anthony Appiah makes a related point when he remarks in his book on cosmopolitanism that the expansion of U.S. products into world markets can have a variety of dynamic effects, including the effect of reverse assimilation, such that U.S. products have to accommodate the desires and preferences of a variety of world consumers.[38] In the case of Ishiguro, he is accommodating consumers, but he is also challenging our sense of what it is that consumers consume: What is the work that we are reading? What is the difference between the work and its many books? What is the appropriate scale for our reading? And what is the relationship between the enlargement of ethics and the enlargement of geography?

Thinking about enlargement does not mean always thinking on a planetary scale, but it does mean acknowledging the many scales that recent globalization has helped to produce. Scholars of U.S. multilingualism such as Werner Sollors, Marc Shell, and Joshua Miller have made this point about American literature, while the Slavicist Harsha

Ram has argued that Russian translations of Georgian literature contributed to regional articulations of Soviet internationalism.[39] These projects suggest that it is not a single "distant reading," to use Franco Moretti's phrase, but a comparison of close readings, in many languages and across many geographies, that studies of world literature may require.[40]

From his novels about Japan to his novel about cloning, Ishiguro has implied that it is inadequate and unethical to treat uniqueness as the defining quality of art, culture, and human life. In *Never Let Me Go*, valuing uniqueness leads to killing clones and preserving people. *The Remains of the Day* suggests a modification of that argument: rather than seeing uniqueness as a property of singular masterpieces or anecdotes or even cultures, we are asked to see it as the property of a work's appearance, as translation, edition, anthology, or excerpt. Ishiguro proposes that comparison, while it elides uniqueness in the service of a larger paradigm, also generates uniqueness, but uniqueness of a different kind: the uniqueness of a translation, the uniqueness of a cassette tape, and the uniqueness of an allegory about political appeasement.

I offer here, really, two accounts of comparison: an account of world literature in which translation and global circulation create many books out of single texts, transforming old traditions and inaugurating new ones; and an account of Ishiguro's novels in which a principle of unoriginality expands the horizon of social relationships, figuring new networks of local and global largeness. Ultimately, Ishiguro's calculation comes to this: uniqueness can persist in the world but only in comparative forms: in the shape of the echo, the copy, the clone, the list, the series, and the translation.

This chapter has explored how books in translation constitute new kinds of groups. The next two chapters consider the relationship between the location of books and the location of audiences.

3

SAMPLING, COLLATING, AND COUNTING

The truth of a myth, your Honor, is not its words but its patterns.

—David Mitchell, *Thousand Autumns*

THE WORLD-SHAPED NOVEL

THIS CHAPTER turns to novels that distribute narrative action across several continents, regions, or national territories. These novels are multistranded: their chapters move back and forth among several points of view. Like an anthology or an atlas, they gather materials drawn from disparate geographies. Multistranded novels of the nineteenth and twentieth centuries, such as *Bleak House* (1853), *Mrs. Dalloway* (1925), and the *U.S.A.* trilogy (1938), distribute their characters within cities and nations. In those works, nation or city drives the theme as well as the shape. Indeed, shape is crucial to theme: Charles Dickens, Virginia Woolf, and John Dos Passos taught readers to understand a social environment by summing up its various perspectives.[1] The works I discuss in this chapter alter both the scope and the structure of multistranded fiction. By encompassing global space while also incorporating histories of global circulation, they develop new models of accumulation. They use these models to address the double logic of parity and expressivity that has been crucial to most understandings of world literature.[2]

Parity has been important because it implies that world literature is a container for different but equivalent traditions. Expressivity has meant that each tradition is imagined to possess specific characteristics that can be communicated and preserved through literary works. Imagining other kinds of containers and other kinds of objects, born-translated novels generate histories of literary production rooted in target rather than source. Emphasizing target—receiving languages as well as receiving cultures—the novels highlight uneven histories of circulation and the role of audiences in the production of literary works. Emphasizing target also becomes a way to reject the principle of diffusion, in which literature begins in one place, typically Europe, and then moves out to other places.[3] Instead of diffusion, theses works introduce rival chronologies that place translation at the source of literary history.

World-shaped novels feature traveling characters who speak different languages, sometimes within the same national space. Notable examples include many first books published at or near the start of the twenty-first century: Ahdaf Soueif's *The Map of Love* (1999), David Mitchell's *Ghostwritten* (1999), Peter Ho Davies's *The Welsh Girl* (2007), Kiran Desai's *Inheritance of Loss* (2006), and Amy Waldman's *The Submission* (2011). They also include novels by Caryl Phillips and W. G. Sebald, whose *Distant Shore* (2004) and *Rings of Saturn* (1995, German; 1998, English), respectively, find ways to incorporate migration into setting and scene. These world-shaped fictions are also world-themed. They present collaborative projects and private undertakings that operate between or across sovereign states. Characters take part in transnational activities such as humanitarian aid, undocumented labor, wartime emigration, architectural design, concert performance, corporate finance, maritime trade, and scientific research. Because characters travel across nations and continents, the novels are saturated by translation, in both explicit and implicit ways. Many feature translators and scenes of translation or intended translation. The three principal actors in *The Welsh Girl* function as translators among speakers of English, German, and Welsh; the narrator in *A Map of Love* creates an anglophone story out of letters and diaries composed in Arabic, English, and French; and a Mongolian folklorist in *Ghostwritten* hopes to get his stories "translated into English and flog them to the tourists."[4]

There are also references in many works to intermedial translation and to the physical and material qualities of language. Waldman's *Submission* asks us to consider what happens when artworks and parts of artworks are adapted across architecture, site-specific sculpture, documentary film, and narrative fiction. *A Map of Love* varies its typography to signal the appearance of handwriting in different languages. Mitchell's later novel, *Black Swan Green* (2006), reflects on the mechanisms of speech. Pointing at the embodiment of words, the novels ask us to notice the kinds of translation that take place within what appears to be a single language. When thought becomes voice, when manuscript becomes typescript, and when Japanese characters become Roman letters on the page, circulation precedes and shapes production. Above all, world-shaped novels explore translation by asking how people, objects, ideas, and even aesthetic styles move across territories, and how that movement alters the meaning and form of collectivity.

Three devices have been crucial to the development of multistranded fiction: sampling, collating, and counting. Before we consider the transformation of these devices as they have moved from nation-shaped to world-shaped novels, it is useful to understand what these devices have done and why they have been effective. Sampling allows literary works to make very large-scale claims using relatively small-scale data. As readers encounter a narrative strand, they encounter both an individual and a kind of individual. The strand projects a population in miniature. I call the arrangement of these strands collating because the multistranded novel curates as well as collects. By segmenting and ordering strands, collating adds meaning rather than simply organizing it. In a novel, collating requires decisions about category and order. What are the principles of organization? How will each strand be arranged? And it also requires decisions about duration and interval. How many chapters or sections will each strand occupy? How frequently will each strand appear? Collating implies reciprocity: that each part is geographically, linguistically, or ethically comparable, and that the novel has generated a plausible system or container for those parts. Collating also anticipates counting, both the right to be enumerated and the gesture of enumeration. The parts of a multistranded novel should add up;

they also deserve to be added. By including the interior monologue of Miss Kilman, for example, Woolf's *Mrs. Dalloway* assigns value to Miss Kilman's experience and places that experience alongside the experiences of other characters. Countability is thus assumed, but it is also affirmed. This operates formally, too. Chapters appear to be independent units within a quantifiable system. Both the units and the system have to be relatively static since it is difficult to count if the units change or if the premises of the system are altered.

In world-shaped novels, an awareness of translation and an emphasis on global circulation, including the global circulation of artworks, have created new conditions for sampling, collating, and counting. These devices remain active, but they sometimes fail to function or they function in extravagant ways. Sampling is often muted or ambiguated. Instead of unmediated voices, novels that begin in translation present us with distant, paraphrased, or disabled voices, or they may produce what Timothy Bewes has called a *"restriction* of voices."[5] Whereas sampling may be constrained, collating is often multiplied. Many world-shaped novels introduce competing arrangements across geographic, calendric, or linguistic systems. Translation, which has traditionally affirmed countability, such as the countability of two languages, in these works impedes accumulation. Through translation the individual unit becomes part of a collective, and the features of the literary system are transformed by the incursion of other systems. Accumulation is impeded because there is too much information rather than too little. Competing arrangements establish comparative worlds, not only different ways of holding units together but also different ways of imagining global space.[6] Sebald's multistranded novel *The Emigrants* (1992, German; 1996, English) invites readers to count up its kinds—emigrants, Jews, Germans, English—and then explores the historical and ethical impediments to social calculation.[7] Sebald is known for folding many voices into what appear to be monologues and for incorporating long passages from other literary works without quotation or other typographical markers. In his works, sampling is overrun: weaving together several voices, drawn from different literary traditions and geographies, he produces the effect of translated writing. By calling attention to the relationship between literary and social classifications, Sebald extends the problem of enumeration from the citizenship of books to the citizenship of people. He suggests that limiting the citizenship of books halts, blocks, or erases translation in ways that contribute to practices of xenophobia and racism.

Muted in some ways and garrulous in others, world-shaped novels are post-multicultural.[8] Developed as an alternative to universalism, the doctrine of multiculturalism sought to protect minority rights by granting a "permanent political identity or constitutional status" to specific ethnic groups.[9] Multiculturalism offered a model of the collective that fits well with Romantic understandings of world literature since both assume that groups possess specific characteristics that can be communicated and preserved, and that the whole consists of different but equivalent groups.[10] In the early 1990s philosophers and social theorists began to worry that the "recognition" of minority groups also demanded their "survival" as groups, and thus their consistency over time.[11] The survival of groups can have pernicious effects on the survival of individuals since people are offered the opportunity to be "acknowledged publicly as what they already are" but may not be given the opportunity to become something else.[12] Critics argue that multiculturalism tends to presuppose and conserve "cultures."[13] Multiculturalism thus assumes countability, but countability undermines the principle of "acculturation" or mutability that is also crucial to the ethos of multiculturalism.[14] World-shaped novels are multicultural insofar as they distribute chapters according to national or ethnic categories and present themselves as an accumulation of those categories. But they are post-multicultural insofar as they emphasize circulation and audience as well as origin. Circulation interferes with both expressivity and parity.

An emphasis on audiences and readers leads world-shaped novels to weigh competing models of translation, to generate alternatives to source- or diffusion-oriented literary histories, and to revisit the logic of inheritance that has been so important to prior novels and to the national collectives imagined by the novel. A concern with inheritance leads many of these novels to focus on significant nationalist turning points: *The Inheritance of Loss* takes place during the struggle for Gorkha independence in West Bengal (1980s); *Welsh Girl* concerns the final years of the Second World War (late 1944–1947); and *The*

Map of Love shuttles between late-twentieth-century struggles in the Middle East and the uprisings against British occupation of Egypt in and around 1906. The title of Desai's novel refers to the experience of exploitation and absence that the novel associates with colonialism's legacy. The work is full of migrants who think their stories are theirs alone, and it is part of the fiction's project to reject the characters' solipsism: "Never again could she think there was but one narrative and that narrative belonged only to herself."[15] *Inheritance of Loss* alternates between scenes in New York City and scenes in the Indian Himalayas, connecting regional rather than national spaces and insisting that geopolitical conflicts, both small and large, need to be understood locally as well as comparatively.

Desai's novel uses histories of circulation to unsettle histories of inheritance, but Davies's and Souief's novels are even more explicit in their engagement with translation as a model for thinking about the world. *The Welsh Girl* begins with a bilingual screening of *Triumph of the Will* and ends with the embrace of *cynefin*, a Welsh-language term that refers to the way sheep establish their territory through the female line. The choice of a Welsh word within an English-language novel initially seems to emphasize an exclusive localism, yet in the novel the local functions as an alternative to the language of "fatherland" circulated by British soldiers, Welsh nationalists, and Nazi propagandists.[16] Indeed, the chief examples of inheritance involve adoption, one ewe caring for another's lamb, and a German prisoner of war substituting (as father) for a Welsh soldier, who is in fact substituting for a British soldier. *Cynefin*, it turns out, is a model of solidarity that relies on social practice rather than biological origin. It draws on circulation to generate production. Souief's *Map of Love*, for its part, presents erotic and literary transactions between Egypt and Britain, and later between Egypt and the United States. It highlights the ways that translation both served and helped to defeat colonialism.[17]

In novels by Souief, Davies, Desai, Sebald, and many others, we can observe translation's presence as a fictional conceit, a historical practice, and a social ideal. The remainder of this chapter turns to Caryl Phillips, David Mitchell, and Amy Waldman, whose novels place traveling artworks and translated books at the source of national traditions. In these novels, the accumulation of territories creates the impression of comparative worlds.

LIMITED PARTICIPATION

The expansion from nation to world in multistranded fiction has not, in fact, reduced sampling. Even when they write about migration, novelists who compare across continents sample more deliberately, more extensively, and more elaborately than ever. This is certainly true for the Caribbean-British-U.S. writer Caryl Phillips, who has been writing multistranded novels since the 1980s. Not all of Phillips's novels are multistranded, but most of them are. In addition to his novels, many of his works in other genres—anthologies, essay collections, memoir, and fictional biography—distribute their parts geographically. Phillips is one of the most persistent and prolific architects of "comparison literature," a term I have used to describe literary works that attribute their beginnings to several national geographies.[18] By creating works that are located comparatively rather than uniquely, Phillips places activities we usually associate with reception—classifying, mapping, distributing, and comparing—squarely within production.

World-themed as well as world-shaped, Phillips's books collate multiple instances of migration; they also promote different strategies of distribution and arrangement. In his works, these are related enterprises. Desequencing circulation and production, Phillips suggests that migration should be understood not simply as a desire for citizenship, or its abdication, but instead as citizenship's foundation, in two ways: first, because the constituents, wealth, and culture attributed to one place originated in many places and through many agents; and, second, because political collectivities depend for their recognition on processes of accumulation, promotion, and reception. Phillips's born-translated works are also born-migrated works: they argue for the primacy of migration in the history and sovereignty of nations.

Phillips initially comes to world-shaped fiction through narratives about the slave trade and its legacies. His early works reach out to various corners of the Atlantic and allocate their narratives to a range of actors and historical periods. Thinking about the slave trade requires thinking not only about several continents but also about the movement of people and objects among those continents. Whereas Phillips's novels tend to focus on experiences of social and political exclusion, his literary anthologies and historical biographies of "foreigners" within Britain focus on changing the terms of inclusion. Phillips's career has thus followed two paths: documenting the negative experience of migration while using the resources of literature in several genres to affirm more inclusive models of participation. Over the past fifteen years Phillips has extended his awareness of literary circulation from the national context of the print anthology to the global context of satellite television and the Internet. In his introduction to a 2001 volume of essays, *A New World Order*, Phillips imagines a new "global conversation" in which the experience of "limited participation," once the domain only of migrants and exiles, will be "open" to everyone.[19] The openness Phillips imagines is produced in part through greater access to travel but more substantially through greater access to visual and social media. This is an ironic kind of openness. It is not simply that the world, however mediated, will belong to more people, but that more people will be introduced to the experience of partial belonging. Awareness of the limit, feeling more limited, becomes in Phillips's work both prescription and description. By emphasizing the effects of global reception on the meanings of national location, Phillips tries to extend limited participation from his characters to his readers.

Appearing in French, German, Japanese and many other languages, Phillips's books are widely translated. They are also born translated, though not because they take any direct interest in the translation of national languages. Most of his characters are migrants, but dialogue is not accented or inflected; no one refers to words they are speaking or that they cannot speak, and everyone seems to understand the words that other characters are using. Instead the novels produce the impression of a target language because they seem to be quoting or paraphrasing stories rather than telling them. The novels thus resemble anthologies, both in their shape and in their accumulation of circulated objects. Of course, any multistranded novel could be said to resemble an anthology insofar as it collates multiple voices and transforms selections into examples. However, Phillips's novels engage not only with the anthology's form, its structure of distribution, but also with its project, in particular its role in gathering and affirming social groups. Historically, anthologies have both honored patrimony and helped to invent it. For this reason they serve as a strategic framework for showing how circulation instantiates production at the very moment it seems simply to celebrate it.

Phillips's novels, memoirs, anthologies, and biographies share many characteristics, including the effort to create new orders of semi- or "limited" belonging. This effort is visible in the language of his book titles over many years, which imply exclusion as an element of participation and distance as a characteristic of proximity. Relevant titles include *Extravagant Strangers: A Literature of Belonging*, an anthology from 1997; *A Distant Shore*, a novel from 2004; *Foreigners: Three English Lives*, a speculative biography from 2007; and *Color Me English: Migration and Belonging Before and After 9/11*, a volume of collected essays published in 2011. *Extravagant Strangers* is typical of Phillips's approach. He brings together selections from the works of nonnative British writers, creating a tradition of negative affiliation. The writers have different ways of being "strangers" in Britain, and some seem to be strangers only by technicality, like William Makepeace Thackeray, who was born in Calcutta before moving to England at the age of five. *Extravagant Strangers* does more to deflate the coherence of other anthologies than it does to assert its own. In this sense it is an anthology in conversation with other anthologies. It aims to bring a new tradition to light, if there can be a tradition of not belonging, and to identify the role of migrants in the tradition of British literature. For this reason Phillips includes both less-famous strangers, such as Ignatius Sancho, born on a slave ship sailing from the West African coast to the West Indies, and long-established English writers, such as Rudyard Kipling, George Orwell, and Thackeray. The anthology is notable for its inclusion of many novelists. Unlike most anthologies, which tend to avoid excerpting by drawing on poetry or short fiction, Phillips's book privileges longer works of narrative prose, or at least parts of those works. Phillips's anthology creates a new order of literary belonging for which his own fiction can serve as a future example.

Five of Phillips's novels to date, beginning with *Higher Ground* (1989) and extending through *A Distant Shore*, operate as historical fictions and distribute chapters across continents. The novel *Dancing in the Dark* (2006), while not distributed across continents, draws out Bert Williams's binational history and his itinerary from Bahamas–California upbringing to iconic performer of Southern minstrel stereotypes. Phillips wants his readers to understand how regional and international migration complicates the geography of African American culture, which includes the story of Williams and the frame of that story, a novel by Caryl Phillips.[20] *Dancing in the Dark* records the regional and international journeys that create the typical artifacts of national culture. In this case, the African American minstrel performer par excellence turns out to be a native not of the American South and not of a northern city but of the Caribbean and the Pacific coast. *A New World Order* is a collection of reviews and essays rather than a novel, but it makes a similar point about the meanings of geography. It organizes four locations—the United States, the Caribbean, Africa, and Britain—into several different orders, title notwithstanding, to suggest that the world contains many itineraries, rather than only one. Marketed as fictional reportage, *Foreigners* retells the "English lives" of three African British celebrities, one from the eighteenth century and two from the mid-twentieth. Again, the national appears both regional and global. In the U.S. edition of *Color Me English*, the subtitle ("migration and belonging after 9/11") implies that Englishness has been "colored" by an event that took place in lower Manhattan and whose actors, causes, and interpretations have tested the concept of territorial agency. All of these works feature "extravagant strangers," a tautology ("strange strangers") that encapsulates Phillips's career-long interest both in limited participation and in the ways that limited participation has supported and helped to create what counts as full participation.

In addition to collating various narratives of migration, Phillips's books represent the life of any single migrant, including their author, as yet another collated account.[21] There is a lot of overlap between Phillips's anthologies and his novels, not only in the ways they distribute examples geographically but also in the ways they combine history, biography, and speculation. Before turning at greater length to the anthological aspects of his fiction, it is worth noting the fictional aspects of his anthologies and essay collections. Unlike other anthologies, which create a single series, Phillips's books ask us to notice several possible trajectories. He often uses his own history as an example. In the short biographies that preface each of his books, Phillips mentions the places through which he has moved and continues to move. The biography from *Extravagant Strangers* is typical: "Caryl Phillips was born in St. Kitts, West Indies. Brought up in England, he has written for television, radio, theater, and cinema. . . . He divides his time between London and New York."[22] In *A New World Order*, Phillips describes his collated self as "one harmonious entity" (6). And yet there is something not especially harmonious about the relationship among the parts he names, or about the collective stories that these places are meant to represent. Phillips intimates this discord by registering what Theodore Mason has called the "historicity" of anthology production: the procedures of selection, arrangement, and framing that allow one series to emerge rather than another.[23] Instead of a single progression through places whose meanings are fixed, Phillips presents multiple progressions through places whose meanings vary according to the framework he establishes for them.

The structure of Phillips's introduction to *A New World Order* presents an autobiographical story of migration that is substantially different from the ones that appear in the biographies placed at the edges of the text. Emphasizing fantasy and memory rather than legal homes, the introduction begins and ends with anecdotes set in different parts of Africa. In one case a British official serving as Phillips's host is eager to display his graciousness toward an African porter; in another, Phillips is served by an African waiter who assumes that he, like any other loyal subject of the British Crown, must be mourning the death of Princess Diana. Each of these anecdotes serves to register Phillips's discomfort with the emphatic affiliations that seem to be available to him, whether he identifies with the official, the porter, the waiter, or the bereaved patriot. In addition to affiliations organized by nativity, genealogy, and residence, he also describes those organized by technology and travel. He considers the places made accessible through worldwide CNN broadcasts, inexpensive airplane travel, and a tourism industry in the former slave ports of West Africa.

These different ways of arranging geography and of arranging people's movements through geography establish the several anthologies in which Phillips's story takes part. The chapters of Phillips's book follow another order, beginning in the United States and moving to Africa, to the Caribbean, and then finally to Britain. Taken as a narrative, the chapters seem to tell the history of Phillips's intellectual development, whereas the series in the biography and in the introduction display the history of his postcolonial consciousness, the history of his passports, and the history of the African diaspora. With its multiple framings and allegorical constructions, Phillips's anthology aspires to the ingenuity and artifice of fiction.

His fiction, in turn, hews to the anthology in several ways. First, the collection is the message. Readers have to compare internal narratives to discover what kind of group they make, what experiences they share, and what histories they help to draw together. Action is sparse. The novels are far more interested in the arrangement of parts and in the ways that arrangement generates plot. Second, the narratives contained by many of the novels resemble historical biographies. They refine stories we know, whether focused on real-life figures such as Bert Williams, famous dramatic characters such as Othello, or generic representatives such as Eva, a concentration camp survivor. The parts of the book point outward not only to lives we have to imagine beyond the text but also to lives we have already imagined in other texts. There is no sharp distinction between the stories the novels are making and the stories they are distributing, circulating, or translating.

The Nature of Blood (1997), one of Phillips's most geographically expansive novels, asks readers to compare five stories that stretch across several centuries and places. The stories are held together by analogies of feeling: the desire to belong, and the experience of not belonging. The self-injuring alienation of Othello, depicted as an isolated African in early modern Venice, chimes with the psychic disintegration of Eva, who emigrates from Germany to postwar Britain. A montage of narratives, several of which are first-person monologues, displays the common experience of racism across African and Jewish diasporas. The novel touches down in Germany, Britain, Israel, Venice, and Cyprus. In many ways, sampling, collating, and counting operate conventionally: we are introduced to distinctive but analogous experiences distributed over several geographies. But the novel eventually departs from its initial distribution: first, a Jewish ghetto appears in Othello's Venice; and, second, an Ethiopian Jew arrives in late-twentieth-century Israel. Instead of equivalent but separate histories, we are asked to recognize a deviation from the novel's formula. It is not only that Jewish ghettos can be found in the sixteenth as well as the twentieth centuries, or that the Jewish experience of racism is historically simultaneous with the African experience of racism. Israel's reluctant acceptance of Ethiopian Jews, described in the final pages of the novel, changes what Israel symbolizes in the novel, and changes retrospectively the meanings assigned to Germany and Venice. For a moment we glimpse other ways of organizing the novel's geography, and other characters—Jews in Venice, or Ethiopians in Israel—whose stories are crowded out by more dominant actors. When Phillips asks us to understand his narratives metonymically rather than metaphorically, as related histories rather than as fixed analogues, we can recognize a surprising overlap with Sebald, with whom we are more likely to associate a critique of multicultural distribution.

Unlike *The Nature of Blood*, which briefly and belatedly raises questions about the territorial categories that have structured it, Phillips's *Distant Shore* begins by affirming the contingency of place. The novel begins with the sentence, "England has changed."[24] While Phillips's narrator seems to be referring to the sheer fact of mutability—what has changed about England is the fact that it is now changeable, she believes—the novel suggests that it is scale rather than object that has been altered. *A Distant Shore* proposes in its opening pages that the meaning of location is established externally as well as internally; that migration can operate across towns, villages, regions, and nations; and that locations are defined not only by maps but also by constituents. Phillips places a story about the strangeness of an English woman in a new housing development alongside the story about the strangeness of her neighbor, a man who is a refugee from genocidal violence in an African country, perhaps Rwanda. When the first narrator, Dorothy, observes, "it's difficult to tell who's from around here and who's not," she is referring not to waves of migrants from India, Nigeria, or Eastern Europe, as we might expect of a novel of this title, but to her own arrival on the edges of an older English village (3). The reader assumes that the novel's title will focus on distant nations, whereas initially it refers to (less) distant counties and villages. It is only later that we are introduced to Solomon, who has entered England illegally, and by this time we have come to understand that the proximate shore is not a static environment even for those who belong legally to the state.

Dorothy finds the locals difficult to identify because people keep arriving and because so many kinds of arrival seem to matter. But identification is also difficult because the meaning of "here" keeps changing, both geographically in terms of physical boundaries and symbolically in terms of the reputations assigned to those boundaries. There is some disagreement, Dorothy tells us, about the municipal status of the new housing development. Those who live in the development believe they are part of a separate community called "Stoneleigh," while those who live in the village insist that the newcomers are actually part of the established town of "Weston." Like any place, the housing development is in fact part of several geographies, as local road signs proclaim. One sign takes us from the regional to the geopolitical: we learn that the village is "twinned with some town in Germany and some village in the south of France" (4).

A Distant Shore begins by attributing complexity not to the boundaries of a strife-torn African nation but to the space of an English village. In this way England becomes more distant. But it also becomes less inert. We learn that the town in Germany was utterly destroyed by wartime bombing and that the village in France deported its Jews to extermination camps. The identity of the English town seems to depend on its status as a place where bombing and deportation did not take place. But the descriptions of the German and French towns hint at an incongruity that reflects on England. By selecting a victimized town to represent Germany and a victimizing village to represent France, Phillips asks us to consider the difference between what we assume about English hospitality—its comparative liberalism, for example—and what we will learn in the novel about the villagers' treatment of strangers. The novel seeks to question above all the cultural heritage that the villagers think they are preserving. It is in some ways disturbing that Phillips would compare Solomon's experience of racism with Dorothy's experience of loneliness and ostracism, but the comparison allows Phillips to suggest that the village's exclusion of strangers like Dorothy is motivated by nativist values that are similar to those that motivate attacks on strangers from other nations and other cultures. Routing England through Germany and France, the novel asks us to see that national symbolism functions comparatively. It has to be translated.

To be sure, Phillips is answering abstraction with more abstraction. Instead of replacing the overgeneralized "here" with physical descriptions of place or meticulous characterization, he introduces competing symbolic geographies. He responds to the rigidity of distribution not by withdrawing taxonomies but by adding them. The novel feels "global" in part because it seems more interested in the arrangement of its actors than in the deep histories of their separate lives. There seems to be no alternative to classification. Throughout the work, Phillips emphasizes the way people are described rather than the way people describe themselves. Dorothy hears of a doctor who was excluded by other villagers because she is Jewish, though the fact of her Jewishness is never mentioned directly (9). A pub owner finds it sufficient to mention that she was called "Dr. Epstein" and that her children were "Rachel and Jacob" (10).[25] There is something extravagantly unsubtle about these monikers. As the pub owner says, "They weren't even trying" (9). The same can be said of the novel. Phillips seems to be more interested in the invocation and arrangement of categories—the Jewish doctor, the "Irish nurse," the lesbian sister—than he is in replacing them (8, 17). Of the doctor and her children, we learn little more than their names.

Approaching Phillips's novels through the history of the anthology, we can see why his work might be more committed to an aesthetic of arrangement than to an aesthetic of expressivity.[26] He is not telling a story about expressivity at all. Instead of unmediated voices, his novels present us with stories that have been circulated, collected, and compared. It is participation, rather than voice, that generates belonging. This would explain why places seem to be the true subjects of Phillips's novels, as many of his works' titles and section headings suggest. At the end of A Distant Shore, Solomon dies at the hands of xenophobic teenagers, and Dorothy has a psychological collapse, but "England" has in fact become changeable, at least for Phillips's readers. In the final pages of *The Nature of Blood*, the Ethiopian-Jewish Malka and the German-Jewish Uncle Stephan seem stuck in their roles as new and old migrant, but "Israel" has greater texture than it did at the beginning. Phillips seems to believe in the political legitimacy of states—Germany, Britain, Israel, Venice—but the meaning of those states, their cultures and symbolic values, appear as effects rather than as sources of the novels. Narrating reception, Phillips creates a body of work whose locations are dynamic and purposefully distant.

Phillips's novel-anthologies eschew two aspects of the anthology tradition: its claim to express a distinctive literary culture based on race or national origin, and its tone of celebration, which has tended to affirm a group's heritage without acknowledging the violent history of such affirmations. This ambivalence about the celebration of heritage helps to explain Phillips's choice to put a black minstrel performer at the center of a story about the history of African American theater. Phillips's anthologies emphasize exclusion rather than sympathy. Phillips seems to value the collective for its capacity to nourish individuals and provide a refuge from violence, but the solidarities represented in his novels are fragile, provisional, and temporary. He offers no model of unmediated or unmodified participation.

Creating anthologies of limited belonging, Phillips tests the distinction between container and object. His books may seem like objects, but they are full of containers: comparative frameworks that impose new classifications and ask us to question what we know about the location of literature. Instead of suggesting that books by new arrivals simply expand literary histories based on the nation, Phillips suggests that these works can help us imagine new literary histories, ones whose scale includes the town, the region, and the housing development, and whose content includes not only the production of narratives but also their translation, circulation, and reception. Emphasizing arrangement rather than expression, Phillips suggests that the "global conversation" is not so new after all. His novels and anthologies associate the mediation of place not only with television and tourist junkets and digital media but also with the institutions of literary history. By incorporating anthologies into his novels, Phillips suggests that limited participation can create a new kind of full participation in which collectives are generated by past arrivals and by arrivals that have not yet taken place. In Phillips's novels, this means placing migration before citizenship so that participation appears limited from the start.

ENGLISH AS A FOREIGN LANGUAGE

Phillips produces remarkably similar books in many genres, whereas David Mitchell produces very dissimilar books in only one genre, the novel. The two writers are also part of relatively distinct literary generations. This is visible in Mitchell's themes, which address translation and global circulation in the most explicit ways, and in his publication history and reception. About a decade younger than Phillips, Mitchell published his first novel, *Ghostwritten*, in 1999. Four years later he was included alongside Zadie Smith, Sarah Waters, Peter Ho Davies, and Adam Thirlwell in *Granta*'s prestigious "Best of Young British Novelists," a list that has appeared every decade since 1983. Phillips appeared in the 1993 list alongside luminaries of the 1980s such as Hanif Kureishi, Kazuo Ishiguro, and Jeannette Winterson. Phillips is arguably the most well-known novelist of the black Atlantic. Mitchell is a novelist of the Pacific. A resident of Japan for many years, he was born in England and now lives in Ireland. Most of Mitchell's novels—there are six to date—feature the circulation of people and books among Asia, Europe, and the United States. To be sure, Mitchell is not the only British novelist who writes about East Asia. Kazuo Ishiguro's first two novels focused on U.S.-occupied Japan, and his fifth on the international settlement in Shanghai; the Japan-based British novelist David Peace is writing a trilogy of novels about Tokyo in the years immediately following the Second World War. There are also many U.S.-based novelists, from Maxine Hong Kingston and Amy Tan to Chang-Rae Lee and Monique Truong, who write about twentieth-century emigrations from the Pacific to the United States, and occasionally, as in Truong's case, from the Pacific to Europe. However, Mitchell's novels are unusual in their attention to longer histories of European-Asian contact, to transactions both within and across those regions, and to the multilingual and multigeneric sources of the British novel.

Unlike Phillips's *Distant Shore*, whose several territories appear only as the novel unfolds, Mitchell's *Ghostwritten* announces this structure right away. Keenly attuned to the uses of paratext—chapter titles, epigraphs, section breaks, illustrations, and other parts of the novel that appear to organize rather than constitute the work—Mitchell introduces the novel's planetary scale in the table of contents. Before reaching the narrative, readers learn of ten chapters divided among three continents and nine sovereign or semi-sovereign territories: "Okinawa," "Tokyo," "Hong Kong," "Holy Mountain," "Mongolia," "Petersburg," "London," "Clear Island," "Night Train," and "Underground." The quantity and range of places suggests a trip around the world. Yet the places are not parallel: some are cities, some are semi-autonomous islands, one is a nation, one is a religious monument somewhere in the Chinese mainland, and another, "Night Train," is a radio program broadcast from Manhattan. In fact, the "Night Train" chapter is not a broadcast or even a recording but a printed transcript. The novel seems to sample the world, but it is difficult to accumulate units of various sizes or units whose location cannot be specified. Media dislocate, or relocate: "Night Train" is no longer attached to Manhattan, nor was it exclusively produced there since satellite has both distributed and diverted its source.

Ghostwritten's final chapter, "Underground," also takes place in more than one location, and in a moving location. A narrator finds himself in a traveling subway car beneath the streets of Tokyo. Words printed on the walls of the car and on the possessions of other passengers recap details and phrases that have appeared in each of the preceding chapters. "Underground" seems to be both part and whole: a new sample as well as a sampling of all of the prior samples. *Ghostwritten*'s first nine chapters are roughly chronological and obliquely contiguous: characters from one episode appear at least tangentially in others. These glimpses help readers sew the episodes together. But since the events of the final chapter take place before the events of the first and other chapters, the book's recapitulation turns out to be the narrative's instantiation, and this discrepancy interferes with the sense of accumulation. As in many anthologies, counting seems retrospectively to have generated the novel's units: it creates the occasion for them. While it is understandable that readers might hold the "Underground" episode apart from the preceding chapters, treating it as a coda, it is important to the fiction that we should have to include it among the others.[27] Only by trying to enumerate the novel's parts do we notice its competing models of accumulation. There may be nine chapters, or ten, or perhaps only one, if the first nine are regarded as branches rather than roots of the last. The novel's circulation of images and words, instead of holding the world together, keeps the world from adding up.

Mitchell interferes with the accumulation of geographies not only by adding and subtracting chapters but also by including multiple languages within individual territories. In this way the individual parts, which make up the collective of the novel, themselves appear collective. There is nothing new about novels that incorporate foreign languages and even episodes of translation. Writers have developed various strategies for making multilingual conversations legible to monolingual readers, including serial translation, in which the narrator repeats the phrases in translation, and contextualization, in which another character's response allows readers to deduce what has been said. And of course multilingual conversations are sometimes legible only to some readers, and that is the point. These strategies work well when the novel is addressed to a regional audience, whose knowledge of one language and lack or partial knowledge of another can be assumed. But many contemporary novels are addressed to audiences whose languages cannot be known in advance. How do you represent the fact that characters are speaking different languages to readers who will encounter the novel in yet more languages?

Instead of citing foreign words directly, as if readers could hear them, Mitchell registers the presence of foreign words through various devices of pointing and narrating. In Mitchell's novels, no word is ontologically foreign since the stories seem to take place in several different languages.[28] *Ghostwritten* has no consistent source language, and there are often several mediating languages. A language can also play multiple roles: a source in one chapter is sometimes a target in another; sometimes a character's source will be the reader's target. For example, a reference to "a new Murakami translation of

Fitzgerald's short stories" in the "Tokyo" chapter tells us that the dialogue is taking place in Japanese (47). While characters refer to English as a source language, readers experience English as a target (for
the Japanese conversation we are reading). Similarly, in "Petersburg,"
we know that a narrator is speaking Russian because she recognizes
English words but cannot reproduce them. She reports that "Jerome
said something in English," but we learn nothing about what he said
(219). In the "Holy Mountain" chapter, set in China, a Japanese soldier's speech is described as "animal noises," whereas Cantonese
counts as "real words" (116). In these moments, the languages that
characters do not speak and cannot understand carry greater significance than the languages they do speak. Through references to books
that cannot be read or to comments that cannot be repeated or even
paraphrased, the novel passes its characters' incomprehension onto
its readers. Lack of comprehension rather than fluency registers the
multilingualism of the episode. In "Holy Mountain," the incomprehensibility of Japanese allows Mitchell to present Cantonese as the
lingua franca of his English-language text.

Yet translation is not confined simply to the text, and this is important too. In "Night Train," the words used by a Japanese-speaking
caller appear on the page in italicized English (406). The italic font
implies that the novel's English is the narrative's Japanese. In this
way the words appear *as if* they are foreign. Translation is a function
of the book rather than the text, though here the book seems to be
not only the novel we hold in our hands but also the transcript of the
radio broadcast contained in that novel. Japanese is the language of
the caller's words as they are broadcast; English is the language of
those words as they appear in the transcript. By italicizing, Mitchell
gets to have it both ways. The chapter is born translated twice: not
only has it been transmitted worldwide by satellite broadcast, it has
been adjusted in print for its target audience. By emphasizing this
process, Mitchell untranslates translation. He uses the typographical
resources of the book to show how translation operates in the text.

Mitchell's recourse to typography resembles J. M. Coetzee's visual
strategies in *Diary of a Bad Year*, and we can see similar techniques
in Mitchell's second novel, *Number9Dream* (2001), which takes place
entirely in Japan. Despite the title, *Ghostwritten* largely points at

speech, whereas *Number9Dream*, whose title is taken from a John Lennon song, more often points at writing. I take this development as a sign of the latter novel's interest in new media, especially the English-dominated Internet, and its effort to consider more substantially what texts look like when they circulate globally as books. Like *Ghostwritten*, *Number9Dream* makes English into a target language by representing it as a source. For example, one character explains to another, "*Imho* stand for the English: 'In my humble opinion.'"[29] The italic font and quotation marks let readers know that English is not the narrative's principal tongue.[30] Later in the novel we are shown an English inscription on a cigarette lighter, and it too appears in italics (219). Pointing at English provincializes the novel by reminding readers that the globe is multilingual and by reminding them of what it would be like to read English as a foreign language, or, for that matter, *as a language at all*. English becomes a material rather than simply a medium. It begins to have substance.

English becomes even more substantial when Mitchell shifts from representing dialogue to representing script. He asks us to notice the contrast between the appearance of words on the pages of the book and the appearance of words on pages or walls or screens described in the book. The novel refers to a message scrawled in "characters" on a hotel room mirror (118), but that message is spelled out in Roman letters. Readers are told that a contract mentioned later in the novel has been signed with brush and calligraphy paper (177). The main character's name, Eiji, is written "not in the commonplace manner" but with "highly unusual kanji," though those characters, and that distinction, is explained rather than shown (243). Mitchell could have silently translated both language and script. Instead, he creates the impression of a translated book and implies that we are reading a translation within a translation: an English-language version of a Japanese-medium novel featuring a character whose life is saturated by the English-language, especially U.S. and U.K. music, fiction, and digital culture.

Number9Dream has only one narrator, and the narrator does not travel beyond Japan. However, the work registers global circulation in several ways: thematically, by showing how Japanese culture appropriates English-language artifacts in the service of Japanese multilingualism; formally, by incorporating non-Japanese words or descriptions of words that are incomprehensible to its narrator; and structurally, by promising nine dreams but enumerating only eight. At the end of the novel, after the eighth chapter has concluded, there is simply a title page printed with the word "nine"; blank pages follow. The novel seems to imply that the life of the book, like the life of the narrator, is still being written. In some ways, this is a cliché of postmodern fiction. But Mitchell's work has a less abstract point to make: the uncountability of the chapters matches the uncountability of its audience.[31] Mitchell suggests that his novel's incompleteness is a function not only of "the reader" but also of "readers," those within the novel who consume translations of stories by F. Scott Fitzgerald in twenty-first-century Tokyo and those who are holding the novel in any one of the editions in which it appears. The most telling model for the book's projected future is the computer virus that Eiji and his hacker friend use to expose an organ-selling mob. The virus causes Eiji's exposé to travel to all the people in the address book of each addressee, up to ninety-nine generations. The end of the novel, like that of the virus, is unpredictable.

EMBEDDED VOICES

In his first two novels Mitchell projects an uncountable world by assigning foreignness to many languages, especially English, and by presenting global circulation as an engine rather than an afterthought of the work. He thus keeps geographical parts from fitting together and from adding up. Subsequent novels find other ways to represent global sources: pointing at the circulation of books; pointing at the mechanics of language; and pointing at literary, biological, social, and chronological models of translation. They also differ from the earlier works because they deploy characteristics we tend to associate with regional rather than with global fiction: vernacular dialogue and narration, local place names and terminology, and details of social custom and social process. Instead of being restricted, distant, or simply absent, voices are now artifacts: they are embedded in social environments and embodied by speakers as well as by media.

Instead of "bleaching out" the local, as global novels are often said to do, Mitchell's later novels generate color by narrating languages and by introducing new kinds of serial translation.[32]

Cloud Atlas (2004), which collates six narratives, is Mitchell's most well-known novel. Translated into many languages and adapted for the screen by the Wachowski siblings, the book's global circulation now matches the global circulation imagined and solicited diegetically by the text. The novel's opening pages introduce readers to selections from "Adam Ewing's Pacific Journal," Ewing's account of his sea journey from Sydney to California, undertaken around the 1850s. Later in the novel readers will learn that the journal has been published, edited, and transported to Europe, and thus global circulation appears as a method as well as a theme of the narrative. Adam Ewing's journal is succeeded by Robert Frobisher's letters from early-twentieth-century Belgium, which are in turn succeeded by a pulp thriller set in late-twentieth-century California, and so on. The "Cloud Atlas" of the title refers to a six-part musical composition, devised by Frobisher, whose interrupted melodies and nested parts echo in advance the structure of the novel as a whole. To accomplish this nesting, each of the novel's first five chapters ends abruptly in the middle of a story, sometimes in the middle of a sentence. The sixth chapter presents an entire narrative. The seventh through eleventh chapters feature the second halves of the five initial stories. The first part of the novel moves forward in time; the second part of the novel moves backward. Distributed across the world and across centuries, *Cloud Atlas* is held together not by circulating characters, as in *Ghostwritten*, but by circulating books. Each story is thus also an object: a journal, a packet of letters, the manuscript of a novel, a memoir, a recorded interview, and an oral narrative. In the first half, each narrator reads or views the prior truncated story. In the second half, each narrator reads or views the remainder of that story, which appears subsequently.

Initially, *Cloud Atlas* seems like a global novel because it features so many spaces: in addition to the Pacific Islands, readers visit Belgium, the United States, Scotland, and regions that appear to be South Korea and Hawai'i. It also features traveling characters. The chapters recount the experiences of people who have moved, by force or by choice, from one part of the world to another. From the perspective of the text in our hands, then, the novel is global twice over, and it seems to be diachronic. However, from the perspective of the texts in the characters' hands, the novel is very local indeed. And also synchronic: since each character is contained in a book or a video that is read or viewed or heard by subsequent characters, the entire work could be said to take place in Hawai'i, the setting of the future-most chapter. The Hawai'i chapter is addressed in the second person to an unidentified audience, "you." The novel thus seems to take place wherever it is being seen. In the chronology of the story, the final word is "Look."[33] But the narrative's final word is a rhetorical question: "Yet what is any ocean but a multitude of drops?" (509). Both endings put their faith in an uncountable collective and in the unpredictability of words, which can travel the proverbial ocean and can also, potentially, change it.

The conceit of mediated *editions* rather than sourced *manuscripts* allows Mitchell to suggest that we are reading documents that have been translated in all sorts of ways. The two narratives whose diction seems most foreign are also the ones set in the future. The chapters are doubly translated: first, by medium (digital projection and oral storytelling rendered in print) and, second, by time (some not-yet-existent language rendered in a version of a language we have now). In all of the chapters, global circulation both constrains and stimulates local action. Constrains, as when invading armies and corporations absorb indigenous cultures. Stimulates, as when those who experience slavery abroad learn to support abolition at home. Yet the novel does not choose between global and local, collective and individual. It is not originality or idiosyncrasy that wins the day. Instead of global conglomerates, Mitchell imagines multivoiced collectives, chapter by chapter: the ocean, the sextet, the countercorporate initiative, the collaborative escape, the underground political movement, and the serial audience. Like novels that begin translated, these units are comparative from the start.

Focused on provincial spaces, Mitchell's fourth and fifth novels place translation within realist genres such as the *Bildungsroman* and the historical novel. In these works, history creates a kind of foreign language: usage changes across time as well as across space.

Narrated by thirteen-year-old Jason Taylor, *Black Swan Green* (2006) begins in a small Midlands village, and both dialogue and narration are suffused with English idiolect, circa 1982. It is the age of Thatcher, the Falklands War, and the Australian duo "Men at Work." Engrossed in period slang, the novel seems unsuitable for readers beyond English. Its phrases are regional as well as ephemeral, featuring words such as "waz, "naff," "homo," and "grass off."[34] Vernacularisms such as "s'pose" (for suppose) and "'cause" (for because) are also common. An adolescent poet and future novelist, Jason is attentive to sound: cobwebs "snaptwanged" (72); his mind moves sideways from "French" as a language to "French kissing" (163); someone invites him to call home on the "jellybone" (232). In these moments, English becomes the topic as well as the medium of the novel, and Mitchell seems to be privileging both fluency and voice.

Yet the novel's syntax and plot tell a different story. Jason has a stammer. His verbal approximations and work-arounds dramatize the kinds of translation that operate within any language. Throughout the novel Jason generates synonyms in order to avoid words whose initial letters are likely to prove difficult. He attributes his stammer's strangulating effects to a principle he calls "Hangman": "The only way to outfox Hangman," he explains, "is to think one sentence ahead, and if you see a stammer-word coming up, alter your sentence so you won't need to use it" (27). Jason's sentences thus proceed by proleptic translation. Asked by his father why he would answer a ringing telephone in a room he was told never to enter, Jason replies, "'But I thought it might be an emergency so I picked it up and there was'—Hangman blocked 'someone'—'a person on the other end . . .'" (14). Elsewhere, he tells a neighbor that "'it's a—Hangman blocked 'nice'—'a—pleasant morning . . .'" (69). Trying to explain who he is to a confused stranger, he exclaims, "'No, you're mistaking me for someone else. My'—Hangman stopped me from saying 'name'—'I'm called Jason'" (95). By introducing the stammer word as well as the replacement, Mitchell creates subjunctive editions: glimpses of sentences that might have been, or might be, which consist of Jason's unused words and of words that he has not yet imagined.

Narrating Jason's efforts to control his stammer, the novel displays the social consequences of deploying—and failing to deploy—specific words. However, it is audiences rather than words that most absorb the novel's attention. Like speech, writing is circumscribed by social cues and social rules, and by the apprehension of readers. Jason stands out because he has to think about this process all the time. A *Kunstlerroman* as well as a *Bildungsroman*, the story tracks Jason's development both as artist and as young man: he learns what words can do, "Just words" (268), and, at the story's climax, a visual image of handwriting on lined paper appears as the embryonic version of a page in the novel we have previously read (261). In this way Mitchell generates an analogy between the book's translation and the narrative's: both the words on the page (Mitchell's) and the words in the story (Jason's) are unoriginal; they have been transformed through editing, printing, and distributing. Those words appear to be part of a source language, the original productions of writer or speaker, but they are in fact part of a target language, embedded in collaborations with readers and audiences. Put another way, Mitchell suggests that source languages *are* target languages insofar as speech implies listeners and novels imply books. Late in the story Jason arrives at this idea when he realizes that his stammering is caused by worry about "*the other person*" (289, emphasis in text). It is his sensitivity to other people—his keen understanding not of production but of circulation—that makes him a successful writer.

In order to stop stammering, Jason has to care less about his listeners, but it is by stammering that he comes to understand the social dynamics of language. That understanding allows him to develop as a poet, someone who realizes that words have to be used, and to become the person who could be the author of the novel we are reading. There are many echoes of Joyce's *Portrait of an Artist as a Young Man*, including an unhappy family, intimations of colonialism, and the narrator's social isolation, though at the end of the novel Jason triumphs against his opponents not by acquiring silence, as Stephen Dedalus does, but by learning how to speak. In fact, his speech appears most effective when it produces other people's silence, reversing the silence that had been produced in him: "That appalled silence was *my* handiwork. Words made it" (268). Instead of suggesting that some people communicate naturally while others do not, Mitchell argues for the ontological primacy of the speech impediment.[35] Everyone in the novel has to translate, which means not only selecting among synonyms but also matching selection to audience. In the story we see this every time a character points to someone else's worn-out slang ("Nigel, *nobody* says 'epic' anymore" [55]; "don't say 'Soz'" [64]) and every time Jason notices that his parents have been trying to adopt an upper-class idiom ("salt and pepper magically turned into 'the condiments'" [47]). Possessing social leverage involves capturing the wave of language. Jason admires those who know that words have currency and who know how to predict the end of that currency before others can. He is initially excluded from this dynamic because he is unable to voice his words at will, but he is knowledgeable about the structure because he gets used to planning his language and to moving nimbly among versions of language.

Translation is not limited to the speech of the characters. The novel appears as a translated edition in several respects. First, by introducing visual representations of handwriting and typescript within the printed lines of the chapters, Mitchell suggests that the novel has its source in notes, drafts, and prior editions, including fictional editions that are the product of the novel itself. Second, at one point Mitchell introduces a minor character from *Cloud Atlas*, suggesting that his novel constitutes an episode in a multinovel collective rather than a self-contained object. (All of Mitchell's novels feature objects or characters from prior novels, as his reviewers have noted.[36]) Third, Mitchell includes a scene of translation within the novel—Jason translates the first chapter of *Le grand meaulnes* from French into English—and thus asks us to consider that the conceit of enchanted adolescence has its origins in other languages and other times. Each of these strategies emphasizes paratext: those elements of the book that may or may not be elements of the novel and that put into question the boundaries and medium of the work. By drawing our attention to multilingual sources and possible futures, Mitchell also draws our attention to global constituents: not only the occasional Belgians and gypsies, who appear as characters, but also the Falklands War, which is mentioned directly throughout the text, and the Iraq War, which is implied. Disabling English, the novel provincializes Britain.

The Thousand Autumns of Jacob de Zoet (2010) also features a regional space, but this time it is late-eighteenth-century Dejima, a Dutch-controlled, Japanese-owned trading island off the coast of Nagasaki. The setting of the novel, an island whose sovereignty can be understood both as shared and as compromised, establishes one of the many impediments to location as we have known it. The story begins in 1799 and follows the adventures of the eponymous Jacob de Zoet, a young Dutch clerk who learns Japanese over the course of eighteen years and 479 paperback pages. The novel focuses on the economic, political, scientific, literary, and interpersonal exchanges between Dejima merchants, mostly Dutch and other Europeans, and the Japanese, who are the merchants' only source for trade, food, entertainment, and, initially, translation. *Thousand Autumns* presents translation as the condition of its narrative. The story begins with a Japanese midwife's interpretation of a Dutch obstetrics manual. It ends with the production of two books, one real and one imagined: a Japanese-Dutch dictionary, and a conjectured autobiography of Jacob's final decades in Holland. Born-translated works appear in the story and motivate the plot, but they are also models for the plot because they present adoption as a source of inheritance. Even the Dutch East India Company, Jacob's employer, appears to be born translated: many of the servants, sailors, and officers hail from nations and colonial spaces well beyond Holland; indeed, over the course of the novel, as imperial fortunes change, the Dutch company is also a French company.[37]

Thousand Autumns consists of at least three, perhaps four, foreign tongues. One of those foreign tongues is the invented language of "bygone-ese," a term that Mitchell uses to describe the "inaccurate but plausible" style of early nineteenth-century English that he places in the mouths of his characters (489). However, the bygone-ese of the novel's discourse is meant to represent the Japanese and Dutch speech of all but a few of the novel's characters. Throughout the narrative, readers are reminded frequently that characters are speaking in a foreign language, but foreignness changes over the course of the novel. In the sections devoted to an English naval officer, for example, Mitchell has to mention that a Dutch character is speaking English (331). By speaking in the language we are reading, the Dutchman is speaking a target language, and Mitchell goes out of his way to register this in the text. In *Ghostwritten*, there is no native tongue because the novel's setting changes. In *Thousand Autumns*, there is no native tongue because the characters inhabit a multilingual environment, and the novel is mimetic of that environment. Even at the very end of the novel, when Jacob is able to speak both Japanese and Dutch, there are still languages that are opaque to him, and thus to us. As Jacob prepares to leave Nagasaki Bay, a sailor shouts "in a Scandinavian language," and several other sailors reply with laughter, but neither the language nor the meaning of the shout appears on the page (476).

Most of the chapters follow characters whose first language is Japanese or Dutch. One chapter follows Javanese, and a small handful follow English. The novel signals source and target languages by reproducing dialogue that is understood by the chapter's principal character and by withdrawing or paraphrasing dialogue that she or he does not understand. Source languages are marked; target languages are treated as the language of the novel. In the first chapter, we have to be told that the Japanese midwife is using a "Dutch term," but Japanese conversation can be taken for granted (4). On the page, all of the words appear in English. When Jacob speaks Dutch in a chapter narrated from the perspective of a monolingual Japanese, the novel records only the Japanese translation (413); Jacob's words are absent. We learn that, "De Zoet directs his answer to Iwase in Dutch," and then Iwase's speech appears as if it were the novel's native tongue (413). In an English chapter, the ship's captain describes the Dutch language as "a gagged, mud-slurped thing," but the reader does not have direct access to those sounds. In one of the Dutch chapters, the word "*kanji*" is italicized because it is a Japanese term spoken in a Dutch setting (94). As a rule, *Thousand Autumns* is more interested in the dynamics of foreignness than in its specific instantiations. This is especially notable on the very few occasions when characters discuss pronunciation. In a chapter organized around Dutch, the Japanese midwife, Orito, confuses the words "lewdness" and "rudeness," but it does not seem to matter that the rhyme has no exact equivalent in the conversation's fictional idiom (49).

While the novel largely ignores the phonological history of languages, it is very much interested in their political and literary histories, and especially in their histories of translation. Before we open the book, the title, *The Thousand Autumns of Jacob de Zoet*, announces that translation will be a central concern. "The Land of a Thousand Autumns," as one character explains, is a translation of a Japanese aphorism about Japan. Understood one way, the title refers to Jacob's experience of a nation that has been both translated and self-mythologized. For English readers, the title promises further mediation, since Jacob's language is actually Dutch. The title also implies a life span, whose unusual extension—one thousand autumns—adds to the sense that the novel takes place in a world foreign to our own. Finally, the title evokes that translation-evolved original, *The Thousand and One Nights*, a book whose French edition appears, near *Candide*, on a bookshelf belonging to the Dutch company's resident surgeon and naturalist (145).[38] (The French edition of Mitchell's novel, *Les mille automnes de Jacob de Zoet* [2012], echoes the original title of the surgeon's book, *Les mille et une nuits*.[39]) While *Candide* begins as a fictional translation, attributed on its title page to the German "Dr. Ralph," *Thousand and One Nights* begins as an actual translation, the accumulation of stories from many languages. Placing this reference in his title, Mitchell places his novel within a long tradition of literature born in translation. Of course, his novel differs from many of its precedents because it incorporates that tradition within its narrative. More than this, *Thousand Autumns* emphasizes translation's role in the history and development of Dutch mercantilism, Japanese imperialism, Enlightenment science, and, indeed, the British novel.

The opening scene of *Thousand Autumns*, an episode that will be crucial to the development of the plot, introduces a Japanese midwife who saves the magistrate's newborn child by using techniques she has learned from a Dutch translation of a Scottish treatise, William Smellie's *Observations*, first published in London in 1754. For us, the scene takes place in English, but we are told throughout the episode that she is speaking both in Dutch and in Japanese, creating a code that includes the bilingual doctor but excludes the monolingual patient and her maid. At the other extreme, in the acknowledgments that constitute one of the novel's endings, Mitchell explains that his research was guided by various translations of travelogues about late-eighteenth-century life in Japan, including *Kaempfer's Japan*, an extraordinarily influential text composed in German but first published and widely circulated in English in 1727.[40] *Kaempfer's Japan*, which also appears in the novel, became available in German only through the mediation of a French edition. In several ways, then, translated works not only shape Mitchell's novel; they are its precedent.

The novel suggests that the circulation and translation of books about obstetrics, political economy, maritime adventures, and botany, among many other topics, nourished both cosmopolitan and imperialist impulses, often at the same time and through the same book. Translations have both negative and positive connotations in the novel, and translators appear from the beginning as ambassadors and guards, scholars and swindlers. The *Bildung* of the novel includes Jacob's realization that translations can be used for lying as well as truth-telling. There is no politics of translation, as such, only uses. We learn of Jacob's Dutch-language edition of *The Wealth of Nations*, which his friend, a Japanese interpreter, longs to translate as a contribution, he says, to the Japanese field of Dutch science. The Japanese interpreter is surprised to learn that Adam Smith wrote his book in English and even more surprised that Smith, despite his language, cannot be called an "Englishman" (28). The lesson here is complex, but we are meant to understand that what the translator values about Smith's book is not its models of self-interest and international trade but the occasion it provides both for learning Dutch and for creating transcultural conversations within Japan. Lending his book, Jacob cements his friendship with the translator. We see here that translations help to create new traditions ("Dutch science") as well as extend old ones (Scottish political economy). Mitchell also uses this occasion to show how many "English" books, including Smith's and Smellie's, began in spaces outside England.

The theme of translation is impossible to miss in *Thousand Autumns*. References to multiple languages, translated dialogue, professional translators, bilingual dictionaries, and translated books ensure this. Yet, as in his earlier novels, Mitchell suggests that the principle of translation changes the shape as well as the subject of the work. Multiplying source languages and emphasizing its own status as a version of other novels, *Thousand Autumns* incorporates translation into its sense of history. The most striking example is the novel's use of several calendars to introduce each of its sections and chapters. The five parts of the novel are labeled sometimes with Gregorian dates, sometimes with dates that correspond to Japanese dynasties, and sometimes with both. The novel begins in "1799" and in "the eleventh year of the Era of Kansei" (1). Gregorian and Lunar dates introduce the chapters. Those introduced by Lunar dates follow characters who speak Japanese; and those with Gregorian dates follow characters who speak Dutch or English. The dates announce the target language of the text that follows, but they also indicate which languages will be presented in translation. As usual, multilingualism is handled through narration and paratext: calendars change, but grammar and syntax remain consistent. By assigning the units of the novel to different calendars, Mitchell impedes accumulation as well as parity. There is no simultaneity. Characters do not act or speak at the same moment, since there is translation even in a single time zone.

Thousand Autumns appears born translated not only through its incorporation of translated books such as *The Wealth of Nations* and Smellie's *Observations*, and not only through its shifting roster of foreign tongues, spaces, and chronologies, but also through its invocation of one of Mitchell's earlier novels. As Jacob prepares to leave Dejima, he meets a young sailor named Boerhaave, who appears as a seasoned officer in the first and last chapters of *Cloud Atlas*. In the 2004 novel, Boerhaave is a sadistic bully who rapes a young recruit; in the later novel, he is a sympathetic midshipman with a bright future. In case there is any uncertainty that the characters are the same, Mitchell tells us that the name of the ship carrying the Dutch-speaking Jacob is the "Profetes" (475); the vessel carrying Adam Ewing goes by the same name, but in English (the "Prophetess," 4). The device of carrying characters and even phrases across novels is not in itself notable, but the arc of development is striking: Boerhaave grows up by becoming less hospitable. The knowledge of *Cloud Atlas* changes our impression of Jacob's equilibrium and creates a larger ambit for the novel we are reading.

To be sure, we do not need to know about Boerhaave's future to question Jacob's persistent faith in human sympathy. There are other signs: for example, the fact that Jacob's son, born to a Japanese woman, cannot return with him to Holland and is likely to be ostracized in Nagasaki. But the appearance of Boerhaave allows us to imagine *Thousand Autumns* as a prequel to the earlier novels, as a version or outgrowth of those novels, or as their alternative trajectory. In this moment, Mitchell finds yet another way to add the history of the book to the novel's historical fiction. We have to imagine the text as one of many books, not only as an edition of *Thousand Autumns* but also as an edition or adaptation of other books, past and future. This gesture is recognizable: it seems to plunge the novel into an abyss of origins. However, it also has a realist edge since Mitchell associates the desire for original books and natural languages with biological literalism: the belief that physical bodies are containers for nationality, family, and other social traits. In the story, biological literalism justifies the Europeans' slave system and the Japanese segregation of disfigured women. But it can also be found in Jacob's youthful assumption that empirical calculation guarantees ethical action. "The restoration of the [company] ledgers," he believes, will lead to justice since he puts his faith in the denotative quality of numbers (36). Over the course of the novel Jacob comes to realize that he will need art to counter art, but moreover that a ledger may "hide a lie or an error, even when the totals appear to balance" (117). Jacob learns to read and manipulate codes, which involves not only translation among natural languages but also translation across the registers of one language. Multilingualism, Mitchell suggests, alerts readers and speakers to the limits of native usage.

Jacob has to learn both what words are and what words do. Speaking in the Japanese he has learned over the course of the novel, he tells Nagasaki's magistrate, "The truth of a myth, your Honor, is not its words but its patterns" (512). This remark could function as the motto of any novel that presents translation as a source of innovation, but it also fits the novel's emphasis on adoption. *Thousand Autumns* values history when it asks readers to learn about the translated sources of national literatures. But it is through myth and other collaborative fictions that it generates new models of collectivity. Mitchell suggests that philosophies of individualism, expressed as the belief in unique beginnings and separate futures, support regimes of slavery, violence, and exploitation that persist into the present. We see this in the Japanese emphasis on national identities, and in the European deployment of racial classification as an alibi for brutality and theft. Privileging patterns over words, the novel privileges social relations over intrinsic affinities. We are told of "scholars glimpsing truth in fragile patterns" (451). The patterns, Mitchell suggests, not only organize knowledge, they generate it.

All of the principal characters in the novel are orphans: Jacob has been raised by his uncle; Marinus is taken in by a distant aunt; the translator Owaga relinquishes his biological family to become the legal heir of a prominent translator; and the midwife Orito loses both of her parents and is sold into slavery by her stepmother. One might argue that these characters are attuned to translation and open to transcultural contact because they have no natural family. But the novel asks us to notice that every character is adopted, from the concubine's baby depicted in the opening scene of childbirth to the second "eldest son" to whom Jacob imagines giving his family bible at the end of the novel (479). Jacob himself is adopted a second time, when the English captain Penhalgion withdraws his canons after noticing a resemblance between Jacob's red hair and the red hair of his beloved son, who died at sea. Mitchell uses adoption to distinguish between good and bad translators. The bad translators believe in hospitality, which grants access to foreigners but retains the distinction between friend and foe. The good translators do not distinguish between natural and artificial systems of belonging. They imagine nations without natives.

Thousand Autumns begins with the belief in "literal truth" (14), a phrase used by Jacob's uncle to describe how the family Bible prevented a musket ball from tearing into Jacob's grandfather's flesh. The Bible's powers are "literal," the uncle explains, because its intercession was both physical (the book got in the way of the bullet) and spiritual (the text summoned an act of God). At the end of the novel, Jacob reads the same Bible while waiting for Penhalgion's canons to fire. By this point, we know that texts, including Bibles, are never literal. As Marinus points out, Jacob's psalter is a "rattle-bag of uneven translations from the Aramaic" (439). But the book is another matter. Books can stop bullets, the novel suggests, not only because they protect someone's flesh from oncoming injury but also because, as objects whose meanings depend on circulation as well as production, they invite affiliation across nations and across languages. Mitchell's novel concludes by invoking its book-ness and addressing its readers. The title of the last section, "The Last Pages" (473), associates Jacob's future, imagined by Jacob on the deck of the departing ship, with the book's future. The "last pages" are conjectured rather than confirmed. The time of reading will never overlap with the time of imagining. In this way, among many others, Mitchell suggests that circulation is a source of future production.

THE CITIZENSHIP OF BOOKS

Recent work on the transnational origins of national literatures has asked us to think of an artwork's "citizenship" in several new ways. In addition to considering an author's legal affiliations as determined by birthplace, residency, and immigration status, Jahan Ramazani suggests that we need to consider an author's imagined affiliations as determined by factors as various as ethnicity, travel, political solidarity, and intellectual sympathy. These two kinds of belonging will sometimes overlap, but they can also lead to conflicting assignments so that, for example, a poet such as T. S. Eliot might be properly described as American in the first instance and British or European in the second. Or, still speaking of Eliot, the author's political affiliations may vary, depending whether one measures at the beginning or at the end of a life. However, even this more expansive account of origins depends on the author's place, whereas Ramazani also asks us to reflect on the place or "citizenship" of the text. "The citizenship of a poem," he argues, "should not always be presupposed . . . in advance."[41] Ramazani means by this that the poem's themes, forms, and figures may belong to traditions, or may help to forge traditions, that are both smaller and larger than states. A writer may have a national passport, Ramazani suggests, but a "transnational poetics." Readers, he suggest, need to avoid reducing the second kind of citizenship (the poem's) to the fraught and constraining rules of the first (those established by governments). In a similar vein, Wai Chee Dimock argues that readers need to engage with literary materials "as not yet classified."[42]

The turn from authors to texts may seem familiar, though what Ramazani actually has in mind is an expansion rather than an explosion of classification.[43] He calls for organizing citizenship by language rather than by nation. The "poem" in his account is understood to be the poem in its original language, and specifically the poem in English. Ramazani and Dimock are principally concerned with the circulation of traditions within texts, and with the reception of individual readers, who later become writers. Caryl Phillips and David Mitchell, while they also suggest that works of literature can belong to more than a single nation and can give voice to "aggregates" at various scales, add reception and institutions of reception to the story of literary citizenship.[44] They ask us to consider how the citizenship of books has shaped the citizenship of texts, and they show how the circulation and reception of texts, by establishing legitimate categories, help to produce the citizenship of authors. In Phillips's case, this means thinking about the production and circulation of literary anthologies, which confer belonging as well as affirm it, and about the geopolitics of national symbolism. In Mitchell's case, this means thinking about the uptake of literary works through translation and adoption, in spaces throughout the world, and about the multilingual origins of British fiction.

Questions about the citizenship of artworks have tended to focus on scale. Ramazani and Dimock argue that the nation may not be the most sensible or most flexible container for understanding literary history. But there is also an implicit question about how the location of an artwork is measured. Is place external to the artwork? Is it produced by the artwork? Is it a function of the artwork's audience? What is the relationship among these three "places"? And to what extent can books be said to have or make "citizenship"? Amy Waldman's *Submission*, a counterfactual novel about efforts to choose an appropriate memorial to the World Trade Center attacks, addresses these concerns at the level of genre and plot as well as theme. By shifting the conversation from *citizenship* to *character*, Waldman's novel invokes the rich and longstanding association between artworks and people, character as imprint or signature and character as dramatic actor. But Waldman also uses the problem of art's character to reframe the problem of art's citizenship since her story con-

cerns above all a debate about what kind of memorial will best represent the experiences of the collective. Which aesthetic traditions
are appropriate to that collective? And where do aesthetic qualities
come from?

The Submission initially presents itself as a classic example of city-
shaped fiction. Chapters alternate among a repertoire of New York
City types: the undocumented Bangladeshi immigrant, the wealthy
WASP widow, the secular Jewish philanthropist, the Irish firefighter's
brother, the Muslim architect, and so forth. We seem to be in the
presence of a multicultural novel, in the older sense. This is implied
not only by the apparent distribution of roles but also by the theme
of social conflict and by an explicit reference, in the very first chapter, to an exemplary precedent, the 1987 blockbuster *The Bonfire of
the Vanities*.[45] Yet the reference is ironic. The philanthropist doubts
his "literary" credentials because he hasn't read a novel since *Bonfire*, published more than a decade earlier (6). Waldman casts doubt
on his doubt, suggesting that it is not only the quantity but also the
complexity of his reading list that may be lacking. Waldman is taking
a swipe both at *Bonfire* and at its overimpressed readers. She seems to
have another lineage in mind. This is suggested by a less explicit allusion, in the same chapter, to the "dark horse" of Joyce's *Ulysses* (15).

The Submission starts off with allusions to prior novels, but it
approaches the question of locating art not through a story about
literary works or literary institutions but through a story about international architecture. The plot is organized around a jury's selection of the memorial design. It is important to the plot that the
competing plans have been entered anonymously. The first chapter
concludes with the revelation that the author of the winning submission, called the "Garden," is named Mohammad Khan. Most of
the subsequent chapters take place in New York City and focus on a
heated debate about whether Khan is a "Muslim architect," whether
it matters that a memorial to bombings perpetrated by Muslims is
created by a Muslim, and whether an artwork produced by a Muslim
architect is therefore expressive of Islamic history, values, or theology. Does the character of the architect, the novel asks, inform the
meaning or character of the artwork? Do artworks have character in
the same way that people do? Is Khan's "submission" (the design)

also a "submission" (an Islamic gesture—"Islam" means "submission")? And what of Waldman's *Submission*? The questions of character that Waldman attaches to Khan's creation fan out to encompass other artworks within the text as well as the novel itself. We should note, for example, that Waldman's narrative is full of memorials but that it too is a memorial: it was published less than a month before the tenth anniversary of the World Trade Center attacks. While the novel's title surely refers to Khan's submission, it can also refer to Waldman's, and the overlap calls for comparison. What do these artworks have in common? What is the appropriate context for understanding each memorial?

As I suggested at the start of this chapter, multicultural fictions typically imply a kind of rigid exemplarity in which social categories are doled out among the principal actors and in which those categories govern to a large degree what those actors think and do. Culture seems to determine character. Waldman approaches this paradigm by asking what happens when the problem of character migrates from persons to literary and visual art. Some members of the memorial jury wonder whether Khan's use of arches and canals that feature in Islamic architecture means that his design is also Islamic. They imagine that the terrorism they associate with Islamic fundamentalism might permeate Khan's work. Can an arch or a canal support terrorism? Claire Burwell, the wealthy WASP widow who initially champions Khan's work, worries that his memorial might be "quoting" (this is initially his term) details from architectural gardens in Afghanistan (267). Because those gardens celebrate an Islamic paradise, perhaps a "martyrs paradise" (268), she asks, is his "Garden" also a paradise? Khan responds by drawing two intersecting lines and then holding his paper at two different angles. Claire sees a cross; then she sees an X. Khan adds more lines, and Claire sees a window, a checkerboard, or a grid, perhaps Manhattan. "It's all of those things, or maybe none of them. It's lines on a plane, just like the Garden," Khan explains. "Lines on a plane. Geometry doesn't belong to a single culture" (269).

In this exchange, histories of circulation and reception add a new dimension to the question of character. If an arch was used to convey Islamic paradise in sixteenth-century Afghanistan, does this feature carry the same meaning when it reappears in mid-twentieth-century New York (as it did in the original World Trade Center buildings) or in twenty-first-century Mumbai (featured at the end of the novel)? What happens to an artwork's meaning when it is adopted into new artworks and in new places and when it is read, viewed, or experienced by new audiences? By asking these questions, Waldman's novel interferes with character as usual in three ways. First, it questions the relevance of character by asking us to imagine right away that the work of art we are reading extends beyond the object in our hands and beyond the identity of its author. Waldman does this by framing her novel ambiguously, beginning with an epigraph attributed to "an unidentified Pashto poet" (n.p.) and ending with an author's note that directs us to the book's "sources of information and inspiration" (n.p.). Like the speaker in the epigraph, the novel is "not bound by its attachments." Its origins seem to be various and to some extent "unidentified."

Yet what is the epigraph telling us? That origins do not matter? What about the origins of the epigraph itself? When one sees on the copyright page that the untitled fragment of uncertain "Pashto" origin comes from a specific book by a named author of precise origin—"*The Afghans*, by Mohammed Ali, Kabul, 1969" (n.p.)—it becomes clear that the abstraction, withholding, display, and proliferation of origins is crucial to the novel's project. Waldman is interested in the difference between categories and individuals, between the "Pashto poet" and the individual writer publishing in Afghanistan. The architect Khan argues that sources are not at all relevant. But Waldman's novel does not dismiss sources so quickly. Instead it suggests that sources enlarge the meanings of art; instead of defining the work, once and for all, sources can help us see how an artwork's meanings are established, and how those meanings might change in the future.

Waldman interferes with character in a second way by aligning her fiction not only with the novel of multiculturalism but also with several of its precursors, including that modernist novel of colonial anti-Semitism, *Ulysses*. When Paul Rubin first sees the name of the winning architect, he says to himself, "A dark horse indeed," echoing the phrase used to describe the uncircumcised Irish-Jewish Leopold Bloom in Joyce's work (15). By having the Jewish chairman apply this

epithet to the secular Muslim American architect Mo Khan, Waldman asks readers to compare anti-Semitic and anti-Islamic preju-
dice. She asks us to notice, as Joyce did, that being victimized does
not preclude victimizing others. She also asks us to consider that racism tends to assign definitive identities. How Jewish is Bloom? How
Muslim is Khan? Most interesting, Waldman's use of a well-known
literary allusion gestures to the idea—so central to *Ulysses*—that the
circulation of objects, including words, through citation and appropriation generates meanings far in excess of the original source. In
this way, too, *The Submission* suggests that we cannot judge the character of the artwork by the implied character of the artist.

Finally, Waldman takes on character by suggesting that narrative,
because it develops over time and integrates different moments of
remembering, interrupts the potentially stagnant quality of position-
taking and position-keeping. Monuments fix, narratives unfold; this
novel turns monuments into narratives. The most effective memorial for the terrorist attack, we learn in the novel's final chapter, is a
documentary film. Twenty years after the architectural competition,
Claire Burwell's son William and his girlfriend Molly are producing
a film about the events that occupied the first 280 pages of the novel.
Their documentary breaks from the traditional mold. Instead of editing and collating separate interviews, they create what we might call
a "living" documentary, in which subjects watch and respond to each
other's interviews. An effective memorial, Waldman suggests, solicits
audience participation. Yet it is part of the brilliance of Waldman's
novel that the documentary, which seems to trump the site-specific
sculpture as a medium of memorialization, actually echoes Khan's
design. William and Molly fly to Mumbai to interview Khan, who left
the United States after withdrawing from the New York competition
and has made his fortune building towers and gardens all over the
world. He has built a version of his Garden, which the filmmakers
include in their video. As William tours the grounds, we see that the
Garden is a kind of narrative, both because its materials grow and
because it is meant to be used as well as to be observed.

Because the novel's final chapter takes place almost exclusively in
Mumbai, it asks us to consider that the city-shaped text has been
world-shaped all along. Moreover, it suggests that the circulation

of artworks and parts of artworks throughout the world means that the conceptual life of the text is inseparable from the historical life of the book. Understanding art as fundamentally target rather than source, Waldman suggests that architectural designs, like words, are drawn from multiple places and enter into multiple audiences and environments; they can thus participate, at any one time, in several traditions. *The Submission* registers its own status as a collective object through allusions to prior works of literature and through discussion of artworks in other media. It appears global, not only by activating several literary and cultural traditions of memorialization, and not only by nesting New York within Mumbai, and later Mumbai within New York, but also by reaching out, in the final instance, to the agency of readers and users. The last image of the novel is Claire's screening of William's documentary footage, in which he shows himself visiting Khan's Garden. William's reception of the Garden, we see, constitutes a new production. He has added to the artwork by placing in one corner what his mother calls a "cairn," the Celtic term for stones used to mark and remember (83, 299). A small pile of stones placed in remembrance invokes many traditions, including the Jewish custom of placing small stones at a grave. It also recalls William's memorial to his father, who had taught him about the cairn when he was a child. The stones' significance is visible to William and to his mother but perhaps to no one else. The cairn appears as the novel's final reminder of reception's effects on the citizenship of art.

By asking readers to question whether a Muslim artist produces a Muslim artwork, Waldman invites us to ask whether a Jewish novelist produces a Jewish novel. *The Submission* responds to both of these questions by insisting that the work of art is not reducible to the artist's geographic location and biographical history, in part because those locations and histories draw on traditions from many cultures and in part because artworks live in the future as well as the past. For all its irony about the multicultural novel, *The Submission* does not leave it entirely behind, and yet Waldman updates the genre by emphasizing points of contact rather than points of view. Instead of distinguishing among categories, she shows how they overlap, share histories, and develop into something new. *The Sub-*

mission believes in character, but it is the kind that art makes, not the kind that makes art.

World-shaped novels incorporate global audiences in order to emphasize the role of readers and translators in the production of literary works. By reflecting on the circulation of books and other media, these works identify translation as a source of literary and political collectivities. They also imagine themselves as part of future collectivities in several languages and traditions. Whereas this chapter has focused on how readers make and remake books, the next chapter will turn to how books make readers. Does a born-translated novel have a native reader, or, for that matter, a foreign one?

4

THIS IS NOT YOUR LANGUAGE

These are all words, all of them, these words are my own.

—Jamaica Kincaid, *Mr. Potter*

RELATIVE FLUENCY

No one is born a native reader. This is true in part because no one is born reading. But it is also true because access to a national language is neither guaranteed nor foreclosed by birth. There are many people who read one language and speak another, or who find that they function better in a language they learned at school or in the workplace than in the language they learned at home. Some people read several languages well, and some do not read at all. This is a point that language educators and theorists of translation have been making for some time, but the idea that readers have intrinsic access to one and only one language is remarkably persistent.[1] In an interview about her career, poet and essayist Meena Alexander has suggested that the concept of multilingualism, which typically refers to the expansive use of several languages, will need to incorporate variations in proficiency, occasion, and medium.[2] In addition, she presents incomprehension as rule rather than exception. We tend to assume that civic participation and linguistic fluency go hand in hand. One is born into a language the way one is born into a community. This is the idea at the heart of the concept of "native" speaker or reader. But, as we see in Alexander's work and in the projects of many other multilingual writers, there is nothing automatic about fluency. It is not natural to place. It requires context as well as education.[3] These two claims, that there are no native languages and that fluency is relative, have been crucial to a new understanding of audiences, both in recent novels that make characters out of readers and in the new emphasis on readers within translation studies.

Fluency is relative in Alexander's case because her languages vary with the conversation, the medium, and the social space in which she is operating, and because she is not necessarily proficient in the languages she is using. Moreover, she is at home with relative fluency:

> I have always grown up in a world where there were things one did not understand, because there were languages that were not completely accessible; you use one language in the marketplace, another in the kitchen, another in the bedroom or the study. And then your friends are those who often speak some of those languages as well and it just gives you a particular sense of being in a world where you can be comfortable even though linguistically the world is not really knowable.[4]

Instead of equating comfort with comprehension, Alexander describes being "comfortable" within a linguistic milieu that is "not completely accessible." She is not exiled from language because she expects to find foreignness where she lives. In addition, while she uses several languages, she does not privilege speech as the most authentic or most important medium of expression. She has a first language, Malayalam, which she learned as a child, but she neither reads nor writes in that tongue. Alexander writes poetry and essays in English. It seems wrong—that is, imprecise—to call English her native language. Yet it seems also unfair, somehow demeaning or withholding, to say that it isn't.

Alexander claims that she "inhabits" languages.[5] She does not claim to own them. Instead of a native writer, then, perhaps we should call her a *resident writer*. Or, if we follow the logic of naturalization, we might call her *a citizen writer*. By emphasizing context and agency, the idea that one might employ different languages and versions of language for different purposes, Alexander's comments open up literary history in two ways: they suggest that writers should not be limited to their first language or to the language spoken by their parents; and they suggest that readers, too, should not be classified by birthplace or by the language they acquired at home. The argument works both ways: access is not blocked by foreignness, but neither is it ensured by nativity. In Alexander's case, expertise complements environment, since she grew up in a place where the occasional use of several languages was the norm.

Alexander is telling a story about multilingual speaking, though as she turns from "marketplace" to "study," she encompasses multilingual reading and writing too. And she is telling a story that does not only belong to her. The shift from the first-person to the second-person voice, from "I have always grown up" to "your friends are those," implies both her experience (*you* as a version of *I*) and the experience of others, the "you" who are reading her interview. She is arguing, beyond her own case, that many English-language writers begin their lives as foreign readers. They do not expect to master languages, and indeed they associate the expectation of mastery with linguistic provincialism, in which an emphasis on fluency obscures the many nonfluent uses of language that function within the most intimate spaces. Alexander is a foreign reader on purpose because she feels at home with partial comprehension and because she believes that partial comprehension should constitute home. This is both a descriptive and a prescriptive point. Because universal fluency is neither a precondition nor an ideal of citizenship, foreignness is a necessary principle of democratic sociability.[6] Literary works may solicit foreign readers not because they bypass national collectives but because they understand translation as a characteristic of those collectives.

The translation scholar Naoki Sakai has long argued against the assumption that literary works in the original address a unified audience. Instead, he has insisted, readers are always a "nonaggregate community."[7] In essays published over the past few years, he has cautioned against postulating "the innateness of cognitive capacity in terms of spatial belonging," by which he means that there is no necessary relationship between a person's ability to speak or read a language and her geographic location.[8] Whereas scholars of translation have typically distinguished between "two kinds of audiences . . . one for whom the text is comprehensible, at least to some degree, and the other for whom it is incomprehensible," Sakai explains, "'not comprehending' takes place everywhere."[9] By placing noncomprehension within a single geography or audience, Sakai argues that translation operates inside, and not only between, languages. This premise leads him to eschew the concept of "native competency," which he associates with "prescription": not how people do speak but how they should speak, or how they are required to speak, in order to be recognized as members of a group.[10]

Other scholars have argued in similar terms that the concept of the "mother tongue," often used synonymously with "native language," misconstrues the relationship between birthplace and fluency, and between fluency and social belonging. It is striking that many of the most forceful advocates for this position are specialists in languages other than English. Language educators and often translators point out that so-called natives may speak different languages (from each other) and may associate those languages with isolation as well as solidarity. Some have argued that there is nothing special about a first language, and that indeed some people may feel alienated from that tongue while others may feel more comfortable operating in several languages.[11] They also observe that an emphasis on birthplace can serve to denigrate migrant communities and the idiomatic variations those speakers and writers introduce into their acquired languages.[12] Moreover, associating languages with birthplace can imply that languages come before people, that they are "fixed" objects best mastered by those who already possess them.[13] Scholars who distinguish between native and nonnative access to languages often do so as a way of insisting on the agency of colonial and postcolonial subjects, and as a way of protecting minor languages from encroachment or erasure by dominant languages.[14] But second-language educators and scholars of migrant writing, working from the perspective of dominant languages, have argued that the demand for native fluency constrains new users, leading to prohibition in some cases and to obligation in others. In place of "native" speakers or readers, who acquire languages unconsciously or intrinsically, they emphasize students or "experts," who acquire language through education of various kinds.[15] The distinction between native and nonnative languages impinges on writers as well as readers. It implies that writers have only one language and that they have a duty to use it.[16]

In this chapter, I ask, first, what it means to read intrinsically or natively, and, second, how and why contemporary novels might choose to impede this practice, especially for English-language readers. The *locus classicus* for these questions is surely James Joyce's *Portrait of the Artist as a Young Man*, in which the Irish Stephen Dedalus realizes, at the end of the novel, that he knows "English" better than the English, who nevertheless subject him to the violent pedagogy of colonialism.[17] Joyce draws attention to the assumption that language is natural to place or ethnic origin; he associates that assumption with the mechanics of political servitude; and he refutes it by outperforming and remaking the English-language novel. Out of someone else's language, Joyce creates his own voice. The novels I consider, by Jamaica Kincaid and Mohsin Hamid, approach the concept of native languages not through voice but through the circulation of voice. They dramatize the geopolitics of reading, and the practical conditions of being—or not being—an audience. They write about audiences, those who might read their works, and also about non-audiences, those for whom their works are not accessible. Fictionally, their stories invoke audiences in the most direct way: they use the second-person voice—the address to "you"—to generate an ambiguous intimacy between the novel and its interlocutors. The novels' intimacy is ambiguous for two reasons. First, "you" seems to reside both inside and outside the text: as a fictional character, and as someone holding that fiction in her hands. Second, the nature of the intimacy remains unspecified: the narrator speaks to a person whose gender and nationality are unmarked.[18] The reader encounters "you," instead of the third-person "Juan," "Jean," or "John," or even "him" or "her."[19] Kincaid's and Hamid's novels create a surfeit of possible relationships—professional, sexual, geopolitical—between readers and texts. This makes the novels seem translated, written for someone else, from the start.

There are many literary works that generate the sense of absent readers or listeners. We might think in this context of lyric poetry, in which the use of apostrophe ("O Wild West Wind") has the effect both of invocation (pointing at the existence of an absent listener) as well as animation (attributing agency to that listener).[20] But there is also what Irene Kacandes has called *narrative apostrophe*, which, like lyric apostrophe, summons the listener as a "partner" in conversation.[21] This is what happens in second-person fiction. Famous examples include Italo Calvino's *If on a Winter's Night a Traveler*, Albert Camus's *The Fall*, and Jay McInerney's *Bright Lights, Big City*. More recent examples are Lorrie Moore's *Self Help*, parts of Naruddin Farah's *Maps*, and stories by Lydia Davis ("Break It Down") and Chimamanda Ngozi Adichie ("The Thing Around Your Neck").[22] Whereas second-person narration is rare in literary fiction, it's more common in popular genres such as children's stories, travel guides, self-improvement manuals, and fantasy books such as the Choose Your Own Adventure line, which Hamid has singled out as an influence on his work.[23] In some cases, the narrative's address to "you" turns out to be the narrator's address to himself, or herself, as in McInerney's *Bright Lights* and Adichie's "The Thing." But in Calvino's and Moore's works, which adopt the imperative voice of the tourist and self-improvement guides, respectively, the narrator is speaking to a distinct character: "you," the reader.[24]

Whether an address to an external character or an ambiguous interior monologue, the second-person narrative can produce the impression of speech—someone talking—because it constitutes a fictional encounter between "I" and "you" and because that encounter seems to be taking place, *now*, in the course of the fiction itself. Second-person writing creates a tension between story and event, between the representation of a happening and the production of that happening. The happening of the artwork becomes its own story, trumping the message, and thus the narrative implies that, to paraphrase John Stuart Mill on poetry, the reader is "overhearing" rather than "hearing."[25] We are not the first audience but the audience of an audience. In this way, second-person works reflect on "the situation of communication itself."[26]

It would be tempting to see second-person narrative—rare as it is within the entire breadth of modern literature, including the literature of the past few decades—as an extreme outlier within the postcolonial tradition. But in fact it makes better sense to understand second-person fiction as the quintessence of that tradition as it has entered the twenty-first century. Postcolonial fiction presupposes the "situation of communication" because it has always needed to compare and translate among regions, languages, and literatures. In fact, it is not only "inherently comparative," as Robert Young has recently argued; it is inherently translated.[27] Using the second-person voice, Kincaid and Hamid bring that history into view. Their work fits with a more pervasive staging of the anglophone novel that is taking place across the field of contemporary postcolonial fiction.[28] Examples include the use of a blog addressed to U.S. readers in Chimamanda Ngozi Adichie's *Americanah* (2013); narrative presented as letters "in English" in Aravind Adiga's *White Tiger* (2008); and the conceit of translated audiotapes, from Hindi to English, in Indra Sinha's *Animal's People* (2007). Distributing second-person narration throughout their works, Kincaid and Hamid build the problem of audience into the structure of the work and use narrative structure to test some of the most tenacious assumptions of U.S. and European literary studies: namely, the distinction between native and foreign audiences, and between native and foreign languages.[29] In their fiction, the process of globalization has permeated event as well as story. The second-person narrative evokes the dramatic quality of oral tradition, which has been so important to expressive cultures in the Caribbean and South Asia, while also registering the institutional pathways of today's global conversations. Moreover, the second-person voice creates a framework for thinking about the history and politics of print.

Classified as U.S. writers by the Library of Congress, Kincaid and Hamid began their lives in Antigua and Pakistan, respectively. Kincaid has lived in the United States for many years, but almost all of her writing focuses on characters living in the Caribbean. Hamid, who attended university in the United States and published his first novel while living in New York City, now lives in Lahore. He holds both U.K. and Pakistani passports. Translated across multiple spaces and languages, Kincaid and Hamid narrate the conditions of world literature, in which there are readers and nonreaders, and in which some readers—those who operate in dominant spaces—expect to be fluent all of the time. Their novels stand out because they generate world literature from the perspective of literacy, understood both as the mechanical knowledge that turns letters into stories and as the rhetorical knowledge that makes it possible to understand those stories comparatively. Caroline Levine has recently noted that world literature as a paradigm excludes "'the great unwritten,' the vast quantity of cultural material that has circulated for centuries in oral form."[30] For Levine, the problem is not that oral materials are never available in writing—and thus are unread altogether—but that "their lives as oral texts" are forgotten. Levine points out that a concept of world literature that includes oral expression and performance would include more of the world (226). To this end, she calls for "negative representativeness," which would involve "self-conscious attention to the limits of the 'world' expressed by a strict definition of 'world literature'" (227). She asks that world literature scholars "recognize the global importance and diffusion of orature [oral literature]" and that they "defamiliarize literacy" (232). Above all, she argues, "what is most politically worrying for [the study of] world literature is not literacy itself but the tendency to take literacy for granted" (234).

Kincaid and Hamid draw attention to literacy, to oral traditions that emphasize the relationship between narrator and audience, and to intermedial as well as interlingual acts of translation. Their novels retract fluency through an emphasis on the negative, the subjunctive, and the virtual—what we don't know, or what we might—as well as an emphasis on the geopolitical arrangements that shape what we know, and what we think about. They ask readers to imagine themselves as residents rather than natives, even in their own tongues. In previous chapters I argue that novels address themselves to the world by creating the impression of a work that begins in a foreign language or in more than one language; by distributing narrative action across several continents, regions, or nations; and by showing how the global circulation of narratives, even within a single novel, produces new locations for literature. In this chapter, I turn to novels that address readers competent in multiple languages, and the related distinction between native and foreign audiences. It is not enough to read a language, they suggest; you have to know "who is responsible for what."[31] Knowing who is responsible for what involves an analysis of agency but also of genre, political economy, and social relations. The problem with intrinsic reading, these novels suggest, is threefold: first, it presumes universal literacy, blurring together speaking, reading, and writing; second, it obscures the social and economic conditions that make literacy possible; and third, it allows us to forget that even monolingual literacy requires knowledge both of additional languages and additional geographies. This last point is crucial. To know the nation, in these texts, one has to know something of the world.

Kincaid and Hamid are novelists of two different literary generations—Kincaid's first book was published in 1983, Hamid's in 2000—but they share an interest in the second-person voice and in the relationship between local characters and foreign audiences. Their novels also share another feature: they make the American reader into an object of global attention. They spotlight American readers not to replace them with other, more appropriate readers, such as Pakistanis or Antiguans, but to suggest that there is something American about native reading. This is because Americans, who rarely read translations, expect to be at home with their books. But in books of relative fluency, everyone has to read in translation at least some of the time.

READING IN TRANSLATION

Serious readers are anxious about reading in translation, which seems to lack rigor of several sorts. It lacks scholarly rigor because we are blocked from analyzing the metaphors and idioms that have seemed crucial to any substantial investigation of literature. It lacks educational rigor because we have failed to learn the languages that would allow more direct access. And it lacks ethical rigor because the failure to learn a sufficient number of languages bespeaks a failure of interest in and engagement with the imaginative life of strangers. Of course, it is not only the reader of the translated object but also the object itself that is implicated. For after all, what kind of literary work could be read—read in any way that would count—in some language other than its own?

Yet, since works of literature now circulate into new languages faster and more extensively than ever, reading in translation happens all the time. Some of my best friends read in translation. I bet some of your best friends do too. And maybe that's okay, as David Damrosch, Lawrence Venuti, and many others have recently suggested, if reading in translation introduces us to works beyond our own literary tradition and beyond the literary traditions of languages we can read fluently. Reading in translation can lead us to learn the languages of works we've come to love, and it can create literary, cultural, and, sometimes, political solidarities that extend beyond the borders of fluency. To help us read in translation better, Damrosch and Venuti have penned instructional essays designed to make our experience with translated works more appreciative and more complex.[32] While Venuti calls for translations that keep their distance, what he has termed "foreignizing" translations, Damrosch encourages readers to nourish distance in a variety of ways.[33] This involves eschewing the practice of intrinsic reading, at least for readers of translations; proposing new reading methods for nonnative audiences; and making readers aware of translation's role within literary history (asking them to think about the distance that is already part of what passes for proximity). There's nothing new about reading in translation. But these approaches are striking because they suggest that the characteristics of translations may not be restricted to translations themselves: native readers might in fact be hard to distinguish from foreign readers.

Echoing the title of Mortimer Adler's classic *How to Read a Book*, from 1940, Venuti's "How to Read a Translation," from 2007, updates and rejects the New Critical emphasis on the author's singular genius by asking us to understand the translation "as a work in its own right" (n.p.).[34] Venuti proposes that readers of translations need "a more practical sense of what a translator does," though Venuti has for many years been trying to change what translators do, and what readers expect from them. Continuing the argument he set out in his groundbreaking work *The Translator's Invisibility*, Venuti calls for strategies of translation that decrease the invisibility of the translator and increase the value of the translator's labor. The critique of invisibility extends from the translator to the process of translation itself. Venuti wants readers to confront the "foreignness" of the original work and to value translations that register, rather than conceal, that foreignness. Translators should resist the temptation to create new works that seem to have been written in their target languages. For Venuti, making the original's foreignness visible is an ethical as well as an intellectual achievement.[35] Advocating the production of translations that read like translations, Venuti associates the success of translated works with the failure of fluency. He asks translators to cultivate failure by withholding fluency on purpose, and thus he rejects the longstanding and in many ways intuitive premise that translations are supposed to pass for original works.[36]

Venuti's call for more visible translations has helped to raise important questions about what translations should achieve, but it has also served to affirm what we know about originals. In this sense, "How to Read a Translation" could serve as an epilogue to *How to Read a Book*. Both take for granted that the reader of an original work is supposed to have access to its language, and that all books have a single language in which they begin. The distinction Venuti offers between the "native" and the "foreign" reader, for example, relies on New Critical standards of comprehension while also invoking confidently the boundaries between insiders and outsiders, between one's own literary tradition and the literary traditions that belong to others.[37] Most significantly, Venuti distributes literary works into single-language editions: that is, original works that appear in one language and translated works that appear in subsequent monolingual versions.

However sensitive to the creative and sometimes political work of translators, then, Venuti's practice of reading in translation seems to reinforce another kind of invisibility, what we might call the invisibility of the original. We think about writing all the time, of course, but whenever we talk about translation we seem to know and to agree what a translator translates from. In a book chapter on "reading in translation," from 2009, David Damrosch begins to undo this consensus by drawing our attention to the ways that translation has functioned within as well as between literary histories. Damrosch offers a helpful corrective to Venuti's rhetoric of foreignness by replacing the distinction between native and nonnative languages with the distinction between first and subsequent "homes" (66). His emphasis on "homes" avoids the association between expressivity and birthright, the idea that books—and, for that matter, people—have a natural language that corresponds to the place in which they begin.[38] Damrosch suggests that translated books, like migrants, can make their homes many times, though not without effort, and some more easily than others. Also like migrants, translated books insert rival temporalities into established histories. Translations remind us that books can begin more than once, and that literary traditions are regularly interrupted, transformed, and initiated by the circulation of works into and out of many languages and many versions of languages.

Damrosch's most important contribution to the idea of reading in translation is his call for thinking about reading the translations of works that, diegetically speaking, are already translated. His examples include José Ortega y Gasset's well-known essay "The Misery and the Splendor of Translation," which was written in Spanish but presents itself as a conversation taking place in French; and Voltaire's *Candide*, whose title page assigns authorship to one "Dr. Ralph," originally writing in German. In both of these cases, the conceit of translation implies that the works' social transgressions can be attributed to someone else's culture. Damrosch also points to texts that have evolved through translation. In these, translation has to be understood as part of the work's ongoing production rather than part of its story or reception. His example is *The Thousand and One Nights*, for which translation from Arabic into French and then back into Arabic involved the addition of new tales as well as the revision of old ones. In *Thousand and One Nights*, foreign languages are there in the original.

Yet it may be that Damrosch has underestimated the consequences of his own intervention. After all, not only actual translations but also diegetic ones such as *Candide* depend on the relationship among national languages. We can therefore understand *Candide* as a novel that is both literally and fictionally multilingual. It is fictionally multilingual because it is a French novel pretending to be a German novel. But it is literally multilingual because the French text's references to German activate a longstanding rivalry between the two languages, and between the two nations. To be at home with the novel, one needs to be fluent in French as well as French ideas about German. And of course, French is a changing language. As Damrosch points out, twenty-first-century readers, no matter what languages they know, are likely to find Voltaire's eighteenth-century terminology difficult to follow.[39] In this way, history creates another kind of foreign tongue. Reading originals that have evolved through translation such as *One Thousand and One Nights* and fictional translations such as *Candide* turns out to require the very skills that Damrosch and Venuti assign to reading translations proper: knowledge about national rivalries and geopolitical conflicts; an understanding of other languages and the social relations among several languages; the ability to compare among editions of texts; and a sense of historical development both within and across language. To be an accomplished reader of these originals, one needs to incorporate the methodology of reading in translation.

Because original works may register not only the conceit but also the process of translation, terms in the past assigned exclusively to unsuccessful translations are now sometimes assigned to originals. *Translatese* and its sisters, *translatorese* and *translationese*, are catchalls for unidiomatic writing that seems either like some other language (from which the work was translated) or like no language in particular (to which the work might be translated in the future). While translatese often refers to the language of a translation that cannot pass for an original, it can also apply to translations that have no aspiration to pass. Translatese is therefore not simply a failed language. Venuti does not embrace the term explicitly; in fact, he suggests that one wouldn't want to "incur a judgment of translationese," but he argues that translatese can be an intended, even ideal effect when it is deployed as an aesthetic strategy, either by translators or by authors.[40] Writers may use specialized, archaic, or idiosyncratic diction to demonstrate competing standards of fluency. Translations should remain comprehensible, Venuti insists, while challenging the norms of comprehensibility. To be sure, this is a paradox, or at least a tightrope. How can a work be comprehensible and challenge comprehension at the same time? But it makes some sense if we imagine that translatese, because it operates at the edges of fluency, is ephemeral. Like other languages, translatese changes over time as new words and new syntactic variations become normalized while other variations fall out of favor. Comprehensible incomprehensibility always risks becoming, simply, comprehensibility, but for Venuti this would be the best—that is, most foreignizing—outcome. Yesterday's translatese can become today's standard idiolect.

But in fact we don't need to wait. Books in translatese can theoretically precede and in some ways anticipate the process of translation. This is because translatese has a secondary meaning. It can refer to the language of works that seem designed for translation, that seem to resemble actual translations, or that seem to have incorporated the process of translation within them.[41] Sometimes translatese designates "bad writing," as in the bad writing that appears in some translations but which may appear in any kind of work. Often it refers not to lack of clarity or grammatical infelicity but to a style that seems insufficiently local.[42] For some observers, translatese constitutes both an aesthetic and an ethical problem. Writing critically of what he calls "the new global novel," Tim Parks dismisses any literary work that does not "revel," as he puts it, in "the subtle nuances of its own language."[43]

Unlike Parks, Venuti rejects the assumption that nonfluent or nonidiomatic writing has to be bad; therefore, he suggests that translatese could have a more neutral meaning, and sometimes a positive one. Books in translatese may be literary works whose deviation from standard usage promotes the impression of translation even when the literal process of translation hasn't taken place. As we move from causes to effects, it is worth noting that this emerging use of translatese, to encompass the language both of translated works and of works made to be translated, interferes with the distinction between native and foreign readers. This interference can be read politically in several ways. For books that begin in smaller languages, measured by number of speakers and writers, translatese can create a path toward dominant languages and toward readers of those languages. In this sense, translatese can seem to demote the agency of writers and readers in smaller languages. However, for books that begin in dominant languages such as English, translatese can be a way of emphasizing debts to prior translations, reducing the significance of dominant languages, and inviting future translations. Translatese can register the geopolitics of reading by drawing attention to divergent audiences.

If translatese includes books that pretend to be translated, books that were produced through translation, and books that sound or look translated even in their original language, how do we know when we are reading a translation? For starters, we can no longer expect to learn from a book's diction whether it began in one language or in another. David Bellos has argued that readers fail in this assessment all the time, so that nontranslated books are sometimes celebrated as excellent translations.[44] There may be no correspondence between the language of a book and a book's "home," whether home is understood as the location of a book's production or as the location of its author's birth. For example, novelist Elif Shafak, who lives both in London and in Istanbul, writes some works in English and some in Turkish. Her novels establish "home" in several different ways. To say that there is no correspondence between language and home, then, does not mean that books no longer have homes, only that homes are not reducible to languages. Additionally, because languages are not conduits or indices for homes, we can no longer expect that reading should offer access to "foreignness." If we follow Alexander's example, the experience of partial understanding should be understood as a domestic phenomenon: part of what we expect in our own community. Recall that, for Damrosch, home is another word for natural language (the novel's "first home"), whereas, for Alexander, home involves the use of several languages. This raises another question. If translation is internal to national literatures, because national literatures are multilingual and because they operate across multiple geographies, is it ever appropriate to read in the original? Put another way, what would reading in translation look like if we did it all the time?

Reading originals the way we read translations would mean treating every text as if its location were not simultaneous with our own. We would want to keep in mind the presence of several languages and nonstandard uses of language. But we would also pay attention to the appearance of variant editions, historical changes to the meanings of language and the relationship among languages, paratextual features of the work, and the kinds of collaboration that have contributed to the work's ongoing production and circulation. We would consider how the work has been influenced by translation and mediation, and how the work calculates its audiences. In a word, we would have to read subjunctively, as if other audiences exist, or will exist in the future. Of course, if we have to treat all originals as potential translations, where does that leave translations? Do we treat them as potential originals, too?

According to many translators, the answer is yes. Instead of separating out translations from originals, as Venuti suggests, we should instead understand originals differently. Edith Grossman, the distinguished English-language translator of Miguel de Cervantes and Gabriel García Márquez, asks readers to include among the category of original works the translations of original works, which now have two rather than only one author.[45] Nancy Huston, who translates her own novels and essays from French to English, writes that her translations have actually improved the first version of the work.[46] And Alastair Reid, a poet, essayist, and English-language translator of Jorge Luis Borges and Pablo Neruda, writes in a bilingual poem about translation that "*lo que se pierde* what gets lost / is not what gets lost in translation but more / what gets lost in language itself *lo que se pierde*."[47] In her gloss on this poem, Grossman suggests that, for Reid, writing is in fact a species of translation. Huston and Reid come to their accounts of translation as writers who have lived in multiple places. Huston was born in Calgary but has lived in Paris for many years. Reid was born in Scotland and has lived in several regions, including the United States, Latin America, and Spain. Both are also, like Alexander, residents of several languages, and perhaps for this reason they associate the process of translation with the process of revision. They treat variant editions in several languages the same way they treat variant editions in one language: both are part of the ongoing production of the work. But here's what's surprising: instead of arguing for a new appreciation of circulation and reception, or for greater attention to the target language of a text, these translators argue for a more robust account of production, both the production of the first author and the later production of editors and translators, who bring the work into subsequent languages and editions.

Thinking about the labor of translation when we read any literary work would allow us to pay closer attention to the work's address to audiences and readers. It would also allow us to value translations as extensions of the work, in which multilingualism—"foreignness"—functions both diegetically and semantically. The books I discuss in the remainder of this chapter, principally Kincaid's *Mr. Potter* (2002) and Hamid's *The Reluctant Fundamentalist* (2007), fit the expanded meaning of translatese, though they generate this effect not through diction or syntax but through negative, reluctant, and virtual strategies of characterization. They seem global or world-oriented because, while they focus our attention on one nation, they also insist that nations operate at several scales and include global as well as local agents. Translation implies an understanding about understanding: what it means to know a language, and what it means not to know it.[48] Kincaid and Hamid enrich the meanings of translation by suggesting that their works, even in their first language, require both more expertise and less fluency. They ask how circulation has shaped production, and they emphasize the condition of relative fluency within as well as across national spaces. While Kincaid highlights intermedial translation (from speech to print), institutions of literacy, and distinctions among English-language audiences, Hamid incorporates in addition multilingualism and linguistic translation. These are American novels that are foreign above all to American readers. They aim to exclude Americans from the experience of reading in the original by narrating scenes of translation that are present from the start.

NEGATIVE CHARACTER

Kincaid's novels enter the world by chronicling the personal and systemic obstructions to their ability to enter the world. This leads her to tell stories about literacy. This is one of the chief ways that her works contribute to thinking about world literature. They calculate the relationship between local and global geographies, and they consider the place of the world within the nation. They also consider the geopolitical, social, economic, and educational arrangements that shape which stories are told and who is able to tell them. Incorporating relative fluency within her texts, making her texts mimetic of that relativity, Kincaid generates an excessive literalness that I have associated with translatese. She points at words, but she also reminds us that many of her characters could not have produced those words, either in speech or in writing, and could not have read them. Her *Mr. Potter*, from 2002, measures the distance between the characters' language and the narrator's language, though the novel rarely compares idioms or allows us to compare them.[49] Instead Kincaid narrates the gaps. There is the frequent refrain, "Mr. Potter could not read" (10), "he could not read or write" (20), "because Mr. Potter could neither read nor write, he could not understand himself" (21), and so on. These interjections are literal because they remind us that words are describing Mr. Potter's lack of access to words. They demonstrate the narrator's literacy and point negatively to the subject's illiteracy. Because the narrator often addresses the reader directly and in the present tense, the story of Mr. Potter appears to be happening in a medium in which he could not participate. Relative fluency thus appears as context, topic, and event of the novel. The book we hold in our hands owes its existence to the narrator's learning: while her father and grandfather "could not read or write," the narrator reports, "I can read and I am also writing all of this at this very moment; at this very moment I am thinking of Nathaniel Potter and I can place my thoughts about him and all that he was and all that he could have been into words. These are all words, all of them, these words are my own" (48). We are reading a novel whose production and circulation testify to the history of literacy. Circulation is built into the narrative. It is generated by the difference between book and story, between the narrator who writes and the character who doesn't.

In their address to readers, their emphasis on comparative beginnings, and their themes, Kincaid's works have remained remarkably consistent. Her memoirs, essays, and novels are largely autobiographical. Most focus on Antigua or on nearby islands in the Caribbean. They deploy first- or second-person narration. They often adopt an accusatory or sarcastic tone. They suggest that the interpersonal is structured by the geopolitical. The narrator of her 1996 novel, *The Autobiography of My Mother*, remarks of an English woman she knows, that "she was pleased to be of the English people, and that made sense, because it is among the first tools you need to transgress against another human being—to be very pleased with who you are."[50] Kincaid points at writing, describing it and talking about it, and she emphasizes the locations of writer, readers, and characters.[51] Her memoir *My Brother*, from 1997, communicates the territorial, social, and medical distance between the narrator's comfortable home in Vermont and the squalid existence of her brother, who is dying of AIDS in Antigua.[52]

Mr. Potter, which also focuses on the relative location of writer and character, takes this project a step further by placing a story about the geopolitics of reading at the center of a story about emotional and economic impoverishment. Kincaid has touched on the geopolitics of reading once before, briefly, in "Wingless," one of her earliest published stories, from 1979.[53] Lyrical rather than declarative, "Wingless" prefigures Kincaid's more elaborate critique of the imperialist "you" (associated in the story with colonial-era children's literature) and shows her initial efforts to create a disaggregate "you" of postcolonial fiction. More than two decades later, *Mr. Potter* treats this concern more extensively and emphasizes the drama of writing. In this biographical fiction, there are no native readers because the eponymous character doesn't read, because reading is not something that anyone does from birth (as Kincaid points out), and because the novel takes place both in the United States, home of its narrator and implied reader, and in Antigua, home of its advertised subject. By emphasizing the *reader* in the concept of the *native reader*, Kincaid compares those who are likely to consume her books with those whose lives are presented within them. She also emphasizes the presenting: the way that the narrator's intellectual resources, idiolect, and geography give shape to her ostensible topic, "Mr. Potter." A robust account of the novel's production, Kincaid suggests, has to make news of the fact that the narrator was able to write it.

Mr. Potter is always the narrator's version of Mr. Potter. Yet this is not simply a lesson about consciousness and point of view. The novel asks us to notice, first, that there are resources such as education and literacy that make consciousness possible and, second, that colonialism and its legacies limit access to those resources. By pitting her own access against her father's, the narrator informs her readers that the language of the novel is located somewhere else—not in Antigua, and not in the mind of Mr. Potter. So, for example, even the term "Mr. Potter" is alien to Mr. Potter: "the name by which I know him is the way he will forever be known, for I am the one who can write the narrative that is his life" (87). "Mr. Potter" is not simply a social name like "Mrs. Dalloway." It is a literary name that distinguishes the writing of the novel from the vernacular of the character. The narrator's language—the language of writing—inhabits the novel's title. We would normally call this an example of free indirect discourse since Kincaid has incorporated without attribution the voice of a character into the narrative voice. But the work's title implies both consciousness (what the narrator calls her father) and medium (what the father's name looks like in printed words). The language of Kincaid's novel is thus, in a persistent way, the language of books. Under the best of circumstances, that language has to be acquired. Under challenging circumstances, such as poverty and limited educational resources, acquisition requires a singular effort. There is nothing intrinsic about it.

However, literacy in the novel is not simply a matter of reading and writing pages but also of acquiring the political and social frameworks that facilitate self-reflection, comparison with other lives, and large-scale interpretation. Kincaid's novels ask readers to recognize that self-reflection can be limited by character as well as by circumstance. This information arrives negatively. In addition to learning that "Mr. Potter could not read" (10), we hear about what Mr. Potter did not do, think, say, or feel. When Mr. Potter encounters Dr. Weizenger, a Jewish refugee from Nazi-occupied Europe, he does not consider the doctor's history or recent experience: "Mr. Potter *was not unfamiliar* with upheavals and displacements and murder and terror; his very existence in the world had been made possible by such things, *but he did not dwell on them and he could not dwell on them* any more than he could dwell on breathing" (7, emphasis added). Mr. Potter does not "dwell" because he is absorbed in his existence, but we are asked to dwell, both on "upheavals and displacements" and on the failures of our own sympathy. We are also told that Dr. Weizenger's suitcases are labeled with "the words 'Singapore' and 'Shanghai' and 'Sydney,' *but Mr. Potter could not read and so did not know what they meant*" (10–11, emphasis added). Without literacy, Mr. Potter is unable to recognize the words on the suitcase, but he is also unable to extrapolate from those words or think about how those words add up to a story about genocide. Dr. Weizenger, for his part, is unable to "read" the history of Mr. Potter, not because he lacks access to books but because he does not understand and does not think about British colonialism (11).

"Reading" in these passages is partly a function of mechanics and partly a function of scale. Both characters are absorbed in their immediate circumstances, and it is the project of the novel to introduce larger contexts, European anti-Semitism and the history of slavery, and to make that introduction visible. The novel announces this project in its final pages, when the narrator explains that, because she can read and write, Mr. Potter's "smallness becomes large, his anonymity is stripped away, his silence broken" (189). However, she insists that the novel's words remain hers: "Mr. Potter himself says nothing, nothing at all." This is an important distinction: Kincaid may be speaking for Mr. Potter, writing on his behalf, writing as if he knew what she knows, but his voice is not present. Even on the very few occasions when the novel incorporates direct speech, we have to understand that Mr. Potter's words depend on the narrator's mediation.

The narrator translates Mr. Potter not only by adding words but also by adding history and political economy. As elsewhere, these additions are really negations, and in this way the novel relates a story and impedes the storytelling at the same time. The reader is asked to know more, but knowledge is also associated with presumption.[54] Knowing is persistently negated, limited, and bracketed by the text. The process of impediment has the effect of relating what is, in effect, a second story: not only to do we learn about the life of Mr. Potter, we also learn how difficult it is to learn about that life. We are told, in a paragraph about Mrs. Weizenger's well-made English shoes, that "shoes did not come easily to Mr. Potter" (30). This fact appears as an interjection, almost a non sequitur:

> And May looked down at her feet, she wore shoes that were made of a very good leather from the skin of cow who had been born and raised and then killed with care in the English countryside and how nice the cow's skin now looked after it had been made into something pleasing (a pair of shoes), and into something that offered protection (a pair of shoes), and into something to cause envy (a pair of shoes); a pair of shoes did not come easily to Mr. Potter. And looking down at her feet. . . . (30)

Kincaid is narrating the total process that generates one pair of shoes. She is also pointing at the near-invisibility of that process. In a gesture that has become familiar to readers schooled in commodification, Kincaid asks us to notice the raw materials, the labor, the multiple geographies, and the economy of pleasure and suffering. We learn that the shoes May is wearing in Antigua, most likely purchased in a metropolitan shop far from the Caribbean, were made in a third location, the English countryside. We also learn that "leather" is really "skin," which has been removed from a cow killed for the purpose of creating an enviable shoe. But the novel is also suggesting, within a Naturalist lesson about the human exploitation of animals, that "shoes" mean something different to May than they do to Mr. Potter. "Care," the passage implies ("killed with care"), has been misdirected: whereas some people need clothing (Mr. Potter) and some animals need sympathy (cows raised for leather), it is the shoes that receive the greatest concern. "How nice the cow's skin now looked," the narrator remarks, blending May's consciousness ("how nice") with her own ("the cow's skin"). Later, in another moment of enlargement, we are told that Mr. Potter's trousers were purchased in Antigua and "made of cotton that had been grown in fields not far from the village where he lived" but manufactured in England (46). Talking about trousers, the novel emphasizes the economic arrangements that transform home-grown cotton into an expensive foreign import. Mr. Potter's trousers, like the shoes that he does not own, testify silently and negatively to the economic systems that govern the balance of care. His body, the narrator explains, "was mixed up with the world and *he could not extricate himself from it, not at all could he separate himself from the world*" (46–47, emphasis added).

So far we have seen three kinds of translation. First, there is the intermedial translation that brings vernacular into print, which allows Kincaid to tell a story about the uneven distribution of literacy, both at a local and at a global scale. Second, there is the geopolitical translation between cause and effect, which allows Kincaid to show how a story about Antigua is animated, in part, by events that take place in distant nations, regions, and cities. This is the kind of translation that Robert Young associates with all postcolonial literature.[55] Yet the movement from a general exposure of the global marketplace within postcolonial fiction to the specific exposure of the novel as an object in that marketplace is a more recent turn even within the postcolonial tradition.[56] Third, there is the translation among individual histories, which allows Kincaid to solicit comparisons that the characters themselves are unable or unwilling to consider. Because the narrator knows where economic disparity comes from, to take one example, readers can be introduced to social and political contexts that are outside the novel's plot, the story of Mr. Potter. However, these contexts also point to the secondary plot: the difference between the narrator's education and Mr. Potter's. It is only because the narrator's education is more expansive than Mr. Potter's, the novel insists, that we can consider social frameworks larger than Mr. Potter's immediate world. By pointing at that difference, Kincaid supplements territorial scale (a novel about Antigua) with the scale of action and consequence (the consumption of U.S. and European commodities; the history of slavery; the Holocaust; civil wars in the Middle East). In this way the novel places U.S. and European readers within its geographic scope while also blocking any direct or proprietary access to the narrative, which can no longer be understood as the story of a single individual or place. In a novel about divergent audiences, every reader is foreign.

Indeed, one could argue that all of Kincaid's novels are about her readers, the implied Americans and Europeans whose comfort she seeks to diminish. To be sure, the novels are also about British colonialism, postcolonial Antigua, and U.S. neo-imperialism. But they are about her readers' knowledge of those histories, and about the locations in which readers expect to consider them. She wants American readers to imagine that they understand less: they lack linguistic competency, but they lack geopolitical competency, too. *Mr. Potter* generates the reader's virtual or possible knowledge—animates that knowledge *as virtual*—by emphasizing negative character (the qualities Mr. Potter does not have; the topics he does not think about; the skills he does not possess) and by highlighting the subjunctive experiences of other characters: events that might have taken place, objects that are "like" other objects, and feelings that characters do not have but that we are asked to consider "as if" they did. The narrator tells of Dr. Weizenger's surprise when he thinks about his near-extinction in Europe, "as if such a thing had never happened before, as if groups of people, one day intact and building civilization and dominating heaven and earth, had not the next found themselves erased" (23). The virtual quality of this statement is redoubled by the use of the negative ("had never"; "had not") and the subjunctive grammar ("as if"). It is not Dr. Weizenger who compares his near-extinction to the extinction or near-extinction of others, such as Africans captured for slavery; indeed, the narrator indicts him for not making this comparison. But the reader is asked to compare, and to imagine what Dr. Weizenger could have known, had he been willing or able to know it.

Another subjunctive event is the given name Mr. Potter did not in fact receive. While at first he was called "Rodney," after the "English maritime criminal George Brydges Rodney," finally he was named "Roderick," after no one in particular (64). We learn about a name as well as an interpretation ("the victims of [Rodney's] actions had come to revere him"), neither of which actually applies to Mr. Potter. A final example: the narrator describes the imagination as "the land of the almost," whose elements include "the as if, the like, the in the vicinity of" (107). In the imagination, one cannot hear, the narrator insists. One can only "almost" hear. This idea of almost-hearing, like the idea of almost-reading, is important to the conclusion of the novel, where the second-person address, more or less implicit until this point, becomes explicit. The narrator calls on her readers to "Hear," "See," and "Touch Mr. Potter." But does the novel really want us to imagine that we can have that kind of sensory knowledge? We are reminded, even at this moment, that the novel's language, history, and geopolitical contexts are the products of the narrator's writing, whose agency is emphasized in a final, self-authorizing gesture: "Mr. Potter was my father's name, my father's name was Mr. Potter" (195). Several times, we are told that the narrator was born "with a line drawn through" her (143, and *passim*). On her birth certificate, a line appears in the space that asks for her father's name. The novel tells that story and rectifies it—there is now a name; there is no longer simply a line—though it also reverses the structure of authorization. The daughter now contains the father: "my father's name was Mr. Potter." The narrator does not erase the line; she narrates it.[57] Paradoxically, it is by animating the reader, by asking us to hear, see, and touch, by invoking—that is, the fiction of orality—that Kincaid registers the persistence of writing: Mr. Potter, after all, is made of lines.

The subjunctive is the space of imagination, but in Kincaid's work it is not the space of sympathy, because negativity gets in the way. Kincaid has long insisted that her goal is to make her readers more uncomfortable.[58] Not only negative knowledge, then, her books also cultivate negative affect. She addresses global audiences in order to register the genuine social conflicts that block collective understanding rather than to encourage or expand understanding. She seeks to display all the ways in which characters and readers overestimate their own knowledge and good faith, as when Dr. Weizenger thinks he's the only person whose community ever faced near-extinction. Kincaid uses conjectured action to rehearse new explanations, introduce possible futures, and mark the space where sympathy might have been. Instead of sympathy, Kincaid courts justice: a cool though sometimes biting reckoning of causes and consequences.

Mr. Potter's emphasis on the enlargement of small experiences, on divergent audiences, and on cool reckoning coincides, in 2002, with a surge in commentary about "niceness" and "fairness" that appeared in the wake of the World Trade Center attacks in 2001. Writing in *The New Yorker* in December 2002, Malcolm Gladwell argues that "the practice of niceness . . . has helped to keep other values, such as fairness, at bay."[59] This is so, he explains, because niceness often involves replacing dissent with consensus, whereas "fairness sometimes requires that surfaces be disturbed, that patterns of cordiality be broken, and that people, rudely and abruptly, be removed from their place." For this reason, Gladwell contends, "niceness is the opposite of fairness." In the name of fairness, Judith Butler writes the same year, Americans need to learn how to "narrate" U.S. internationalism in the third-person as well as the first, and how to receive "accounts delivered in the second."[60] Calling for dissent instead of consensus, global views of the United States in addition to U.S. views of the globe, Gladwell and Butler echo Kincaid's principal claims: that U.S. readers need to know more about how other places see themselves; that they need to become less confident about their own knowledge; and that they need to imagine better the various ways that people, commodities, and languages circulate—and do not circulate—throughout the world.

Kincaid's commitment to reading in translation precedes the era of *Mr. Potter*. Most infamously, in *A Small Place* (1988), she berates readers for trying to escape the ordinariness of their own lives while declining to notice the ordinary impoverishment, both banal and constant, of Antiguans' lives.[61] Kincaid analyzes and condemns politeness, which she sees as a cover for racism, and also tries to replace politeness with an impolite explicitness, in which U.S. readers are forced to confront both the harsh judgment of the Antiguans ("They do not like you" [17]) and the savage history of global exploitation (European expansion, colonialism, and slavery) that has made their Caribbean vacations possible. Part of Kincaid's incivility is her implication that present-day tourists are comparable to the slave-traders and exploiters of the past, who are addressed, collectively, as "you" in the text (37). *Mr. Potter* adds a new dimension to the project of aggravating readers by treating them, first of all, *as readers*. This means insisting that any global approach to a novel about Antigua will have to acknowledge the conditions of its own production, circulation, and reception: the fact that some people can read and write a novel, and others, including the eponymous character, cannot; and the fact that the novel will have several beginnings, understood narratively, diegetically, physically, and geopolitically.

Mr. Potter contains the world in a variety of ways. The novel's episodes take place in the Caribbean, but the narrative begins in the United States, where the writer is "living north of the equator and in the temperate zone" (165). The characters trace an even larger ambit: in addition to Mr. Potter, who is born and dies on the island of Antigua, there is Dr. Weizenger, from Czechoslovakia by way of Singapore, Shanghai, and Sydney; his wife May, who was born in England; and Mr. Shoul, from Lebanon by way of Surinam and Trinidad. There is very little dialogue in the novel. We are told that the characters speak the same language, English, but they experience each other's speech as "foreign" because of accent or idiom or intonation (113). Narrating the characters' solipsism, Kincaid presents their individual histories in relation to others and at various geopolitical distances. However, this structure registers dissonance rather than universalism. The point is not to admire Mr. Potter's life so much as to understand its causes, consequences, and relationship to other lives. There is no common language. Instead, there is translation from one circumstance to another.

The emphasis on translation operates at the level of character, context, and medium, as we have seen, but it also operates at the level of syntax—though it is a syntax attributed to character. Because she values the process of comparison, Kincaid prefers simile to metaphor. Simile makes its comparisons visible—it is a happening—and it can create a space for alternative comparisons. Metaphor, Kincaid suggests, can be passive and paralyzing, as when Mr. Potter's indifference becomes "not like a skin, but a skin itself" (93). He does not display indifference; he cannot exert agency over it. Instead of being indifferent, indifference becomes him. By contrast, when we are called upon to "hear" Mr. Potter, we are only overhearing. What we have before us is "almost" Mr. Potter but not in fact Mr. Potter at all. This is a condition of representation, the difference between words and things, but it is also a condition of agency, the robust thinking and writing and comparing that Mr. Potter's daughter is capable of imposing. In this sense, simile comes to structure the novel as a whole.

Placing Mr. Potter in the world, Kincaid narrates the effort to tell his story. She writes expertly, not natively, but she has turned expertise on its head. Instead of knowing more, the novel suggests, the expert has to resist the desire to be all-knowing.[62] Readers are asked to follow this model and, thus, to learn as Kincaid has learned. By focusing on relative fluency, literacy, and audience, Kincaid incorporates world literature. Like many scholars of translation, she writes against intrinsic reading. She emphasizes the materiality of printed words in order to emphasize the political significance of having been able to use them. She is unromantic about birth, which appears as a social artifact rather than a natural phenomenon. Those who are "born with a line drawn through" them, she shows, have to struggle to draw their own lines.

RELUCTANT CHARACTER

Hamid's novels, too, feature the figure of the expert: the guide with ambiguous designs in *The Reluctant Fundamentalist* (2007) and the self-help author in *How to Get Filthy Rich in Rising Asia* (2013). Like Kincaid, Hamid narrates two kinds of expertise: the ability to read and write the words on the page, and the ability to understand the relationship among local and global actions. He also refines the concept of expertise by introducing several incompatible narratives. Even more than Kincaid, Hamid embraces the second-person voice, a preoccupation he has acknowledged in an essay published after the appearance of *Filthy Rich*. His first novel, *Moth Smoke*, alternates among several different narrators but includes three chapters addressed to "you," whom the novel has placed in the role of judge.[63] "You" are part of the action: "You sit behind a high desk, wearing a black robe and a white wig, tastefully powdered" (5). In the later books, the address to "you" saturates the narrative. These are novels about reading and about readers. In his second novel, Hamid asks readers to witness their own reading; in his third, he asks them to imagine themselves as "co-creators," present for the happening of the text but also anterior to that happening.[64]

The Reluctant Fundamentalist introduces global actors who think that they are local actors. But the local is a moving target.[65] National institutions depend on the agency of migrants, who appear variously as government operatives, financial analysts, international students, and taxi drivers. Even the most basic version of the plot suggests a circuit of exchange: an American learns about Pakistan by learning in Pakistan about America. The conceit of the novel is a one-sided conversation between a Pakistani narrator, Changez, and an unnamed American visitor to Pakistan. Changez, now a university lecturer in Lahore, was educated in the United States and worked in New York City as a management consultant before returning to Pakistan after the World Trade Center attacks. The purpose and occupation of the American visitor remain ambiguous. The entire novel takes the shape of a dramatic monologue, which means we never hear from the American, nor do we receive any information apart from Changez's narration. The novel begins in translation, in at least three ways. First, the story takes place in a Pakistani bazaar. The language of currency is Urdu, but Changez announces on the first page that he will be speaking only in English. Addressing his companion, the bilingual narrator offers to provide assistance in "your language" (1).

The entire novel is thus narrated in a tongue foreign to its narrator, as we are reminded several times. The narrator remarks that their waiter's "intimidating" looks are contradicted by the "sweetness of his speech, if only you understood Urdu" (6). Later Changez laments that he is restricted to English, a language that does not possess "a respectful term for the word *you*—as we do in Urdu" (98). The novel's readers, whatever languages they actually speak, are thus constrained by the narrator's constraint: because the American doesn't speak Urdu, Changez keeps the waiter's comments to himself. He never reports them directly, or even indirectly. In this way, English is not only a medium for the book; it is integral to the novel's plot. This is not a story that could have been told in Urdu since the American's ignorance is crucial and since the absence of respectful address appears to be a feature of American solipsism. Indeed, Changez will suggest that monolingualism contributes to solipsism: the American's inability to understand the Pakistani waiter, or even to imagine him as a potential interlocutor, leads to his (the American's) assumption that he is being threatened.

If the first kind of translation is related to the story's implied language, in which Changez has adopted someone else's tongue, the second kind is related to the novel's setting, in which Hamid refracts territorial space through what I have called the space of action and consequence. The narrative remains in Lahore, but the story visits the United States, Greece, the Philippines, and Chile, before returning to Pakistan. Placing U.S. tourism in Greece next to U.S. investment in the Philippines and Chile, *The Reluctant Fundamentalist* draws a straight line from Kincaid's subjects to its own. Visiting Greece with a group of Americans he met at Princeton, Changez is disturbed by the "self-righteousness" of his companions and their rudeness toward "Greeks twice their age" (21). The young Americans' impoliteness, Changez suggests, reflects a worldview that is political as well as social. While evaluating foreign companies for his U.S.-based firm, Changez becomes increasingly concerned that narrowing his analysis to future profitability, as he was taught to do, excludes "the critical personal and political issues that affect one's emotional present" (145). For example, thinking only about finance leads Changez and his colleagues to assess a Chilean publishing concern according to its place in "the media industry" rather than according to the quality of the books it makes, and the place of those books in regional literary cultures (141–42). As Changez begins to think instead about Latin American poetry, he moves away from the narrow evaluation of the publisher's business and toward a comparative evaluation of his own business. Shifting his gaze outward as well as sideways, he compares his firm's economic incursion into the Chilean book industry with the U.S. military incursion into Afghanistan. Later he moves on from comparison to contiguity: "I knew from my experience as a Pakistani," he reports, "that finance was a primary means by which the American empire exercised its power" (156).

From thinking about "parts," Hamid writes, Changez begins to think about the "whole" (157), yet the structure of the novel also obstructs wholeness. Changez considers that the agency of the United States extends well beyond its territorial boundaries, and that one might best understand the United States by learning more about the countries in which it exercises its influence. This insight changes the character's orientation, from finance to activism and from the United States to Pakistan, and it also provides a model for the narrative in which a story about finance and the United States is placed inside a story about activism and Pakistan. Of course, it is not surprising to imagine that events in Lahore have to be understood in relation to events in New York. But it is more unusual to find—and this is the novel's most pressing argument—that New York is already embedded in Lahore, both because it relies on migrant workers such as Changez and because its financial success depends, as the Chilean book publisher puts it, on "disrupting the lives of others" (151).

The Reluctant Fundamentalist seeks to readjust the narrative balance of trade. In the global economy of ideas, it is usually the Americans (or other English-language speakers) who talk, and audiences in the so-called Global South who listen. In Hamid's novel, the U.S. visitor hears but does not speak, at least not in any way that the book records. The American view of the world usually dominates. Hamid's novel subjects that view to scrutiny and displaces it with other views. The American has to encounter the United States from the perspective of a foreigner. Finally, it is the American who is threatening, at least at first, and the Pakistani who appears to be hospitable. The

American is asked to imagine the United States as an agent rather than a victim of violence. The novel seems to be reversing the usual roles, and it encourages this impression through various exercises in chiasmus. Changez introduces himself by noting that the American "seemed to be on a *mission*" (1, emphasis in original). But in the final pages of the novel, the narrator assumes that role, claiming to have "made it my mission to advocate a disengagement from your country by mine" (179). Yet one mission has not exactly trumped the other. Instead the novel introduces two rival narratives: one in which Changez is a potential victim and the American an assassin, and one in which Changez is the assassin or "terrorist" and the American the victim (183). Moreover, the novel sews these narratives together. Changez's mission seems in retrospect to have shaped his approach to the American's since Changez introduces the American to Pakistan by teaching him about the United States.

Hamid's novel identifies and supplements the usual routes of world literature, in which works travel out from dominant languages and spaces into marginal or less dominant ones. In this narrative, we are asked to consider stories that usually go without hearing, and the usual speakers—the Americans—say nothing at all.[66] However, as I've suggested, the novel does not engage simply in a project of replacement. Rather, it generates several narratives at the same time, putting them into conflict and drawing our attention to the political, social, and economic conditions that make one narrative more visible (or audible) than others. When Changez speaks of "that bearded man—who even now, sir, continues to attract your wary gaze" (26), it is unclear whether it is the man or the interlocutor who is most threatening. Is the bearded man an object of pursuit by the American? Or, is the bearded man the pursuer? Put another way, is the man responsible for attracting the American's gaze, or is the gaze a result of the American's interests, concerns, and internal projections? Both explanations are plausible. Not only between characters but also between nations, the origins of violence seem to be multiple, though some stories are presented as villainy while others appear to be heroic. For example, the narrator acknowledges a local plot to assassinate the American coordinator of development aid to the poor while also describing how American bombings of "ill-equipped and ill-fed Afghan tribesmen" are presented in the U.S. media as "a daring raid on a Taliban command post" (181, 99–100). The narrator attributes the uneven distribution of stories to the U.S. influence over "international television news networks" (182).

With its emphasis on global media, the novel is mimetic of world literature, and also seeks to correct what Hamid sees as its limitations, including its tendency to produce, through translation, many monolingual editions. *The Reluctant Fundamentalist* therefore incorporates multilingualism at the level of narration and address. There is only one speaker in the work, but there is always more than one listener. This is in part a function of the dramatic monologue, the way it serves both as content, because we have to question the narrator's motives, and as form, because it is the conduit for the story the narrator tells. But the impression of multiple audiences is also a function of subjunctive characterization. The novel generates several versions of its drama by asking readers to think of themselves as the "you" who is an American and as the "you" who is an audience for Changez's exchange with the American. The second-person address produces a kind of vagueness, to be sure. But it also produces a kind of excess, the possibility of a different audience (not an American) and of a different audience for that audience (someone unlike the fictional American). The other subjunctive character, of course, is the narrator, whose intentions, background, and even actions can be known only through his speech.

The Reluctant Fundamentalist stands out among the literary response to the World Trade Center attacks because it does not actually take place in the United States. Like Kincaid's fictions, it is more concerned with what Americans look like from abroad and in generating new relationships between parts and wholes. Changez plays the role of the ethnographer, though notably he is an ethnographer not of Pakistan, whose customs he is supposed to be describing, but of the United States. He locates in an American's comment about Pakistani "fundamentalism" a "typically *American* undercurrent of condescension" (55, emphasis in original). Later he lists for his interlocutor the behavior that helped him seem "more like an American": speaking impolitely to foreign executives "my father's age," learning "to cut to the front of lines," and claiming that he is from New York

(65). The American has no opportunity to analyze Pakistani customs, both because his voice is not represented in the novel and because, as we are reminded, he doesn't have access to the world that he is visiting. Because Changez expects to be killed or jailed for his views, he describes himself as "a Kurtz waiting for his Marlowe [*sic*]" (183). This is an intriguing association, since, as the only speaker, Changez seems more Marlow than Kurtz, and the United States appears to be the place of darkness. But it is also intriguing because, whether Marlow or Kurtz, there is some other narrator to come: we are reading a story that is always about to be translated.

It is notable that Hamid engages in his correction of world literature not by narrating more explicitly—we learn very little about everyday life in Pakistan, for example—but by narrating reluctantly. The final lines of the novel are typical: "But why are you reaching into your jacket pocket, sir? I detect a glint of metal. Given that you and I are now bound by a certain shared intimacy, I trust it is from the holder of your business cards" (184).

The novel presents details about character and action in the language of possibility or negation rather than in the language of declaration. This is one of the ways that the novel achieves its oxymoronic title. There is a fundamentalist in the text, but we don't know who it is or which worldview he represents. The plot vacillates between attributing menace to the characteristics and intentions of the American and attributing menace to the characteristics and intentions of the narrator and the waiter who is serving them. Supporting the first plot, the narrator mentions the substantial size of his companion's chest, about which he notes, "sportsmen and soldiers of all nationalities tend to look alike" (2). He tells the American, "there is no need to reach under your jacket, I assume to grasp your wallet" (5). He observes that the American is in possession of a mobile phone "capable of communicating by satellite when no ground coverage is available" (30). Supporting the second plot, the narrator tries to put the American at ease—or at least pretends to try—by assuring him that the food is safe ("it is not as if it has been poisoned" [11]), that "nothing sinister" is meant (122), and that the loud sound they heard "was not the report of a pistol" (176). All of these details—and there are many more like them that I have not cited—contribute to the frame narrative, not the story about the United States that is being related to the American but the story about the storytelling for which we are the principal audience. The novel provides details that it will never substantiate, and in fact the narrator reminds his companion, "you should not imagine that we Pakistanis are all potential terrorists, just as we should not imagine that you Americans are all undercover assassins" (183). The novel, however, asks for the opposite, sort of: we're asked to imagine negatively, expertly but not fluently, both of these possibilities.

The narrator's use of the personal pronoun "you" generates reluctance, too, and this creates a third kind of translation. Changez is addressing the American, but "you"—through what one theorist of the second-person voice calls its "referential slither"—implies the book's readers as well.[67] Through the irony of dramatic monologue, the difference between what the narrator says and why he might be saying it, the novel asks us to think about production and circulation at the same time. Because the narrator's voice implies its own fictional audience, the reader is always a second reader. We are the (fictional) audience's audience. Because there are no first, original, or native audiences—only subsequent audiences—the narrative appears to be written in translatese. It is language for another. We are confronted with a story that can only be read at a distance. To be sure, this could be said of any dramatic monologue. But in *The Reluctant Fundamentalist*, "you" is always foreign.

It is difficult to know whether the "fundamentalist" of Hamid's title is meant to refer to Changez, whose determined critique of U.S. foreign policy has been labeled anti-American, or whether it refers to the American, who seems to possess a one-eyed view of the world. In both of these cases, *fundamentalist* is a negative epithet. However, there is another more literal, less negative fundamentalism presented by the text. When Changez gives up financial security and the pursuit of efficiency to nurture interpersonal relationships (support for his family in Pakistan and the effort to help his depressed friend, Erica), he seems to exchange one set of "fundamentals" for another (98). Approving this exchange, the novel promotes its own kind of ironic fundamentalism, though this is a fundamentalism defined by a commitment to comparative wholes rather than distinctive parts, and to the belief that, as Changez puts it in the novel's final pages, "we cannot reconstitute ourselves as the autonomous beings we previously imagined ourselves to be" (174).

The Reluctant Fundamentalist tells a story about American solipsism by showing how actions that seem local have global consequences, both for other nations and for the United States. At the level of narrative, the novel incorporates perspectives beyond the self by addressing a reader who is both singular and plural, the individual "you" and the many versions of "you" among whom the text will circulate. Hamid uses translation to create subjunctive audiences and to suggest that the agency of the self is embedded in other selves. The hovering structure of multiple intentions generates excessive detail about character and action. While one story line is abstracted through this detail, another achieves greater resolution. Translation, which obscures the assassination plot, brings to light the geopolitical dynamics and historical contexts that mobilize that plot.

How to Get Filthy Rich in Rising Asia, published in 2013, extends this approach by narrating, in addition to the life "you" actually lead, paths not taken, characters not considered, and experiences fortunately avoided. *Filthy Rich* presents itself as a self-help book, a book you read in order to improve yourself by yourself, but its actual project is showing how much the self relies on other selves, on collectives such as the state, the school, the family, the hospital, and the audience, and on good fortune. Mechanical literacy is insufficient, Hamid implies. Beyond knowledge of letters, one needs knowledge of cultural production. Watching the end of a television program, the learned audience needs to know that that entertainment has been generated through collaborative labor and institutional sponsorship. Hamid describes a characteristic scene: "Your mother sees a meaningless stream of hieroglyphs. Your father and sister make out an occasional number, your brother that and the occasional word. For you alone does this part of the programming make sense. You understand it reveals who is responsible for what."[68] Hamid places a story about paratext, the actors and institutions that generate the artwork, inside his text. The anecdote operates as an allegory of the novel's form since it mimics the structure of embedded audiences produced by the dramatic monologue. *How to Get Filthy Rich* provides a robust account of literary production by drawing our attention to narrative production, making comparisons among narrative outcomes and understandings of those outcomes, and analyzing how and why narratives circulate, or do not circulate. Hamid reminds us of the people who fail, even while telling us a story about a person, "you," who succeeds. In this sense, the novel is always doubled in two ways: first, the second-person narrative creates an extra narrative, the performance of the narrator's story and the reader's place in that performance; second, the invocation of other outcomes invites us to imagine the many storylines that do not appear but persist as ghostly siblings, like the other TV watchers, of the "get rich" conceit.

Hamid's books are optimistic about circulation. They are not optimistic that everyone will have access to reading and writing—in fact, they often insist that literacy is in some contexts an exception rather than a norm, as when the narrator remarks that "occasionally a literate visitor is to be heard reading to his fellows" from the signs at a municipal zoo (211). At the same time, Hamid treats reading in translation as an opportunity for selves to understand their relationship to other selves. Reading in translation involves being a second audience: engaging both with the story and with the story's history of reception. It involves collaboration, or what Hamid calls "co-creation," so that "in each of a million different readings a book becomes one of a million different books" (98). At the end of the novel, "you" are ready to die because "you have been beyond yourself" (228). The final words of the novel conjugate this model of collectivity as a kind of mutual containment: "I contain you, who may not yet even be born, you inside me inside you, though not in a creepy way, and so may you, may I, may we, so may all of us confront the end" (228). The insertion of the clause "though not in a creepy way" has the effect of deflating the statement's high ethical tone. In dramatic terms, it seems like an aside; in narrative terms, like a metafictional interruption. We are reminded in this moment that the history of genres is part of the novel's story. This is a self-help book that doesn't believe in the premise of self-help books, so a sincere peroration has to be modified to incorporate other registers. Hamid's book believes neither in the autonomy of selves nor in the autonomy of sentences. Mixing two kinds of diction, the final words of the novel produce the impression of a performance, a statement and the saying of a statement.

The Reluctant Fundamentalist has been compared to *One Thousand and One Nights*, and this comparison fits *How to Get Filthy Rich* as well. In each of these works there is an implication that death will come when the storytelling ends. There is the dramatic monologue. There is the conceit of oral literature appearing as written literature. There is the Orientalist narrative (mysterious bazaars; impenetrable bureaucracies) addressed to foreign audiences. There are embedded stories. And there is the impression of a work that has evolved and will continue to evolve through circuits of communication. Pointing to an evolved translation that has been crucial to the evolution of the novel as a genre, Hamid reminds his audiences that the origins of the anglophone novel are not reducible to Europe and that the future of the novel is, at this moment, being read.[69]

THIS IS NOT YOUR LANGUAGE

I am indebted for the title of this chapter to a chapter title in David Bellos's lively book on translation in which he asks "is your native language really yours?"[70] Bellos does not discuss second-person narrative, and only his title adopts that style of address, but the wit of his query depends on the fact that "your native language" means both the language that "you," the reader, acquired first and the language that belongs to "you," the one that is yours and not someone else's. The terms "native language" and "mother tongue," he points out, confuse "the history of an individual's acquisition of linguistic skills with the mystery of what we mean by the 'possession' of a language" (65). The answer he gives to his own question, at least indirectly, is no. Not "no" because the language you are speaking belongs to someone else, but "no" because "your language" is not restricted to a specific "you." In fact, thinking about the uncanniness of second-person address, we can observe that "your language," grammatically, can never be restricted only to one "you," since *you* is a capacious and also an open pronoun.[71] There is always another *you* to come, who shadows the reader at the very moment that she or he enters the conversation. This is why the declaration "this is not your language" is axiomatic as well as descriptive. It is descriptive because readers do not own the language they read. It is axiomatic because the language possesses them: readers, addressed by the second-person voice, observe the sentence while being placed within it. Like Magritte's "*ceci n'est pas une pipe*," which the artist famously inscribed beneath an image of a pipe, "this is not your language" names the counterfactual truth of second-person fiction: identity does not inhabit words. There is no *you* in *this*.

Postcolonial novels have sometimes sought to communicate "a detailed understanding of cultural differences," in Ursula Heise's phrase, through multilingual or hybrid idiolect.[72] For readers, the encounter with words could function as an encounter with differences so that one imagined encountering foreignness, someone else's culture, not in what words express but in the texture of words themselves. In anglophone writing, virtuosic performances of hybrid idiolect (think of Rushdie's *Midnight's Children*, to take one of the most distinguished examples) have been a strategic response to the underrepresentation of English's many histories and to the political exclusions associated with linguistic standardization and monolingualism.[73] Writers have used hybrid idiolect to affirm the sovereignty of nations outside of Europe and the United States and to register political and social collectives that are smaller than, or alternative to, the nation. In a book such as Anthony Burgess's *Clockwork Orange*, not a postcolonial text but influenced by Joyce's use of sound, the reader is pulled into the narrator's group, his "droogs," by becoming comfortable—one might even say fluent—in his slang. Hamid's and Kincaid's novels largely block the equation between words and identity, first of all, by reminding readers that the language on the page has been translated both from other languages and from other media; second, by embedding local details, or what Hamid calls "parts," in geopolitical systems and networks; and third, by placing readers into a round-robin, in which the audience is part of the work and thus not able, in any final way, to receive it.

Once we bracket the idea of native voice, several questions immediately follow. Do foreign languages matter if they don't transmit foreignness, or if foreignness is already present in the languages we think we know? If anglophone novels such as *Mr. Potter* and *The Reluctant Fundamentalist* have incorporated translation, suggesting that multilingualism is present even within what appears to be "your language," do we need to read books in translation or books composed in languages other than English? Have we managed to encounter multilingualism without ever having to leave English? These are important questions, and they touch on both ontological (what is the book I am reading?) and ethical (what book should I read?) concerns.

Hamid's and Kincaid's novels suggest that there is something limiting, and perhaps even pernicious, about the idea that language offers direct access to culture. Indeed, there is nothing *direct* about their novels at all, insofar as they incorporate mediation and translation of several kinds. There is no hearing Mr. Potter in *Mr. Potter*, and Pakistan has to be understood geopolitically, as a territory embedded in many territories, in *The Reluctant Fundamentalist*. Hamid and Kincaid emphasize translation not to ignore American solipsism or to suggest that American solipsism can be undermined by self-estrangement but to insist that Americans need to encounter *other readers rather than other voices*. Put another way, these novels emphasize the comparative beginnings of postcolonial fiction by making their readers into rereaders and into selves whose meaning depends on other selves, and by making their authors into writers rather than speakers. This focus on the relationship between books and audiences reflects a shift in what fiction is trying to achieve: instead of articulating distinctive cultures, Kincaid and Hamid are articulating geopolitical systems, including the systems in which their novels are produced.

Knowing languages—knowing how to write and read any language, and how to speak and understand more than one language—is not inherently ethical since multilingualism can be used to subdue and impose as well as to compromise and receive. But in Hamid's novels, knowing languages is a precondition for conversation across boundaries of class, institution, and nation. Knowing languages makes it more likely that Americans will imagine themselves as target as well as source, receiving narration as well as dictating it. Multilingualism matters because it enhances a speaker's range of expressivity, making it possible to imagine different registers of *you*, for example, and it reminds speakers that there is a range: that *you* can be different. But Hamid and Kincaid also suggest that multilingualism in the service of foreignness is incoherent without multilingualism in the service of knowing what passes for proximity. This does not mean that the rationale for learning languages stops at the door of the nation. Rather, it means that multilingualism has to include knowing the dramatic variety of English languages used throughout the world, what David Damrosch has called "comparative English literature."[74] It has to include knowing something about the many languages that operate within English or as part of the knowledge of English today. And it has to include knowing the many languages that operate within so-called local geographies, territorial units equal to or smaller than the nation. These are important inclusions not because they suggest that multilingualism of the nation or the neighborhood is the same as multilingualism at larger scales, and thus exchangeable for them. They are important because they force us to recognize that even the most local fictions require knowledge of other languages, literary histories, and geographies. There are no languages without foreign languages. Only a comparative literary history can produce a literary history worth the name. Novels that block native fluency invite us to imagine that project: the history of literature in the world.

This chapter focuses on books that use translation to generate relative fluency, to make readers more aware of other readers, and to enhance readers' sense of their role in the ongoing production of the work. The next chapter approaches the literature of ongoing production by turning to digital narratives that seem to thwart or resist monolingualism. "Born Translated and Born Digital" features digital media and post-digital books that are meant to be operated as well as read. They often appear to be multiple books, series, or collaborations. These works are born translated because they are born collective.

5

BORN TRANSLATED AND BORN DIGITAL

MULTILINGUAL COLLECTIVES

Some born-translated works appear to be multilingual because they combine foreign narratives or editions rather than foreign phonemes, words, or phrases. Functioning as a single object and as several objects at the same time, these works consist of multiple literatures as well as multiple languages. How do we determine the group, understood linguistically and geographically, in which works such as these belong? What kind of group do the works themselves constitute? This chapter approaches these questions by turning to the oeuvre of the collaborative Web artists Young-Hae Chang Heavy Industries. This corporate name represents a Seoul-based team, Young-Hae Chang, who is Korean, and her partner, Marc Voge, who is American. Since 1999 Chang and Voge have been creating artworks together using the animation software Flash Player. We tend to imagine that digital technologies offer greater autonomy to writers, readers, and translators, and thus that digital fiction serves as well as celebrates individual expressivity. But Chang and Voge's work suggests that the opposite may be true: that digital technologies often block rather than nurture autonomy, and that digital fiction, by emphasizing its

HAYATIMIZ BØYUNCA ERTELENEBİLECEK HERŞEYİ ERTELERİZ. -- BØRGES

ALL ØUR LIVES, WE PØSTPØNE EVERYTHING THAT CAN BE PØSTPØNED. --BØRGES

FIGURE 5.1

Screenshot from Young-Hae Chang Heavy Industries, *The Art of Sleep*.
Copyright Young-Hae Chang Heavy Industries.

Source: www.yhchang.com. Accessed February 19, 2014.
Used by permission of the artists.

corporate origins, can help us think about the literary and political dimensions of collectivity.

Take *HONEYMOON IN BEPPU*, a multilingual collective that uses the visual culture of facing-page translation, subtitling, and interlineal translation to generate a multivoiced story about a tryst in the Japanese seaside town of Beppu (figure 5.2).[1]

There are two narrators, one male and one female; and two or three narrations, audio (Japanese) and print (Japanese and English). The work consists of interlingual, intermedial, and interpersonal translations. *HONEYMOON* is structured like a couple: its many duos (English and Japanese, his and hers, red and black images) compete for our attention. However, contrasting colors, genders, languages, and even facts suggest competition rather than complementarity.[2] This effect is animated most dramatically by our effort to organize the voices. Do we read one narrative at a time, or do we try to collate narratives as they appear, nearly simultaneously, on the screen?

FIGURE 5.2 Screenshot from Young-Hae Chang Heavy Industries,
Honeymoon in Beppu. Copyright Young-Hae Chang Heavy Industries.

Source: www.yhchang.com. Accessed November 5, 2010.
Used by permission of the artists.

Another of Chang and Voge's multilingual collectives, *TRAVELING TO UTOPIA: WITH A BRIEF HISTORY OF TECHNOLOGY* (figure 5.3), presents three narratives while also presenting three languages (French, Korean, and English). Although they tell different stories and imply different literary genres—roughly, fantasy, science fiction, and realism—the narratives have similar themes: they consider whether technology extends or impedes mobility. The work takes up this question by engaging with debates about political inclusion. It does this by relating anecdotes about thwarted travel, immigration control, and police harassment, and by asking whether its narrative strands should be understood as separate units or as parts of the same unit. Readers have to focus their attention on the work's episodic structure while also considering how many objects and how many languages they have before them. The calculation of objects and languages refines the calculation of citizenship since the work suggests above all that belonging cannot be aligned with linguistic and physical homogeneity.

As these brief examples suggest, Chang and Voge's works are born translated. They engage formally, thematically, and typographically with the theory and practice of translation. They are also self-translated: they participate from the start in several literary histories. On their Web site, www.yhchang.com, which functions as a standing (and

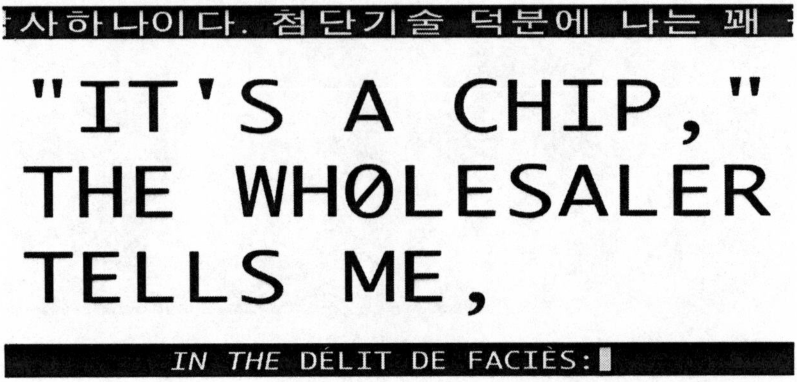

사 하 나 이 다. 첨 단 기 술 덕 분 에   나 는   꽤

"IT'S A CHIP,"
THE WHØLESALER
TELLS ME,

IN THE DÉLIT DE FACIÈS:

FIGURE 5.3 Screenshot from Young-Hae Chang Heavy Industries,
Traveling to Utopia: With a Brief History of Technology (English/Korean).
Copyright: Young-Hae Chang Heavy Industries.

Source: www.yhchang.com. Accessed September 13, 2012.
Used by permission of the artists.

also expanding) gallery, works are sometimes offered in separate language editions: "PORTUGUÊS," "KOREAN," "TURKISH," "ENGLISH,"
"DEUTSCH," "JAPANESE," and so on. Sometimes they are offered
in what seem to be bilingual editions: "PORTUGUÊS/ENGLISH" or
"ENGLISH/KOREAN" or "FRANCAIS/ENGLISH." Sometimes, they are
offered in musical editions: "WITH DRUMS" or "WITH STRINGS"
or "TANGO VERSION." Sometimes a choice among editions is not
offered at all (figure 5.4).

While many of the works began as site-specific installations in
museums or in public spaces, the artists have described the Web as
their primary interface.[3] However, the Web site offers no information
about the chronology or location of the compositions, and in fact
the inventory changes from time to time without notice and without
archiving prior inventories.

The Web page serves both as a portal and as a table of contents. However, unlike the usual table of contents we find in books, this one's chapters or parts are intentionally uncountable. It is impossible to say how
many works or editions of works have been gathered by the page since
what we can identify as a unique object, or even as a unique language,

THE NEW AND IMPRØVED
YØUNG-HAE CHANG HEAVY INDUSTRIES
PRESENTS

DAKØTA ENGLISH ESPANØLA KØREAN PØRTUGUÊS
CUNNILINGUS IN NØRTH KØREA ENGLISH DEUTSCH FRANCAIS ESPANØLA PØRTUGUÊS
LØTUS BLØSSØM ENGLISH KØREAN
THE STRUGGLE CØNTINUES ENGLISH KØREAN FRANCAIS MEXICANØ PØRTUGUÊS
SAMSUNG ENGLISH KØREAN FRANCAIS DEUTSCH ESPANØLA TANGØ VERSIØN
SAMSUNG MEANS TØ CØME ENGLISH KØREAN FRANCAIS
ARTIST'S STATEMENT NØ. 45,730,944: THE PERFECT ARTISTIC WEB SITE ENGLISH KØREAN FRANCAIS ESPANØLA
ØPERATIØN NUKØREA ENGLISH KØREAN
METABLAST
NIPPØN
THE SEA ENGLISH PØRTUGUÊS
RIVIERA ENGLISH CHINESE
BECKETT'S BØUNCE
ALL FALL DØWN
RØYAL CRØWN SUPER SALØN
SUPER SMILE
ØRIENT ENGLISH KØREAN JAPANESE
THE INLAND SEA
JØNGNØ ENGLISH KØREAN
SAUL
RAIN ØN THE SEA ENGLISH KØKEAN ESPANØLA
HALF BREED APACHE
BUST DØWN THE DØØRS! ENGLISH DEUTSCH FRANCAIS
BUST DØWN THE DØØR AGAIN! WITH DRUMS WITH STRINGS GATES ØF HELL-VICTØRIA VERSIØN
THE END ENGLISH KØREAN GALEGØ
VICTØRIA DEFILED: PERFECT VICTØRIA VICTØRIA'S FIRE
SUBJECT: HELLØ ENGLISH ESPANØLA
PAØ! PAØ! PAØ! ENGLISH FRANCAIS RUSSIAN
MISS DMZ
WHAT NØW? ENGLISH SVENSKA ENGLISH/FRANCAIS
THE LAST DAY ØF BETTY NKØMØ
JØE JØNES
TRAVELING TØ UTØPIA: WITH A BRIEF HISTØRY ØF THE TECHNØLØGY ENGLISH/KØREAN FRANCAIS/ENGLISH
SØ, SØ SØULFUL ENGLISH TURKISH
THE ART ØF SLEEP TURKISH
AØMØRI AMØRI
(ØUT ØF THE INTERNET AND) INTØ THE NIGHT
MØRNING ØF THE MØNGØLØIDS DEUTSCH/ENGLISH PØRTUGUÊS/ENGLISH

FIGURE 5.4 Screenshot from Young-Hae Chang Heavy Industries,
main Web page, www.yhchang.com. Copyright: Young-Hae Chang
Heavy Industries.

Source: www.yhchang.com. Accessed February 19, 2014.
Used by permission of the artists.

is not self-evident. For example, the work called *SAMSUNG* appears in
six versions: "ENGLISH," "KOREAN," "FRANCAIS," "DEUTSCH," "ESPA-
NOLA," and "TANGO VERSION." The several versions are not comprehensible within a single system of differences.[4] Perhaps the soundtrack
functions like a language? Or, perhaps we should regard the verbal text
not as the primary medium but as lyrics attached to a score?[5] The work
consists of editions that have to be understood collectively in relation
to each other and also collectively in relation to other texts in the same
language, the same instrument, and the same rhythm.

Not only is it difficult to count the works, it is also difficult to order them. Because there are no publication or composition dates, the editions seem to exist synchronically. In no case do we have a work offered first in "the original," as it were, and then, later, "in translation." Refusing the priority of original languages, the artists seem to suggest that differences of geography and culture are irrelevant in an age of electronic literature. Judging by their Web page, we might assume that translation doesn't matter; that there is no significance in the choice among Japanese, Korean, English, Dutch, Portuguese, and Swedish; and that we need not notice when a text moves from a dominant language to a language that has fewer speakers or fewer writers. Yet the narratives contradict this impression by reversing the usual hierarchy between original and translation, by reflecting on stories of migration and thwarted migration, and by reminding audiences that translation has already taken place even within what seem to be original-language works. In addition, if translatability typically means that a work can easily travel from one language to another, Chang and Voge's usage is a little different. Appearing in English and Korean as well as Tango, *SAMSUNG* suggests that language is not the only or the most important axis of differentiation. The aggregate work interferes with the impression of equivalence among language editions and with the impression that the difference among editions depends solely on language. In Chang and Voge's works, soundtrack, illustration, and regional languages matter too. The truly global work of literature, like a Samsung stereo, should be the same from Pittsburgh to Prague. Chang and Voge are declining this model of sameness, which they associate with a dominant but by no means necessary agreement about the accumulation and grouping of literary objects.

In addition to being born translated, Chang and Voge's works are also born digital. They have been made on and for the computer, and they use the resources of digital technology to emphasize the computer's special role in the history of translation, in methods of circulation and surveillance, and in assumptions about the ontology of artworks. Jessica Pressman has observed that mechanical translation has always been both "an essential aspect" and a principal goal of digital computing.[6] In this sense, translation is "both a central ambition *for* the computer and a central operating process *of* the computer."[7] While translation allows born-digital texts to think about computing's past, as Pressman suggests, it also allows those texts to think about literature's future. Digital works introduce new genres, new producers, and new dynamics of reading and consuming. They also present an opportunity to test the foundational concepts of the literary field. By engaging with histories of literary translation as well as with the visual culture of print, Chang and Voge place their born-digital works in conversation with paper-bound technologies and within a long tradition of multilingual writing.

Like many born-translated writers in print, Chang and Voge use translation to point at languages and to decouple the relationship between language and citizenship. Deploying the visual and aural culture of translation, their works generate multiple scales of literary and political collectivity. Chang and Voge also invoke translation's past. Ezra Pound, Vladimir Nabokov, Jorge Luis Borges, and Samuel Beckett, who rewrote, adapted, and translated both their own and other writers' works, appear in Chang and Voge's oeuvre by name and by allusion. Emphasizing this lineage, Chang and Voge seem to be celebrating translation as the modernists did, because it enlivens languages, because it renovates literary traditions, and because it helps to generate solidarities both smaller and larger than the nation. Yet Chang and Voge take this celebration further by refusing to identify source languages and by bringing multilingual experimentation to a large, heterogeneous, and undetermined audience. Embracing translatability, Chang and Voge not only demote the word, they also demote the reader, or at least the image of the knowing reader that we have inherited from modernism. No longer a master of many languages, the reader of born-translated fiction is expected to understand less because understanding all the languages of the globe would be impossible, and to understand differently because new units of the book become meaningful.

Studies of Chang and Voge's work have focused on two contexts: the development of literary and cinematic modernism at the start of the twentieth century and the flourishing of electronic literature at the century's end. Pressman has singled out the pair's homage to Pound and their appropriation of modernist values such as difficulty, autonomy, and canonicity.[8] Katherine Hayles has emphasized their aversion to interactivity and their use of digital resources such as timed sequence and "the synergistic interplay of text, music, color, motion, and animation."[9] To consider Chang and Voge's relationship to ideas of collectivity, this chapter introduces two additional frameworks: the history of U.S. and European contact with East Asia and the national, regional, and transpacific history of South Korea. Thinking about these locations and approaches to location will allow us to consider why Chang and Voge create works in multiple languages without demanding fluency in those languages. What kind of literature are they creating, and what reading strategies does it require?

THE ART OF THE CORPORATION

Even before we examine the artworks themselves, we know from the artists' moniker that histories of translation and transpacific contact will be significant to the work. Chang and Voge present their compositions and give all interviews as Young-Hae Chang Heavy Industries. This multinational corporation, as it were, allows them to register their antagonism both to European and to Asian traditions of cultural production. The artists conspicuously decline the Romantic individualism of European literary history and, at the same time, edgily appropriate the impersonal legacy of South Korea's global conglomerates. Yet this corporate self is hardly impersonal. As Chang and Voge show, corporate universalism is more guise than guarantee. The artists' name calls to mind Korea-based companies such as Hyundai Heavy Industries and Samsung Heavy Industries. These firms are known the world over, but their origins are regional. They were nourished in the late twentieth century by Korea's commitment to large-scale growth in the so-called heavy industries of electronics, shipbuilding, automobiles, machinery, and chemicals.[10] On a Web site that advertises their work, Chang and Voge wryly signal this allusion: "Besides building ships," they explain with tongue in cheek, their company "combines text with jazz to create Web pieces."[11] As historians of contemporary Korea know well, Hyundai and Samsung benefitted from a command economy whose success is now associated with a national tradition of military dictatorship and an international tradition of treaties favoring the United States and Japan.[12] The relationship between digital technology and state coercion is addressed thematically in a number of Chang and Voge's works. But the corporate name, which appears at the start of every one of their compositions, attaches this theme to the entire oeuvre. Chang and Voge thus locate their project within a tradition of state-mandated and state-controlled transnationalism.

The very language of the corporate moniker, a mixture of anglicized Korean and business English, encapsulates a transpacific regionalism that is at once utterly Korean and utterly global. The moniker is global because its hybrid appearance and phonology register the generic signs of transnational commerce. But it is Korean because it reproduces a usage that is specific to Korean companies, after the practice of Japanese companies. The phrase "heavy industries" is an estrangement of English that is native only to non-anglophone speakers; it is a translation with no original. Chang and Voge's moniker thus conveys a kind of individualism in the weak sense because it can be distinguished from, say, French or Scandinavian corporate names, but it stands apart from individualism in the strong, philosophical sense because its characteristics are hardly unified, sovereign, or consistent.[13] The corporation, as Henry Turner reminds us, is in legal terms both a group of persons and a collective person. Because it is conceived as a system rather than an organism, Turner remarks, it has "no depth and no inside" (120); "it is a person without personality," where personality refers to the possession of desires, preferences, and will that are imagined to be coherent and enduring (112). Corporations tend to obscure individuals but reify individualism by claiming for themselves the qualities of unanimity typically attached to persons.

Through the corporation, Chang and Voge resist the demand for unanimity that they associate both with the individual and with the state. That said, throughout their works, Chang and Voge are critical of both actual and invented corporations. They take aim at the ways that corporations have dominated Korean domestic policy and geopolitical history. They express concern about the gender politics of corporate socialization. They display wariness about governments ceding to corporations the right to invent, produce, distribute, use, and monitor digital technologies. In *CAMPBELL'S SOUP TOWN*, with a nod to Andy Warhol, they imagine a futuristic world in which the mayor of Cambelltown (an actual place, near Sydney, Australia) invites the Campbell's Soup Company to invest in the city in exchange for naming rights and unfettered access to development. The narrators, who relocate to Campbell's Soup Town after receiving financial incentives, find that all of the city's major buildings look like soup cans and that, through technological advancement, everything in them has been manufactured from soup. As this piece implies, instead of seeing the individual and the state as antidotes to corporate practices, Chang and Voge see them as part of the problem. Their works therefore deploy the corporation's structure of irreducible collectivity against the corporate valorization of the individual and especially the individual nation.

We can see this strategy in the artists' self-presentation. Two individuals lead the corporation known as Young-Hae Chang Heavy Industries, but each individual is presented as a container for multiple geographies, languages, affiliations, and histories. This model of disaggregate individualism shapes their treatment of authorship, political collectivity, national identity, and, above all, literary history, in which translations seem to be both internal and external to the text. When translation is external, the artwork appears to be a unique object that travels into several languages. When translation is internal, the artwork appears to be a collection of related objects in different languages, although those languages are not always reducible to one or another national idiom. Chang and Voge are engaged in what we might call "the art of the corporation," both in the literal sense of exploring the details of corporate life and in the more conceptual sense of exploring the relationship between the individual and the collective and among different kinds of collectives.[14]

The complex interface between different scales of collectivity is perhaps most visible on the artists' Web page (figure 5.4). The inventory calls to mind Borges's famous "Chinese encyclopedia," whose classification of animals—"(a) those belonging to the Emperor, (b) embalmed ones, (c) those that are trained, (d) suckling pigs, (e) mermaids, (f) fabulous ones, (g) stray dogs, (h) those that are included in this classification, (i) those that tremble as if they were mad, (j) innumerable ones, (k) those drawn with a very fine camel's hair brush, (l) others, (m) those that have just broken a flower vase, (n) those that resemble flies from a distance"—shows us, in the first place, that what we can think about is limited by our organization of thought and that, perhaps more significantly, the unexpected organization of thought has the capacity to create new objects.[15] Chang and Voge's inventory asks us to consider both sides of this equation: how we collect works of art and how we make them.

FAKE ORIGINALS AND FEINT TRANSLATIONS

Let us return for a moment to *HONEYMOON IN BEPPU* (figure 5.2). Appearing as a work in Japanese with English subtitles, *HONEYMOON* thwarts classification by presenting its audience with a familiar conceit: the fake translation. The screenshot shows two simultaneous narratives, "his" and "hers." In the animation, male and female speakers give voice to the Japanese text. Of course, literary history is full of European works pretending to be taken from some exotic language such as Arabic, Italian, or, indeed, Japanese.[16] But what we have here is actually something more unusual. *HONEYMOON IN BEPPU* is not a fake or pseudotranslation. Not really. Instead, it's a fake original: a Japanese work claiming to need translation into English. Chang and Voge achieve this pretense by offering the Japanese translation as the primary text, both visually and conceptually. Visually, the Japanese appears in large font with the English in smaller font below. Conceptually, Japanese has been allowed to replace English as the language of publication, even though an English version was produced first.[17] There is nothing in the text that would tell you that English is the primary or original language. In fact, the Japanese translation has become an original in even the most literal sense: when the Japanese translator misunderstood one of the English idioms, Chang and Voge allowed it to stand in the published version.[18] Since the English translation now differs from the Japanese, the mistake—or the variation—has become theirs.

While the fake originality of *HONEYMOON IN BEPPU* is largely invisible to the casual reader, questions of precedence and competition are highlighted by the text's verbal and visual motifs. Think, first of all, of the red and black images, the subtitled text, and the doubled his-and-her narratives. Moreover, each narrative is double-voiced. The two speakers recall a tryst they shared in the Japanese tourist town of Beppu, known for its hot springs and its sex industry. Both remember pretending to others that they were on a honeymoon (they had in fact just met) and to each other that they were telling the truth about themselves (they were in fact both lying). The authors collaborate with their characters by giving the work a misleading title. *HONEYMOON IN BEPPU*, we come to realize, is not about a honeymoon at all. Like Kurosawa's *Rashomon*, *HONEYMOON* presents no marriage of persons, languages, media, or narratives. Instead, it offers if not an absence of truth then a new conception of truth based on incompatible perspectives. The art of the corporation, which appears in this text as the aggregation of voices, is also an art of translation. Images and themes of translation register fantasies of social, sexual, and linguistic transparency.

HONEYMOON takes up the politics of language in an indirect way, through the visual and aural culture of translation and through themes of doubling/duping, but Chang and Voge's other works focus much more explicitly on the misfit between language and citizenship. These works show how languages are embedded in political debates about belonging and exclusion. For example, *MORNING OF THE MONGOLOIDS* presents a narrator—he describes himself as "white"—who wakes up after a night of drinking to find that he and everyone around him now speak a language he doesn't recognize. He assumes that the words he's hearing are Chinese. Only later does he realize he's hearing Korean and living in Seoul. The change in language is accompanied by a change in physical appearance. His nose is flatter; his hair is darker and straighter; his cheeks are rounder (figure 5.5). This piece tells a familiar story of anxious transformation from one so-called race to another. It pokes fun at anti-Asian racism, but it also registers the regional fate of Korea, which has been dominated at one time or another by China and Japan. The narrator can't tell the difference between Chinese and Korean because, for him, all Asians sound alike. But it would never occur to him to think about Korean in the first place, and in this sense the story is less familiar: in addition to Western generalizations about the East,

PØRQUE ESTAØ AS MINHAS BØCHECHAS TÃØ REDØNDAS?

WHY ARE MY CHEEKS SØ RØUND?

FIGURE 5.5   Screenshot from Young-Hae Chang Heavy Industries, *Morning of the Mongoloids* (Portuguese/English). Copyright: Young-Hae Chang Heavy Industries.

Source: www.yhchang.com. Accessed September 13, 2012. Used by permission of the artists.

its target is also the so-called East's own histories of imperialism and cultural hierarchy.

It is important to note that Chang and Voge's response to both kinds of ignorance is not better or more concrete knowledge. They don't replace the narrator's generalizations about East Asian languages and cultures with some more literal access to them. Instead we receive a text in Portuguese and English, in the version I'm showing you here, with the understanding that both languages are, diegetically speaking, translations of Korean—the language that the narrator is supposedly speaking.[19] We never learn what language the narrator spoke before the morning in question; nor do we learn where he used to live, though we suspect it was some U.S. or European city where people who look Asian seem, to the narrator, out of place. Fictionally as well as literally, the text's beginnings are obscured. The effort to assign and fix national origins is associated with the speaker's anti-Asian prejudices. Only in the narrator's racist fantasy, the artists suggest, do language and physical appearance imply a specific geography.

The racist narrator is monolingual—before the morning in question, he didn't speak Korean—but he is not a racist because he's monolingual. He is a racist because he assumes that everyone in his community speaks the same language and because he associates political community with physical and linguistic homogeneity. This point is relevant for readers as well. We don't need to know Korean in order to recognize the work's dramatic irony. In truth, we don't need to know both English and Portuguese either. Chang and Voge do not require mastery. If anything, they require less mastery. In political terms, we are asked to recognize that incomprehensibility operates within, and not simply between, communities. In an age of global migration, it is impossible to know all languages or even to comprehend all versions of the same language. In literary terms, we are asked to recognize that born-translated works will operate in more languages than any one reader could expect to acquire. There are at least two consequences to the withdrawal of mastery. First, we have to assume that different readers will have access to different versions or different parts of the work, and the relativity of access becomes part of the work's project. Second, because no single reader can comprehend the work in all of its languages, reading in translation becomes a condition of literary history, not simply an exception for those who have failed to acquire a sufficient number of tongues.

Chang and Voge are critical of what we might call the ethos of multilingualism, the idea that only speakers of many languages are adequate to the task of reading world literature, that literature that seeks to engage with the politics of language will require native fluency, and that all works of literature have a single language in which they can be said to begin. While Chang and Voge turn away from idiolect and from the cult of originality, as we've seen, they are also wary of utopian approaches to translation and digital media. They do not romanticize original languages, nor do they romanticize technologies of circulation that seem to promise new and unfettered agency. We see both of these points in *TRAVELING TO UTOPIA: WITH A BRIEF HISTORY OF TECHNOLOGY*, which appears in two bilingual versions, marked as "ENGLISH/KOREAN" and "FRANCAIS/ENGLISH."[20] The English/Korean version of *TRAVELING* is somewhat different from its sibling, and in fact it's utterly different from the texts we've examined so far. The artists' Web inventory promises a single narrative in two languages (English and Korean), but audiences are presented instead, as I've suggested, with three narratives drawn from three languages (English, Korean, and French).[21] This is a fake translation or what we might call a *feint* translation: a text that promises one kind of comparison (between two versions of the same story) but in fact offers another (between three different stories, three different languages). *TRAVELING TO UTOPIA* evokes the print culture of interlineal translation and encourages viewers to consider the kinds of comparison that take place within—as well as between—literary texts.

The screenshot (figure 5.3) shows a Korean narrative at the top, an English narrative in the middle, and narrative that mixes French and English below. Since the effect of the feint translation requires both a specific language (Korean) and a specific group of readers (who don't read Korean), the work is in some ways difficult to render in new languages. Yet there are many elements in the visual display and in the narratives themselves that serve to convey the idea of feinting to a much larger group of readers. In the Korean narrative the speaker claims that the Internet has allowed him or her to choose his or her race, gender, and other physical traits. It reads: "I am a man. It hasn't always been like this, but thanks to technology I am now a man. Thank you so much God of digital technology. I am a white man. It hasn't always been like this, but thanks to technology I am now a white man. Thank you so much God of digital technology. I am a charming woman. It hasn't always. . . ."[22] The speaker goes on to thank the God of digital technology for making him or her attractive, no longer a loser, sexy, and hot. And then she or he says it all over again. The English text in the middle begins as an odd but harmless anecdote about a woman living abroad who learns to send faxes and, later, email to her family back home. As the technology develops, the narrative becomes a dystopian fiction about global positioning systems that invade and monitor our bodies without our consent. In a bizarre twist, the speaker finds that a Samsung microchip has been implanted in her stomach. She sets off the alarms at airport security and is thus unable to travel home, or to travel at all. At the bottom of the screen, the third narrative presents a counterpoint of fantasy and paranoia. A speaker reports that he has been stopped by the police while inserting his magnetic ticket at the entrance to the Seoul subway. This encounter with Korean officers triggers the narrator's memories of the Paris Metro and of the French officers who make a "mission," he says, out of intimidating undocumented aliens. Like the speaker in the middle narrative, the speaker in the third lives abroad, but he seems to know Korean. When the Seoul policeman speaks, he hears "a language that is foreign" but that he understands "only too well."

The story at the bottom is presented mostly in English, but it is punctuated by two untranslated French idioms. (The text presents them as untranslated by displaying them in a contrasting font.) Those phrases—*contrôle d'identité* and *délit de faciès*—appear to mark the limits of the narrative's translatability. They can be rendered in English, roughly, as "identity check" and "traveling while black." Because state officials use the language of identity both to thwart and to monitor circulation, these phrases function in the text mimetically as well as literally. That is, they are translatable because they mean, simply, exclusion. And they are untranslatable because they point to a history of racism whose exclusions are managed through a French hierarchy of color. The narrator uses these incomparable phrases to compare Korean and French methods and to suggest that belonging in both nations is rooted in an assumption of linguistic and physical homogeneity.

Visually, *TRAVELING TO UTOPIA* resembles the magnetic ticket of the third narrative. Many other technologies are also implied. An archaic cursor, a digital billboard, a television crawl, and cinema come immediately to mind. But the image of the ticket, stripes at top and bottom, invites us to consider that the artwork solicits as well as describes circulation. Traveling between three stories, two or three languages, and three media, we are asked to make comparisons among various materials, themes, and geographies. Young-Hae Chang Heavy Industries suggests that the refusal to do so, the refusal to approach born-translated works as artifacts that belong to several collectivities, limits our understanding of those works and supports a logic of possessive individualism. That logic favors exclusive models of citizenship, in which a person or an artwork is called upon to match unique characteristics that define and delimit the nation. That one might speak "a language that is foreign" or "travel while black" implies some language or some "color" that is natural both to citizenship and to literary history.

Furthermore, by equating "traveling" and "technology" in the title of the work, the artists ask us to consider together the digital media that circulate texts with the digital media that identify, supervise, and obstruct the circulation of their authors. By placing a comparison between Seoul and Paris policemen in the bottom narrative, *TRAVELING* alludes to the transnational history of metropolitan surveillance as well as to a substantial literary history of East–West comparison. In Chang and Voge's narrative, the direction of comparison has been reversed: cheerful fantasy is located in Paris while gritty realism resides in Seoul.[23] The work as a whole is critical of idealizations, both the effort to fix identities and the effort to evade them. The free-wheeling claims of the Korean-language narrative at the top are contradicted by its structural place in a comparison among several languages and by its diegetic counterpoint to narratives about surveillance and classification.

Since it is impossible to read the three narratives at the same time, we might say the work resists close reading or that it requires a more intensive version of it.[24] But actually I think it solicits both new strategies and new objects: new strategies, because most readers will be able to read closely only some parts of the text, and thus the work intimates a kind of closeness that is either partial or collaborative, and new objects, because readers are asked to consider larger units of text and to weigh the relationship among those units. It is the structure of the work that is most accessible, and indeed any engagement with the narratives apart from that structure risks missing the text's emphasis on dynamics of grouping. In *TRAVELING*, the three narratives are not distinct insofar as they all speak to technologies of circulation and surveillance, but they are not simply versions of the same story either. And of course the "ENGLISH/KOREAN" version is not, properly speaking, translated at all. Rather, it invites us to consider translation as a process of aggregation and comparison. If subtitling has tended to ossify national collectivities by suggesting that narratives begin in one language and are simply mirrored in another, the negation of subtitling insists on new ways of grouping both within texts and across them.

BUST DOWN THE DOOR!

FIGURE 5.6 Screenshot from Young-Hae Chang Heavy Industries, *Bust Down the Doors!* (English). Copyright: Young-Hae Chang Heavy Industries.

Source: www.yhchang.com. Accessed September 13, 2012.
Used by permission of the artists.

FROM THE WORD TO THE EPISODE

Chang and Voge's works are distinctive because they reflect on the political dynamics of translation while inviting and accommodating circulation into new languages. It is in this sense that they try to keep being translated. They solicit a readership that is large, heterogeneous, and indeterminate by eschewing bilingual puns and emphasizing formal and thematic aspects of literature that do not depend on a specific national language. But they also go out of their way to make proper names and vernacular phrases as accessible as possible. While many aspects of their work surely remind us of modernism, this is not one of them. Chang and Voge may invoke Pound and Beckett as literary role models, but their approach to colloquial language is rather more like Helen Fielding's than Gertrude Stein's.[25] The pair's works are full of idiolect, as Fielding's and Stein's and certainly Pound's are, but they offer context or parenthetical translation so that readers unfamiliar with local terminology will be able to follow along.

A reference to a street called Palpan-Dong in *DAKOTA* accompanies a discussion of the "Korean geishas" who hang out on the sidewalk below the authors' apartment. The beach Hae-oondae appears

TRETET DIE TÜR EIN!

FIGURE 5.7 Screenshot from Young-Hae Chang Heavy Industries, *Bust Down the Doors!* (German). Copyright: Young-Hae Chang Heavy Industries.

Source: www.yhchang.com. Accessed September 13, 2012.
Used by permission of the artists.

in the work *RIVIERA* alongside a reference to the "Korea straight's sea stink." The word "Ahjuma" in *SAMSUNG* is immediately followed by the explanation, "Korean for married woman." Literary allusions are treated casually rather than reverently, and this too aids translation. In *SAMSUNG*, the narrator declares, "Samsung, light of my life, fire in my loins." Versions in other languages reproduce this approximate but inexact quotation from Nabokov's *Lolita*.[26] References to "*amour*" in the English *SAMSUNG* are neatly rendered as "love" in the French, no matter that French signifies something different as a language of love than English does. Because they make vernacular terms accessible, because they do not fetishize the sound of language even when they are citing authors who do, and because they are happy to preserve approximations and even mistakes, the strategies of translatability featured in Chang and Voge's works really owe more to popular and middlebrow genre fiction than to the last century's experimental prose.

The best example of this debt comes in a work called *BUST DOWN THE DOORS!*, which exists in three single-language versions identified on the artists' Web page as "ENGLISH," "DEUTSCH," and "FRANCAIS." Unlike *HONEYMOON* or *TRAVELING*, which invoke the visual culture of translation and feature multiple languages within the text, *BUST* appears to be multilingual because it gathers several language-

ENFØNÇØNS LA PØRTE!

FIGURE 5.8 Screenshot from Young-Hae Chang Heavy Industries, *Bust Down the Doors!* (French). Copyright: Young-Hae Chang Heavy Industries.

Source: www.yhchang.com. Accessed September 13, 2012.
Used by permission of the artists.

versions under a single heading. The languages seem to be interchangeable and potentially infinite.

The portability implied by Chang and Voge's inventory is affirmed by the work's diction and story. There are almost no proper names and no vernacular phrases to worry over. The speaker refers at one point to a dream of sea breezes and "an unbearably sweet Bossa Nova," but the music is never played, and the Brazilian-born genre becomes, here as elsewhere, a catchall for globalized jazz. The English version of *BUST DOWN THE DOORS!* tells of a person or group of people—secret police, perhaps—who "bust open the door," drag "you" into the street, and prepare to shoot "you" in the head while neighbors shout, "kill the traitor!" Chang and Voge invoke this kind of authoritarian nightmare in many of their works, but in others they place their story in specific locations such as Seoul, Paris, and the U.S. border with Canada. *BUST DOWN THE DOORS!* lacks particularity, and thus the work seems both translatable and unconcerned with translation.

But this most translatable of texts possesses its own kind of multilingualism. It approaches the history and practice of translation not through foreign idioms or doubled images but through patterns of narrative repetition and comparison. These patterns operate at the level of episode or chapter. *BUST DOWN THE DOORS!* is

THEY BUST ∅PEN

FIGURE 5.9 Screenshot from Young-Hae Chang Heavy Industries, *Bust Down the Doors!* (English). Copyright: Young-Hae Chang Heavy Industries.

Source: www.yhchang.com. Accessed September 13, 2012.
Used by permission of the artists.

plural, as the title announces. When the first narrative comes to an end, the program loops back to the artists' title sequence. Once the second narrative begins, however, we see that several key pronouns have changed. The initial conceit, "they bust open the door and drag you out," becomes "you bust open the door and drag him out," which, in a third iteration, becomes "I bust open the door and drag her out."

Readers have to consider new actors, victims, and contexts. The work thus contains several stories. Or it contains several versions of the same story. Or it contains one story composed of several versions, each looped into the next. Comparing each version suggests not the universality of authoritarianism so much as its pervasiveness, its variety, and the incongruities among those varieties. We are asked to notice that a single word changes the meaning of the story; at the same time we are asked to notice that the structure trumps any one example. Put another way, the difference between "they," "you," and "I" is significant, but so is the fact of that difference. No single broken door tells the whole story. It is the potentially infinite series of "doors"—plural—that we are to consider.

BUST DOWN THE DOORS! is in this sense a work about near-simultaneous translation. Unlike all of Chang and Voge's other

YØU BUST ØPEN

FIGURE 5.10   Screenshot from Young-Hae Chang Heavy Industries, *Bust Down the Doors!* (English). Copyright: Young-Hae Chang Heavy Industries.

Source: www.yhchang.com. Accessed September 13, 2012.
Used by permission of the artists.

works, this one is constituted by various editions or copies, suggesting by analogy that we might understand the English, French, and German versions both individually and collectively, as translations of a unique text and as a multilingual conglomerate. If we take *BUST DOWN THE DOORS!* as an occasion to reflect on Chang and Voge's oeuvre, we can see that translation operates in several ways. Themes of translation are fundamental to Chang and Voge's project, but the artists also use translation to probe the nature of artworks as they circulate throughout the world. On the group's Web site and in compositions like this one, circulation is internal to production. Their works are thus better understood in terms of a future-oriented process than a completed or fixed object.[27] In *BUST DOWN THE DOORS!*, multilingualism functions as a property of the work and also as a property of the work's editions, translations, and copies.

Chang and Voge's approach to translation depends on their strategic use of digital media, which allows them to emphasize the complex interaction among aural, visual, and verbal systems. Because they serve as their own publishers and are not subject to the usual rules of copyright and cataloguing, they can superimpose multiple-

I BUST
ØPEN

FIGURE 5.11 Screenshot from Young-Hae Chang Heavy Industries, *Bust Down the Doors!* (English). Copyright: Young-Hae Chang Heavy Industries.

Source: www.yhchang.com. Accessed September 13, 2012.
Used by permission of the artists.

language editions and decline to distinguish among versions, either chronologically or legally. At the same time, by pointing at the history of literature and literary translation, they are making an argument that extends to analog works and to the strategies of analysis we bring to literature in many formats.

AGAINST INTERACTIVITY

Many viewers experience *BUST DOWN THE DOORS!* as a manifesto. The commanding title and the futurist pace of the animation certainly contribute to this effect. And so does the story of arrest and political assassination. Formally and thematically, the work calls us to action. But what kind of action? And how much?

As a story, *BUST DOWN THE DOORS!* suggests that the artful imagination can provide a fleeting but substantive refuge from state aggression. As a narrative, however, the singular dream of imaginative oasis (sea breezes, the sounds of bossa nova) is displaced by the accumulation and reversal of actors and victims. The persistent looping of the narrative, which the reader can turn off but can't slow down, aligns the digital work with anonymous power rather than with the individual's exception to that power. The piece may seem to call for action but, in dramatic ways, it forestalls action, especially interaction.

To pursue this observation further, we need to return both to the history of digital media and to the history of modernism. Hypertext and interactivity have been hallmarks of electronic literature. Viewers of digital art expect to do something as well as see something. Early digital artists used electronic links and embedded options to transfer control of the text from creator to reader and to distribute control by making readers into creators. When supporters of digital culture point to the radical differences between digital and analog production, as they often do, they single out interactivity as a distinct characteristic of digital art. Supporters celebrate digital culture's capacity for decentered agency, global access, and what Mark Poster has called "the detachment of the body from its location in space."[28] Poster has written enthusiastically of "global media culture," which he says "[violates] assumptions about center and periphery, North and South, First and Third Worlds, Western and non-Western, imperial and subaltern, colonizer and colonized."[29] George Landow, one of the first scholars of early electronic literature, argues that democratic principles are inherent to the form of interactive writing.[30] He claims that hypertext, with its branches and links, possesses an "essential multivocality, decentering, and redefinition of edges."[31] Digital culture's supporters assume its pervasive translatability and support for translatability: the way it allows people and ideas to travel, the way it allows consumers to become producers, and the way it transcends politics, nations, and the borders of race, class, and gender.

Unlike many born-digital artists, Chang and Voge don't urge their readers to become producers, and they don't suggest that digital technology frees people from bodies or allows people to evade the experience of bodies. MORNING OF THE MONGOLOIDS and TRAVELING TO UTOPIA explicitly reject this notion, make fun of it, and offer in its place fantastic narratives of digital embodiment. Chang and Voge refuse the kind of interactivity we have come to associate with hypertext links and social networking. They take advantage of Flash Player's relative accessibility and its capacity for multimedia animation. But they offer readers very little choice beyond the Web page inventory, and they don't encourage readers to view themselves as makers. Instead, they use their works to explore the contraction of agency. We can understand this in at least two ways. As digital media scholars have argued, the resistance to interactivity can be seen as a claim for literariness, difficulty, autonomy, and cultural capital.[32] In this light, Chang and Voge are expanding their own agency while contracting the agency of their audience.

However, if we place the European history of modernism in conversation with the transpacific history of heavy industries, the turn away from interactivity looks less like a story about authors than like a story about institutions. Chang and Voge preserve the experience of coercion, which they associate with the corporate origins of digital technology. Responding to an interviewer's question about interactivity, Chang and Voge remark that "societal strictures and problems without evident solutions . . . inspire our longings and musings."[33] In a general way, they want to deflate the ambitions of the digital consumer who views technology as a source of self-fashioning and self-extension. They share David Golumbia's sense that there has been "uncritical enthusiasm for computers" and a romanticization of interactivity, which in its limited agency distracts us from the much more substantive agency of governments and corporations.[34] Chang and Voge suggest, in addition, that digital technologies in Korea, which are widely accessible but highly supervised, have developed hand in hand with antidemocratic social policies and the expansion of state-sponsored surveillance. Corporations and states, their works propose, have been both the principal engines and the principal beneficiaries of digital innovation.

By focusing attention on the authoritarian uses of digital media, Chang and Voge both indulge in the dream of autonomy and emphasize the fictiveness of that dream. By refusing interactivity, they modestly extend their own autonomy by exerting greater control over the distribution of their works. They also reflect on the limits of autonomy for any work. But there is also a more positive way to understand their insistence on the semiaccessible text. Without the unpredictability of branching and linking, they are able to preserve causality and characterization. Interactive art, as Landow has remarked, is fundamentally inhospitable to narrative.[35] In addition, it is inhospitable to an expansive readership that is imagined as collective as well as large. The interactive text, Landow explains, "conceives of its audience, unlike that of cinema, as an audience of one" because each reader creates a new object in the act of consuming it.[36] To be sure, all digital works can be understood as unique objects. They have to be viewed or "run" on individual computers that vary in speed, memory, screen size, software, and quality. Chang and Voge draw attention to those variables by pointing at the materiality of digital production such as cursors, fonts, and flashes. But by privileging theme, plot, and episode, the artists ensure that some aspects of their works are relatively impervious to translation across devices as well as languages. This imperviousness allows them to solicit many readers and to produce narratives of migration that can survive global circulation. To survive global circulation is not necessarily to ignore it. Chang and Voge's call to action is thus perhaps best understood as a call to compare. Their works present readers with more languages, editions, narratives, episodes, and media than they can possibly absorb. Instead of choosing among versions or making new ones, readers are asked to consider the practices of translation that have distinguished works in the past and to imagine new practices, new arrangements in the future.

TRANSLATION'S FUTURES

Young-Hae Chang Heavy Industries collates a literary history of the twentieth century in which translation and translators play a central role. Pound, Beckett, Borges, and Nabokov composed and adapted their works in multiple languages, and all produced important works as translators as well as authors. Like Beckett and Nabokov, Chang and Voge practice self-translation; and like them, they treat the translated versions as new productions rather than as derivations. Yet, for Chang and Voge, the value of the translation does not depend on uniqueness. That is, while Beckett insisted that rendering *En Attendant Godot* in English involved writing a completely new play, Chang and Voge take a page from Borges, suggesting that translations are part of the work, that they remake the work, or that they are indistinguishable from it.

Because they suggest that translation is integral to production, Chang and Voge are altering the politics as well as the practice of translation. While Pound and other Anglo-American modernists encouraged translation into English, most were far less interested in the circulation of their own works beyond English. Pound translated in order to enrich anglophone literary culture, but Chang and Voge often demote English by concealing or removing the distinction between original and target languages. This is not to say that English is not central to their creations and to the production and circulation of those creations. English is the principal language of the Web site, and it appears at some point in most of their work. But Chang and Voge emphasize the regional and political histories in which languages function. By amplifying themes of translation and non-translation, they make languages less neutral, and in this sense they register the inequality of languages, including the inequality that functions within their own works. Pound's commitment to incorporating multiple languages and multiple vernaculars led to a multilingualism with English at its center.[37] Narrating translation and muting idiolect, Chang and Voge make Pound's dream of multilingualism function multilingually. They create works not only for English literary history but also for the many other literary histories in which their works travel and in which they begin.

Chang and Voge's renovation of literary modernism is perhaps nowhere more visible than in their approach to generalizations about Asia. Whereas Pound imagined that Chinese characters functioned literally rather than semiotically—that they visually resembled or embodied what they named—Chang and Voge use multiple layers of translation to deactivate associations between language and culture and to critique fantasies of authenticity and unmediated knowledge.[38] *MORNING OF THE MONGOLOIDS* reverses rather than replaces stereotype: it generalizes about white metropolitan racists and declines to represent Korean speech directly. Instead of fantasies of the Orient, *TRAVELING TO UTOPIA* offers us a fantasy of French pluralism and then goes out of its way to point out the fallacy of pitting French liberty against Korean constraint. Chang and Voge resist national synecdoche—the association of physical or linguistic characteristics with a single collectivity—by creating parts or versions of works that cannot be allocated neatly or placed within coherent wholes. A final thought about synecdoche: it would be difficult to anthologize Chang and Voge's works in any strict collection of Korean writing, women's writing, or even global anglophone writing. The works fit uneasily into categories of this sort. They also clash with an additive model of world writing in which expansion includes everything, and on the same terms.

The works of Young-Hae Chang Heavy Industries route the future of world literature through the history and technology of translation. There are many differences between digital and print media, but in this chapter I emphasize some of the formal, political, and literary continuities. Chang and Voge's digital artworks share many of the born-translated qualities I have discussed in prior chapters. They emphasize the relationship between language and citizenship. They explore technologies of reproduction. They incorporate visual and verbal cultures of translation. And they use global circulation as an opportunity to generate new models of literary and political belonging.

PRINT AFTER DIGITAL

Claiming that digital art is "the opposite of digital media," Young-Hae Chang Heavy Industries responds to the celebration of freewheeling circulation by emphasizing the embodiment of users, the constraints of the medium, and the impediments to circulation.[39] Writers in print, too, have begun to push back against the apparent disembodiment and effortless flow of digital production. This has led to the development of what N. Katherine Hayles and Jessica Pressman have termed "an aesthetic of bookishness."[40] To be sure, most books in print are indebted to digital production, circulation, and reception, whether we're speaking of the microprocessors with which books are composed, the online retailers that distribute those books, or the digital readers and listening devices used to consume them. Digital production has also shaped the themes and forms of the novel, as we see in the integration of email, instant messaging, viruses, and blogs. But "bookish" books are post-digital in a different way. They call attention to the properties of bound paper and ask readers to do more, in fact, than read. Readers have to become handlers and viewers, and indeed these works force readers to establish the text rather than to assume it. For example, in Jonathan Safran Foer's *Tree of Codes* (2010), whose physical properties Hayles has catalogued and analyzed, sentences are not always legible since each page features holes—actual cutouts—that display words and phrases from subsequent pages.[41] Which words are we meant to be reading? And in what order? Salvador Plascencia's *The People of Paper* (2005), another "bookish" book, obscures words with inkblots and scratchings; it also makes use of simultaneous narrators whose stories are printed in side-by-side vertical columns.[42] Adam Thirlwell's *Kapow!* (2012) places some of its text at angles, forcing readers to interrupt one narrative, rotate the book, and engage with a tangential narrative or metafictional comment; sometimes, the text runs off one page onto additional pages, which have to be unfolded.[43] Because they require turning, folding, and peering through, these books seem to be the very opposite of digital art. They are designed to be inhospitable toward electronic distribution. They are lavishly attuned to the resources of paper. They achieve their "narrative complexity," as Hayles puts it, not only from "the semantic register of words" but also from the "physical forms" in which those words are presented.[44] However, all of these works make use of digital technology at some point. It is difficult to imagine producing a work such as Foer's without the resources of word and image processing software.

There is also some common cause between Chang and Voge's born-digital project and today's post-digital artworks. They share a commitment to staging and to some extent interrupting the global circulation of literature. They treat editing, translating, reprinting, and curating as species of making. They incorporate circulation within production while also drawing attention to circulation's histories, practices, and futures. Plascencia writes a Chicano novel that worries about the commodification of Chicano novels.[45] Thirlwell's *Delighted States* (2007), which also features upside-down text and metafictional commentary, traces the history of its topic—translation and the novel—by

including title pages and excerpts from prior novels as well as a translation of a self-translated story by Vladimir Nabokov.[46] The subtitle of
Thirlwell's work tells readers that they are holding a book "of novels,
romances, & their unknown translators, containing ten languages,
set on four continents." Nodding to the lengthy titles of eighteenth-
century fiction, *The Delighted States* encourages readers to imagine
that they are visiting, or perhaps even occupying, an era of unsettled
vernaculars, promiscuous reprinting, and transitional genres. Thirlwell's book celebrates paper by sampling, in photocopied images, the
history of fiction in print. Foer's *Tree of Codes* is an unusual case since
the book involves the cutting down rather than building up of a prior
work. This is so in the most explicit way. Foer has taken the pages of
Bruno Schulz's 1934 collection of short stories, *The Street of Crocodiles*,
and removed about 90 percent of its text as well as several letters from
its title, making his own shorter work, *Tree of Codes*.[47] Foer's work is
"bookish" because his creative agency (cutting) was inspired by an
edition made of paper and because he uses the paper of his own edition to create gaps or blank presences that are crucial to his narrative.

However, for all its memorialization of a past text and the texts that
Schulz, murdered by a Gestapo officer in 1942, did not have a chance
to circulate or write, *Tree of Codes* also erases its debts to prior books
and intervening geographies. The book that Foer has cut down is
not—or not only—Bruno Schulz's 1934 collection. Foer's book has
been published in English. Schulz wrote in Polish. Foer has cut down,
in fact, Celina Wieniewska's English translation of Schulz's collection, first published in 1963 and reprinted several times in a paperback edition issued in the United States by Penguin.[48] *Tree of Codes*
is a tribute to the resources of paper. It aspires to stimulate readers'
awareness of bodies: the text's, the author's, and their own. It is a
record of Foer's reading across time and place. The physical depth of
the pages registers the trace of other pages, which Foer's later work
replaces and also honors. A note from the publisher supports this formulation by describing *Tree of Codes* as a "new story" that was "cut"
from "an English language edition" of Schulz's work (4). This is the
book's only reference to multiple editions, and nowhere in the text or
paratext—not even in Foer's afterword, entitled "This Book and the
Book"—does the name of the translator or the language of composi-

tion appear. So, while Foer's project may emphasize the production, materiality, and history of "the book" in some substantial ways, it occludes the production, materiality, and history of the book in translation. Put another way, whereas *Tree of Codes* was made by hands in Poland (Schulz), the United Kingdom (Wieniewska), the Netherlands (die-cutting and binding), Belgium (printing), and the United States (publishing; Foer), Foer attributes the work to a much more local and more limited collaboration: his private encounter with Schulz's writing (139). Making the translator and the process of translation nearly invisible, *Tree of Codes* omits the itinerary of Schulz's stories, implying that the book began in English and that it offers access, however mediated through gaps and holes, to an original work (Schulz's text), a single time (1934, the era of the Third Reich), a definitive place (Drohobycz, in what is now Poland), and a simultaneous collective (animated by the common experience of absence). Foer remembers Schulz, but, like most anglophone writers, he forgets about Polish, and thus he allows his readers to forget about Polish, too.

While it might seem perverse to call Chang and Voge's project "bookish" since their works are not produced on paper, there is something purposefully old fashioned about their emphasis on the bodies of readers, authors, and texts and their reluctance to engage in a celebration of universal mobility.[49] Unlike Foer, Chang and Voge register the friction of medium while also acknowledging the friction of language and geography. They present their works as a disaggregate corporation rather than a unified corpus. *HONEYMOON IN BEPPU* and *TRAVELING TO UTOPIA* can't be mass produced in any medium or language. They are not born universal. Instead, they are born collective: they identify translation as a source of production and as a drag on simultaneous reading. Their works try to represent that drag. Thinking about the post-digital in the light of the born digital, we might say that Plascencia and Thirlwell are bookish not because they generate singular works but because they know that they don't. Like Young-Hae Chang Heavy Industries, they aim to keep being translated.

EPILOGUE

MULTIPLES

A viewing, a reading, a rendering has to be /
a translation of what's there into what it's like that it's there. /
Nothing exists without translation.

—"Manifesto of the New Translation"

MOST OF the works I discuss in this book negotiate the translation pathways of multinational publishing. But many of the most significant works of born-digital and post-digital fiction have been nurtured and first published by independent Web sites and small coterie presses. The works of Young-Hae Chang Heavy Industries are presented, as they often announce, by Young-Hae Chang Heavy Industries, founded in 1999. Jonathan Safran Foer's *Tree of Codes* and Adam Thirlwell's *Kapow!* were released by Visual Editions in London, an independent book publisher founded in 2010.[1] Salvador Plascencia's *The People of Paper* was first published by the books division of McSweeney's, the San Francisco–based company that also publishes the periodical *McSweeney's Quarterly*, edited by Dave Eggers.[2] McSweeney's was founded in 1998. The born digital and the post-digital may seem like parallel but separate developments, but that's not really the case. The new coterie presses, for all their interest in exploiting the visual and sensory experience of paper, have also produced born-digital works. This is true for Visual Editions, which has designed, in both paper and digital formats, medium-specific, even medium-distinctive editions of a single book.[3]

Like Young-Hae Chang Heavy Industries, for which collaboration is both process and product, the independent publishers that support born-translated works are interested in the event as well as the outcome of producing art collectively. Indeed, this is one of the ways that contemporary literature incorporates circulation: it is social from the start; or, better, it makes sociability into a feature of content.[4] For example, McSweeney's books and periodicals go out of their way to build design into the conception of the work: the objects that readers hold in their hands are not simply containers for a verbal or two-dimensional text. Writers and designers are co-producers, rather than actors in sequence. This collaboration plays out in the work because, for readers, it is no longer clear which part serves as illustration or format and which as message or story. Even the words themselves, presented colorfully and dynamically on the page, seem to be visually as well as verbally expressive. These collaborative works are not blocking or diminishing the agency of producers so much as they are presenting agency as a social rather than a sovereign phenomenon.

The independent presses also emphasize collaboration through their approach to translation. "Manifesto of the New Translation," produced by the Brooklyn-based poets and publishers Sharmila Cohen and Paul Legault, treats rewriting, homage, and adaptation as methods of translation, and indeed translation as a method of rewriting.[5] Cohen and Legault's manifesto argues that an artwork enters the world through translation because only through translation do we know "what it's like that it's there." This is not simply a phenomenological argument, in which the work exists because someone is there to interpret it. Rather, it is an argument about history and comparison, in which the work has meaning because we place it alongside other works and other languages; we give it history and form by claiming it for the present. Cohen and Legault's project corresponds to one of the central tenets of book history, Pierre Bourdieu and Roger Chartier's claim that "a book changes by the fact that it remains changeless while the world changes."[6] Bourdieu and Chartier are not discounting transformations in technology and format. Rather, they are noting that new "reading modes" alter both approaches to the object and what counts as the object itself.

Cohen and Legault are the founders of a Web site, a journal, and a publishing venture called Telephone Books. Their manifesto appears on the Web site http://distranslation.com. Telephone Books shares many characteristics with McSweeney's, including a penchant for literary production that combines as well as crosses media. There is also a professional connection: McSweeney's published Legault's book *The Emily Dickinson Reader: An English-to-English Translation of Emily Dickinson's Complete Poems* in 2012.[7] Committed to "works of radical translation," Telephone Books has published one edition: the anthology *The Sonnets: Translating and Rewriting Shakespeare*, also released in 2012.[8] Like the *Dickinson Reader*, *The Sonnets* consists of English-language adaptations of English-language works, in this case translations and rewritings based on an unauthorized edition of Shakespeare's *Sonnets*.[9] Whereas in the *Dickinson Reader* Legault produces his own adaptations of Dickinson's poems, in *The Sonnets* he and Cohen invite 154 "poet-translators" to rewrite Shakespeare.[10] As the editors point out in the anthology's introduction, their poet-translators are pirating a piracy.[11]

It may seem all too conventional or all too clever to produce "English-to-English" translations, but that venture is in many ways continuous with the project of interlingual translation that Cohen and Legault have sponsored through the three extant issues of their journal *Telephone*.[12] Translating within English, they imply, serves to provincialize English in ways that complement and also modify the practice of translation between English and other languages.[13] In the journal issues, published in paper and digital formats in 2010 and 2011, several poet-translators working in English were invited to translate several poems by writers working in other languages. The translations are serial: each poem always appears in several English-language versions. The first two issues focus on younger contemporary poets, presenting multilingual German poems by Uljana Wolf (b. 1979) in the fall 2010 issue and French poems written collaboratively by Renée Gagnon (b. 1978) and Steve Savage (b. 1970) in the spring 2011 issue. The third issue, published in the fall of 2011, rewrites works by the distinguished Portuguese-language poet Augusto de Campos (b. 1931), one of the founders of the Brazilian concrete poetry movement. The serial element of each issue is significant: each poem can be compared across languages and also within languages, and creativity across genre is encouraged. Indeed, concrete poetry's emphasis on the physical and typographical expressivity of words, what shapes and meanings they can make when they no longer hew to standard lineation, seems to influence *Telephone*'s project well beyond the issue committed to de Campos. The journal serves not only to introduce German, French, and Portuguese works to English readers but also to introduce the varieties of English and English-language interpretation that these non-English works inspire. It is not simply a matter of moving between separate literature traditions but of the convergences and divergences that appear when literatures are brought into contact.

By calling their journal *Telephone*, Cohen and Legault allude to the children's game in which the circulation of a story, whispered from one person to the next, leads to the story's extravagant, often nonsensical transformation. In that game the transformation is part of the entertainment and part of the point. Cohen and Legault's *Telephone* involves transformations that are more intentional and less mediated (each translator works from the original), but their title retains the game's premise, that literary circulation is both social and unpredictable. They make production social and unpredictable too. They mean for the journal to serve "as a home for foreign poetry, as a tool for developing new work, and as an experiment in translation." Multiple translations complement interlingual translation by demonstrating, through many versions, the richness and openness of what the original is "like."

Cohen and Legault are nourishing avant-garde poetry and introducing "foreign poetry" to English-language readers. That's their remit. But it is notable that their approach to the translation of poetry depends on strategies of comparison, dilation, and exegesis that we more commonly associate with narrative or visual art. In this light, their interest in concrete poetry is telling, since the visual formatting of words and lines (think here of Bolaño's fictional poem discussed in the introduction) is one of the ways that poetry makes itself portable. At the risk of overstatement, we might say that the closer poetry comes to the novel, the closer it comes to translatability. Engaging with format and medium, then, Cohen and Legault are in conversation with fiction. But they are also in conversation with fiction by way of philosophy. Their approach to translation as a source of literary production and as an opportunity to rebalance, however incrementally, the flow of literary trade is shared by digital periodicals that are committed to translating a range of genres.

One such periodical is the international quarterly *Asymptote*, which debuted online in 2011. According to the Web site, www.asymptotejournal.com, they have featured work from fifty-four languages and seventy-five countries.[14] *Asymptote*'s geometric name is meant to convey the approximate nature of all translations (never reaching the original), the creative act of translation (making its own line), and the more abstract postulate that "all texts . . . are approaching fundamental truths that we attempt to express through language."[15] The editors write that they are "interested in encounters between languages and the consequences of these encounters."[16] While most of their "encounters" involve English as the target language, sometimes the journal translates works into other global language such as Spanish and Chinese. They are engaged in two kinds of rebalancing: encouraging English-language readers to become acquainted with literature composed in other languages and developing alternative pathways that do not address English at all. Another more established digital periodical is *Words Without Borders*, launched in 2003, whose title lends humanitarian purchase ("cultural understanding") to the project of literary translation from many world languages into English.[17] Like *Asymptote*, *Words Without Borders* provides an international platform for non-English literature, but *Asymptote* differs in two important respects: it prints originals and translations together; and, by including essays from the translators, it presents readers with competing histories and practices of translation. In these ways, *Asymptote* shares with many born-translated novels a commitment to probing translation while also facilitating it.

Asymptote and *Telephone* emphasize serial production and comparison: serial production, because readers are presented with multiple versions, which sometimes include multiple translations; and comparison, because those versions are bound together, as it were, by facing-page or linked-page formatting. To be sure, there are printed books that offer multiple versions and translations of a single work. University presses sometimes release translations of poetry in facing-page format, and there is the impressive *Multilingual Anthology of American Literature*, which presents all of its entries in English as well as in the original.[18] There are also rare projects, such as *19 Ways of Looking at Wang Wei*, a collection of translations and transliterations of a seventeenth-century version of an eighth-century poem by Wang Wei. No original "way" is presented in the book: the first three "ways" are versions of the Chinese; two "ways" are versions in French and Spanish; and fourteen others are versions in English. First produced by Asphodel Press, out of Kingston, Rhode Island, *19 Ways* is another small-scale project, though it has been presented by the eminent translator Eliot Weinberger and the Nobel poet Octavio Paz.

Serial and comparative translations are certainly easier in the digital medium, where extra pages do not generate extra shipping costs. For *Asymptote* and *Telephone*, comparative formats are crucial because they dramatize intralingual variation and nurture the relative fluencies of readers across languages. Suggesting that differences between languages have to be modified by differences within languages, these journals exchange an ethics of translation based on foreignness, one language distinct from the other, for an ethics of translation based on convergence, one approach to a language interpreting one approach to another. Instead of relying on target languages to register the history of translation, the relationship among versions, and the collaboration among makers, the journals rely on format and design. They narrate translation's histories rather than describe them. Whereas *Asymptote* and *Telephone* both function as hosts, *Telephone* also functions as curator in the sense of providing a space that inspires new content and creating the framework that makes new content accessible to readers. Since the editors of *Telephone* seek out foreign-language poetry that has integrated translation in semantic or visual ways, the journal is both a conduit for and an example of born-translated literature.[19]

Young-Hae Chang Heavy Industries, *Telephone*, *Asymptote*, and *Words Without Borders* are creating new pathways for translation through nonprofit digital publishing. Producing (mostly) editions in paper, Telephone Books, McSweeney's, and Visual Editions also operate relatively independently of the largest publishing conglomerates. Their works stage and often jettison the norms of trade production such as standard book sizing, regular margins, consistent typography, and monochrome printing. Periodicals such as *Asymptote* and

Telephone and books such as *Tree of Codes*, *The Sonnets*, and *The Emily Dickinson Reader* highlight an essential feature of the large-scale publishing business: the separation of original from derivation; writing from rewriting, adapting, and translating. These magazines and books highlight this feature by making literature out of it: the *Reader* is a collection of Emily Dickinson's poems (reader as anthology) and also a record, in poems, of the experience of one reader (reader as one who has viewed or interpreted). The title names the anthology and the experience of a prior anthology at the same time.

Perhaps the most striking recent example of a born-translated work produced by a small-scale publisher is Thirlwell's insouciant anthology, "Multiples," which was released in 2013, first in the United States as a special issue of *McSweeney's Quarterly Concern* and later in the United Kingdom as a clothbound book by the independent press *Portobello Books* (which also publishes the distinguished literary journal *Granta*).[20] The covers of "Multiples" tell you much of what you need to know: "twelve stories appearing in up to six versions each" (U.S.) and "12 stories in 18 languages by 61 authors" (U.K.). The book appears in twelve sections. The first eleven sections contain a series of translations, each based on a preceding version, though the initial version—the original story—is not reprinted. Each series involves several English translations as well as translations between English and other languages. The final section contains a single translation, from Italian into English, attributed to Thirlwell, who does not speak Italian, and the Italian novelist Francesco Pacifico, who is also the translator of an earlier story from English into Italian. The collection's many translators are established and sometimes eminent international writers. Some, such as Lydia Davis and J. M. Coetzee, are also eminent translators, whereas Zadie Smith seems to be a first-timer. Both editions offer facing-page translation as well as illustrations, short essays about the process of translation, and sometimes footnotes and suggestions for further reading. However, in the *McSweeney's* version, "Multiples" is also physically irregular: the issue is printed in a large, horizontal format, and its pages, which feature a mixture of red and black type, are bound by several half-covers of different lengths.

Thirlwell's anthology is an experiment in translation. It asks what happens when a work of literature moves, serially, from one language to the next, and it also asks what happens when translators are urged to write rather than to rewrite. To encourage writing, Thirlwell has gone out of his way to include among his translators, called "authors" on the book's covers, those who are not "uniformly fluent" in the original languages (4). But how shall they write? One answer is provided by the illustrations. The anthology's U.S. edition is covered—several times, since there are six covers, including back and front—by images of telephones. Not one telephone, mind you. Or even several versions of the same kind of telephone. Rather, what readers see on the covers are many different genres of telephone—a push-button handset attached to a long, tangled cord; a flip phone with monochrome screen; an analog ear-and-mouthpiece whose wire extends beyond the end of the page; and so on—all of which correspond to historical eras prior to the one in which the book has been published. There's not a smartphone among them. Anachronistic and various, the images suggest, first, that there is no single technology of transmission and, second, that even the game of telephone has a history. Thirlwell encourages his contributors to invent, but invention turns out to be a profoundly social project.

Like *Telephone*, "Multiples" is deliberately uncountable. The volume appears to be an anthology, but it is hard to say how many flowers have been gathered. The titles promise "twelve stories," but the first originals—the stories—aren't present at all. From the perspective of its readers, there are sixty-one stories because there are sixty-one author-translators. However, from the perspective of each translator, there is only one story, though it is never the same one for any two participants. So perhaps "twelve stories" are present after all, but there is no single aggregation. Indeed, it is difficult to imagine the anthology's intended reader since it will be a rare reader indeed who can compare every contribution. Encouraging collaborative reception as well as collaborative writing, Thirlwell conceives of his project as a "throwback to the modernist days of multilingual magazines" (6). But "Multiples" is contemporary in at least two ways: in its incorporation of languages beyond Europe and the United States and of scripts beyond Roman, and in its effort to displace the one original, many translations model that is featured in most histories of translation. Instead of multiple translations of a single work, Thirlwell makes each installment function both as translation and as original. He forces readers to confront various languages on the page, including several non-European languages such as Chinese, Hebrew, and Urdu. And he reverses the usual order of global circulation, bringing many more works into English than he has sent out into other languages. The twelve original works, whose titles appear in their first languages, are from Danish, Spanish, Dutch, Japanese, German, Arabic, Russian, Serbo-Croat, Italian (2), Hungarian, and English.

While Thirlwell invokes the history of modernist translation, his project differs substantially from the engagement with modernism we see in many multilingual novels. Unlike Junot Díaz's fiction, Thirlwell's anthology treats natural languages as single units. For example, the Spanish of Barcelona-based Enrique Vila-Matas, the author of one of the unprinted originals, is undifferentiated from the Spanish of the Chilean-based Alejandro Zambra, who translates an English version of a story by Franz Kafka. The many versions of English and French also go unremarked, though the translators hail from different regions, nations, and continents. How many multiples is that? Like Ben Lerner's fiction, Thirlwell's project blocks access to the original language, but, unlike Lerner, he treats all languages equally: no one language is more ripe for blocking or deflating than any other. Thirlwell promotes, above all, universal domestication. In his utopia, "literature will become the pure international—oblivious to the problems of time and space—and somehow the language in which you write or read your literature will be less important than the singular, multiple structures those languages happen to form" (8). Thirlwell hopes that someday the territorial, political, and social differences among languages will no longer matter.

Thirlwell's ground rules for translators reflect this aspiration. Here are two. No translator is allowed to see the version prior to the one she is translating or to know anything about the first author or text. All translators are encouraged to take liberties and to produce a work they could have written. One of the contributors compares the project to some complex Oulipo conceit, and that seems right (95). Despite the collaborative format, Thirlwell's vision seems ascendant. However, the work as it has been published contains historicizing practices, commentaries, and illustrations that operate in tension with the editor's formalizing impulses. Thirlwell acknowledges this tension when he reflects that his book has become "an anthology and a notebook, at the same time" (6). Among the historicizing practices are Lydia Davis's instance on including footnotes that allow her to retain the Dutch locations of the original and her use of a Dutch collaborator to help with idiom and syntax (93). David Mitchell honors the original Japanese by including a list of supplementary texts for readers eager to learn more about the Japanese author (134). Nadeem Aslam, who translates one of the stories from English into Urdu, includes a longish essay about the political charge of that transaction (135–36). His comment, "I vote every time I write a sentence," is particularly memorable (136). Francesco Pacifico produces his translation from English into Italian by imitating the diction of previous English-to-Italian translations (206). Other writers perform their refusal to create new originals by interrupting their own voice with other voices, in one case with the voice of photographs, and in another, with Twitter-generated alternatives to the initial translated ending. A. S. Byatt, perhaps the most recalcitrant, utterly rejects Thirlwell's premises, arguing that a translation should be "adding nothing and subtracting nothing" (351–52).

Emphasizing the translator's invention, Thirlwell's book asks readers to hear new words rather than to hear how they have circulated. Yet the structure of the book, with its interruptions and paratexts and multiple translations, pulls in the other direction. "Multiples" is an interesting and timely volume for the way it testifies to the uneasiness and conflict that is part of world literature's ongoing development. Thirlwell may imagine his anthology as a throwback to modernism, but he's interested in only one side of that legacy: he wants translation without the history of translation.

Why should readers encounter the history of translation? Cohen and Legault's "Manifesto of the New Translation" suggests that translation augments the work of art by assessing its reception. The history of translation would be a history of those assessments across time and place, and a history of the differences that time and place have made: "what it's like" now and here, and what it has been like then and there. This principle finds its complement in a comment made by the translator and scholar Catherine Porter, who claims that "to know any language in its intricacy is at some point to translate it and to translate into it."[21] Intricate knowledge, Porter suggests, involves knowing more—and also knowing less. Speaking as president of the Modern Language Association, Porter argues that Americans should learn additional languages and read literatures in translation because knowing "English is not enough" even for knowing English.[22] When Porter claims that the economic and political might of the United States is being compromised by monolingualism, she suggests that Americans need to learn other languages in order to preserve their access to the world.[23] However, when she argues that bilingualism not only increases a language user's expressive range but also makes apparent the limits of that range, she suggests that Americans should learn additional languages as a way of becoming more knowledgeable, but less knowing.[24] Additionally, she suggests that an intricate understanding of language requires an understanding of the historical and cultural contexts that shape what that language expresses well, and what it doesn't.

This kind of argument, that English-only users should give up dominance in order to acquire worldliness, matches the ethical project of many born-translated novels. These works use facing-page translation, serial translation, minor-to-major translation, diegetic translation, and English-to-English translation as ways of imagining other literary histories and other audiences. Born-translated fiction in English asks readers to *unforget* those audiences. This means learning new languages. It also means engaging with English as a medium of circulation while learning about the history and future of that medium. Making circulation the basis for contemporary anglophone production, born-translated novels place English in the world. They stake their claim to originality not by asserting uniqueness but by sharing it. While entering new languages and new versions of language, these works also trace the paths of translation. In this way they ask us to think about how, rather than where, novels belong.

NOTES

INTRODUCTION

1. And this is true at the level of composition, too. N. Katherine Hayles has argued that "print books are now so interpenetrated with digital media at every stage of their production that they may more appropriately be considered an output form of digital texts than a separate medium." N. Katherine Hayles, "Combining Close Reading and Distant Reading: Jonathan Safran Foer's *Tree of Codes* and the Aesthetic of Bookishness," *PMLA* 128, no. 1 (2013): 226.

2. The study of audio books is an emerging field. In 2012 James English taught an undergraduate course devoted to listening rather than reading novels. The first full-length study of the phenomenon is Mikko Keskinen, *Audio Book: Essays on Sound Technologies in Narrative* Fiction (Lanham, MD: Lexington Books, 2008). Focusing on novels in which accent or sound is part of the story, Christopher Pizzino and Sydney Bufkin have shown how audiobook versions of novels have differed remarkably from print versions. Christopher Pizzino, "Alien Stereo: China Miéville's *Embassytown*," presentation at the Annual Conference of the Modern Language Association, Chicago, IL, January 9–12, 2014; and Sydney Bufkin, "'Fully Fleshed out and Filled with Emotion': Accent, Region, and Identification in the Reception of *The Help*," presentation at the Annual Conference of the Modern Language Association, Chicago, IL, January 9–12, 2014.

3. Franco Moretti, *Atlas of the European Novel, 1800–1900* (London: Verso, 1998), 171–73.

4. Isabel Hofmeyr, *The Portable Bunyan: A Transnational History of the Pilgrim's Progress* (Princeton, NJ: Princeton University Press, 2004), 240–43.

5. Martin Puchner, *Poetry of the Revolution: Marx, Manifestos, and the Avant-Gardes* (Princeton, NJ: Princeton University Press, 2006), 62–65.

6. Moretti, *Atlas of the European Novel*, 176. *Uncle Tom's Cabin*, first published as a book in 1852, was part of this phenomenon, too. The U.S. periodical *Putman's Monthly* estimates there were "thirty different editions published in London, within six months of the publication of the work here," "four rival editions" in Paris, and two in Italy. Charles Frederick Briggs, "Uncle Tomitudes," *Putnam's Monthly* 1 (January 1853): 99. Meredith McGill argues that the international translation and reprinting of *Uncle Tom's Cabin* was instrumental in convincing U.S. publishers to support an international copyright treaty with Britain. Meredith McGill, *American Literature and the Culture of Reprinting* (Philadelphia: University of Pennsylvania Press, 2003), 270–77.

7. Bethany Wiggin, *Novel Translations: The European Novel and the German Book, 1680–1730* (Ithaca, NY: Cornell University Press, 2011), esp. 185–205.

8. The fascinating story of *Robinson Crusoe*'s appearance and circulation in Japan is told in Jonathan Zwicker, "Japan, 1850–1900," in *Novel*, vol. 1, *History, Geography, and Culture*, ed. Franco Moretti, 509–20 (Princeton, NJ: Princeton University Press, 2006).

9. Of the top twenty-five translated authors listed in UNESCO's "Index Translationum," twenty-two are novelists or writers of fiction. The others are Vladimir Lenin, Pope John Paul II, and Shakespeare, accessed February 28, 2014, http://portal.unesco.org/culture/en/ev.php-URL_ID=7810&URL_DO=DO_TOPIC&URL_SECTION=201.html.

10. Rowling's sixth "Harry Potter" novel, *Harry Potter and the Half-Blood Prince*, was published worldwide in English on July 16, 2005, but there is a gap of more than two months before the translations began to appear. When they did appear, however, there were many, including Vietnamese (September 24), German (October 1), French (October 1), Ukrainian (October 6), Danish (October 15), simplified Chinese (October 15), Portuguese (October 15), Swedish (November 9), Afrikaans (November 15), Greek (November 15), Dutch (November 19), Norwegian (November 19), Portuguese-Brazil (November 26), Estonian (November 26), and Hebrew (December 22). Source: publishers and booksellers.

11. The novel was published in Dutch in February 2013. British and Australian editions followed in March; Brazilian and French editions, in April and August; U.S. and Spanish editions, in September. By the end of the year, editions had also been published in Chinese, German, Italian, Polish, and Portuguese.

12. In the United States alone, *Harry Potter and the Half-Blood Prince* sold 6.9 million copies in its first twenty-four hours, a record. Edward Wyatt,

"Harry Potter Book Sets Record in First Day," *New York Times*, July 18, 2005, accessed April 3, 2014, http://www.nytimes.com/2005/07/18/books/18sale. html?_r=0; and Holly Williams, "Heads Up: The Childhood of Jesus," *Independent*, February 10, 2013, accessed April 3, 2014, http://www.independent.co.uk/arts-entertainment/books/features/heads-up-the-childhood-of-jesus-8488433.html.

13. J. K. Rowling's books appeared in non-English editions less quickly because she released them to translators only when she released them to (English-language) consumers. Hillel Italie, "Harry Potter and the Slow Translation: Non-English Stores Await Bestseller," *Washington Post*, July 27, 2005, http://www.washingtonpost.com/wp-dyn/content/article/2005/07/26/AR2005072601793.html.

14. Coetzee's previous book, *Diary of a Bad Year*, also appeared first in Dutch, as I discuss in the next chapter.

15. The history of the novel may have become national, but it didn't start that way. Bethany Wiggin shows, for example, that German novels around 1700 were really French novels: some were actual translations from the French, some were knockoffs of French books, and others adapted themes associated with French novels (*Novel Translations*, 6). French novels, for their part, were also often translated, adapted, and borrowed (ibid., 4). Emphasizing translation has led theorists of the novel to argue against a single chronology of the novel's "rise." For important accounts of the novel's "multichronological" history, see Srinivas Aravamudan, *Enlightenment Orientalism: Resisting the Rise of the Novel* (Chicago: Chicago University Press, 2012), 253; and Margaret Cohen and Carolyn Dever, eds., *The Literary Channel: the International Invention of the Novel* (Princeton, NJ: Princeton University Press, 2002).

16. Matthew Kirschenbaum, *Mechanisms: New Media and the Forensic Imagination* (Cambridge, MA: MIT Press, 2008).

17. Born-digital works are generally distinguished from literary works that are typed or composed on computers because they aren't simply digital versions of analog texts. They have to be "run," as we say, as well as read.

18. This question and my effort to answer it are indebted to Franco Moretti's self-translated study, *Atlas of the European Novel*, in which he asks: "How is it, I mean, *that geography shapes the narrative structure of the European novel.*" Moretti, *Atlas of the European Novel*, 8, emphasis in original. Moretti first published the book as *Atlante del romanzo europeo 1800–1900* (Turin: Giulio Einaudi, 1997).

19. Simón's comment to his young charge, David, that learning to read involves knowing "27 letters" serves as one of many reminders that the characters are operating in a language other than English. J. M. Coetzee, *Childhood of Jesus* (London: Harvill Secker, 2013), 161. I say a language "other than English," because even English-language readers who don't know Spanish will know that he can't be referring to an anglophone alphabet.

20. Coetzee, *Childhood of Jesus*, 67.

21. Unlike the author, who writes in one and reads the other fluently. J. M. Coetzee, "Roads to Translation," *Meanjin* 64, no. 4 (December 2005): 149–51.

22. Jorge Luis Borges, "Pierre Menard, Author of the *Quixote*," trans. James E. Irby, in *Labyrinths: Selected Stories and Other Writings* (New York: New Directions, 1962), 39.

23. Ibid., 42–44.

24. The early seventeenth-century English play *Cardenio*, whose title character is drawn from a story recounted in *Don Quixote*, is sometimes attributed to Shakespeare. *Don Quixote* was published in English translation in 1612, but a draft of the translation may have circulated much earlier, perhaps as early as 1607. "As early as 1605 or 1606," Roger Chartier argues, "a number of English readers must have been able to acquire and read *Don Quixote* in its original language, with the aid of the many dictionaries, grammars, and handbooks designed to teach Spanish that were produced by London publishers from 1590 onwards." Roger Chartier, *Cardenio Between Cervantes and Shakespeare: The Story of a Lost Play*, trans. Janet Lloyd (Cambridge: Polity Press, 2013), 18. It is unlikely that Cervantes "read" Shakespeare, since the first substantial printing of the plays, the First Folio, was produced in 1623, seven years after Cervantes's (and Shakespeare's) death in 1616. The first Spanish translation of a Shakespeare play was published in 1772; it was based on a French translation. But it is also unlikely that Cervantes watched Shakespeare's plays. The first Shakespeare play produced in Madrid was *Hamlet*, also in 1772. Thomas A. Fitzgerald, "Shakespeare in Spain and Spanish America," *Modern Language Journal* 35, no. 8 (December 1951): 590.

25. Coetzee's South African novel, *In the Heart of the Country*, also features Spanish, of a kind. The narrator uses made-up Spanish, spelled out in rocks, to communicate with airplanes she believes are flying overhead. Some critics have referred to this language as a kind of Esperanto. Rita Barnard, "Coetzee in/and Afrikaans," *Journal of Literary Studies* 25, no. 4 (December 2009): 84–105.

26. *Hamlet* owes its plot to Scandinavian tales that circulated in Latin. *The Pilgrim's Progress* adapts the New Testament (translated out of Greek and Aramaic) into English prose. *Absalom, Absalom!*, whose title is taken from the Hebrew Bible, was influenced by Faulkner's reading of Balzac. Edith Grossman attributes Faulkner's popularity in Latin America to his adaptation of Cervantes, whom he in turn helped to introduce to later Latin American writers. Woolf was reading Proust while she was writing *Mrs. Dalloway*. David Michael Walter, "Strange Attractions: Sibling Love Triangles in Faulkner's *Absalom, Absalom!* and Balzac's *La fille aux yeux d'or*," *Comparative Literature Studies* 44, no. 4 (2007): 484–506; Edith Grossman, *Why Translation Matters* (New Haven, CT: Yale University Press, 2010), 19–21; and

Pericles Lewis, "Proust, Woolf, and Modern Fiction," *Romantic Review* 99, no. 1 (2008): 77–86.

27. In this sense, born-translated novels try to bring about what Yasemin Yildiz has called "the postmonolingual condition." Yasemin Yildiz, *Beyond the Mother Tongue: The Postmonolingual Condition* (New York: Fordham University Press, 2012).

28. Miéville's novels incorporate translation through the conceit of overlapping, multilingual, or "crosshatch" worlds. This phrase comes from his novel *The City, The City* (New York: Del Rey, 2010), 26. Miéville's first novel, *King Rat* (1998), amalgamates trickster stories gathered from several geographies (Irish, German, West African) to present a magical realm of disenfranchised animals that exists beneath and within the nonmagical realm of human London. *Embassytown* (2011) concerns a colonized species on a distant planet, whose inability to conceive of multiple languages or even figurative language (puns, lies, metaphor) renders its members unable to imagine an alternative political order. In this novel, Miéville suggests that the principle of translation—more than one way of speaking—is crucial to the principle of democratic self-governance.

29. Miéville, *The City, The City*, 12; emphasis added.

30. Ibid., 45; emphasis added.

31. The languages are Italian, Turkish, Spanish, German, Greek, Chinese, Hebrew, Norwegian, and French. They appear in four different scripts: Greek, Chinese, and Hebrew, and Roman. Details courtesy of curator Lydie Diakhaté. The exhibit was presented by the NYU/Kimmel Center Windows Gallery, freely visible to passersby on the street, from June 10–August 1, 2013.

32. Pascale Casanova, "What Is a Dominant Language? Giacomo Leopardi: Theoretician of Linguistic Inequality," trans. Marlon Jones, *New Literary History* 44 (2013): 380.

33. This doesn't mean that all circuits are global circuits. For a discussion of translation histories that don't involve major languages, or in which entry into a dominant language is not the ultimate goal, see Gayle Rogers, "Translation," in *A New Vocabulary for Global Modernism*, ed. Eric Hayot and Rebecca L. Walkowitz (New York: Columbia University Press, forthcoming); and Aparna Dharwadker, *Theatres of Independence: Drama, Theory, and Urban Performance in India Since 1947* (Iowa City: University of Iowa Press, 2005). For an important discussion of translation and adaptation within English, see Priya Joshi, *In Another Country* (New York: Columbia University Press, 2002). On "the geography of prestige," see James F. English, *The Economy of Prestige* (Cambridge, MA: Harvard University Press, 2009).

34. Jan Walsh Hokenson and Marcella Munson describe this history in their excellent study, *The Bilingual Text: History and Theory of Literary Self-Translation* (Manchester, U.K.: St. Jerome Publishing, 2007). They note the shift

toward vernacular languages, which came to be understood as national languages ("the language of the 'fatherland,'" in Friedrich Schleiermacher's terms), in the early nineteenth century (142–43).

35. On Iranian philosophy in Arabic, see Hamid Dabashi, "Found in Translation," *New York Times*, July 28, 2013, accessed April 3, 2014, http://nyti.ms/1gp03A8. On the dominance of the Chinese language in East Asia, see Karen Thornber, *Empire of Texts in Motion: Chinese, Korean, and Taiwanese Transculturations of Japanese Literature* (Cambridge, MA: Harvard University Asia Center, 2009), 7.

36. Steven G. Kellman, *Switching Languages: Translingual Writers Reflect on Their Craft* (Lincoln: University of Nebraska Press, 2003).

37. Schleiermacher, cited in Yildiz, *Beyond the Mother Tongue*, 8–9.

38. There are many examples of writers composing in their second or third language. Sometimes this is prompted by migration, as in Nabokov's case, Conrad's (composing and publishing in English instead of Polish or French), or, to take a more recent example, Marjane Satrapi's (composing and publishing the graphic novel *Persepolis* in French instead of Persian). In each case, the writer's choice reflects a combination of commercial, political, and personal factors.

39. Edith Grossman, [Interview with] "Jaime Manrique," *Bomb* 121 (Fall 2012), accessed April 3, 2014, http://bombmagazine.org/article/6771/.

40. Corydon Ireland, "Borders, Books, and the Balkans." *Harvard Gazette*, April 12, 2013. http://news.harvard.edu/gazette/story/2013/04/borders-books-and-the-balkans.

41. [Vinay Dharwadker], "Premchand" in *The Norton Anthology of World Literature*, 3rd ed., ed. Martin Puchner, Suzanne Conklin Akbari, Wiebke Denecke, Vinay Dharwadker, Barbara Fuchs, Caroline Levine, Pericles Lewis, and Emily Wilson (New York: W. W. Norton, 2012), vol. F., 311–14.

42. Michelle Woods, *Translating Milan Kundera* (Clevedon, U.K.: Multilingual Matters, 2006), 151. Woods discusses all of the ways that translation has generated production in Kundera's oeuvre.

43. Ibid., ix.

44. Email correspondence with the author, October 31, 2012.

45. Andrew van der Vlies, *South African Textual Cultures: White, Black, and Read All Over* (Manchester, U.K.: Manchester University Press, 2007), 135–54.

46. As David Chioni Moore points out, "le boy" refers to "a male of African descent of any age in domestic service." Moore argues that there is no way to "render the Anglo-coloniality of many of Oyono's Anglo-French words in any English version." David Chioni Moore, "An African Classic in Fourteen Translations: Ferdinand Oyono's *Une vie de boy* on the World Literary Stage," *PMLA* 128, no. 1 (2013): 104–5.

47. Ibid., 104.

48. She won the Canadian Governor General's Award for French-language fiction for *Cantiques des Plaines* (1993), which she wrote originally in English and published as *Plainsong* (1993). Jane Koustas notes Huston's insistence that the later editions are "rewritings" rather than translations. Jane Koustas, *Les belles étrangères: Canadians in Paris* (Ottawa: University of Ottawa Press, 2008), 65.

49. Nancy Huston, *Losing North: Musings on Land, Tongue and Self* (Toronto: McArthur, 2002). Huston's novels have been very successful in France, but her choice of French over English was intellectual and political as well as commercial. She wanted to write in a language she had to acquire and that she would have to write consciously. Elizabeth M. Knutson, "Writing in Between Worlds: Reflections on Language and Identity from Works by Nancy Huston and Leïla Sebbar," *Symposium* 65, no. 4 (2011): 266–67, doi:10.1080/0 0397709.2011.628589. To be sure, some intellectual projects are likely to have a larger audience in French than they will in English. Given its length and subject matter, it is hard to imagine that *Les bienveillantes*, the 2006 blockbuster by the New York-born novelist Jonathan Littell, would have done as well had it appeared first in English. The 983-page novel, narrated by a former SS officer, won two prestigious French literary awards, including the Prix Goncourt. The novel received mixed reviews when it was published in English as *The Kindly Ones* in 2009. Jonathon Littell, *Les bienviellants* (Paris: Gallimard, 2006); and Jonathon Littell, *The Kindly Ones*, trans. Charlotte Mandell (New York: Harper Collins, 2009).

50. Rebecca Suter, *The Japanization of Modernity: Murakami Haruki Between Japan and the United States* (Cambridge, MA: Harvard University Press, 2008), 41.

51. Anna Zielinska-Elliott and Mette Holm, "Two Moons over Europe: Translating Haruki Murakami's *1Q84*," *AALITRA Review: A Journal of Literary Translation* 7 (November 2013): 7.

52. For example, *1Q84*, published in Japan in 2009, evokes in its title George Orwell's international bestseller *1984*. *1Q84* was published in Dutch, Polish, Norwegian, and German in 2010 before entering French, Russian, and English in 2011. Zielinska-Elliott and Holm, "Two Moons," 5.

53. According to Anna Zielinska-Elliott, Murakami's translator into Polish, *IQ84* was advertised with a "matrix style" trailer in Spain but with an "urban romantic" style trailer in Italy. Anna Zielinska-Elliott, Session on "Challenging the Hegemony of English: Translating Haruki Murakami's *1Q84* in Europe." Harvard University, October 2, 2012.

54. Ika Kaminka, who translates Murakami's works into Norwegian, has argued that English "vanishes" in English translation. Ika Kaminka, Session on "Challenging the Hegemony of English: Translating Haruki Murakami's *1Q84* in Europe." Harvard University, October 2, 2012. In addition, the

English versions often involve abridgement, as Zielinska-Elliott and Holm explain ("Two Moons," 7).

55. Zielinska-Elliott and Holm, "Two Moons," 31; Suter discusses Murakami's use of "polygraphy" in *The Japanization of Modernity*, 62–93.

56. For the debate about whether Murakami's novels are "Japanese" or Americanized Japanese, see Will Slocombe, "Haruki Murakami and the Ethics of Translation," *CLCWeb: Comparative Literature and Culture* 6, no. 2 (June 2004), accessed April 3, 2014, doi:10.7771/1481-4374.1232.

57. Murakami, in Zielinska-Elliott and Holm, "Two Moons," 9.

58. List-makers rank language dominance in all sorts of ways, from the number of "native" or first-language speakers to the aggregate of all users (even those who know only a little bit, and may only use the language for reading). Different strategies lead to different lists, so that Chinese will top lists that privilege fluent speakers, whereas English will top lists that emphasize both fluent and partial use. Another way to measure dominance is to see which languages top the list of translations. The Index Translationum, maintained by UNESCO, evaluates all works published between 1979 and 2012. In that list, more books are translated from English than from any other language in the world, with five times as many translations as books in the next most translated language, French. Turkish books come in thirty-sixth.

59. Erdağ Göknar, "Occulted Texts: Pamuk's Untranslated Novels" in *Global Perspectives on Orhan Pamuk: Existentialism and Politics*, ed. Mehnaz M. Afridi and David M. Buyze (New York: Palgrave, 2012), 192. Istanbul is often invoked as the paradigmatic city of world literature. This is partly because of its geography, divided between Europe and Asia, and partly because it has served as a host for two of the twentieth century's most distinguished theorists of world literature, Erich Auerbach and Leo Spitzer. Indeed, Göknar argues, because some of Pamuk's novels have not been translated and because he presents himself in recent essays and books "as a student and practitioner of an international canon," it can seem as if his career has been shaped (only) by Istanbul rather than by Republican Turkey. Ibid., 192–93; and Erdağ Göknar, "The Untranslated Novels of a Nobel Laureate," in *Orhan Pamuk, Secularism and Blasphemy: The Politics of the Turkish Novel* (London: Routledge, 2013), 50–88. Sevinç Türkkan argues that later translators of Pamuk's novels have contributed to Pamuk's reception as a world writer by producing editions that use "straightforward and unadorned" diction instead of a mixed diction that imitates Pamuk's hybrid Turkish. Sevinç Türkkan, "Orhan Pamuk's *Kara Kitap* [The black book]: A Double Life in English" in *Global Perspectives on Orhan Pamuk: Existentialism and Politics*, ed. Mehnaz M. Afridi and David M. Buyze (New York: Palgrave, 2012), 170.

60. Gloria Fisk, "Orhan Pamuk and the Good of World Literature," unpublished manuscript, 50.

61. The shift in written Turkish from Arabic script to Latin alphabet was a cornerstone of Mustafa Kemal Atatürk's modernization process. Pamuk discusses the "erasure of the past" through Westernization in *Istanbul: Memories and the City*, trans. Maureen Freely (New York: Knopf, 2006), 29.

62. David Kurnick, "Bolaño to Come," *Public Books*, September 5, 2012, accessed April 3, 2014, http://www.publicbooks.org/fiction/bolano-to-come.

63. For example, in *2666*, the chapter called "The Part About Fate" appears to be taking place entirely in English, though there are no English words in the Spanish version. There is not even italicization, a common feature in texts that are pretending to render words in a foreign language. Brett Levinson argues that this section of the novel is "written in English" but "with Spanish signifiers." Brett Levinson, "Case Closed: Madness and Dissociation in *2666*," *Journal of Latin American Cultural Studies* 18, nos. 2–3 (December 2009): 181.

64. Roberto Bolaño, *The Savage Detectives*, trans. Natasha Wimmer (New York: Picador, 2007), 297, 173, 180, 181, 222, 228.

65. For more on the use of second-person narration in born-translated novels, see chapter 4.

66. Bolaño, *The Savage Detectives*, 424.

67. As scholars such as Lydia Liu and Gayle Rogers have shown, translation projects may operate across vast distances without operating globally or universally. It is not a matter of choosing between roots and rootlessness. Gayle Rogers, *Modernism and the New Spain: Britain, Cosmopolitan Europe, and Literary History* (New York: Oxford University Press, 2012); and Lydia Liu, *Translingual Practice: Literature, National Culture, and Translated Modernity—China, 1900–1937* (Palo Alto, CA: Stanford University Press, 1995).

68. Index Translationum, UNESCO, http://portal.unesco.org/culture/en/ev.php-URL_ID=7810&URL_DO=DO_TOPIC&URL_SECTION=201.html.

69. Casanova, "What Is a Dominant Language?": 380.

70. Anthony Pym argues that "the sheer size of English could mean that much of the variety and new blood that other language groups seek through translation, English-language cultures may be receiving through distribution without translation." Anthony Pym, *The Moving Text: Localization, Translation, and Distribution* (Amsterdam: John Benjamins, 2005), 200.

71. Even writers in a global language such as Spanish aspire to publication in English. The Madrid-based publisher Hispabooks, launched in the spring of 2013, focuses solely on the translation of Spanish novels for English-language audiences. The imprint's tagline is "Spanish literature for worldwide readers." Hispabooks Web site, accessed April 3, 2014, www.hispabooks.com.

72. Some scholars have insisted that studies of translation should include both works that were actually translated and original works that have been treated as translations by their readers. Gideon Toury, *Descriptive Translation Studies and Beyond* (Amsterdam: John Benjamins, 1995), 32; and Reine Meylaerts, Roundtable on "Multilingualism and the Object of Translation Studies," MLA conference, January 9, 2014.

73. Reine Meylaerts, "Heterolingualism in/and translation: How Legitimate Are the Other and His/Her Language? An Introduction," *Target: International Journal on Translation Studies* 18, no. 1 (2006): 1–15. Stefan Helgesson asks, "How is literature constructed as a *distinct* literature?" in "Linguistic Desire and Literary Identity," Roundtable on "Multilingualism and the Object of Translation Studies," Modern Language Association conference, January 9, 2014. David Chioni Moore treats Ferdinand Oyono's francophone novel *Une vie de boy* as a translation, both because it integrates so many other languages into its version of French and because it pretends to have been written in the indigenous language of Ewondo. Moore, "An African Classic in Fourteen Translations," 103.

74. As Stefan Helgesson has rightly noted, the invitation to translation should not be confused with an extension or preservation of the author's agency. You can invite someone to translate without determining in advance what that translation will do. Stefan Helgesson, "Clarice Lispector, J. M. Coetzee, and the Seriality of Translation," *Translation Studies* 3, no. 3 (2010): 328. I will be using "multilingualism" to refer to the presence of several languages at once, even when those languages are not necessarily countable or distinct, as in my discussion of the presence of Spanish and English in Junot Díaz's work.

75. Casanova, "What Is a Dominant Language?" 393.

76. *Asymptote*, www.asymptotejournal.com.

77. Lawrence Venuti champions this kind of foreignization as an ethics of translation. See my discussion in chapter 4.

78. M. M. Bakhtin, *The Dialogic Imagination: Four Essays*, trans. Michael Holquist (Austin: University of Texas Press, 1982), 295.

79. Ibid., 61–62. In fact, Bakhtin concludes, the novel "arose" not through a struggle over competing "world-view" but through a struggle over competing cultures and languages (83). Much more recently, Srinivas Aravamudan has made a similar point, arguing that Oriental tales were a principal source of English fiction (*Enlightenment Orientalism*, 22).

80. Benedict Anderson, *Imagined Communities: Reflections on the Origin and Spread of Nationalism*, 3rd ed. (London: Verso, 2006).

81. Rosemary Coombe, *The Cultural Life of Intellectual Properties: Authorship, Appropriation, and the Law* (Durham, NC: Duke University Press, 1998), 225. Coombe's use of this phrase is derived from Richard Handler, "Who Owns

the Past? History, Cultural Property, and the Logic of Possessive Individualism," in *The Politics of Culture*, ed. Brett Williams, 63–74 (Washington, DC: Smithsonian Institution Press, 1991).

82. Richard Handler, *Nationalism and the Politics of Culture in Quebec* (Madison: University of Wisconsin Press, 1988), 39–41.

83. Coombe, *The Cultural Life of Intellectual Properties*, 224–25.

84. Anderson, *Imagined Communities*, 25.

85. Jonathan Culler, "Anderson and the Novel," in *Grounds of Comparison: Around the Work of Benedict Anderson*, ed. Pheng Cheah and Jonathan Culler (New York: Routledge, 2003), 50.

86. On *Imagined Communities* as an argument, see Wai Chee Dimock, *Through Other Continents: American Literature Across Deep Time* (Princeton, NJ: Princeton University Press, 2006); Jahan Ramazani, *A Transnational Poetics* (Chicago: University of Chicago Press, 2009); and Brent Hayes Edwards, *The Practice of Diaspora: Literature, Translation, and the Rise of Black Internationalism* (Cambridge, MA: Harvard University Press, 2003).

87. We might consider those nineteenth-century books such as anthologies, periodicals, and episodic novels in which the experience of a single container is disrupted by the perception of alternative collectivities, both within the nation as well as across nations. In modernist literature, the apprehension of simultaneity in time and space is regularly breached by free indirect discourse, by the importation of multiple languages, and by multiple frames of narration. In the decades since the Second World War, with the expansive circulation of anglophone writing, transnational novelists have developed structures of "meanwhile" that are not only "relative," as Wai Chee Dimock has put it, but recursive and rivalrous. On the integration of regional articles within national magazines as a disruption of the homogeneous, empty time/space of national consciousness, see James Buzard, *Disorienting Fiction: The Autoethnographic Work of Nineteenth-Century British Novels* (Princeton: Princeton UP, 2005), 172-173; and Wai Chee Dimock, "Literature for the Planet," *PMLA* 116. 1 (2001): 174.

88. Moretti calls world literature "a problem" rather than "an object"; he also calls it a "system." Pascale Casanova's work posits a "republic of letters." According to Damrosch, it is because of the "network," the several literary systems that share a single text, that the work can be called world literature. Building on Goethe's theory of *Weltliteratur*, Martin Puchner writes in a similar vein: "world literature is not written but made—made by a marketplace" (*Poetry of the Revolution*, 49). See also Pascale Casanova, *The World Republic of Letters*, trans. M. B. DeBevoise (Cambridge, MA: Harvard University Press, 2005); Moretti, "Conjectures on World Literature," *New Left Review* 1 (2000): 55, 66; and David Damrosch, *What Is World Literature?* (Princeton, NJ: Princeton University Press, 2003), 3.

89. David Damrosch has put it most succinctly: "Virtually all literary works are born within what we would now call a national literature." Damrosch, *What Is World Literature?* 283.

90. Emily Apter, *Against World Literature: On the Politics of Untranslatability* (New York: Verso, 2013), 2, 4, 41.

91. Capitalization designates the institutional category. Caroline Levine, "For World Literature," *Public Books*, January 6, 2014, accessed April 3, 2014, http://www.publicbooks.org/fiction/for-world-literature.

92. Apter, *Against World Literature*, 9.

93. Ibid., 15.

94. The nineteenth-century novel provides the crucial example in Moretti, *Atlas*; Anderson, *Imagined Communities*; and Casanova, *World Republic of Letters*.

95. The robust practice of self-translation in early modern Europe suggests that many literary works of that period entered the world in several languages as well as in several editions. Hokenson and Munson, *Bilingual Text*. Thinking synchronically, Damrosch has begun calling for "the comparative study of world literatures," acknowledging that the theory of world literature, too, has begun in many places. David Damrosch, "Comparative World Literature," in *The Canonical Debate Today: Crossing Disciplinary and Cultural Boundaries*, ed. Liviu Papadima, David Damrosch, and Theo D'haen, 169–78 (Amsterdam: Rodopi, 2011), 177. Thinking diachronically, scholars such as Margaret Cohen, Gayle Rogers, and Karen Thornber have considered how world literature looks from the perspective of other periods, including the eighteenth and twentieth centuries. Margaret Cohen, *The Novel and the Sea* (Princeton, NJ: Princeton University Press, 2012); Rogers, *Modernism and the New Spain*; and Thornber, *Empire of Texts in Motion*. Bethany Wiggin answers this question by looking back at late seventeenth- and early eighteenth-century fiction.

96. I have explored the idea of a work's translations as a kind of "series" in "Unimaginable Largeness: Kazuo Ishiguro, Translation, and the New World Literature" *Novel* 40, no. 3 (2007): 216–39. Stefan Helgesson develops the idea of literary translation as a "serial collective endeavor" in "Clarice Lispector," 320.

97. Helgesson argues that translated editions "undercut the writer's authority even as they expand the work." Helgesson, "Clarice Lispector," 319. Translating can be seen as a robust and more durable version of reading, in which the audience not only enters into the text but also produces a new version of it. In this sense, the emphasis on translated editions focuses on readers, as book history has done, while also focusing on new writers. For a foundational account of readers as users, see Roger Chartier, "Laborers and Voyagers: From the Text to the Reader," trans. J. A. González, in *Diacritics* 22, no. 2 (Summer 1992): 49–61. For a discussion of the turn to "target" in translation studies, see Cecelia Alvstad, Stefan Helgesson, and David

Watson, "Introduction: Literature, Geography, Translation," in *Literature, Geography, Translation: Studies in World Writing*, ed. Cecilia Alvstad, Stefan Helgesson, and David Watson, 1–12 (Cambridge: Cambridge Scholars Publishing, 2011).

98. Martin Puchner describes Orhan Pamuk's novel *The Museum of Innocence* as a "triptych" that includes a museum, an exhibition catalogue, and a book. Martin Puchner, "Orhan Pamuk's Own Private Istanbul," *Raritan* 33, no. 3 (Winter 2013): 97–108.

99. Martin Puchner reports that Orhan Pamuk's novel *The Museum of Innocence* and his museum by the same name were imagined simultaneously as an engagement with "the idea of a museum." The space is an "extension" of the book, but the book and space can also be understood as versions, in different media, of Pamuk's "museum." Martin Puchner, "World Literature in Istanbul," *Inside Higher Ed*, August 27, 2012, accessed April 3, 2014, https://www.insidehighered.com/views/2012/08/27/essay-teaching-world-literature-istanbul.

100. For debate about whether readers of world literature remain themselves or enter into new selves, see Apter, *Against World Literature*, 329–34.

101. Levine, "For World Literature."

102. New approaches to literary sequencing put to the test old approaches to literary periodization. For an account of why literary history needs to move beyond universal periodization, see Eric Hayot, *On Literary Worlds* (Oxford: Oxford University Press, 2012).

103. Pankaj Mishra, "Beyond the Global Novel," *Financial Times*, September 27, 2013, accessed April 3, 2014, http://www.ft.com/cms/s/2/6e00ad86-26a2-11e3-9dc0-00144feab7de.html#axzz3CsMRGIsx. Emily Apter also registers this concern when she writes that artists producing for a global audience help to create "a problem-based monocultural aesthetic agenda that elicits transnational engagement." Emily Apter, "Translation in a Global Market," *Public Culture* 13, no. 1 (2001): 3.

104. Tim Parks, "The Dull New Global Novel," *New York Review Blog*, February 9, 2010, accessed April 2, 2014, http://www.nybooks.com/blogs/nyrblog/2010/feb/09/the-dull-new-global-novel/. In a later essay, Parks writes, "What I'm getting at is that style is predicated on a strict relation to a specific readership and the more that readership is diluted or extended, particularly if it includes foreign-language readers, the more difficult it is for a text of any stylistic density to be successful." Tim Parks, "Literature Without Style," *New York Review Blog*, November 7, 2013, accessed April 3, 2014, http://www.nybooks.com/blogs/nyrblog/2013/nov/07/literature-without-style/.

105. Rita Barnard, "On Public and Private in J. M. Coetzee" in *Cultural Studies* 27, no. 3 (2013): 456.

106. Except, as Pascale Casanova and others have pointed out, translation is an index of dominance. This is why a *Time* magazine article linking the

decline of France with the decline in translations of French literature caused such a ruckus when it was published in 2007. Donald Morrison, "In Search of Lost Time," *Time*, November 21, 2007, http://content.time. com/time/magazine/article/0,9171,1686532,00.html. Among responses, see Agnès Poirier, "Vive la dissidence," *Guardian*, December 4, 2007, accessed April 3, 2014, http://www.theguardian.com/commentisfree/2007/ dec/05/comment.usa; and Elise Barthet, "Internautes et intellectuels s'insurgent contre 'la mort de la culture française," *Le Monde*, December 18, 2007, accessed April 3, 2014, http://www.lemonde.fr/culture/article/2007/12/18/internautes-et-intellectuels-s-insurgent-contre-la-mort-de-la-culture-francaise_990480_3246.html.

107. Brian Lennon, *In Babel's Shadow: Multilingual Literatures, Monolingual States* (Minneapolis: University of Minnesota Press), 2.

108. Ibid., 9.

109. Doris Sommer, *Proceed with Caution, When Engaged by Minority Writing in the Americas* (Cambridge, MA: Harvard University Press, 1999), ix. Joshua Miller also claims that multilingual works aim to reduce the importance of dominant languages such as English and to emphasize instead "ethnic particularism and cultural pluralism." Joshua L. Miller, "The Transamerican Trail to *Cerco del Cielo*: John Sayles and the Aesthetics of Multilingual Cinema," in *Bilingual Games: Some Literary Investigations*, ed. Doris Sommer, 121–48 (New York: Palgrave, 2003), 125.

110. Particularist writing, Sommer argues, does not assume "cultural continuity between writer and reader" but does assume that it can identify and reach its "target audience" (*Proceed with Caution*, 2).

111. One might imagine that the opposite of works designed for particular languages would be works designed for universal languages such as Esperanto (introduced by L. L. Zamenhof in the 1880s) and Europanto (introduced by Diego Marani in the 1990s). Consisting of words and syntax taken from Romance languages with a little help from German and Slavic, Esperanto blends together several different tongues in the service of transnational communication. It would seem to facilitate translation, but in fact it tries to make translation redundant. A language that could work for all Europeans would require, for Europeans, no translation at all. Such a language produces a larger collective, but it is a single collective all the same. Utopian works such as the *Communist Manifesto* likewise imagine a future in which differences among readers would no longer matter. While universal languages skip over translation by creating a language for everyone (relatively speaking), advocates of "post-exotic" and "minor" languages have sought to make translation obsolete by dislocating or "impoverishing" language altogether. These languages, too, are resisting national or tribal consolidations. However, instead of expressing an alternative collective, as Esperanto does, "minor literature" expresses foreignness: the experience of those who "live

in a language that is not their own." Minor writing is not translated; it is blocked or "underdeveloped." Minor works aim to hold back or pare down, but they are generally aimed at a specific national language. Gilles Deleuze and Félix Guattari, *Kafka: Toward a Minor Literature*, trans. Dana Polan (Minneapolis: University of Minnesota Press, 1986), 22–23; 19; 26. Writing in this tradition, contemporary French writer Antoine Volodine calls for "foreign literature in the French language." Volodine aspires to write, he says, in a "translated language [lange de traduction]," but he means by this that he is using French, a language whose "genius" [genie] he celebrates, to resist the habits and customs of French society. Antoine Volodine, "Écrire en français une littérature étrangère," *Chaoïd*, no. 6 (Autumn–Winter 2002). For an analysis of Volodine's "post-exotic" project, see Christy Wampole, "Self-Begetting Theory: Volodine's Post-Exotic Aesthetics," presentation at the "Actuality and the Idea" conference, Princeton University, May 11–12, 2012.

112. Emily Apter, "Philosophical Translation and Untranslatability: Translation as Critical Pedagogy," *Profession* (2010), 61.

113. Ibid., 54.

114. Ibid., 61.

115. Barbara Cassin, "Untranslatables and their Translations," trans. Andrew Goffey, *Transeuropéennes: Revue international de pensée critique*, September 14, 2009, accessed April 3, 2014, http://www.transeuropeennes.org/en/articles/83. Two alternate translations of this phrase, one by Michael Wood and one by Barbara Cassin herself, emphasize even more strongly the sense of interminable engagement: "what one keeps on (not) translating" (Wood) and "what never stops being (not) translated" (Cassin and Walkowitz). Barbara Cassin, Introduction to *Dictionary of Untranslatables: A Philosophical Lexicon*, trans. Michael Wood, ed. Barbara Cassin (Princeton, NJ: Princeton University Press, 2013), xvii; and Rebecca L. Walkowitz, "Translating the Untranslatable: An Interview with Barbara Cassin," *Public Books*, June 15, 2014, http://www.publicbooks.org/interviews/translating-the-untranslatable-an-interview-with-barbara-cassin.

116. Barbara Cassin, "Introduction," xvii.

117. It is beyond the scope of these pages to consider why such very different models of untranslatability might emerge at this moment in the United States and France. However, the ban on translation fits well with a U.S. commitment to multiculturalism, emphasizing difference, while the insistence on translation fits well with the French commitment to republicanism, emphasizing collectivity above all.

118. Apter and Cassin seem to present substantially different versions of untranslatability, though sometimes Apter associates untranslatable works with "creative failure," an oxymoron that seems closer to Cassin's "translating, still" than to the rhetoric of territorial blockage. Apter, *Against World Literature*, 20.

119. Samuel Beckett, "Dante . . . Bruno, Vico, Joyce," in *Disjecta: Miscellaneous Writings and a Dramatic Fragment*, ed. Ruby Cohn (New York: Grove Press, 1984), 27, emphasis in the original.

120. To consider how literary texts have embraced one or another kind of untranslatability, it is useful to look at some examples. The first page of the eighth chapter of *Ulysses* is a good place to start. The page is important: the typography and spacing contribute to the impression of hearing both a character's interior monologue and the ambient sounds of Dublin.

We should notice, first, that the novel privileges sound: that is, the way a character from a distinctive group speaks within that group at a particular time and place. We are meant to imagine ourselves as listeners as well as readers. In this passage, sound holds ideas together at the level of phoneme as well as well as phrase. The parts of this passage the resist translation would be the sideways movement of phonemes, which allows Joyce to gather together high and low, imperial anthems such as "God Save the King" and menacing images of a "king" sucking red juice out of candies. Or, the way that Bloom, the character, initially imagines that the phrase he sees on a piece of paper, "Blood of the Lamb," could be about it him. Or, the way his mind associates, through the words "blood" and the phrase "is coming," evangelical doctrine, his breakfast that morning, pagan rituals, and an adulterous scene that will take place later in the day. But it is also important to notice how the novel incorporates and even solicits translation. This includes the novel's emphasis on metempsychosis, in which matter is transformed into new matter. It also includes the various systems and institutions of circulation, from the body's processing of blood and food to the Church's processing of souls and the city's processing of a "throwaway," which blows in the street and flows down the river. Over the course of *Ulysses*, we are asked to notice an enormous number of semantic details, but we are also asked to consider the political histories that have organized language and that have shaped what languages do, and who gets to use them. Joyce is engaged not only in the trumping of fluency in his own case: I speak English better than the English; or, my English will replace their English. He is also engaged in a conceptual project, the decoupling of fluency and citizenship: no one owns language; language does not belong. James Joyce, *Ulysses* (1922; repr., New York, Vintage, 1990), 151.

121. My use of the terms *description* and *narration* is indebted to Georg Lukács's "Narrate or Describe?" Description refers in that essay to the accumulation of detail, at the very smallest scale, that is typical of the naturalist novel and its legacy. Because description strips away omniscient narration, it "levels," in Lukács's phrase, and thus brackets the history of causes and consequences. Narration, Lukács insists, tends to focus on social mechanisms, and is thus more attentive to the question of how things happen, and how they don't. Lukács was wrong to insist that novels would have to

choose between these two projects, as my very telescopic account of *Ulysses* is meant to suggest (see the previous note), but he is right to notice that there is some conflict between them, and that description is more attuned to the accidents of language than to the habits and institutions that shape what can be said, and what can be read. Georg Lukács, "Narrate or Describe?," in *Writer and Critic and Other Essays*, trans. Arthur Kahn, 110–48 (Lincoln, NE: iUniverse, 2005).

122. Anthony Burgess, *A Clockwork Orange* (New York: Norton, 1995), 8.

123. Junot Díaz, *This Is How You Lose Her* (New York: Riverhead, 2012), 101.

124. In fact, the Spanish translator of *This Is How You Lose Her* has written of his efforts to acquire fluency in Dominican Spanish (he is Cuban) so that the Spanish edition would "sound Dominican." Achy Obejas, "Translating Junot," *Chicago Tribune*, September 14, 2012), accessed April 3, 2014, http://articles.chicagotribune.com/2012-09-14/features/ct-prj-0916-book-of-the-month-20120914_1_dominican-republic-oscar-wao-spanglish.

125. Joshua L. Miller, *Accented America: The Cultural Politics of Multilingual Modernism* (New York: Oxford University Press, 2011).

126. Junot Díaz described his negotiations with the *New Yorker* during a presentation at the 2011 Jaipur Literature Festival. Díaz, cited in "Create Relevant Literature for Future Gen: Junot Díaz," in *Times of India*, January 11, 2011, accessed April 3, 2014, http://timesofindia.indiatimes.com/city/jaipur/Create-relevant-literature-for-future-gen-Junot-Diaz/articleshow/7337450.cms.

127. Junot Díaz, *La breve y maravillosa vida de Oscar Wao*, trans. Achy Obejas (New York: Vintage Espanol, 2008). Díaz discusses the translation process in Anna Barnet, "Words on a Page: An Interview with Junot Díaz," *Harvard Advocate* (Spring 2009), accessed April 3, 2014, http://www.theharvardadvocate.com/category/author/anna-barnet.

128. Barnet, "Words on a Page."

129. Junot Díaz, *Así es como la pierdes*, trans. Achy Obejas (New York: Vintage Espanol, 2013), 107.

130. Junot Díaz, *Guide du loser amoureux*, trans. Stéphane Roques (Paris: Plon, 2013).

131. Ibid., 97.

132. Ibid.

133. Yildiz, *Beyond the Mother Tongue*, 35; emphasis original.

134. Theodor Adorno, "Words from Abroad," in *Notes to Literature*, vol. 1, trans. Shierry Weber Nicholsen (New York: Columbia University Press, 1991), 185.

135. Ben Lerner, *Leaving the Atocha Station* (Minneapolis: Coffee House Press, 2011).

136. Roland Barthes, *Image, Music, Text*, trans. Stephen Heath (New York: Hill and Wang, 1977), 121; and Moretti, "Conjectures on World Literature," 65.

137. Jahan Ramazani argues persuasively that "form" is also sensitive to place. Ramazani focuses on poetry, as when the sonnet comes into contact with

calypso, but his point is relevant for the novel, too, where the effect of "foreignness" can be produced in many different ways. Moreover, as Ramazani notes, "the equation of 'form' with 'plot' simplifies the novel—which has other vital elements down to the level of syntax and sentence" (chapter 7). In Lerner's novel, plot modifies form: the encounter with Spanish, a feature of the plot, alters the novel's approach both to dialogue and to free indirect discourse, features typically associated with form. The structure of the narrator's encounter—listening and beholding—is in turn crucial to the story. Jahan Ramazani, "Form," in *A New Vocabulary for Global Modernism*, ed. Eric Hayot and Rebecca L. Walkowitz (New York: Columbia University Press, forthcoming).

138. Lerner, *Leaving the Atocha Station*, 13–14.

139. Gayle Rogers, "An Interview with Ben Lerner," in *Contemporary Literature*, 54, no. 2 (2013): 228.

140. Ibid.

141. Ibid., 229.

142. My use of "provincializing" here and elsewhere is indebted to Dipesh Chakrabarty, *Provincializing Europe: Postcolonial Thought and Historical Difference* (Princeton, NJ: Princeton University Press, 2000).

143. Ben Lerner, *Saliendo de la estacion de Atocha*, trans. Cruz Rodríguez Juiz (Barcelona: Mondadori, 2013), 14.

144. Lerner, *Leaving the Atocha Station*, 9.

145. Ibid., 180.

146. Ibid., 181.

147. Modernist fiction is a diverse category, and there are important examples that diverge from the emphasis on idiolect. One thinks right away about the novels of D. H. Lawrence and E. M. Forster. Yet surveys of modernism regularly note that puns, portmanteau words, vernacular diction, and a heightened consciousness about the social uses of heroic language are central features of the modernist novel. James Joyce's *Ulysses*, Zora Neale Hurston's *Their Eyes Were Watching God*, and Virginia Woolf's *Mrs. Dalloway* are prime examples. "Many modernists embraced the idea of the literary work as a particularly sophisticated sort of language game, in which the relations among words were more important than the relations of words to nonlinguistic reality," Pericles Lewis argues in *The Cambridge Introduction to Modernism* (Cambridge: Cambridge University Press, 2007), 10. In the *Cambridge Companion to Modernism*, Michael Bell writes of "the linguistic turn" within modernist literature, in which language became the subject and not simply the medium of representation. Michael Bell, "The Metaphysics of Modernism," in *The Cambridge Companion to Modernism*, ed. Michael Levenson (Cambridge: Cambridge University Press, 2011), 16.

148. Naoki Sakai, "How Do We Count a Language? Translation and Discontinuity," *Translation Studies* 2, no. 1 (2009): 73. Stefan Helgesson uses Sakai's

work to discuss the relationship between counting languages and count-ing translations in "Clarice Lispector," 320–21.

149. Dimock, *Through Other Continents*; Puchner, *Poetry of the Revolution*; and Ramazani, *A Transnational Poetics*.

150. Grossman, *Why Translation Matters*, 49.

151. For a comparison of these two different modes of translation history, see Zwicker, "Japan, 1850–1900." A collaborative study of this kind, tracking fourteen translations of Ferdinand Oyono's *Une vie de boy*, is discussed in Moore, "An African Classic in Fourteen Translations," 101–11.

152. "Multiples" was first published as an oversized, four-color paperback, in a special issue of *McSweeney's Quarterly Concern*.

1. CLOSE READING AT A DISTANCE

1. Stefan Helgesson refers to works and their (ongoing) translations as "open-ended series" in "Clarice Lispector, J. M. Coetzee and the Seriality of Trans-lation," *Translation Studies* 3, no. 3 (2010): 320.

2. The two features that seem most essential to programmatic accounts of close reading, several of which I discuss at the end of this chapter, are the distinction between "intrinsic" and "extrinsic" features of a text (and the reader's emphasis on the former); and the privileged encounter with the smallest units of a text, its individual words (even if readers are also meant to analyze "larger" features such as theme, structure, and narrative voice). For a recent overview of the intrinsic/extrinsic distinction, see Andrew Du-bois, introduction to *Close Reading: A Reader*, ed. Frank Lenricchia and An-drew Dubois (Durham, NC: Duke University Press, 2002), 8. For a classic ac-count of how book history complicates this distinction, see D. F. McKenzie, "The Book as an Expressive Form," in *The Book History Reader*, ed. David Finkelstein and Alistair McCleery (London: Routledge, 2003), 27–38.

3. Lawrence Rainey and Aaron Jaffe have used the phrase "not reading" to refer to all the ways we might analyze the meaning of a literary work with-out paying attention to the words on the page. "Not reading" a literary text, then, means "reading" something else—for example, book reviews, adver-tisements, typescripts, and other paratextual materials. Close reading at a distance retains close reading as a practice but suggests that it may be difficult to discern the boundaries between "the text" and something other than the text. Lawrence Rainey, *Institutions of Modernism: Literary Elites and Public Culture* (New Haven, CT: Yale University Press, 1998); and Aaron Jaffe, *Modernism and the Culture of Celebrity* (Cambridge: Cambridge University Press, 2005).

4. J. M. Coetzee, *Diary of a Bad Year* (London: Harvill Secker, 2007). Unless oth-erwise indicated, all future references to the text will refer to this edition.

5. Like *Childhood of Jesus* (2013), *Diary* was first published in Holland. It appeared in Dutch in August 2007 and within fourteen months appeared in Australia, the United Kingdom, Canada, Spain, the United States, German, Japan, and France. J. M. Coetzee, *Dagboek van een slecht jaar* (Diary of a bad year), trans. Peter Bergsma (Amsterdam: Cossee, 2007). A sticker affixed to the front cover proclaims the Dutch edition *"Wereldprimeur de nieuwe roman van de Nobelprijswinnaar"* (a rough translation of which would be "world premier of the new novel by the Nobel Prize winner"). In 2007 *Diary* was published in Australia on September 3; the United Kingdom on September 6; Canada on October 23; Spain on October 30; and the United States on December 27. In 2008 the book appeared in Germany on April 1, Japan on September 9, and France on October 1.

6. J. M. Coetzee, *Doubling the Point: Essays and Interviews*, ed. David Attwell (Cambridge, MA: Harvard University Press, 1992), 90.

7. J. M. Coetzee, *White Writing: On the Culture of Letters in South Africa* (New Haven, CT: Yale University Press, 1988), 118.

8. In *Slow Man*, as I discuss below, Marijana, a recent migrant from Croatia, often speaks in accented English, which is registered in the text by missing articles and imperfect word choice ("flesh" for "flash"; "book saver" for "book collector"). These are the least translatable moments in the novel—however, not because of what they convey about Croatian but because of what they convey about English: that it functions as a medium of translation rather than as the character's or the novel's natural language. However, this is not really "language transfer" since Marijana is not speaking Croatian here; rather, she is speaking English translated from Croatian. J. M. Coetzee, *Slow Man* (New York: Viking, 2005), 54, 47. To represent speech in other languages, Coetzee often incorporates foreign (non-English) words or phrases. However, most of these words and phrases will be translated in the text. Otherwise, Coetzee tends to render all characters in the same idiom. Coetzee's first novel, *In the Heart of the Country*, offers an interesting case: sections originally published in Afrikaans were translated into English when the novel moved from its South African to its British edition. For an excellent discussion of this translation within so-called English-language editions, see Rita Barnard, "Coetzee in/as Afrikaans," *Journal of Literary Studies* 25, no. 4 (2009): 438–62.

9. Andrew van der Vlies, South African Textual Cultures: White, Black, Read All Over (Manchester, U.K.: Manchester University Press, 2007), 5. Two of the best recent studies of multilingualism, book history, and the South African context of Coetzee's work are van der Vlies's *South African Textual Cultures* and Rita Barnard's "Coetzee in/and Afrikaans."

10. J. M. Coetzee, *Inner Workings: Essays 2000–2005* (London: Harvill Secker, 2007).

11. J. M. Coetzee, "Roads to Translation," *Meanjin* 64, no. 4 (December 2005): 141–52.

12. Peter McDonald, "The Ethics of Reading and the Question of the Novel," in *NOVEL* 43, no. 3 (2010): 493.

13. Timothy Bewes calls *Elizabeth Costello* a "novel" even though the subtitle pronounces it a "fiction." Timothy Bewes, *The Event of Postcolonial Shame* (Princeton, NJ: Princeton University Press, 2010), 150; and J. M. Coetzee, *Elizabeth Costello: Fiction* (New York: Penguin, 2003). The U.S. title of *Summertime* includes the word "fiction" in the subtitle, whereas the U.K. subtitle promises "scenes from a provincial life," which matches the two prior fictional memoirs. J. M. Coetzee, *Summertime: Fiction* (New York: Viking, 2009); and J. M. Coetzee, *Summertime: Scenes from a Provincial Life* (London: Harvill Secker, 2009). McDonald notes that the cover of *Diary*'s Australian edition promises a "novel," whereas the U.S. and U.K. editions promise "fiction" (493). The Dutch edition promises a "novel" too. Both *Elizabeth Costello* and *Summertime*, arguably the least novelistic of the four books considered in this chapter, were chosen as finalists for the Man Booker Prize (given to "the best novel of the year," according to the Man Booker Web site). As Coetzee well knows, the disavowal of the novel is a recognizable and longstanding gesture of the anglophone novel itself. But the genre also changes as it travels: a truly global approach to this question would have to acknowledge that, in French and Dutch, *roman* signifies differently and much more capaciously than "novel" does.

14. Benedict Anderson, *Imagined Communities: Reflections on the Origin and Spread of Nationalism*, 3rd ed. (London: Verso, 2006), 34, 30.

15. Stefan Helgesson has argued that Coetzee's *Waiting for the Barbarians* (1980) "is, in important respects, *an already translated novel*" (his emphasis) because its setting and historical period are intentionally vague. While the novel is designed to be "read *out of context*," Helgesson argues, actual translation creates new contexts and new versions of the work ("Clarice Lispector," 324–26).

16. Modeled on a fictional letter penned by the Austrian poet Hugo von Hofmannsthal in 1902, Elizabeth's dispatch (like Hofmannsthal's, addressed to Francis Bacon) suggests that a writer's obsession with the resources of language ultimately obstructs both agency and community. It obstructs translation too.

17. See my discussion of these paradigms in the introduction.

18. In an episode that is in some ways untranslatable, we learn in *Elizabeth Costello* that the novelist has selected the unusual word "acidulous" as the perfect term to describe herself (37). It is impossible to transmit into another language the exact properties of this term—its strangeness within English as well as its denotative meaning—but the fact of choosing it and pointing at it diegetically can survive in many languages and can have the effect of reminding us that even writers who choose their words carefully, as Elizabeth does, cannot control what happens to them. Moments like this one chime

with others in which Elizabeth seems to regret the globalization of culture: the way a Russian singer, speaking English, rhymes "dove" with "stove" rather than "love," or the way the singer's so-called Russian song "sounds everything but Russian" (49). The novel's interest in pronunciation, including pronunciation it will not represent directly, suggests its resistance to global circulation, or at least its ambivalence. For Coetzee, the Russian song's failure to be Russian is less worrying than the difference between the claim to authenticity and the generic "sounds" that seem to effect its achievement. The novel's ambivalence about the homogenization of art and the disappearance of vernacular idiom can be seen too in the way it toys with puns that appear as if by accident: a hotel elevator that leads to a bedroom tryst is casually described as a "shaft" (23); on her way to meet her sister who has become a nun, the nonbelieving Elizabeth worries that she has contracted a stomach bug but "prays she is wrong" (117). These episodes are difficult to translate in good part because they use the resources of English to make their point, though their point largely supports the idea that words, even in their original language, will always exceed the meanings attributed to them.

19. J. M. Coetzee, "Diary of a Bad Year," *New York Review of Books*, July 19, 2007.

20. In the U.K. edition, the table of contents appears at the start of the book. It guides our reading. However, in the French edition, it appears—as is common in French books—at the end.

21. Patrick Denman Flanery, "J. M. Coetzee's autre-biography," *Times Literary Supplement*, September 9, 2009.

22. For an excellent account of Coetzee's insistence on "modesty" as a critical disposition, see Thom Dancer, "Between Belief and Knowledge: J. M. Coetzee and the Present of Reading," in *Minnesota Review* 77 (2011): 131–42.

23. The chronology of interviews as they appear in the text runs from May 2008 to June 2008 to December 2007 to September 2007 to January 2008, whereas the interviews themselves run from September 2007 through June 2008. Put another way, the table of contents introduces us to Julia, Margot, Adriana, Martin, and Sophie, whereas the biographer met Martin, Margot, Adriana, Sophie, Julia, and then Margot (again).

24. There are two hints of this later production. First, the notebooks are described by the biographer as "notebooks for the years 1972–75," which leaves open the possibility that they are not from these years but only about them (19). Second, Mr. Vincent reads to Martin from a new entry which, like the others, is written in the present tense about the 1970s. He says of that entry, "It is undated, but I am pretty sure he wrote it in 1999 or 2000" (208).

25. The French translation of the book is J. M. Coetzee, *L'été de la vie*, trans. Catherine Luaga Du Plessis (Paris: Seuil, 2010).

26. The direct quotation of Stephen's comment, "Agenbite of inwit," signals this connection. J. M. Coetzee, *Summertime: Scenes from a Provincial Life* (London: Harvill Secker, 2009), 4.

27. Timothy Bewes has argued persuasively that Coetzee would regard critical detachment as a new occasion for shame because detachment distributes shame elsewhere and because it claims for itself a kind of self-knowing wisdom. Bewes, *The Event of Postcolonial Shame*, 138. Peter McDonald has shown that Coetzee has a long track-record of rejecting the authoritative, unaffiliated role of the author. McDonald, "The Ethics of Reading," 496.

28. Dubois, Introduction to *Close Reading*. The longstanding equation between "reading" and "words on the page" seems understandable when we consider the New Critical preference for short poems, in which all of a text's words can often be encountered on a single page. For a brief discussion of close reading's institutional history, see John Guillory, "Close Reading: Prologue and Epilogue," *ADE Bulletin*, no. 149 (2010): 9.

29. Jane Gallop, "Close Reading in 2009," *ADE Bulletin*, no. 149 (2010), 16; and Jonathan Culler, "The Closeness of Close Reading," *ADE Bulletin*, no. 149 (2010), 24.

30. On the turn toward books in the study of texts, in the field of world literature alone, see Brent Hayes Edwards, *The Practice of Diaspora: Literature, Translation, and the Rise of Black Internationalism* (Cambridge, MA: Harvard University Press, 2003); Isabel Hofmyer, *The Portable Bunyan: A Transnational History of the Pilgrim's Progress* (Princeton, NJ: Princeton University Press, 2004); McDonald, "The Ethics of Reading"; Franco Moretti, "Conjectures on World Literature." *New Left Review* 1 (2000): 54–69; and Martin Puchner, *Poetry of the Revolution: Marx, Manifestos, and the Avant-Gardes* (Princeton, NJ: Princeton University Press, 2006). On dominant practices of close reading, in addition to essays by Culler, Gallop, and Guillory, see Stephen Best and Sharon Marcus, "Surface Reading: An Introduction," *Representations* 108, no. 1 (Fall 2009): 1–21; and Bewes, *The Event of Postcolonial Shame*.

31. Daniel Hack, "Close Reading at a Distance: The African-Americanization of Bleak House," *Critical Inquiry* 34, no. 4 (Summer 2008): 729–53.

32. This phrase appears in a related essay, Daniel Hack, "Close Reading at a Distance: Bleak House," *Novel* 42, no. 3 (2009): 429.

33. Best and Marcus, "Surface Reading," 1.

34. Timothy Bewes, "Reading with the Grain: A New World in Literary Criticism," *Differences: A Journal of Feminist Cultural Studies* 21, no. 3 (2010): 1–33.

35. Best and Marcus, "Surface Reading," 5.

36. Culler, "The Closeness of Close Reading," 22.

37. Ibid., 23.

38. Gallop, "Close Reading in 2009," 17.

39. Ibid., 16.

40. Naomi Schor, *Reading in Detail: Aesthetics and the Feminine* (1987; repr., New York: Routledge, 2007).

41. Ibid., xlii.

42. Ibid., xli.

43. Ibid., 76–77.

44. Gallop, "Close Reading in 2009," 16.

2. THE SERIES, THE LIST, AND THE CLONE

1. Steven Owen, "What Is World Poetry?," *New Republic*, November 19, 1990, 28–32; Gayatri Chakravorty Spivak, *Death of a Discipline* (New York: Columbia University Press, 2003); Emily Apter, "On Translation in a Global Market," *Public Culture* 13, no. 1 (Winter 2001): 1–12; Jonathan Arac, "Anglo-Globalism?," *New Left Review* 16 (July–August 2002): 35–45; and Timothy Brennan, "The Cuts of Language: The East/West of North/South," *Public Culture* 13, no. 1 (Winter 2001): 39–63.

2. Owen, "What Is World Poetry," 31; Spivak, *Death*, 18–19; and Apter, "On Translation," 12.

3. Brennan, "The Cuts of Language," 59–61.

4. The translation data comes from Ishiguro's U.K. publishers, Faber & Faber, accessed April 2, 2014, http://www.faber.co.uk/catalog/author/kazuo-ishiguro.

5. On worrying, see Kazuo Ishiguro and Kezuburo Oe, "The Novelist in Today's World: A Conversation" (1989), in *Conversations with Kazuo Ishiguro*, ed. Brian W. Shaffer and Cynthia W. Wong (Jackson: University of Mississippi Press, 2008), 60. On embracing, see Cynthia F. Wong, "Like Idealism Is to the Intellect: An Interview with Kazuo Ishiguro" (2001), in *Conversations with Kazuo Ishiguro*, ed. Brian W. Shaffer and Cynthia W. Wong, 174–88 (Jackson: University of Mississippi Press, 2008), 179–81; and "Interview with Claire Hamilton" (2007), cited in Motoyuki Shibata and Motoko Sugano, "Strange Reads: Kazuo Ishiguro's *A Pale View of Hills* and *An Artist of the Floating World* in Japan," in *Kazuo Ishiguro: Contemporary Critical Perspectives*, ed. Sean Matthews and Sebastian Groes (London: Continuum, 2009), 21.

6. Wong, "Like Idealism," 180.

7. Ishiguro has spoken of this, but the publishing history of his novels is also telling. Within six months of its first printing, *Never Let Me Go* was published in U.K. (March 3), Canadian (March 8), Dutch (March), U.S. (April 11), Spanish (June 30), German (August 31), Finnish (September 1), and Swedish editions (September 1). By the end of the calendar year, editions in Polish (October 25) and Portuguese had appeared; French and Japanese editions followed in March and April 2006. For Ishiguro's comments, see Tim Adams, "For Me, England Is a Mythical Place," *Guardian (Observer)*, February 20, 2005, http://www.theguardian.com/books/2005/feb/20/fiction.kazuoishiguro; and Michael Scott Moore and Michael Sontheimer, "*Spiegel*

Interview with Kazuo Ishiguro: I Remain Fascinated by Memory," *Spiegel Online*, October 5, 2005, accessed April 2, 2014, http://www.spiegel.de/international/spiegel-interview-with-kazuo-ishiguro-i-remain-fascinated-by-memory-a-378173.html.

8. Adams, "For Me."

9. The novels are *A Pale View of Hills* (1982) and *An Artist of the Floating World* (1986). The appearance of English in each novel is also significant, as I discuss in *Cosmopolitan Style: Modernism Beyond the Nation* (New York: Columbia University Press, 2006).

10. On *The Remains of the Day*, see Bruce Robbins, "The Village of the Liberal Managerial Class," in *Cosmopolitan Geographies: New Locations in Literature and Culture*, ed. Vinay Dharwadker, 15–32 (New York: Routledge, 2001), 26–30; Walkowitz, *Cosmopolitan Style*, 110–30; James M. Lang, "Public Memory, Private History: Kazuo Ishiguro's *The Remains of the Day*," *Clio* 29, no. 2 (Winter 2000): 143–65; John J. Su, "Refiguring National Character: The Remains of the British Estate Novel," *Modern Fiction Studies* 48, no. 3 (Fall 2002): 552–80; and Cynthia F. Wong, "Kazuo Ishiguro's *The Remains of the Day*," in *A Companion to the British and Irish Novel, 1945–2000*, ed. Brian W. Shaffer, 493–503 (Oxford: Blackwell, 2005).

11. The works most explicitly engaged in geographies of imperialism are *A Pale View of Hills* (1982), *An Artist of the Floating World*, *Remains of the Day*, and *When We Were Orphans* (2000). Thematic engagement with philosophies of art is present in some of the earlier volumes, especially *Artist* and *The Unconsoled*, but the topic is most thoroughly explored in *Never Let Me Go*.

12. Kazuo Ishiguro, *The Remains of the Day* (New York: Vintage, 1989), 77.

13. Simon Gikandi, "Globalization and the Claims of Postcoloniality," *South Atlantic Quarterly* 100, no. 3 (Summer 2001): 632–33, at 633.

14. "Geography of the book" is a phrase coined by Leah Price in "The Tangible Page," *London Review of Books*, February 3, 2000, 38.

15. British Council Poland, "Interview with Kazuo Ishiguro," October26, 2005, accessed September 16, 2007, http://www.britishcouncil.org/poland-kazuo-ishiguro.htm. (This material is no longer found at this Web site.)

16. J. M. Coetzee, "Roads to Translation," *Meanjin* 64, no. 4 (December 2005): 141–52.

17. Ibid. The U.K. edition of *Waiting for the Barbarians* appeared in 1980; Chinese editions appeared in 2002 and 2004.

18. Roland Barthes, "The Death of the Author," in *The Rustle of Language*, trans. Richard Howard, 49–55 (Berkeley: University of California Press, 1989).

19. For world literature as a "network," see David Damrosch, *What Is World Literature?* (Princeton, NJ: Princeton University Press, 2003).

20. Stefan Helgesson describes composition as an act of translation because it requires writers to negotiate "between the literary culture to which they aspire and their geographical situatedness." Stefan Helgesson, "Clarice

Lispector, J. M. Coetzee and the Seriality of Translation," *Translation Studies* 3, no. 3 (2010): 322.

21. British Council Poland, "Interview with Kazuo Ishiguro."

22. Marcel Proust, *In Search of Lost Time*, vol. 6. Trans. Andreas Mayor and Terence Kilmartin, rev. by D. J. Enright (New York: Modern Library, 1993), 287.

23. Martin Puchner proposes that the Communist Manifesto should be understood to have an autonomous existence in several languages. Martin Puchner, *Poetry of the Revolution: Marx, Manifestos, and the Avant-Gardes* (Princeton, NJ: Princeton University Press, 2006), 51–52.

24. Peter D. McDonald, "Ideas of the Book and Histories of Literature: After Theory?," *PMLA* 121, no. 1 (January 2006): 214–28.

25. Noël Carroll, quoted in ibid., 223.

26. Ibid., 224.

27. Ibid., 223–25.

28. This has not always been so, but today international copyright law regards translations as "derivative works" rather than works based on new or collaborative authorship. Lawrence Venuti, *The Scandals of Translation: Towards an Ethics of Difference* (London: Routledge, 1998), 55.

29. Walkowitz, *Cosmopolitan Style*, 127–30.

30. Responding to my claim that Coetzee and Ishiguro anticipate translation (Rebecca L. Walkowitz, "Comparison Literature," *New Literary History* 40 [2009]: 567–82), Helgesson rightly points out that actual translations will always "undercut the writer's authority even as they expand the work." Acknowledging the agency of the author as well as the translators, he refers to the literary work in translation as a "serial collective." Helgesson, "Clarice Lispector," 320.

31. Emily Apter associates "translatability" with the condition of objects that can be too readily consumed across "linguistic, cultural, and social contexts." Apter, "On Translation in a Global Market," 1–3.

32. Kazuo Ishiguro, *Never Let Me Go* (New York: Knopf, 2005), 70, 271–72.

33. Frank Kermode, "Outrageous Game," *London Review of Books* 27, no. 8 (April 2005): 21–22.

34. A survey of the editions published in the novel's first year shows only one other cover that does not display an image of a person or of what appears to be part of a person. That is the first Dutch translation, which displays an image of discarded refuse in a field. Kazuo Ishiguro, *Laat me nooit alleen*, trans. Bartho Krieck (Amsterdam: Atlas, 2005). A later Dutch translation, published by Eldorado in 2006, shows what appears to be two human hearts (figure 2.3).

35. Walter Benjamin, *Illuminations*, trans. Harry Zohn (New York: Schocken, 1968), 256.

36. Ibid., 71, 73.

37. Sharon Marcus, *Between Women: Friendship, Desire, and Marriage in Victorian England* (Princeton, NJ: Princeton University Press, 2006). See also Ste-

phen Best and Sharon Marcus, "Surface Reading: An Introduction," *Representations* 108, no. 1 (Fall 2009): 1–21.

38. Anthony Appiah, *Cosmopolitanism: Ethics in a World of Strangers* (New York: Norton, 2006), 109–13.

39. Werner Sollors, ed., *Multilingual America: Transnationalism, Ethnicity, and the Languages of American Literature* (New York: New York University Press, 1998); Marc Shell and Werner Sollors, eds. *The Multilingual Anthology of American Literature: A Reader of Original Texts with English Translations* (New York: New York University Press, 2000); Joshua Miller, *Accented America: The Cultural Politics of Multilingual Modernism* (New York: Oxford University Press, 2011); and Harsha Ram, "Towards and Crosscultural Poetics of the Contact Zone: Romantic, Modernist, and Soviet Intertextualities in Boris Paternak's Translations of T'itisian T'bidze," *Comparative Literature* 59, no. 1 (Winter 2007): 63–89.

40. Franco Moretti, "Conjectures on World Literature," *New Left Review* 1 (2000): 56–57.

3. SAMPLING, COLLATING, AND COUNTING

1. Some later versions of multistranded fiction, though they continue to focus on the city and the nation, begin to retract the impression of wholeness by folding literary history into the plot and by emphasizing the overlap or merging of narrative strands. In Michael Ondaatje's *The English Patient* (1992), Michael Cunningham's *The Hours* (1998), and Zadie Smith's *White Teeth* (2000), for example, the multistranded book in one's hands appears analogous to a multistranded book in the text (Herodotus's *Histories*, *Mrs. Dalloway*, and *The Tempest*, respectively). There is no longer a self-contained object, both because the text seems to belong to many historical periods and because it seems to supplement and in some ways extend a prior text. In these city- and region-shaped books, the principles of distribution and accumulation are part of the story, since the meaning of the characters shifts over the course of the narrative (the "English patient" is not English, after all) and since the collectivity made by the novel includes not only its characters but also its readers.

2. Mariano Siskind analyzes world literature's reliance on these concepts in "The Globalization of the Novel and the Novelization of the Global: A Critique of World Literature," *Comparative Literature* 62, no. 4 (2010): 352.

3. For a critique of the "diffusion" model, see Srinivas Aravamudan, *Enlightenment Orientalism: Resisting the Rise of the Novel* (Princeton, NJ: Princeton University Press, 2012).

4. David Mitchell, *Ghostwritten* (New York: Vintage, 2001), 173.

5. Timothy Bewes, *The Event of Postcolonial Shame* (Princeton, NJ: Princeton University Press, 2010), 71, emphasis in original.

6. See Eric Hayot's account of competing ideas of world and David Damrosch's effort to account for the different ways that world literature is understood throughout the world, through his concept of "global world literature." Eric Hayot, *On Literary Worlds* (Oxford: Oxford University Press, 2012); and David Damrosch, "Toward a History of World Literature," *New Literary History* 39 (2008): 490. Mariano Siskind argues that location inflects the "novel's relationship to globalization" ("The Globalization of the Novel," 337–38). Likewise, Pheng Cheah and John Marx have argued that literature makes worlds as well as enters into them. Pheng Cheah, "What Is a World? On World Literature and World-Making Activity," *Daedalus* 137, no. 3: 36; and John Marx, *Geopolitics and the Anglophone Novel, 1890–2011* (Cambridge: Cambridge University Press, 2012), 11.

7. For an eloquent account of the relationship between counting narrative parts and counting people, see Carol Jacobs, "What Does It Mean to Count? W. G. Sebald's *The Emigrants*," chap. 5 in *Skirting the Ethical* (Stanford, CA: Stanford University Press, 2008), 138–39.

8. Sebald's writing, for example, engages with a long history of minority rights that links late-twentieth-century Britain to mid-twentieth-century Europe and to earlier histories of slavery and colonialism in Africa, the Americas, and Asia.

9. Will Kymlicka, *Multicultural Citizenship: A Liberal Theory of Minority Rights* (Oxford: Clarendon Press, 1995), 10.

10. The model fits well with Romantic understandings of world literature because it is rooted in the idea that literary works give voice to the cultural particularity of the group, traditionally the nation. Siskind rightly describes this model as pluralist. Siskind, "The Globalization of the Novel," 352.

11. Michael Waltzer, "Comment," in *Multiculturalism: Examining the Politics of Recognition*, by Charles Taylor, ed. Amy Gutman, 99–104 (Princeton, NJ: Princeton University Press, 1994), 102.

12. K. Anthony Appiah, "Identity, Authenticity, Survival: Multicultural Societies and Social Reproduction," in *Multiculturalism: Examining the Politics of Recognition*, by Charles Taylor, ed. Amy Gutman, 149–64 (Princeton, NJ: Princeton University Press, 1994), 149. Appiah concludes, "Between the politics of recognition and the politics of compulsion there is no bright line" (163).

13. Werner Hamacher, "One 2 Many Multiculturalisms," trans. Dana Hollander (1994, German; 1997, English), in *Violence, Identity, and Self-Determination*, ed. Hent De Vries and Samuel Weber (Stanford, CA: Stanford University Press, 1997), 295.

14. Ibid., 296–98.

15. Kiran Desai, *The Inheritance of Loss* (New York: Atlantic Monthly Press, 2006), 355.

16. Peter Ho Davies, *The Welsh Girl* (Boston: Houghton Mifflin, 2007).

17. Waïl Hassan addresses the many turns of translation in the novel in "Agency and Translational Literature: Ahdaf Soueif's *The Map of Love*," *PMLA* 121, no. 3 (May 2006): 753–68.

18. Rebecca L. Walkowitz, "The Location of Literature: The Transnational Book and the Migrant Writer," *Contemporary Literature* 47, no. 4 (Winter 2006): 527–45.

19. Caryl Phillips, *A New World Order: Essays* (New York: Vintage, 2001), 5.

20. Phillips makes a similar point in his 2009 novel, *In the Falling Snow*, by tucking an account of the Windrush migration into the latter pages of a narrative about race in contemporary Britain. Caryl Phillips, *In the Falling Snow* (New York: Vintage, 2009).

21. On Phillips's "plural selves," see Louise Yelin, "Plural Selves: The Dispersion of the Autobiographical Subject in the Essays of Caryl Phillips," in *Caryl Phillips: Writing in the Key of Life*, ed. Bénédicte Ledent and Daria Tunca, 57–73 (Amsterdam: Rodopi, 2012); and Louise Yelin, "'Living State-Side': Caryl Phillips and the United States," *Moving Worlds: A Journal of Transcultural Writings* 7, no. 1 (2007): 85–102.

22. Caryl Phillips, *Extravagant Strangers: A Literature of Belonging* (New York: Vintage, 1997).

23. Theodore O. Mason, "The African-American Anthology: Mapping the Territory, Taking the National Census, Building the Museum," *American Literary History* 10 (1998): 191.

24. Caryl Phillips, *A Distant Shore* (New York: Vintage, 2003), 3.

25. Briefly and schematically, Phillips also introduces the lesbianism of the narrator's sister and the sister's abuse by their father.

26. Timothy Bewes argues that Phillips's novels restrict voices because they are dramatizing the impossibility of writing about colonialism, slavery, genocide, and other topics that are, literally, unspeakable. Bewes, *Event of Postcolonial Shame*.

27. For alternative readings of the novel's final section, see Berthold Schoene, *The Cosmopolitan Novel* (Edinburgh: Edinburgh University Press, 2009); and Rita Barnard, "Fictions of the Global," *Novel* 42, no. 2 (2009): 207–15.

28. As Rita Barnard has shown, *Ghostwritten* works to "challenge the normativity of English" by announcing emphatically that a character is speaking some other language (Barnard, "Fictions of the Global," 213).

29. David Mitchell, *Number9Dream* (New York: Random House, 2003), 82.

30. For English readers, multiple fonts do the work of multiple languages. To achieve this effect beyond English is difficult, since translations are unlikely to preserve the acronym and since readers in other languages might not

find it strange to see references to English. However, the story's thematic engagement with translation survives translation relatively well.

31. The titles of the German-language editions of Mitchell's books draw attention to the project of enumeration, though they tend to imply that the number of parts is knowable in advance. *Ghostwritten* is titled *Chaos: Ein Roman in neun Teilen* (A novel in nine parts), while *Black Swan Green* appears as *Der dreizehnte Monat* (Thirteen months). The German edition of *Number9Dream* preserves the English title. The French edition of *Ghostwritten* is titled *Écrits fantômes* and, like other French books, places the table of contents at the end. Readers who move through the French book chronologically (without jumping to the back) are likely to have fewer expectations about the whole. One way of understanding the uncountability of Mitchell's audience, then, is by considering how the novels' presentation of countability is altered as the books move into new editions.

32. David Kurnick, "Bolaño to Come." *Public Books*, September 5, 2012, accessed April 2, 2014, http://www.publicbooks.org/fiction/bolano-to-come.

33. David Mitchell, *Cloud Atlas* (New York: Random House, 2004), 309.

34. David Mitchell, *Black Swan Green* (New York: Random House, 2007), 10, 62, 6, 63.

35. I borrow this reversal of "norms" from Disability Studies. Michael Davidson, *Concerto for the Left Hand: Disability and the Defamiliar Body* (Ann Arbor: University of Michigan Press, 2008).

36. Wyatt Mason, "David Mitchell, the Experimentalist," *New York Times Magazine*, June 25, 2010, accessed April 2, 2014, http://www.nytimes.com/2010/06/27/magazine/27mitchell-t.html?pagewanted=all&_r=0.

37. The Netherlands was under French rule or influence from 1796–1813. David Mitchell, *The Thousand Autumns of Jacob de Zoet* (New York: Random House, 2011), 399.

38. David Damrosch describes the evolution of *The Thousand and One Nights* through translation. Its movement from Arabic to French and back into Arabic involved the addition of new tales as well as the revision of old ones. David Damrosch, *How to Read World Literature* (Chichester, U.K.: Wiley Blackwell, 2008), 75–82.

39. David Mitchell, *Les mille automnes de Jacob de Zoet*, trans. Manuel Berri (Paris: Éditions de l'Olivier, 2012).

40. Aravamudan, *Enlightenment Orientalism*, 8.

41. Jahan Ramazani, "A Transnational Poetics," *American Literary History* 18, no. 2 (Summer 2006): 334–35.

42. Wai Chee Dimock, "Scales of Aggregation: Prenational, Subnational, Transnational," *American Literary History* 18, no. 2 (Summer 2006): 226.

43. Ramazani's project should not be confused, for example, with Barthes's project in "The Death of the Author."

44. On "aggregates," see Dimock, "Scales of Aggregation," 219–28.

45. Amy Waldman, *The Submission* (New York: Farrar, Straus and Giroux, 2011), 6.

4. THIS IS NOT YOUR LANGUAGE

1. For an excellent discussion of what she calls "the monolingual paradigm," see Yasemin Yildiz, *Beyond the Mother Tongue: The Postmonolingual Condition* (New York: Fordham University Press, 2012). See also David Bellos, *Is That a Fish in Your Ear* (New York: Faber and Faber, 2011), especially the chapter entitled "Native Command: Is Your Language Really Yours?," 60–68.

2. Meena Alexander, *Poetics of Dislocation* (Ann Arbor: University of Michigan Press, 2009), 193.

3. In a powerful essay calling for "building a new public idea about language," Mary Louise Pratt, (then) president of the Modern Language Association, argues, "language—including one's own native language—has to be taught with as much effort and seriousness as mathematics and music." Mary Louise Pratt, "Building a New Public Idea About Language," *ADFL Bulletin* 34, no. 3 (Spring 2003): 8.

4. Alexander, *Poetics of Dislocation*, 193.

5. Ibid., her quotation marks.

6. Judith Butler has argued that a "non-nationalist or counter-nationalist mode of belonging," a mode of belonging that does not exclude minorities, will require a "certain distance or fissure," which Butler associates literally and figuratively with translation. Instead of "extending or augmenting the homogeneity of the nation," she asserts, genuine equality requires "a collectivity that comes to exercise its freedom in a language or set of languages for which difference and translation are irreducible" (61–62). Judith Butler and Gayatri Chakravorty Spivak, *Who Sings the Nation-State? Language, Politics, Belonging* (London: Seagull Books, 2007), 58–61. Rey Chow argues that source languages and cultures have to be understood as "comparative" rather than as "monolingual, monocultural, or mononational" (85). Rey Chow, *The Age of the World Target: Self-Referentiality in War, Theory, and Comparative Work* (Durham, NC: Duke University Press, 2006).

7. Naoki Sakai, *Translation and Subjectivity: On "Japan" and Cultural Nationalism* (Minneapolis: University of Minnesota Press, 1997), 4.

8. Naoki Sakai, "Translation as a Filter," trans. Gavin Walker and Naoki Sakai, *Transeuropeennes: Revue internationale de pensée critique*, March 25, 2010, 7. http://www.transeuropeennes.eu/en/articles/200/Translation_as_a_filter.

9. Naoki Sakai, "How Do We Count a Language? Translation and Discontinuity," *Translation Studies* 2, no. 1 (2009): 83–84.

10. Ibid., 74.

11. In a study of "the monolingual paradigm," Yildiz, who is a Germanist and a comparative literature scholar, insists that there is not "one privileged language" and that a language is not special "because one is born into it" (*Beyond the Mother Tongue*, 203). Instead, she argues, one's first language may induce feelings of alienation rather than comfort; or one may feel more comfortable operating in several languages (204). Yildiz acknowledges that the mother tongue "may indeed be experienced as a wholesome unity by some"; "the problem lies," she asserts, "in the monolingual paradigm's insistence that this is always and exclusively the case" (205).

12. Arguing that an emphasis on birthplace can serve to denigrate migrant communities, many critics now place the term "native" in quotation marks, or use it to describe people (someone born in a place) but not languages (a tongue that is natural or intrinsic). For example, see Yildiz, *Beyond the Mother Tongue*; Bellos, *Is That a Fish*; and David Damrosch, *How to Read World Literature* (Chichester, U.K.: Wiley Blackwell, 2008), 128.

13. Emily Brown Coolidge Toker, who teaches second-language acquisition, objects to the idea that a language is "somehow intrinsically, intuitively known" by those who have learned it unconsciously. She contends that the category of the "native speaker," far from protecting minority groups, limits the "agency and ownership" of postcolonial and migrant speakers when they enter into dominant languages such as English. Emily Brown Coolidge Toker, "What Makes a Native Speaker? Nativeness, Ownership, and Global Englishes," *Minnesota Review* 78, no. 1 (2012): 122.

14. Gayatri Chakravorty Spivak, *An Aesthetic Education in the Era of Globalization* (Cambridge, MA: Harvard University Press, 2012), especially the chapters "How to Teach a 'Culturally Different' Book" and "Translation as Culture," 73–96, and 241–255, respectively.

15. Translator and French scholar David Bellos prefers the rhetoric of professionalism, being an "expert," to the rhetoric of origin or birth. Bellos, *Is That a Fish*, 66–68. Mary Louise Pratt points out that while the idea of "natural" or intrinsic language acquisition is in some ways democratic because it presumes that all children have the capacity to learn the language that surrounds them, it also "obscures the roles long-term training and experience abroad play in the development of advanced language abilities, whether in first languages or added ones." Pratt continues, "Whether language training is institutionalized or not, all societies have it." Pratt, "Building a New Public Idea About Language," 8–9.

16. Yildiz, *Beyond the Mother Tongue*, 14.

17. I'm thinking here of the dispute over Stephen's use of the word "tundish." The dean of studies, an Englishman, doesn't know the word and thus assumes it is Irish. Later, Stephen realizes that it is "good old blunt English." Stephen laments that "the language we are speaking is his before it is mine"; but Stephen is the more competent speaker. The irony of "owner-

ship" is registered in Stephen's comment, "What did he come here for to teach us his own language or to learn it from us." James Joyce, *A Portrait of the Artist as a Young Man* (New York: Penguin, 1999), 216.

18. See Fludernik on the "openness" of second-person narrative, and Richardson on its subjunctive quality. Monika Fludernik, "Introduction: Second-Person Narrative and Related Issues," in *Second-Person Narrative*, ed. Harold F. Mosher (Dekalb: Northern Illinois University Press, 1994), 288, accessed May 9, 2014, http://www.freidok.uni-freiburg.de/volltexte/5098/pdf/Fludernik_Introduction_Second_person_narrative.pdf; and Brian Richardson, "The Poetics and Politics of Second Person Narrative," *Genre* 24 (Fall 1991), 319.

19. In love poetry and other erotic writing, Irene Kacandes notes, second-person address can serve to obscure both the speaker's sexuality and the gender of the beloved. Irene Kacandes, "Are You in the Text? The 'Literary Perfomative' in Postmodernist Fiction," *Text and Performance Quarterly* 13 (1993): 151. As Kacandes notes, this works especially well in English, where participles are ungendered. So, for example, the second-person can serve both to express and to conceal homoerotic desire, as it does in many of Frank O'Hara's poems. Conceal, because it is not clear that the speaker is addressing a lover of the same gender. Express, because the work conveys the speaker's desire, introduces the possibility of a homosexual encounter, and refuses the grammatical terms that would close down that possibility.

20. Jonathan Culler, "Apostrophe," chap. 7 in *The Pursuit of Signs: Semiotics, Literature, Deconstruction* (1981; repr., Ithaca, NY: Cornell University Press, 2003), 135–54; and Barbara Johnson, "Apostrophe, Animation, and Abortion," chap. 16 in *A World of Difference* (Baltimore: Johns Hopkins University Press, 1987), 184–200.

21. Irene Kacandes, "Narrative Apostrophe: Reading, Rhetoric, Resistance in Michel Butor's *La modification* and Julio Cortazar's 'Graffiti'," *Style* 28, no. 3 (Fall 1994): 329–49.

22. See the virtuosic chapter on Davis in Lauren Berlant and Lee Edelman, *Sex, or the Unbearable* (Durham, NC: Duke University Press, 2013).

23. Mohsin Hamid, "Mohsin Hamid on His Enduring Love of the Second-Person Narrative," *Guardian*, March 22, 2013, accessed October 2, 2013, http://www.theguardian.com/books/2013/mar/22/mohsin-hamid-second-person-narrative.

24. On the imperative in second-person fiction, see Fludernik, "Introduction," 302; and Richardson, "Poetics and Politics," 319.

25. See Culler, "Apostrophe," 149–50.

26. Culler uses this phrase to talk about apostrophe (ibid., 135), but I'm arguing that it is also true for second-person narrative.

27. Robert Young has made this point eloquently: "Postcolonial literature is inherently comparative, intrinsically more comparative because it is defined

by its comparatism: peau noire, masques blancs." Robert Young, "The Postcolonial Comparative," *PMLA* 128, no. 3 (May 2013): 688.

28. My thanks to Rajeswari Sunder Rajan for suggesting this formulation.

29. These books resist the structure of synecdoche that Robert Young has associated with "Western accounts of contemporary world literature," in which readers encounter "microcosmic portraits" of foreign worlds. Young, "The Postcolonial Comparative," 686.

30. Caroline Levine, "The Great Unwritten: World Literature and the Effacement of Orality," *Modern Language Quarterly* 74, no. 2 (2013): 219.

31. Mohsin Hamid, *How to Get Filthy Rich in Rising Asia* (New York: Riverhead Books, 2013), 33.

32. Lawrence Venuti, "How to Read a Translation," *Words Without Borders* (2004), accessed April 2, 2014, http://wordswithoutborders.org/article/ how-to-read-a-translation; and David Damrosch, "Reading in Translation," chap. 4 in Damrosch, *How to Read World Literature*, 65–85.

33. Lawrence Venuti, *The Translator's Invisibility: A History of Translation*, 2nd ed. (New York: Routledge, 2008), esp. 18–19. See also Lawrence Venuti, *The Scandals of Translation: Towards an Ethics of Difference* (London: Routledge, 1998), esp. chap. 8, "Globalization," 158–89.

34. One hears, too, an echo of Ezra Pound's *How to Read* (London: D. Harsworth, 1931).

35. Thus the subtitle of one of Venuti's influential works, *The Scandals of Translation: Towards an Ethics of Difference*.

36. This argument, while influential among scholars of translation, has been controversial among practicing translators. See, for example, Bellos, who does not mention Venuti directly but does mention "proponents of awkward and foreign-sounding translation styles" in *Is That a Fish*, 59. The most well-known critique is Anthony Pym, "Venuti's Visibility," *Target* 8, no. 1 (1996): 165–77.

37. Lawrence Venuti, "How to Read a Translation," *Words Without Borders: The Online Magazine for International Literature*, July 2004, http:// wordswithoutborders.org/article/how-to-read-a-translation.

38. Damrosch avoids using the word "native" to describe anything other than a place of birth (one's "native country") until the final chapter, when he refers to "near-native fluency," though even here this seems to be a shorthand for a person whose fluency is "near" to fluency of a native (128).

39. Damrosch, "Reading in Translation," 71.

40. Venuti, *The Translator's Invisibility*, 19, 4.

41. Tim Parks does not use the word "translatese," but his description of novels designed for translation—cultural vagueness, linguistic simplicity—fits well with Venuti's description of too-fluent ("immediately recognizable and intelligible" [ibid., 5]) translations. Tim Parks, "The Dull New Global Novel," *New York Review of Books Blog*, February 9, 2010, accessed April 2, 2014, http://

www.nybooks.com/blogs/nyrblog/2010/feb/09/the-dull-new-global-novel/. Venuti points out that Amos Tutuola's *The Palm-Wine Drinkard* was controversial when it was published in 1952 because it was indistinguishable from an "unsystematic" translation. Venuti, *The Scandals of Translation*, 174. Emily Apter uses "translationese" to refer to the original language of literary works produced for the global marketplace. Emily Apter, "Translation in a Global Market," *Public Culture* 13, no. 1: 7. Edith Grossman uses "translatorese" to refer to "robotic pairing," whereby the translation retains too much loyalty to the syntax and sound of the original language, thus failing to produce fluency in the new language. Edith Grossman, *Why Translation Matters* (New Haven, CT: Yale University Press, 2010), 69.

42. Venuti, *The Scandals of Translation*, 4.

43. Parks, "The Dull New Global Novel."

44. Bellos, *Is That a Fish*, 65.

45. Grossman refers to the translator as the "second writer" in *Why Translation Matters*, 49.

46. Nancy Huston, *Longings and Belongings: Essays* (Toronto: McArthur, 2005), 344.

47. Alastair Reid, *Inside Out: Selected Poetry and Translations* (Edinburgh: Polygon, 2008), 168.

48. Sakai, "How Do We Count?" 73.

49. Jamaica Kincaid, *Mr. Potter* (New York: Farrar, Straus and Giroux, 2002).

50. Jamaica Kincaid, *The Autobiography of My Mother* (New York: Farrar, Straus and Giroux, 1996), 156.

51. See Richardson, "Poetics and Politics," 323–24.

52. Jamaica Kincaid, *My Brother* (New York: Farrar, Straus and Giroux, 1997).

53. "Wingless" opens with the narrator's reading of Charles Kingsley's "The Water-Babies," a nineteenth-century children's story narrated in the second person. Kingsley's universal "you" is belied by the story's casual racism. Jamaica Kincaid, "Wingless," *New Yorker*, January 29, 1979, 26–27.

54. My thanks to Philip Tsang for helping me to see this important point.

55. Young, "The Postcolonial Comparative," 688.

56. See Graham Huggan's discussion of "staged marginality" in *The Postcolonial Exotic: Marketing the Margins* (London: Routledge, 2001); and Sarah Brouillette, *Postcolonial Writers in the Global Literary Marketplace* (2007; repr., Basingstoke, U.K.: Palgrave Macmillan, 2011).

57. Kincaid reverses the subject of the sentence, exchanging "Mr. Potter" for "My father's name," as a way to emphasize her ownership of the story. She describes this kind of reversal, or chiasmus, as "an important distinction" in her memoir *My Brother*, 53.

58. For example: "I feel it's my duty to make everyone a little less happy." Jamaica Kincaid, quoted in Marilyn Berlin Snell, "Jamaica Kincaid Hates Happy Endings," *Mother Jones*, September/October 1997, accessed April 2, 2014, http://www.motherjones.com/politics/1997/09/jamaica-kincaid-hates-happy-endings.

59. Malcolm Gladwell, "The Politics of Politesse," *New Yorker*, December 23, 2002, 57.

60. Judith Butler, "Explanation and Exoneration, or What We Can Hear" in *Social Text* 20, no. 3 (Fall 2002): 181.

61. Jamaica Kincaid, *A Small Place* (New York: Farrar, Straus and Giroux, 1988). In her direct address to U.S. and European readers, Brian Richardson observes, Kincaid "is painfully aware of antithetical communities of reception, as well as the ideological codes that typically encase notions like the model reader" ("The Poetics and Politics of Second Person Narrative," 324).

62. I am grateful to Kalyan Nadiminti, whose comments on an early draft of this chapter crystallized this idea for me.

63. Mohsin Hamid, *Moth Smoke* (New York: Riverhead, 2000).

64. Hamid, *How to Get Filthy Rich*, 97; and Hamid, "Mohsin Hamid on His Enduring Love," n.p.

65. Mohsin Hamid, *The Reluctant Fundamentalist* (Orlando, FL: Harcourt, 2008).

66. Or almost nothing. There are a few moments when the narrator seems to be repeating back a phrase uttered by his interlocutor, but these phrases are never cited directly (*The Reluctant Fundamentalist*, 62, 75, 115, 129).

67. Helmut Bonheim, cited in Fludernik, "Introduction," 286.

68. Hamid, *How to Get Filthy Rich*, 33.

69. For the place of *The Thousand and One Nights* in the history of the novel, see Srinivas Aravamudan, *Enlightenment Orientalism: Resisting the Rise of the Novel* (Chicago: Chicago University Press, 2012), 252–53. For *The Thousand and One Nights* as a work that includes its future readers, see Jorges Luis Borges, "The Thousand and One Nights," in *Seven Nights*, trans. Eliot Weinberger, 42–57 (New York: New Directions, 1984).

70. Bellos, *Is That a Fish*, 60.

71. Kacandes, "Are You in the Text?," 140.

72. Ursula Heise, "Globality, Difference, and the International Turn in Ecocriticism," *PMLA* 128, no. 3 (May 2013): 636.

73. For Rushdie's account of this strategy, see "'Commonwealth Literature' Does Not Exist," chap. 3 in *Imaginary Homelands: Essays and Criticism, 1981–1991* (New York: Penguin, 1991), 61–70.

74. David Damrosch, "Global Comparatism and the Question of Language," *PMLA* 128, no. 3 (May 2013): 627.

5. BORN TRANSLATED AND BORN DIGITAL

1. Following Chang and Voge's lead, I have rendered the titles of all of their works in full capital letters. I do this to emphasize medium and form, and to create some discrepancy between the medium of my text and the me-

dium of Young-Hae Chang Heavy Industries. That said, my medium cannot do justice to theirs. Such is the nature of quotation, in any medium. For example, I don't reproduce font, layout, color, or any number of the other qualities that contribute to the distinctiveness of their editions. This selectivity of course applies to citation in previous chapters too.

2. In *NIPPON*, as Jessica Pressman has noted, the rivalry between Japanese and English is even more explicit. Jessica Pressman, "Reading the Code Between the Words: The Role of Translation in Young-Hae Chang Heavy Industries's *Nippon*." *Dichtung-digital* 37 (2007), emphasis in text. Accessed February 14, 2011, http://dichtung-digital.de/2007/Pressman/Pressman.htm.

3. Kelly Shindler, "Interview with Young-Hae Chang Heavy Industries," *Bootprint* 3, no. 1 (Summer 2009), 22–23.

4. All quotations from works by Young-Hae Chang Heavy Industries are taken from their Web site and from animations linked to that site. Since the site is updated frequently and offers no publication dates, I have not provided dates in the text for works I discuss. In addition, standard annotation would give the impression that the first appearance of the work constitutes its unique identity or original state. Young-Hae Chang Heavy Industries goes out of its way to resist this impression. However, for the reader's benefit, I list below approximate dates for the first appearance of each work in one, but of course not all, of its languages, formats, or editions: *SAMSUNG* (2000), *BUST DOWN THE DOORS!* (2000), *RIVIERA* (2002), *DAKOTA* (2002), *TRAVELING TO UTOPIA* (2005), *MORNING OF THE MONGOLOIDS* (2007), *HONEYMOON IN BEPPU* (2009), and *CAMPBELL'S SOUP TOWN* (2011).

5. George Dillon makes this suggestion. Audiences might thus regard national language as one of several modes of aesthetic classification alongside musical genre and visual image. George L. Dillon, "'Think Locally, Act Globally'—a Conundrum for web.art," in *Writing with Images: Towards a Semiotics of the Web*, course outline (2003), accessed April 2, 2014, http://courses.washington.edu/hypertxt/cgi-bin/book/contexts/koreansatire.html.

6. As Pressman notes in "Reading the Code," Chang and Voge allude to the foundational role of translation in digital computing by using the numerical zero "0" (Monaco font) where the alphabetic letter "O" would usually appear. They do this to remind us that electronic literature is constituted by "the translation of computer code into human language." Chang and Voge use English and Japanese in *NIPPON*, Pressman argues, to draw our attention to the materiality of electronic literature. Another digital work that uses translation between human languages to emphasize translation between computer code and human language is John Cayley's, *Translation* (2004), which is available from his Web site: http://programmatology.shadoof.net/. Katherine Hayles discusses *Translation* in N. Katherine Hayles, *Electronic Literature: New Horizons for the Literary* (Notre Dame, IN: University of Notre Dame Press, 2008), 145–54.

7. Pressman, "Reading the Code," emphasis in the original.
8. Pressman published the first print article on Young-Hae-Chang Heavy Industries: "The Strategy of Digital Modernism: Young-Hae Chang Heavy Industries's *Dakota*." *MFS Modern Fiction Studies* 54, no. 2 (Summer 2008): 302–25. A version of this essay also appeared as Jessica Pressman, "Pacific Rim Digital Modernism: The Electronic Literature of Young-Hae Chang Heavy Industries," in *Pacific Rim Modernisms*, ed. Mary Ann Gilles, Helen Sword, and Steven Yao, 316–32 (Toronto: University of Toronto Press, 2009).
9. Hayles, *Electronic Literature*, 128.
10. Robert Castley, *Korea's Economic Miracle: The Crucial Role of Japan* (Basingstoke, U.K.: Macmillan, 1997), 2; Seung-Ho Kwon and Michael O'Donnell, *The Chaebol and Labour in Korea: The Development of Management Strategy in Hyundai* (London: Routledge, 2001), 20–21; and Martin Hart-Landsberg, Seongjin Jeong, and Richard Westra, eds., *Marxist Perspectives on South Korea in the Global Economy* (Aldershot, U.K.: Ashgate, 2007), 1–2.
11. Multimedia Art Asia Pacific Web site for Festival 2002, accessed February 14, 2011, http://maap.asia/2002/english/html/fa_young_hae_chang.php.
12. Castley, *Korea's Economic Miracle*, 252.
13. Henry Turner discusses "corporate form" in "Toward an Analysis of the Corporate Ego: The Case of Richard Hakluyt," *Differences: A Journal of Feminist Cultural Studies* 20, nos. 2 and 3 (2009): 103–46.
14. They are also engaged in corporate art. They have accepted the hospitality of corporate-sponsored museums and galleries, including the Samsung Museum of Art in Seoul. Their work is supported in part by the philanthropic system and makes use of technologies developed by the computer and electronics industries.
15. Jorge Luis Borges, "The Analytical Language of John Wilkins," in *Other Inquisitions, 1937–1952*, trans. Ruth L. C. Simms (Austin: University of Texas Press, 2000), 103.
16. Canonical examples include parts of *The Thousand and One Nights* (written in French but pretending to be from Arabic), *Candide* (French pretending to German) and *Castle of Otronto* (English pretending to Italian). A more recent example is *Double Flowering* (English pretending to Japanese). For a discussion of the latter, see Eric R. J. Hayot, "The Strange Case of Araki Yasusada: Author, Object," *PMLA* 120, no. 1 (January 2005): 66–81. For a discussion of the logic of "exposure" that surrounds fraudulent translations, see Emily Apter, "Translation with No Original: Scandals of Textual Reproduction," chap. 14 in *The Translation Zone: A New Comparative Literature* (Princeton, NJ: Princeton University Press, 2006), 210–25.
17. Shindler, "Interview," 23.
18. Ibid.
19. There are two bilingual editions of the narrative: one is marked "Português/English" and one "Deutsch/English."

20. The second version presents a fake original that is similar to the ones we see in *HONEYMOON* and *MORNING*: there are two streams of text, a French narrative in large font with English subtitles below.
21. But perhaps there are four rather than three languages in play. The English in the *FRANCAIS/ENGLISH* version is different from the English in the *ENGLISH/KOREAN* one. The French version refers to British English: in the text, we see "travelling" instead of "traveling."
22. Translation by Nami Shin.
23. A more recent example of reverse appropriation and comparison: Chang and Voge's *DOWN IN FUKUOKA WITH THE BELARUSIAN BLUES*, which premiered at the Gallery Hyundai in Seoul in October 2010, adapts Arthur Rimbaud's deposition against his lover, Paul Verlaine, from French to English, adds some words in Korean, and moves the narrative to Japan and Russia. A teaser for this work, called *TEASER*, mingles English text with French-accented English voiceover and photographs of various urban scenes, including French cafés in Japan. A description of *DOWN IN FUKUOKA*, which is not yet available on Chang and Voge's Web site, can be found in Ines Min, "A Visceral Experience of Web Art," *Korea Times*, October 15, 2010, accessed February 15, 2011, http://www.koreatimes.co.kr/www/news/art/2010/10/148_74601.html. *TEASER* used to be available on the Web site of the Gallery Hyundai.
24. For this argument, see Hayles, *Electronic Literature*; and Pressman, "The Strategy of Digital Modernism."
25. In U.S. and U.K. editions of *Bridget Jones's Diary*, readers are accommodated by localized spelling, punctuation, slang, measurement, and cultural references. Johanna Seppala, "Differences in the British and American Versions of *Bridget Jones's Diary* by Helen Fielding," Department of Translation Studies, University of Tampere, Fall 2008, accessed April 20, 2014, http://www15.uta.fi/FAST/US1/P1/js-jones.html.
26. The opening phrases of *Lolita* are: "Lolita. Light of my life. Fire of my loins." Vladimir Nabokov, *Lolita* (New York: Vintage, 1989), 9.
27. Some cultural forms are "better grasped as processes than as products," Sharon Marcus writes in an important essay on theater and comparative literature (137). Marcus's argument about the transnational production and circulation of nineteenth-century plays fits well with Chang and Voge's digital art, which show how translations, editions, versions, and adaptations help to generate the work. Sharon Marcus, "The Theater of Comparative Literature," in *A Companion to Comparative Literature*, ed. Ali Behdad and Dominic Thomas, 136–54 (Chichester, U.K.: Wiley-Blackwell, 2011).
28. Mark Poster, "Global Media and Culture," *New Literary History* 39, no. 3 (Summer 2008): 685–703.
29. Ibid., 700.

30. George Landow, *Hypertext 3.0: Critical Theory and New Media in an Age of Globalization* (Baltimore: Johns Hopkins University Press, 2006), 343.

31. Ibid., 356.

32. Pressman, "The Strategy of Digital Modernism," 303.

33. Young-Hae Chang Heavy Industries, quoted in Hyun-Joo Yoo, "Interview with Young-hae Chang Heavy Industries," in *dichtung-digital* 2 (2005), accessed April 2, 2014, http://www.dichtung-digital.org/2005/2/Yoo/index-engl.htm.

34. David Golumbia, *The Cultural Logic of Computation* (Cambridge, MA: Harvard University Press, 2009), 145–47.

35. Landow, *Hypertext 3.0*, 265.

36. Ibid., 254.

37. Ming Xie, "Pound as Translator," in *The Cambridge Companion to Ezra Pound*, ed. Ira B. Nadel (Cambridge: Cambridge University Press, 1999), 219; and Lawrence Venuti, *The Translator's Invisibility: A History of Translation*, 2nd ed. (New York: Routledge, 2008), 178.

38. On Pound, see Yunte Huang, *Transpacific Displacement: Ethnography, Translation, and Intertextual Travel in Twentieth-Century American Literature* (Berkeley: University of California Press, 2002), 90. For a discussion of Chineseness in Pound's *Cantos*, see Eric Hayot, *Chinese Dreams: Pound, Brecht, Tel Quel* (Ann Arbor: University of Michigan Press, 2003; Yunte Huang, *Transpacific Displacements: Ethnography, Translation, and Intertextual Travel in Twentieth-Century American Literature* (Berkeley: University of California Press, 2002); and Christopher Bush, *Ideographic Modernism: China, Writing, Media* (New York: Oxford University Press, 2010).

39. Hyun-Joo Yoo, "Interview with Young-hae Chang Heavy Industries," *dichtung-digital* 2 (2005). http://www.dichtung-digital.org/2005/2/Yoo/index-engl.htm.

40. N. Katherine Hayles, "Combining Close Reading and Distant Reading: Jonathan Safran Foer's *Tree of Codes* and the Aesthetic of Bookishness," *PMLA* 128, no. 1 (2013): 226–31; and Jessica Pressman, "The Aesthetic of Bookishness in Twenty-First Century Literature," *Michigan Quarterly Review* 48, no. 4 (2009): 465–82. See also Jessica Pressman, "CODA—Rereading: Digital Modernism in Print, Mark Z. Danielewski's *Only* Revolutions," in *Digital Modernism: Making it New in New Media* (Oxford: Oxford University Press, 2014), 158–74; doi:10.1093/acprof:oso/9780199937080.003.0007.

41. Jonathan Safran Foer, *Tree of Codes* (London: Visual Editions, 2011); and Hayles, "Combining Close Reading," 226–31.

42. Salvador Plascencia, *The People of Paper* (Orlando: Harcourt, 2006).

43. Adam Thirlwell, *Kapow!* (London: Visual Editions, 2012).

44. Hayles, *Electronic Literature*, 227.

45. Ramón Saldívar shows how Plascencia's concern with "the commodification of sadness" structures the form and medium of the novel. Ramón

Saldívar, "Historical Fantasy, Speculative Realism, and Postrace Aesthetics in Contemporary American Fiction," *American Literary History* 23, no. 3 (Fall 2011): 574–99.

46. Adam Thirlwell, *The Delighted States: A Book of Novels, Romances, & Their Unknown Translators, Containing Ten Languages, Set on Four Continents, & Accompanied by Maps, Portraits, Squiggles, Illustrations, & a Variety of Helpful Indexes* (New York: Picador, 2010). Thirlwell's novel is post-digital insofar as it asks us to handle the book (turn it upside-down, for example) and reproduces title pages, typography, squiggles, and copyright notices from the pages of other books. However, these pages are two-dimensional photocopies. They are recognizable as parts of other books made of paper, but they don't need to be made of paper.

47. For the exact proportions, see Hayles, "Combining Close and Distant Reading," 227.

48. Ibid., 231.

49. Pressman acknowledges that born-digital works can be "bookish" too, as when they integrate "the appearance of paper" and "print-based reading strategies" ("The Aesthetic of Bookishness," 467). Consider, in this light, Young-Hae Chang Heavy Industries' display of static photographs in works such as *HONEYMOON IN BEPPU* and the way they borrow, throughout their works, the visual format of facing-page and interlineal translation. Their most bookish work—and the work in which they seem to be trying to be most bookish, thus perhaps postbookish—is their *PACIFIC LIMN* e-book, which was released to accompany the 2013 installation of the Flash Player video *PACIFIC LIMN*. The "cover" of the e-book displays—and coincides with—the image of slightly worn cloth dust jacket. When you advance the pages (by clicking arrows to the right), the pages of the book appear to turn. In what appears to be the inside of the book, there is a small revolver resting within a space cut into the pages. Clicking the revolver executes a video about homelessness in San Francisco. The e-book is available for free through iTunes. However, it has to be viewed on an iPad or on a Mac.

EPILOGUE

1. Jonathan Safran Foer, *Tree of Codes* (London: Visual Editions, 2011); and Adam Thirlwell, *Kapow!* (London: Visual Editions, 2012).

2. Salvador Plascencia, *The People of Paper* (San Francisco: McSweeney's Books, 2005). Only later was *People of Paper* republished by Harcourt, which has since merged with the conglomerate Houghton Mifflin to become Houghton Mifflin Harcourt. Harcourt was founded in 1919.

3. Marc Saporta's *Composition No. 1*, published by Visual Editions in 2011, is available as box with 150 loose pages and as an iPad app.

4. Amy Hungerford argues that social networks have been crucial to the production of contemporary U.S. fiction. Amy Hungerford, *Making Literature Now* (Stanford, CA: Stanford University Press, 2015).

5. Sharmila Cohen and Paul Legault's "Manifesto of the New Translation" is available on the Web site of Translation Books, accessed February 25, 2014, http://www.distranslation.com/index.php?/folder-name/the-new-translation-manifesto/.

6. Pierre Bourdieu and Roger Chartier, cited in Roger Chartier, "Laborers and Voyagers," *Diacritics* 22, no. 2 (Summer 1992): 56–57.

7. Paul Legault, *The Emily Dickinson Reader: An English-to-English Translation of Emily Dickinson's Complete Poems* (San Francisco: McSweeney's Books, 2012).

8. The index page of the Web site for Telephone Books announces at the top, "Telephone Books publishes works of radical translation." Accessed April 2, 2014, http://distranslation.com.

9. Sharmila Cohen and Paul Legault, *The Sonnets: Translating and Rewriting Shakespeare* (Brooklyn: Telephone Books, 2012).

10. Ibid., back cover.

11. Ibid., i.

12. We might consider as a precedent Raymond Queneau's French-to-French translations, *Exercises de Style* (1947), which presents a short anecdote in ninety-nine different versions of French. The book's English translator, Barbara Wright, describes Queneau's project "as an exercise in communication patterns." Raymond Queneau, *Exercises in Style*, translated by Barbara Wright (New York: New Directions, 1981), 16.

13. For a recent discussion of the importance of "provincializing English," insisting that "there are many varieties of English" and articulating English's role "as part of the diversity and plurality of world languages," see Simon Gikandi, "Editor's Column: Provincializing English," *PMLA* 129, no. 1 (2014): 13.

14. Contributors have included luminaries such as J. M. Coetzee and Haruki Murakami, but the journal has also introduced numerous less-known writers.

15. *Asymptote*, "About" page, under FAQ, accessed April 2, 2014, http://www.asymptotejournal.com/about.php.

16. *Asymptote*, "About" page, under Mission, accessed April 2, 2014, http://www.asymptotejournal.com/about.php.

17. "About Words Without Borders," accessed April 2, 2014, http://wordswithoutborders.org/about/.

18. For example, the translation series "Facing Pages," edited by Nicholas Jenkins for Princeton University Press. See also Marc Shell and Werner Sollors, eds., *The Multilingual Anthology of American Literature: A Reader of Original Texts with English Translations* (New York: New York University Press, 2000).

19. Sharmila Cohen and Paul Legault, "On Telephone: A Message from the Editors," *Telephone* 1 (Spring 2010), 1.

20. "Multiples," special issue edited by Adam Thirlwell, in *McSweeney's Quarterly Concern* 42 (2012): 1–219; Adam Thirlwell, *Multiples: An Anthology of Stories in an Assortment of Languages and Literary Styles* (London: Portobello, 2013). Parenthetical citations in the text refer to the U.K. edition.

21. Catherine Porter, "Presidential Address 2009: English Is Not Enough," *PMLA* 125, no. 3 (2010), 553.

22. Ibid., 554.

23. Ibid., 550.

24. Simon Gikandi notes that "to be monolingual is to be recognized as a sovereign subject," whereas being bilingual "marks one as a stranger." Simon Gikandi, "Editor's Column: From Penn Station to Trenton: The Language Train," *PMLA* 128, no. 4 (2013): 870.

BIBLIOGRAPHY

Adams, Tim. "For Me, England Is a Mythical Place." *Observer*, February 20, 2005. http://www.theguardian.com/books/2005/feb/20/fiction.kazuoishiguro.

Adorno, Theodor. "Words from Abroad." In *Notes to Literature*, vol. 1. Trans. Shierry Weber Nicholsen, 185–199. New York: Columbia University Press, 1991.

Alexander, Meena. *Poetics of Dislocation.* Ann Arbor: University of Michigan Press, 2009.

Alvstad, Cecelia, Stefan Helgesson, and David Watson. "Introduction: Literature, Geography, Translation." In *Literature, Geography, Translation: Studies in World Writing*, ed. Cecilia Alvstad, Stefan Helgesson, and David Watson, 1–12. Cambridge: Cambridge Scholars Publishing, 2011.

Anderson, Benedict. *Imagined Communities: Reflections on the Origin and Spread of Nationalism*, 3rd ed. London: Verso, 2006.

Appiah, Anthony. *Cosmopolitanism: Ethics in a World of Strangers.* New York: Norton, 2006.

——. "Identity, Authenticity, Survival: Multicultural Societies and Social Reproduction." In *Multiculturalism: Examining the Politics of Recognition*, by Charles Taylor, ed. Amy Gutman, 149–64. Princeton, NJ: Princeton University Press, 1994.

Apter, Emily. *Against World Literature: On the Politics of Untranslatability.* New York: Verso, 2013.

——."On Translation in a Global Market." *Public Culture* 13, no. 1 (Winter 2001): 1–12.

——. "Philosophical Translation and Untranslatability: Translation as Critical Pedagogy." *Profession* (2010): 50–63.

——. "Translation in a Global Market." *Public Culture* 13, no. 1 (2001): 1–13.

——. "Translation with No Original: Scandals of Textual Reproduction." In *The Translation Zone: A New Comparative Literature*, 210–25. Princeton, NJ: Princeton University Press, 2006.

Arac, Jonathan. "Anglo-Globalism?" *New Left Review* 16 (July–August 2002): 35–45.

Aravamudan, Srinivas. *Enlightenment Orientalism: Resisting the Rise of the Novel.* Chicago: Chicago University Press, 2012.

Bakhtin, M. M. *The Dialogic Imagination: Four Essays*. Trans. Michael Holquist. Austin: University of Texas Press, 1982.

Barnard, Rita. "Coetzee in/and Afrikaans," *Journal of Literary Studies* 25, no. 4 (2009): 84–105.

——. "Fictions of the Global." *Novel* 42, no. 2 (2009): 207–15.

——. "On Public and Private in J. M. Coetzee." *Cultural Studies* 27, no. 3 (2013): 438–62.

Barnet, Anna. "Words on a Page: An Interview with Junot Díaz." *Harvard Advocate* (Spring 2009). http://www.theharvardadvocate.com/content/words-page-interview-junot-diaz.

Barthes, Roland. "The Death of the Author." *The Rustle of Language*. Trans. Richard Howard, 49–55. Berkeley: University of California Press, 1989.

——. *Image, Music, Text*. Trans. Stephen Heath. New York: Hill and Wang, 1977.

Barthet, Elise. "Internautes et intellectuels s'insurgent contre 'la mort de la culture française.'" *Le Monde*, December 8, 2007. http://www.lemonde.fr/culture/article/2007/12/18/internautes-et-intellectuels-s-insurgent-contre-la-mort-de-la-culture-francaise_990480_3246.html.

Beckett, Samuel. "Dante . . . Bruno, Vico, Joyce." In *Disjecta: Miscellaneous Writings and a Dramatic Fragment*, ed. Ruby Cohn, 19–34. New York: Grove Press, 1984.

Bell, Michael. "The Metaphysics of Modernism." In *The Cambridge Companion to Modernism*, ed. Michael Levenson, 9–32. Cambridge: Cambridge University Press, 2011.

Bellos, David. *Is That a Fish in Your Ear? Translation and the Meaning of Everything*. New York: Faber and Faber, 2011.

Benjamin, Walter. *Illuminations*. Trans. Harry Zohn. New York: Schocken, 1968.

Berlant, Lauren, and Lee Edelman. *Sex, or the Unbearable*. Durham, NC: Duke University Press, 2013.

Best, Stephen, and Sharon Marcus. "Surface Reading: An Introduction." *Representations* 108, no. 1 (Fall 2009): 1–21.

Bewes, Timothy. *The Event of Postcolonial Shame*. Princeton, NJ: Princeton University Press, 2010.

——. "Reading with the Grain: A New World in Literary Criticism." *Differences: A Journal of Feminist Cultural Studies* 21, no. 3 (2010): 1–33.

Bolaño, Roberto. *The Savage Detectives*. Trans. Natasha Wimmer. New York: Picador, 2007.

Borges, Jorge Luis. "The Analytical Language of John Wilkins." In *Other Inquisitions, 1937–1952*, trans. Ruth L. C. Simms, 101–5. Austin: University of Texas Press, 2000.

——. "Pierre Menard, Author of the *Quixote*." In *Labyrinths: Selected Stories and Other Writings*. Trans. James E. Irby, 36–44. New York: New Directions, 1962.

——. "The Thousand and One Nights." In *Seven Nights*, trans. Eliot Weinberger, 42–57. New York: New Directions, 1984.

Brennan, Timothy. "The Cuts of Language: The East/West of North/South." *Public Culture* 13, no. 1 (Winter 2001): 39–63.

Briggs, Charles Frederick. "Uncle Tomitudes." *Putnam's Monthly* 1 (January 1853): 97–102.

Brouillette, Sarah. *Postcolonial Writers in the Global Literary Marketplace*. 2007. Reprint, Basingstoke: Palgrave Macmillan, 2011.

Bufkin, Sydney. "'Fully Fleshed Out and Filled with Emotion': Accent, Region, and Identification in the Reception of *The Help*." Presentation at the Annual Conference of the Modern Language Association, Chicago, IL, January 9–12, 2014.

Burgess, Anthony. *A Clockwork Orange*. New York: Norton, 1995.

Bush, Christopher. *Ideographic Modernism: China, Writing, Media*. New York: Oxford University Press, 2010.

Butler, Judith. "Explanation and Exoneration, or What We Can Hear." *Social Text* 20, no. 3 (Fall 2002), 177–88.

Butler, Judith, and Gayatri Chakravorty Spivak. *Who Sings the Nation-State? Language, Politics, Belonging*. London: Seagull Books, 2007.

Buzard, James. *Disorienting Fiction: The Autoethnographic Work of Nineteenth-Century British Novels*. Princeton, NJ: Princeton University Press, 2005.

Casanova, Pascale. "What Is a Dominant Language? Giacomo Leopardi: Theoretician of Linguistic Inequality." Trans. Marlon Jones. *New Literary History* 44, no. 3 (Summer 2013): 379–99.

——. *The World Republic of Letters*. Trans. M. B. DeBevoise. Cambridge, MA: Harvard University Press, 2005.

Cassin, Barbara. Introduction to *Dictionary of Untranslatables: A Philosophical Lexicon*, xvii–xx. Trans. Michael Wood, ed. Barbara Cassin. Princeton, NJ: Princeton University Press, 2013.

——. "The Philosophical Vocabulary of Europe." Trans. Valerie Henituk. *In Other Words* 29 (2007): 15–21.

——. "Untranslatables and Their Translations." Trans. Andrew Goffey. *Transeuropéennes: Revue internationale de pensée critique* (August 2009). http://www.transeuropeennes.eu/en/articles/voir_pdf/83.

Castley, Robert. *Korea's Economic Miracle: The Crucial Role of Japan*. Basingstoke, U.K.: Macmillan, 1997.

Chakrabarty, Dipesh. *Provincializing Europe: Postcolonial Thought and Historical Difference*. Princeton, NJ: Princeton University Press, 2000.

Chartier, Roger. *Cardenio Between Cervantes and Shakespeare: The Story of a Lost Play*. Trans. Janet Lloyd. Cambridge: Polity Press, 2013.

——. "Laborers and Voyagers: From the Text to the Reader." Trans. J. A. González. *Diacritics* 22, no. 2 (Summer 1992): 49–61.

Cheah, Pheng. "What Is a World? On World Literature and World-Making Activity." *Daedalus* 137, no. 3: 26–38.

Chow, Rey. *The Age of the World Target: Self-Referentiality in War, Theory, and Comparative Work*. Durham, NC: Duke University Press, 2006.

Coetzee, J. M. *Childhood of Jesus*. London: Harvill Secker, 2013.

——. *Dagboek van een slecht jaar* (Diary of a bad year). Trans. Peter Bergsma. Amsterdam: Cossee, 2007.

——. *Diary of a Bad Year*. London: Harvill Secker, 2007.

——. *Diary of a Bad Year*. Melbourne: Text Publishing, 2007.

——. "Diary of a Bad Year." *New York Review of Books*, July 19, 2007. http://www.nybooks.com/articles/archives/2007/jul/19/diary-of-a-bad-year/.

——. *Doubling the Point: Essays and Interviews*. Ed. David Attwell. Cambridge, MA: Harvard University Press, 1992.

——. *Elizabeth Costello: Fiction*. New York: Penguin, 2003.

——. *In the Heart of the Country*. London: Vintage, 1977.

——. *Inner Workings: Essays 2000–2005*. London: Harvill Secker, 2007.

——. *L'été de la vie* (Summertime). Trans, Catherine Luaga Du Plessis. Paris: Seuil, 2010.

——. "Roads to Translation." *Meanjin* 64, no. 4 (2005): 141–151.

——. *Slow Man*. New York: Viking, 2005.

——. *Summertime: Fiction*. New York: Viking, 2009.

——. *Summertime: Scenes from a Provincial Life*. London: Harvill Secker, 2009.

——. *White Writing: On the Culture of Letters in South Africa*. New Haven, CT: Yale University Press, 1988.

Cohen, Margaret. *The Novel and the Sea*. Princeton, NJ: Princeton University Press, 2012.

Cohen, Margaret, and Carolyn Dever, eds. *The Literary Channel: The International Invention of the Novel*. Princeton, NJ: Princeton University Press, 2002.

Cohen, Sharmila, and Paul Legault. "Manifesto of the New Translation," *Translation Books*. Accessed February 25, 2014. http://www.distranslation.com/index.php?/folder-name/the-new-translation-manifesto/

——. "On Telephone: A Message from the Editors." *Telephone* 1 (Spring 2010): 1.

——. *The Sonnets: Translating and Rewriting Shakespeare*. Brooklyn: Telephone Books, 2012.

Coombe, Rosemary. *The Cultural Life of Intellectual Properties: Authorship, Appropriation, and the Law*. Durham, NC: Duke University Press, 1998.

Culler, Jonathan. "Anderson and the Novel." In *Grounds of Comparison: Around the Work of Benedict Anderson*, ed. Pheng Cheah and Jonathan Culler, 29–52. New York: Routledge, 2003.

——. "Apostrophe." In *The Pursuit of Signs: Semiotics, Literature, Deconstruction*, 135–54. 1981. Reprint, Ithaca: Cornell University Press, 2003.

——. "The Closeness of Close Reading." *ADE Bulletin* 149 (2010): 20–25.

Dabashi, Hamid. "Found in Translation." *New York Times*, July 28, 2013. http://nyti.ms/1gpo3A8.

Damrosch, David. "Comparative World Literature." In *The Canonical Debate Today: Crossing Disciplinary and Cultural Boundaries*, ed. Liviu Papadima, David Damrosch, and Theo D'haen, 169–78. Amsterdam: Rodopi, 2011.

——. "Global Comparatism and the Question of Language." *PMLA* 128, no. 3 (May 2013): 622–28.

——. "Reading in Translation." In *How to Read World Literature*, 65–85. Chichester, U.K.: Wiley Blackwell, 2009.

——. "Toward a History of World Literature." *New Literary History* 39, no. 3 (Summer 2008): 481–495.

——. *What Is World Literature?* Princeton, NJ: Princeton University Press, 2003.

Dancer, Thom. "Between Belief and Knowledge: J. M. Coetzee and the Present of Reading." *Minnesota Review* 77 (2011): 131–42.

Davidson, Michael. *Concerto for the Left Hand: Disability and the Defamiliar Body*. Ann Arbor: University of Michigan Press, 2008.

Davies, Peter Ho. *The Welsh Girl*. Boston: Houghton Mifflin, 2007.

Deleuze, Gilles, and Félix Guattari. *Kafka: Toward a Minor Literature*. Trans. Dana Polan. Minneapolis: University of Minnesota Press, 1986.

Desai, Kiran. *The Inheritance of Loss*. New York: Atlantic Monthly Press, 2006.

Dharwadker, Aparna. *Theatres of Independence: Drama, Theory, and Urban Performance in India Since 1947*. Iowa City: University of Iowa Press, 2005.

Dharwadker, Vinay. "Premchand." In *The Norton Anthology of World Literature*, 3rd ed., vol. F, 311–14. Ed. Martin Puchner, Suzanne Conklin Akbari, Wiebke Denecke, Vinay Dharwadker, Barbara Fuchs, Caroline Levine, Pericles Lewis, and Emily Wilson. New York: W. W. Norton, 2012.

Díaz, Junot. *Así es como la pierdes*. Trans. Achy Obejas. New York: Vintage Espanol, 2013.

——. *Guide du loser amoureux*. Trans. Stéphane Roques. Paris: Plon, 2013.

——. *La breve y maravillosa vida de Oscar Wao*. Trans. Achy Obejas. New York: Vintage Espanol, 2008.

——. *This Is How You Lose Her*. New York: Riverhead, 2012.

Dimock, Wai Chee. "Literature for the Planet." *PMLA* 116, no. 1 (January 2001): 173–89.

——. "Scales of Aggregation: Prenational, Subnational, Transnational." *American Literary History* 18, no. 2 (Summer 2006): 219–28.

——. *Through Other Continents: American Literature Across Deep Time*. Princeton, NJ: Princeton University Press, 2006.

Dubois, Andrew. Introduction to *Close Reading: The Reader*, ed. Frank Lentricchia and Andrew DuBois, 1–42. Durham, NC: Duke University Press, 2002.

Edwards, Brent Hayes. *The Practice of Diaspora: Literature, Translation, and the Rise of Black Internationalism.* Cambridge, MA: Harvard University Press, 2003.

English, James F. *The Economy of Prestige.* Cambridge, MA: Harvard University Press, 2009.

Fisk, Gloria. "Orhan Pamuk and the Good of World Literature." Unpublished manuscript.

Fitzgerald, Thomas A. "Shakespeare in Spain and Spanish America." *Modern Language Journal* 35, no. 8 (December 1951): 589–594.

Flanery, Patrick Denman. "J. M. Coetzee's autre-biography." *Times Literary Supplement*, September 9, 2009.

Fludernik, Monika. "Introduction: Second-Person Narrative and Related Issues." In *Second-Person Narrative*, ed. Harold F. Mosher, 281–311. Dekalb: Northern Illinois University Press, 1994. http://www.freidok.uni-freiburg.de/volltexte/5098/pdf/Fludernik_Introduction_Second_person_narrative.pdf.

Foer, Jonathan Safran. *Tree of Codes.* London: Visual Editions, 2011.

Gallop, Jane. "Close Reading in 2009." *ADE Bulletin* 149 (2010): 15–19.

Gikandi, Simon. "Editor's Column: From Penn Station to Trenton: The Language Train." *PMLA* 128, no. 4 (2013): 865–71.

——. "Editor's Column: Provincializing English," *PMLA* 129, no. 1 (2014): 7–17.

——. "Globalization and the Claims of Postcoloniality." *South Atlantic Quarterly* 100, no. 3 (Summer 2001): 632–33.

Gladwell, Malcolm. "The Politics of Politesse." *New Yorker*, December 23, 2002, 57.

Göknar, Erdağ. "Occulted Texts: Pamuk's Untranslated Novels." In *Global Perspectives on Orhan Pamuk: Existentialism and Politics*, ed. Mehnaz M. Afridi and David M. Buyze, 177–99. New York: Palgrave, 2012.

——. *Orhan Pamuk, Secularism and Blasphemy: The Politics of the Turkish Novel.* London: Routledge, 2012.

——. "The Untranslated Novels of a Nobel Laureate." In *Orhan Pamuk, Secularism and Blasphemy: The Politics of the Turkish Novel* (London: Routledge, 2013).

Golumbia, David. *The Cultural Logic of Computation.* Cambridge, MA: Harvard University Press, 2009.

Grossman, Edith. [Interview with] "Jaime Manrique." *Bomb* 121 (Fall 2012). http://bombmagazine.org/article/6771/jaime-manrique.

——. *Why Translation Matters.* New Haven: Yale University Press, 2010.

Guillory, John. "Close Reading: Prologue and Epilogue." *ADE Bulletin* 149 (2010): 8–14.

Hack, Daniel. "Close Reading at a Distance: The African-Americanization of *Bleak House.*" *Critical Inquiry* 34, no. 4 (Summer 2008): 729–53.

——. "Close Reading at a Distance: Bleak House," *Novel* 42, no. 3 (2009): 423–30.

Hamacher, Werner. "One 2 Many Multiculturalisms." Trans. Dana Hollander. In *Violence, Identity, and Self-Determination*, ed. Hent De Vries and Samuel Weber, 284–325. Stanford, CA: Stanford University Press, 1997.

Hamid, Mohsin. *How to Get Filthy Rich in Rising Asia*. New York: Riverhead Books, 2013.

——. *Moth Smoke*. New York: Riverhead, 2000.

——. "Mohsin Hamid on His Enduring Love of the Second-Person Narrative." *Guardian*, March 22, 2013. http://www.theguardian.com/books/2013/mar/22/mohsin-hamid-second-person-narrative.

Handler, Richard. *Nationalism and the Politics of Culture in Quebec*. Madison: University of Wisconsin Press, 1988.

——. "Who Owns the Past? History, Cultural Property, and the Logic of Possessive Individualism." In *The Politics of Culture*, ed. Brett Williams, 63–74. Washington DC: Smithsonian Institution Press, 1991.

Hart-Landsberg, Martin, Seongjin Jeong, and Richard Westra, eds. *Marxist Perspectives on South Korea in the Global Economy*. Aldershot, U.K.: Ashgate, 2007.

Hassan, Waïl. "Agency and Translational Literature: Ahdaf Soueif's *The Map of Love*." *PMLA* 121, no. 3 (May 2006): 753–68.

Hayles, N. Katherine. "Combining Close Reading and Distant Reading: Jonathan Safran Foer's *Tree of Codes* and the Aesthetic of Bookishness." *PMLA* 128, no. 1 (January 2013): 226–31.

——. *Electronic Literature: New Horizons for the Literary*. Notre Dame, IN: University of Notre Dame Press, 2008.

Hayot, Eric. *On Literary Worlds*. Oxford: Oxford University Press, 2012.

——. *Chinese Dreams: Pound, Brecht, Tel Quel*. Ann Arbor: University of Michigan Press, 2003.

——. "The Strange Case of Araki Yasusada: Author, Object." *PMLA* 120, no. 1 (January 2005): 66–81.

Heise, Ursula. "Globality, Difference, and the International Turn in Ecocriticism." *PMLA* 128, no. 3 (May 2013): 636–43.

Helgesson, Stefan. "Clarice Lispector, J.M. Coetzee, and the Seriality of Translation." *Translation Studies* 3, no. 3 (2010), 318–33.

——. "Linguistic Desire and Literary Identity." Presentation at roundtable on "Multilingualism and the Object of Translation Studies." Annual Conference of the Modern Language Association, Chicago, IL, January 9–12, 2014.

Hofmyer, Isabel. *The Portable Bunyan: A Transnational History of the Pilgrim's Progress*. Princeton, NJ: Princeton University Press, 2004.

Hokenson, Jan Walsh, and Marcella Munson. *The Bilingual Text: History and Theory of Self-Translation*. Manchester, U.K.: St. Jerome Publishing, 2007.

Huang, Yunte. *Transpacific Displacements: Ethnography, Translation, and Intertextual Travel in Twentieth-Century American Literature*. Berkeley: University of California Press, 2002.

Huggan, Graham. *The Postcolonial Exotic: Marketing the Margins*. London: Routledge, 2001.

Hungerford, Amy. *Making Literature Now*. Stanford, CA: Stanford University Press, 2015.

Huston, Nancy. *Cantiques des Plaines*. Montreal: Leméac, 1993.

——. *Longings and Belongings: Essays*. Toronto: McArthur, 2005.

——. *Losing North: Musings on Land, Tongue and Self*. Toronto: McArthur, 2002.

——. *Plainsong*. Toronto: Harper Collins, 1993.

Ireland, Corydon. "Borders, Books, and the Balkans." *Harvard Gazette*, April 12, 2013. http://news.harvard.edu/gazette/story/2013/04/borders-books-and-the-balkans.

Ishiguro, Kazuo. *Alles, was wir geben mussten*. Trans. Barbara Schaden. Munich: Blessing, 2005.

——. *An Artist of the Floating World*. New York: Vintage, 1986.

——. *Laat me nooit alleen*. Trans. Bartho Krieck. Amsterdam: Atlas, 2005.

——. *Laat me nooit alleen*. Trans. Bartho Krieck. Amsterdam: Eldorado, 2006.

——. *Never Let Me Go*. New York: Knopf, 2005.

——. *Never Let Me Go*. London: Faber, 2005.

——. *Nunca me abandones*. Trans. Jesús Zulaika Goicoechea. Barcelona: Editorial Anagrama, 2005.

——. *Ole luonani aina*. Trans. Helene Bützow. Helsinki: Kustannusosakeyhtiö, 2005.

——. *A Pale View of Hills*. New York: Vintage, 1982.

——. *The Remains of the Day*. New York: Vintage, 1989.

——. *The Unconsoled*. New York: Vintage, 1995.

——. *Watashi o hanasanaide*. Trans. Tsuchiya Masao. Tokyo: Hayakawa Publishing, 2006.

——. *When We Were Orphans*. New York: Vintage, 2000.

Ishiguro, Kazuo and Kezuburo Oe. "The Novelist in Today's World: A Conversation" (1989). In *Conversations with Kazuo Ishiguro*, ed. Brian W. Shaffer and Cynthia W. Wong, 52–65. Jackson: University of Mississippi Press, 2008.

Italie, Hillel. "Harry Potter and the Slow Translation: Non-English Stores Await Bestseller." *Washington Post*, July 27, 2005. http://www.washingtonpost.com/wp-dyn/content/article/2005/07/26/AR2005072601793.html.

Jacobs, Carol. "What Does It Mean to Count? W. G. Sebald's *The Emigrants*," In *Skirting the Ethical*, 131–150. Stanford, CA: Stanford University Press, 2008.

Jaffe, Aaron. *Modernism and the Culture of Celebrity*. Cambridge: Cambridge University Press, 2005.

Johnson, Barbara. "Apostrophe, Animation, and Abortion." In *A World of Difference*, 184–200. Baltimore: Johns Hopkins University Press, 1987.

Joshi, Priya. *In Another Country*. New York: Columbia University Press, 2002.

Joyce, James. *A Portrait of the Artist as a Young Man*. New York: Penguin, 1999.

——. *Ulysses*. New York: Vintage, 1990.

Kacandis, Irene. "Are You in the Text? The 'Literary Perfomative' in Postmodernist Fiction." *Text and Performance Quarterly* 13 (1993): 139–53.

——. "Narrative Apostrophe: Reading, Rhetoric, Resistance in Michel Butor's *La modification* and Julio Cortazar's 'Graffiti.'" *Style* 28, no. 3 (Fall 1994): 329–49.

Kaminka, Ika. Session on "Challenging the Hegemony of English: Translating Haruki Murakami's *1Q84* in Europe." Harvard University, October 2, 2012.

Kellman, Steven G. *Switching Languages: Translingual Writers Reflect on their Craft*. Lincoln: University of Nebraska Press, 2003.

Kermode, Frank. "Outrageous Game." *London Review of Books* 27, no. 8 (April 2005): 21–22.

Keskinen, Mikko. *Audio Book: Essays on Sound Technologies in Narrative Fiction*. Lanham, MD: Lexington Books, 2008.

Kincaid, Jamaica. *The Autobiography of My Mother*. New York: Farrar, Straus and Giroux, 1996.

——. *My Brother*. New York: Farrar, Straus and Giroux, 1997.

——. *Mr. Potter*. New York: Farrar Straus and Giroux, 2002.

——. *A Small Place*. New York: Farrar, Straus and Giroux, 1988.

——. "Wingless." *New Yorker*, January 29, 1979, 26–27.

Kirschenbaum, Matthew. *Mechanisms: New Media and the Forensic Imagination*. Cambridge, MA: MIT Press, 2008.

Knutson, Elizabeth M. "Writing in Between Worlds: Reflections on Language and Identity from Works by Nancy Huston and Leïla Sebbar." *Symposium* 65, no. 4 (Winter 2011): 253–70. doi:10.1080/00397709.2011.628589.

Koustas, Jane. *Les belles étrangères: Canadians in Paris*. Ottawa: University of Ottawa Press, 2008.

Kurnick, David. "Bolaño to Come." *Public Books*, September 5, 2012. http://www.publicbooks.org/fiction/bolano-to-come.

Kwon, Seung-Ho, and Michael O'Donnell. *The Chaebol and Labour in Korea: The Development of Management Strategy in Hyundai*. London: Routledge, 2001.

Kymlicka, Will. *Multicultural Citizenship: A Liberal Theory of Minority Rights*. Oxford: Clarendon Press, 1995.

Landow, George. *Hypertext 3.0: Critical Theory and New Media in an Age of Globalization*. Baltimore: Johns Hopkins University Press, 2006.

Lang, James M. "Public Memory, Private History: Kazuo Ishiguro's *The Remains of the Day*." *Clio* 29, no. 2 (Winter 2000): 143–65.

Legault, Paul. *The Emily Dickinson Reader: An English-to-English Translation of Emily Dickinson's Complete Poems*. San Francisco: McSweeney's Books, 2012.

Lennon, Brian. *In Babel's Shadow: Multilingual Literatures, Monolingual States*. Minneapolis: University of Minnesota Press, 2010.

Lerner, Ben. *Leaving the Atocha Station*. Minneapolis: Coffee House Press, 2011.

——. *Saliendo de la estacíon de Atocha*. Trans. Cruz Rodríguez Juiz. Barcelona: Mondadori, 2013.

Levine, Caroline. "For World Literature." *Public Books*, January 6, 2014. http://www.publicbooks.org/fiction/for-world-literature.

——. "The Great Unwritten: World Literature and the Effacement of Orality." *Modern Language Quarterly* 74, no. 2 (June 2013): 217–37.

Levinson, Brett. "Case Closed: Madness and Dissociation in *2666.*" *Journal of Latin American Cultural Studies* 18, nos. 2–3 (December 2009): 177–92.

Lewis, Pericles. *The Cambridge Introduction to Modernism*. Cambridge: Cambridge University Press, 2007.

——. "Proust, Woolf, and Modern Fiction." *Romanic Review* 99, nos. 1–2 (January–March 2008): 77–86.

Littell, Jonathon. *Les bienviellants*. Paris: Gallimard, 2006.

——. *The Kindly Ones*. Trans. Charlotte Mandell. New York: Harper Collins, 2009.

Liu, Lydia. *Translingual Practice: Literature, National Culture, and Translated Modernity—China, 1900–1937*. Palo Alto, CA: Stanford University Press, 1995.

Lukács, Georg. "Narrate or Describe?" *Writer and Critic and Other Essays*. Trans. Arthur Kahn, 110–48. Lincoln, NE: iUniverse, 2005.

Marcus, Sharon. *Between Women: Friendship, Desire, and Marriage in Victorian England*. Princeton, NJ: Princeton University Press, 2006.

——. "The Theater of Comparative Literature." In *A Companion to Comparative Literature*, ed. Ali Behdad and Dominic Thomas, 136–54. Chichester, U.K.: Wiley-Blackwell, 2011.

Marx, John. *Geopolitics and the Anglophone Novel, 1890–2011*. Cambridge: Cambridge University Press, 2012.

Mason, Theodore O. "The African-American Anthology: Mapping the Territory, Taking the National Census, Building the Museum." *American Literary History* 10 (Spring 1998): 185–98.

Mason, Wyatt. "David Mitchell, the Experimentalist." *New York Times Magazine*, June 25, 2010. http://www.nytimes.com/2010/06/27/magazine/27mitchell-t.html?pagewanted=all&_r=0.

McDonald, Peter. "The Ethics of Reading and the Question of the Novel." *NOVEL* 43, no. 3 (September 2010): 483–500.

——. "Ideas of the Book and Histories of Literature: After Theory?" *PMLA* 121, no. 1 (January 2006): 214–28.

McGill, Meredith. *American Literature and the Culture of Reprinting*. Philadelphia: University of Pennsylvania Press, 2003.

McKenzie, D. F. "The Book as an Expressive Form." In *The Book History Reader*, ed. David Finkelstein and Alistair McCleery, 27–38. London: Routledge, 2003.

Meylaerts, Reine. "Heterolingualism in/and Translation: How Legitimate Are the Other and His/Her Language." *Target: International Journal on Translation Studies* 18, no. 1 (2006): 1–15.

——. Presentation at roundtable on "Multilingualism and the Object of Translation Studies." Annual Conference of the Modern Language Association, Chicago, IL, January 9–12, 2014.

Miéville, China. *The City, The City*. New York: Del Rey, 2010.

Miller, Joshua L. *Accented America: The Cultural Politics of Multilingual Modernism*. New York: Oxford University Press, 2011.

——. "The Transamerican Trail to *Cerco del Cielo*: John Sayles and the Aesthetics of Multilingual Cinema." In *Bilingual Games: Some Literary Investigations*, ed. Doris Sommer, 121–49. New York: Palgrave, 2003.

Min, Ines. "A Visceral Experience of Web Art." *The Korea Times*, October 15, 2010. http://www.koreatimes.co.kr/www/news/art/2010/10/148_74601.html.

Mishra, Pankaj. "Beyond the Global Novel." *Financial Times*, September 27, 2013. http://www.ft.com/cms/s/2/6e00ad86-26a2-11e3-9dc0-00144feab7de.html#axzz2zLgmSHWr.

Mitchell, David. *Black Swan Green*. New York: Random House, 2007.

——. *Cloud Atlas*. New York: Random House, 2004.

——. *Ghostwritten*. New York: Vintage, 2001.

——. *Les mille automnes de Jacob de Zoet*. Trans. Manuel Berri. Paris: Éditions de l'Olivier, 2012.

——. *Number9Dream*. New York: Random House, 2003.

——. *The Thousand Autumns of Jacob de Zoet*. New York: Random House, 2011.

Moore, David Chioni. "An African Classic in Fourteen Translations: Ferdinand Oyono's *Une vie de boy* on the World Literary Stage." *PMLA* 128, no. 1 (January 2013): 101–11.

Moore, Michael Scott, and Michael Sontheimer. "*Spiegel* Interview with Kazuo Ishiguro." *Spiegel Online*, October 5, 2005. http://www.spiegel.de/international/spiegel-interview-with-kazuo-ishiguro-i-remain-fascinated-by-memory-a-378173.html.

Moretti, Franco. *Atlante del romanzo europeo 1800–1900*. Turin: Giulio Einaudi, 1997.

——. *Atlas of the European Novel, 1800–1900*. London: Verso, 1998.

——. "Conjectures on World Literature." *New Left Review* 1 (2000): 54–69.

Morrison, Donald. "In Search of Lost Time." *Time*, November 21, 2007. http://content.time.com/time/magazine/article/0,9171,1686532,00.html.

Mosley, Walter. *Alien Script*. Curated by Lydie Diakhaté. NYU/Kimmel Center Windows Gallery. 60 Washington Square South, New York City, NY 10010. June 10–August 1, 2013.

Nabokov, Vladimir. *Lolita*. New York: Vintage, 1989.

Obejas, Achy. "Translating Junot." *Chicago Tribune*. September 14, 2012. http://articles.chicagotribune.com/2012-09-14/features/ct-prj-0916-book-of-the-month-20120914_1_dominican-republic-oscar-wao-spanglish.

Owen, Steven. "What Is World Poetry?" *New Republic*, November 19, 1990, 28–32.

Pamuk, Orhan. *Istanbul: Memories and the City*. Trans. Maureen Freely. New York: Knopf, 2006.

——. *The Museum of Innocence*. Trans. Maureen Freely. New York: Vintage, 2009.

Parks, Tim. "The Dull New Global Novel." *New York Review Blog*, February 9, 2010. http://www.nybooks.com/blogs/nyrblog/2010/feb/09/the-dull-new-global-novel/.

——. "Literature Without Style." *New York Review Blog*, November 7, 2013. http://www.nybooks.com/blogs/nyrblog/2013/nov/07/literature-without-style/.

Phillips, Caryl. *A Distant Shore*. New York: Vintage, 2003.

——. *Extravagant Strangers: A Literature of Belonging*. New York: Vintage, 1997.

——. *In the Falling Snow*. New York: Vintage, 2009.

——. *A New World Order: Essays*. New York: Vintage, 2001.

Pizzino, Christopher. "Alien Stereo: China Miéville's *Embassytown*." Presentation at the Annual Conference of the Modern Language Association, Chicago, IL, January 9–12, 2014.

Plascencia, Salvador. *The People of Paper*. San Francisco: McSweeney's Books, 2005.

——. *The People of Paper*. Orlando: Harcourt, 2006.

Poirer, Agnès. "Vive la dissidence." *Guardian*, December 4, 2007. http://www.theguardian.com/commentisfree/2007/dec/05/comment.usa.

Porter, Catherine. "Presidential Address 2009: English Is Not Enough." *PMLA* 125, no. 3 (May 2010): 546–55.

Poster, Mark. "Global Media and Culture." *New Literary History* 39, no. 3 (Summer 2008): 685–703.

Pound, Ezra. *How to Read*. London: D. Harsworth, 1931.

Pratt, Mary Louise. "Building a New Public Idea About Language." *ADFL Bulletin* 34, no. 3 (Spring 2003): 5–9.

Pressman, Jessica. "The Aesthetic of Bookishness in Twenty-First Century Literature." *Michigan Quarterly Review* 48, no. 4 (Fall 2009): 465–82.

——. "CODA—Rereading: Digital Modernism in Print, Mark Z. Danielewski's *Only* Revolutions," in *Digital Modernism: Making it New in New Media* (Oxford: Oxford University Press, 2014), 158–74. doi:10.1093/acprof:oso/9780199937080.003.0007.

——. "Pacific Rim Digital Modernism: The Electronic Literature of Young-hae Chang Heavy Industries." In *Pacific Rim Modernisms*, ed. Mary Ann Gilles, Helen Sword, and Steven Yao, 316–32. Toronto: University of Toronto Press, 2009.

——. "Reading the Code Between the Words: The Role of Translation in Young-hae Chang Heavy Industries's *Nippon*." *Dichtung-digital* 37 (2007). http://dichtung-digital.de/2007/Pressman/Pressman.htm.

——. "The Strategy of Digital Modernism: Young-hae Chang Heavy Industries's *Dakota*." *MFS Modern Fiction Studies* 54, no. 2 (Summer 2008): 302–25.

Proust, Marcel. *In Search of Lost Time*, vol. 6. Trans. Andreas Mayor and Terence Kilmartin. Rev. D. J. Enright. New York: Modern Library, 1993.

Puchner, Martin. "Orhan Pamuk's Own Private Istanbul." *Raritan* 33, no. 3 (Winter 2014): 97–108.

——. *Poetry of the Revolution: Marx, Manifestos, and the Avant-Gardes*. Princeton, NJ: Princeton University Press, 2006.

——. "World Literature in Istanbul." *Inside Higher Ed*, August 27, 2012. http://www.insidehighered.com/views/2012/08/27/essay-teaching-world-literature-istanbul.

Pym, Anthony. *The Moving Text: Localization, Translation, and Distribution*. Amsterdam: John Benjamins, 2005.

——. "Venuti's Visibility." *Target* 8 no. 1 (1996): 165–77.

Queneau, Raymond. *Exercises in Style*. Trans. Barbara Wright. New York: New Directions, 1981.

Rainey, Lawrence. *Institutions of Modernism: Literary Elites and Public Culture*. New Haven, CT: Yale University Press, 1998.

Ram, Harsha. "Towards a Crosscultural Poetics of the Contact Zone: Romantic, Modernist, and Soviet Intertextualities in Boris Paternak's Translations of T'itisian T'bidze." *Comparative Literature* 59, no. 1 (Winter 2007): 63–89.

Ramazani, Jahan. "Form." In *A New Vocabulary for Global Modernism*, ed. Eric Hayot and Rebecca L. Walkowitz. New York: Columbia University Press, forthcoming.

——. "A Transnational Poetics." *American Literary History* 18, no. 2 (Summer 2006): 332–59.

——. *A Transnational Poetics*. Chicago: University of Chicago Press, 2009.

Reid, Alastair. *Inside Out: Selected Poetry and Translations*. Edinburgh: Polygon, 2008.

Richardson, Brian. "The Poetics and Politics of Second Person Narrative." *Genre* 24 (Fall 1991): 309–30.

Robbins, Bruce. "The Village of the Liberal Managerial Class." In *Cosmopolitan Geographies: New Locations in Culture and Literature*, ed. Vinay Dharwadker, 15–32. New York: Routledge, 2001.

Rogers, Gayle. "An Interview with Ben Lerner." *Contemporary Literature* 54, no. 2 (June 2013): 218–39.

——. *Modernism and the New Spain: Britain, Cosmopolitan Europe, and Literary History*. New York: Oxford University Press, 2012.

——. "Translation." In *A New Vocabulary for Global Modernism*, ed. Eric Hayot and Rebecca L. Walkowitz. New York: Columbia University Press, forthcoming.

Rushdie, Salman. "'Commonwealth Literature' Does Not Exist." In *Imaginary Homelands: Essays and Criticism, 1981–1991*. New York: Penguin, 1991, 61–70.

Sakai, Naoki. "How Do We Count a Language? Translation and Discontinuity." *Translation Studies* 2, no. 1 (2009): 71–88.

——. "Translation as a Filter." Trans. Gavin Walker and Naoki Sakai. *Transeuropéennes: Revue internationale de pensée critique*, March 25, 2010. http://www.transeuropeennes.eu/en/articles/200/Translation_as_a_filter.

——. *Translation and Subjectivity: On "Japan" and Cultural Nationalism*. Minneapolis: University of Minnesota Press, 1997.

Saldívar, Ramón. "Historical Fantasy, Speculative Realism, and Postrace Aesthetics in Contemporary American Fiction." *American Literary History* 23, no. 3 (Fall 2011): 574–99.

Saporta, Marc. *Composition No. 1*. London: Visual Editions, 2011.

Satrapi, Marjane. *Persepolis Monovolume*. Paris: L'Association, 2007.

Schoene, Berthold. *The Cosmopolitan Novel*. Edinburgh: Edinburgh University Press, 2009.

Schor, Naomi. *Reading in Detail: Aesthetics and the Feminine*. 1987. Reprint, New York: Routledge, 2007.

Seppala, Johanna. "Differences in the British and American Versions of *Bridget Jones's Diary* by Helen Fielding." Department of Translation Studies, University of Tampere, Fall 2008. Accessed April 20, 2014. http://www15.uta.fi/FAST/US1/P1/js-jones.html.

Shell, Marc, and Werner Sollors, eds. *The Multilingual Anthology of American Literature: A Reader of Original Texts with English Translations*. New York: New York University Press, 2000.

Shibata, Motoyuki, and Motoko Sugano. "Strange Reads: Kazuo Ishiguro's *A Pale View of Hills* and *An Artist of the Floating World* in Japan." In *Kazuo Ishiguro: Contemporary Critical Perspectives*, ed. Sean Matthews and Sebastian Groes, 20–31. London: Continuum, 2009.

Shindler, Kelly. "Interview with Young-Hae Chang Heavy Industries." *Bootprint* 3, no. 1 (Summer 2009): 22–23.

Siskind, Mariano. "The Globalization of the Novel and the Novelization of the Global: A Critique of World Literature." *Comparative Literature* 62, no. 4 (2010): 336–61.

Slocombe, Will. "Haruki Murakami and the Ethics of Translation." *CLCWeb: Comparative Literature and Culture* 6, no. 2 (June 2004). doi:10.7771/1481-4374.1232.

Snell, Marilyn Berlin. "Jamaica Kincaid Hates Happy Endings." *Mother Jones*, September/October 1997. http://www.motherjones.com/politics/1997/09/jamaica-kincaid-hates-happy-endings.

Sollors, Werner, ed. *Multilingual America: Transnationalism, Ethnicity, and the Languages of American Literature*. New York: New York University Press, 1998.

Sommer, Doris. *Proceed with Caution, When Engaged by Minority Writing in the Americas*. Cambridge, MA: Harvard University Press, 1999.

Spivak, Gayatri Chakravorty. *An Aesthetic Education in the Era of Globalization*. Cambridge, MA: Harvard University Press, 2012.

——. *Death of a Discipline*. New York: Columbia University Press, 2003.

Su, John J. "Refiguring National Character: The Remains of the British Estate Novel." *Modern Fiction Studies* 48, no. 3 (Fall 2002): 552–80.

Suter, Rebecca. *The Japanization of Modernity: Murakami Haruki Between Japan and the United States*. Cambridge, MA: Harvard University Press, 2008.

Thirwell, Adam, *The Delighted States: A Book of Novels, Romances, & Their Unknown Translators, Containing Ten Languages, Set on Four Continents, & Accompanied by Maps, Portraits, Squiggles, Illustrations, & a Variety of Helpful Indexes*. New York: Picador, 2010.

——. *Kapow!* London: Visual Editions, 2012.

——, ed. "Multiples." *McSweeney's Quarterly Concern* 42 (January 2013).

——. *Multiples: An Anthology of Stories in an Assortment of Languages and Literary Styles*. London: Portobello, 2013.

Thornber, Karen. *Empire of Texts in Motion: Chinese, Korean, and Taiwanese Transculturations of Japanese Literature*. Cambridge, MA: Harvard University Asia Center, 2009.

Toker, Emily Brown Coolidge. "What Makes a Native Speaker? Nativeness, Ownership, and Global Englishes." *Minnesota Review* 78, no. 1 (2012): 113–29.

Toury, Gideon. *Descriptive Translation Studies and Beyond*. Amsterdam: J. Benjamins, 1995.

Türkkan, Sevinç. "Orhan Pamuk's *Kara Kitap* [The black book]: A Double Life in English." In *Global Perspectives on Orhan Pamuk: Existentialism and Politics*, ed. Mehnaz M. Afridi and David M. Buyze, 159–77. New York: Palgrave, 2012.

Turner, Henry. "Toward an Analysis of the Corporate Ego: The Case of Richard Hakluyt." *Differences: A Journal of Feminist Cultural Studies* 20, nos. 2 and 3 (2009): 103–46.

van der Vlies, Andrew. *South African Textual Cultures: White, Black, Read All Over*. Manchester, U.K.: Manchester University Press, 2007.

Venuti, Lawrence. "How to Read a Translation." *Words Without Borders: The Online Magazine for International Literature*, July 2004. http://wordswithoutborders.org/article/how-to-read-a-translation.

——. *The Scandals of Translation*. London: Routledge, 1998.

——. *The Translator's Invisibility: A History of Translation*, 2nd ed. New York: Routledge, 2008.

Volodine, Antoine. "Écrire en français une littérature étrangère." *Chaoïd*, no. 6 (Autumn–Winter 2002): 52–58.

Waldman, Amy. *The Submission*. New York: Farrar, Straus and Giroux, 2011.

Walkowitz, Rebecca L. "Comparison Literature." *New Literary History* 40 (2009): 567–82.

——. *Cosmopolitan Style: Modernism Beyond the Nation*. New York: Columbia University Press, 2006.

——. "The Location of Literature: The Transnational Book and the Migrant Writer." *Contemporary Literature* 47, no. 4 (Winter 2006): 527–45.

——. "Translating the Untranslatable: An Interview with Barbara Cassin." *Public Books*, June 15, 2014. http://www.publicbooks.org/interviews/translating-the-untranslatable-an-interview-with-barbara-cassin.

——. "Unimaginable Largeness: Kazuo Ishiguro, Translation, and the New World Literature." *Novel* 40, no. 3 (2007): 216–39.

Walter, David Michael. "Strange Attractions: Sibling Love Triangles in Faulkner's *Absalom, Absalom!* and Balzac's *La Fille aux yeux d'or*." *Comparative Literature Studies* 44, no. 4 (December 2007): 484–506.

Waltzer, Michael. "Comment." In *Multiculturalism: Examining the Politics of Recognition*, by Charles Taylor, ed. Amy Gutman, 99–104. Princeton, NJ: Princeton University Press, 1994.

Wampole, Christy. "Self-Begetting Theory: Volodine's Post-Exotic Aesthetics," presentation at the "Actuality and the Idea" conference, Princeton University, Princeton, NJ, May 11–12, 2012.

Wiggin, Bethany. *Novel Translations: The European Novel and the German Book, 1680–1730*. Ithaca, NY: Cornell University Press, 2011.

Williams, Holly. "Heads Up: The Childhood of Jesus." *Independent*, February 10, 2013. Accessed April 3, 2014, http://www.independent.co.uk/arts-entertainment/books/features/heads-up-the-childhood-of-jesus-8488433.html.

Wong, Cynthia F. "Kazuo Ishiguro's *The Remains of the Day*." *A Companion to the British and Irish Novel, 1945–2000*, ed. Brian W. Shaffer, 493–503. Oxford: Blackwell, 2005.

——. "Like Idealism Is to the Intellect: An Interview with Kazuo Ishiguro." In *Conversations with Kazuo Ishiguro*, ed. Brian W. Shaffer and Cynthia W. Wong, 174–88. Jackson: University of Mississippi Press, 2008.

Woods, Michelle. *Translating Milan Kundera*. Bristol, U.K.: Multilingual Matters, 2006.

Wyatt, Edward. "Harry Potter Book Sets Record in First Day." *New York Times*, July 18, 2005. http://www.nytimes.com/2005/07/18/books/18sale.html.

Xie, Ming. "Pound as Translator." In *The Cambridge Companion to Ezra Pound*, ed. Ira B. Nadel, 204–23. Cambridge: Cambridge University Press, 1999.

Yelin, Louise. "'Living State-Side': Caryl Phillips and the United States." *Moving Worlds: A Journal of Transcultural Writings* 7, no. 1 (2007): 85–102.

——. "Plural Selves: The Dispersion of the Autobiographical Subject in the Essays of Caryl Phillips." In *Caryl Phillips: Writing in the Key of Life*, ed. Bénédicte Ledent and Daria Tunca, 57–73. Amsterdam: Rodofi, 2012.

Yildiz, Yasemin. *Beyond the Mother Tongue: The Postmonolingual Condition*. New York: Fordham University Press, 2012.

Yoo, Hyun-Joo. "Interview with Young-hae Chang Heavy Industries." *dichtung-digital* 2 (2005). http://www.dichtung-digital.org/2005/2/Yoo/index-engl.htm.

Young, Robert. "The Postcolonial Comparative." *PMLA* 128, no. 3 (May 2013): 683–89.

Young-Hae Chang Heavy Industries, Young-Hae Chang and Marc Voge. *BUST DOWN THE DOORS!* 2000. Flash Animation. http://www.yhchang.com/BUST_DOWN_THE_DOORS!.html.

——. *CAMPBELL'S SOUP TOWN*. 2011. Flash Animation. http://www.yhchang.com/CAMPBELLS_SOUP_TOWN.html.

——. *DAKOTA*. 2002. Flash Animation. http://www.yhchang.com/DAKOTA.html.

——. *DOWN IN FUKUOKA WITH THE BELARUSIAN BLUES.* Gallery Hyundai, Seoul, South Korea, October 2010. Flash Animation.

——. *HONEYMOON IN BEPPU.* 2009. Flash Animation. http://www.yhchang.com/ HONEYMOON_IN_BEPPU.html.

——. *MORNING OF THE MONGOLOIDS.* 2007. Flash Animation. http://www.yh-chang.com/DAS_ERWACHEN_DER_MONGOLIDEN.html.

——. *PACIFIC LIMN.* 2013. E-book designed for iBooks. Kadist Art Foundation. Available for download through iTunes.

——. *RIVIERA.* 2002. Flash Animation. http://www.yhchang.com/RIVIERA.html.

——. *SAMSUNG.* 2000. Flash Animation. http://www.yhchang.com/SAMSUNG_ ENGLISH.html.

——. *TRAVELING TO UTOPIA.* 2005. Flash Animation. http://www.yhchang.com/ TRAVELING_TO_UTOPIA.html.

Zielinska-Elliott, Anna. Session on "Challenging the Hegemony of English: Translating Haruki Murakami's *1Q84* in Europe." Harvard University, October 2, 2012.

Zielinska-Elliott, Anna, and Mette Holm. "Two Moons over Europe: Translating Haruki Murakami's *1Q84.*" *AALITRA Review: A Journal of Literary Translation* 7 (November 2013): 5–19.

Zwicker, Jonathan. "Japan, 1850–1900." In *Novel*, vol. 1, ed. Franco Moretti, 509–20. Princeton, NJ: Princeton University Press, 2006.

INDEX

f denotes figure

Absalom, Absalom! (Faulkner), 5,
  250–251n26
absent readers/listeners, 167
absent structure, 96
accent, 54, 62, 188, 247n2
accented novels/accented writing, 37,
  40
accumulation, models of, 121, 124, 139
Achebe, Chinua, 13
Achterberg, Gerrit, 53
Adichie, Chimamanda Ngozi, 168, 169
Adiga, Aravind, 169
Adler, Mortimer, 172
Adorno, Theodor, 40
aesthetic of arrangement, 135, 136
aesthetic of bookishness, 230
aesthetic production, 61, 95
Against World Literature (Apter), 29
Alexander, Meena, 163, 164, 165, 177, 178
Alien Script (Mosley), 7, 8*f*, 9*f*, 10, 31
All about H. Hatterr (Desani), 35
Americanah (Adichie), 169

Anderson, Benedict, 25, 26, 27, 28–29,
  56, 83
anglophone novels, as more likely to
  appear in translation, 20
anglophone writers: as followers
  of born-translated fiction, not
  leaders, 10; as subject to conditions
  of literary globalization, 21; and
  translations for those located out-
  side largest publishing centers, 13, 21
Animal's People (Sinha), 169
Appiah, Anthony, 119
Apter, Emily, 29, 33, 34, 35, 42, 272n31
arrangement, aesthetic of, 135, 136
The Artist of the Floating World
  (Ishiguro), 95
The Art of Sleep (Young-Hae Chang
  Heavy Industries), 204*f*
Ashbery, John, 40
Aslam, Nadeem, 244
Asphodel Press, 240
Asymptote (journal), 23, 24, 239, 240
Atlas of the European Novel (Moretti),
  249n18

Atxaga, Bernardo, 13
audiences, role of in production, 66,
    83, 122, 162, 202
audio books, 247n2
Auerbach, Erich, 254n59
authorship, relationship of to
    nationhood, 26
The Autobiography of My Mother
    (Kincaid), 180

Bakhtin, M. M., 24, 25
"Ballade van de gasfitter" (Achterberg),
    53
bantering, 115, 116
Barthes, Roland, 41, 97, 100
Beckett, Samuel, 14–15, 34, 209, 220, 228
"Before the Law" (Kafka), 57
Bellos, David, 177, 199
Benjamin, Walter, 93, 113, 116, 119
Best, Stephen, 88
Bewes, Timothy, 124
big picture, 91
Bildung, 151
Bildungsroman, 144, 146
bilingualism, 36, 245, 289n24
biological literalism, 153
Black Swan Green (Mitchell), 123,
    145–147
Bleak House (Dickens), 86, 87, 121
"The Boarding House" (Joyce), 37
Bewes, Timothy, 88
Bolaño, Roberto, 16, 17–20, 18*f*, 19*f*, 23,
    238
The Bonfire of the Vanities (Wolfe), 157
book history, 22, 83, 84, 86, 236, 265n2,
    266n9
bookish books, 231, 232, 233, 287n49
bookishness, aesthetic of, 230
Book of Salt (Truong), 37
books: bookish books. *See* bookish
    books: citizenship of, 155–162;
    as counting as part of several
    traditions and media, 23

Borges, Jorge Luis, 5, 178, 209, 212, 228,
    229
born-digital artists, 226
born-digital literature, 3
born-digital texts/works, 3, 47, 48, 209,
    235, 249n17, 287n49
born-migrated works, 127
born translated, defined, 3
born-translated novels: as asking
    us to conceive of details more
    broadly and more variously, 90; as
    designed to obstruct traditional
    alignment among language,
    territory, and nation, 88–89; *Diary
    of a Bad Year* as, 51; as engaging
    in project of unforgetting, 23; as
    generating histories of literary
    production rooted in target,
    122; as implying intersection of
    methodologies, 83; as introducing
    new ontologies, 23; Ishiguro's
    fiction as, 94, 95; originality of, 83,
    85; as redirecting attention, 49; as
    repelling attention and impeding
    reader's mastery or knowledge of
    the work, 49
Botchorichvili, Elena, 13
Bourdieu, Pierre, 236
Boyhood (Coetzee), 57, 72
"Break It Down" (L. Davis), 168
Bridget Jones's Diary (Fielding), 285n25
*The Brief and Wondrous Life of Oscar
    Wao* (Díaz), 38
Bright Lights, Big City (McInerney), 168
Burgess, Anthony, 35, 41, 200
BUST DOWN THE DOORS! (Young-Hae
    Chang Heavy Industries), 40, 220*f*,
    221–225, 221*f*, 222*f*, 223*f*, 224*f*, 225*f*
Butler, Judith, 187, 277n6
Byatt, A. S., 244

Call It Sleep (Roth), 37
Calvino, Italo, 168

CAMPBELL'S SOUP TOWN (Young-Hae Chang Heavy Industries), 212

Camus, Albert, 168

Candide (Voltaire), 150, 174, 175

Cantiques des Plaines (Huston), 253n48

Cardenio, 250n24

Carroll, Noël, 99

Casanova, Pascale, 20, 259–260n106

Cassin, Barbara, 33–34, 35, 42

Cayley, John, 283n6

Cervantes, Miguel de, 4, 178

Cha, Theresa Hak Kyung, 35

Chang, Young-Hae, 203, 205, 208–211, 213–216, 219, 220, 222, 226–230, 233

character, according to Waldman, 158, 159, 160, 162

Chartier, Roger, 236

Chekhov, Anton, 98

Childhood of Jesus (Coetzee), 3, 4, 5, 22, 31, 51

Choose Your Own Adventure series, 168

circulation: as basis for contemporary anglophone production, 245; as built into narrative in *Mr. Potter*, 180; of Coetzee's book compared to of Rowling's book, 3; contemporary literature as incorporating, 236; desequencing of, 127; global circulation. *See* global circulation: Hamid's books as optimistic about, 198; histories of, 47, 65, 122, 126, 158; of *Imagined Communities*, 28; impediments to, 230; as incorporated within production, 231; individual voices as modified by, 72; as instantiating production, 128; as interfering with expressivity and parity, 125; as internal to production, 202; literary traditions as interrupted, transformed, and initiated by, 174; Murakami's incorporation of histories of into production,

15; planetary circulation, 47; as preceding and shaping production, 123; as producing citizenship of authors, 156; of *Robinson Crusoe*, 3; as shaping production, 51, 57, 61, 126, 179; as source of production, 64, 155; *Summertime* as building of into production, 80, 82; technologies of, 216, 219; tip toward, 24; as trailing production in dominant model of literary sequencing, 31; transnational circulation, 28, 83, 95

citizenship (of books), 155–162

citizen writer, 164

The City, The City (Miéville), 6, 7, 31

classification, 24, 56, 78, 80, 88, 89, 98, 124, 135, 136, 154, 156, 213, 219

A Clockwork Orange (Burgess), 35, 200

close reading, 46, 49, 83, 84, 85, 86, 88, 89, 90, 91, 120, 219, 265n2

close reading at a distance, 51, 83, 86, 87, 90, 265n3

Cloud Atlas (Mitchell), 143, 147, 152

Coetzee, J. M., 3, 4, 5, 6, 10, 13, 14, 22, 31, 40, 49, 50*f*, 51, 52*f*, 53–54, 68*f*, 77*f*, 79*f*, 90–91, 97–98, 140, 241

Cohen, Margaret, 258n95

Cohen, Sharmila, 236, 238, 244

collaboration, history of, 97, 98

collating, as device crucial to development of multistranded fiction, 123–124, 132, 143

Color Me English: Migration and Belonging Before and After 9/11 (Phillips), 120, 130

The Communist Manifesto (Marx), 2

comparative beginnings, 21, 54, 180, 201

comparative literature, as distinguished from national literature, 101

comparison: according to Coetzee, 72, 83; in Ishiguro's novels, 101, 109, 111, 112, 117, 119, 120

comparison literature, 127
Conrad, Joseph, 73, 252n38
Coombe, Rosemary, 26
copyright law, 2, 26, 224, 272n28
corporation, art of, 210–213
counting, as device crucial to
    development of multistranded
    fiction, 123, 124, 132, 138–139
critical detachment, 269n27
critical distance, 87
crosshatch worlds, 251n28
Culler, Jonathan, 27, 85, 88
cultural homogenization, 32, 93, 113
Cunningham, Michael, 273n1

Dagboek van een slecht jaar (Coetzee), 52f
DAKOTA (Young-Hae Chang Heavy
    Industries), 220
Damrosch, David, 172, 173–175, 177
Dancing in the Dark (Phillips), 130
Dante, Alighieri, 12
Davies, Peter Ho, 122, 126, 137
Davis, Lydia, 168, 241, 244
death of the author, 97
de Campos, Augusto, 237, 238
The Delighted States (Thirlwell), 231, 232
deowned literature, 29
Derrida, Jacques, 89
Desai, Kiran, 122, 126
Desani, G. V., 35
Devil in a Blue Dress (Mosley), 7, 10
Diary of a Bad Year (Coetzee), 50f, 51,
    52f, 53, 55, 66–72, 68f, 82, 84, 85, 140
Díaz, Junot, 35, 36–37, 38, 39, 40, 41, 42,
    243
Dickens, Charles, 121
Dictée (Cha), 35
diegetic translation, 31, 245
digital art, 2, 226, 230, 231
digital culture, 141, 226
digital fiction, 203
digital media, 21, 136, 202, 216, 219, 224,
    226, 227, 230, 247n1

digital narratives, 31, 202
digital production, 228, 230
digital technologies, 203, 208, 211, 212,
    217, 226, 227, 231
digital translation, 1
Dillon, George, 283n5
Dimock, Wai Chee, 44, 155, 156, 257n87
A Distant Shore (Phillips), 120, 122, 130,
    133–134, 138
distant reading, 86, 87, 120
distant reading up close, 87
Don Quixote (Cervantes), 2, 4, 5, 250n24
Dos Passos, John, 121
Dostoyevsky, Fyodor, 98
doubly translated, 144
DOWN IN FUKUOKA WITH THE
    BELARUSIAN BLUES (Young-Hae
    Chang Heavy Industries), 285n23
Dusklands (Coetzee), 57
DVDs, books as, 1

Easy Rawlins mysteries, 8
echo trope, 100, 120
Eggers, Dave, 235
electronic literature, 208, 209, 226,
    283n6
Eliot, T. S., 155
Elizabeth Costello (Coetzee), 55, 57–61,
    82
Embassytown (Miéville), 251n28
embedded voices, 142–155
The Emigrants (Sebald), 124
The Emily Dickinson Reader: An
    English-to-English Translation of
    Emily Dickinson's Complete Poems
    (Legault), 237, 241
En Attention Godot (Beckett), 228
English: according to Coetzee, 88; as
    foreign language, 137–142; as most
    frequent medium of translations,
    21; as world's dominant language,
    20
The English Patient (Ondaatje), 273n1

English-to-English translations, 237, 245

enlarged reading, 119

enlarged thinking, 113, 114, 115, 118

enumeration, 123, 125, 276n31

Esperanto, 250n25, 260–261n111

"The Ethics of Reading and the Question of the Novel" (McDonald), 83–84

Europanto, 260–261n111

Exercises de Style (Queneau), 288n12

expressivity: aesthetic of, 135, 136; association of with birthright, 173; as belonging to unique individuals who in turn belong to unique groups, 26; blocking of, 10; circulation as interfering with, 125; community as not premised on unique expressivity, 63; digital fiction as celebrating, 203; limits of individuality as model for, 66; multilingualism as enhancing speaker's range of, 201; typographical expressivity, 237; and world literature, 121, 122

external multilingualism, 41

Extravagant Strangers: A Literature of Belonging (Phillips), 129, 131

facing-page translation, 51, 204, 241, 245

fake originals, and feint translations, 213–219

The Fall (Camus), 168

Farah, Naruddin, 168

Faulkner, William, 250–251n26

feint translations, fake originals and, 213–219

Fielding, Helen, 220, 285n25

Finnegans Wake (Joyce), 34

first language, 2, 11, 12, 14, 15, 17, 20, 164, 165, 166, 179, 254n58, 278n11

Fitzgerald, F. Scott, 142

Flanery, Patrick Denman, 74

Flash Player, 203, 227

fluency: competing standards of, 175; failure of, 173; logic of, 63; mastery as, 85; near-native fluency, 280n38; oppositional fluency, 35; partial fluency. *See* partial fluency: principle of, 66; relative fluency. *See* relative fluency: trumping of, 262n120

Foer, Jonathan Safran, 231, 232–233, 235

fonts: multiple fonts doing work of multiple languages, 275–276n30; use of different fonts, 140, 141, 213, 218, 283n6

Foreigners: Three English Lives (Phillips), 120, 130

foreignness, 7, 39, 63, 85, 89, 142, 148, 149, 164, 165, 172, 173, 177, 178, 200, 202, 240, 260–261n111, 263–264n137

foreign poetry, 238

foreign words: contemporary novels use of, 62; Mitchell's use of, 139; as no longer distinguished typographically, 37

formats, of books, 1

Forster, E. M., 264n147

French-to-French translation, 288n12

Gagnon, Renée, 237

Gallop, Jane, 85, 88, 90, 91

geopolitical translation, 184

Ghostwritten (Mitchell), 122, 137–141, 143, 148

Gikandi, Simon, 96

Ginzburg, Natalia, 31

Gladwell, Malcolm, 187

global circulation, 16, 23, 32, 46, 48, 62, 66, 86, 94, 95, 120, 121, 124, 137, 141, 142, 143, 144, 170, 228, 230, 231, 243

global comparison, 100

global conversations, 128, 136, 169

global culture, 96

global demand, 3
global invisibility, 81
global novels, 18, 143, 176
global world literature, 274n6
Golumbia, David, 227
Google Translate, 1
Granta (journal), 137, 241
Grossman, Edith, 45, 178
Guide du loser amoureux (Díaz), 38, 39
Guillory, John, 85

Hack, Daniel, 86–87
Hamid, Mohsin, 22, 40, 167, 168, 169, 170, 171, 178, 179, 189–199, 200, 201, 202
Hamlet (Shakespeare), 5, 250–251n26
Handler, Richard, 25
Harry Potter and the Half-Blood Prince (Rowling), 3, 248–249n12, 248n10
Harry Potter novels (Rowling), 100
Hayles, N. Katherine, 210, 230, 231
Hayot, Eric, 259n102, 274n6, 284n16, 286n38
Heart of Darkness (Conrad), 73
heavy industries, 211
Heinemann series, 13
Heise, Ursula, 200
Helgesson, Stefan, 101, 256n74, 258–258n97, 258n96, 265n1, 267n15, 271–272n20, 272n30
Herodotus, 273n1
Higher Ground (Phillips), 130
Hispabooks, 255n71
Histories (Herodotus), 273n1
Hofmannsthal, Hugo von, 267n16
home, as not reducible to languages, 177
Homer, 64
HONEYMOON IN BEPPU (Young-Hae Chang Heavy Industries), 204, 205f, 213–214, 221, 233, 287n49
The Hours (Cunningham), 273n1
How to Get Filthy Rich in Rising Asia (Hamid), 190, 197–199

How to Read a Book (Adler), 172, 173
"How to Read a Translation" (Venuti), 172, 173
Hurston, Zora Neale, 264n147
Huston, Nancy, 14, 178
hybrid idiolect, 200
Hyundai Heavy Industries, 210

idiolect, 16, 33, 41, 44, 51, 62, 85, 145, 175, 181, 200, 216, 220, 229, 264n147
idiom, 11, 14, 17, 35, 37, 62, 64, 69, 70, 75, 86, 147, 149, 166, 171, 180, 188, 212, 213, 218, 222, 244, 267–268n18
Iliad (Homer), 64
Illuminations (Benjamin), 93
illustrations, 49, 85, 138, 208, 236, 241, 242, 243. *See also* visuals
imagined communities, 25, 26–27, 61, 91
Imagined Communities (Anderson), 27–28
"Index Translationum" (UNESCO), 248n9
inheritance, 125, 126, 148
The Inheritance of Loss (Desai), 122, 125, 126
Inner Workings (Coetzee), 54
interactive art, 228
interactive writing, 226
interactivity, 210, 225, 226, 227
intermedial translation, 31, 123, 170, 179, 184, 204
internal multilingualism, 21, 24, 41
In the Falling Snow (Phillips), 275n20
In the Heart of the Country (Coetzee), 13, 250n25, 266n8
intrinsic/extrinsic distinction, 265n2
intrinsic language acquisition, 278n15
intrinsic reading, 170, 172, 189
Ishiguro, Kazuo, 22, 94–120, 137, 270–271n7

Jaffe, Aaron, 265n3
Joyce, James, 35, 36, 37, 57, 146, 157, 159, 160, 167, 200, 264n147

Kacandes, Irene, 168, 279n19
Kaempfer's Japan (Kaempfer), 150–151
Kafka, Franz, 40, 57, 243
Kaminka, Ika, 253–254n54
Kapllani, Gazmend, 12
Kapow! (Thirlwell), 231, 235
Kermode, Frank, 103
Kincaid, Jamaica, 21, 22, 40, 163, 167, 169, 170, 171, 178, 179–189, 190, 200, 201, 202
Kindle editions, 1
King Rat (Miéville), 251n28
Kingston, Maxine Hong, 137
Kipling, Rudyard, 129
Kundera, Milan, 13, 14
Kunstlerroman, 146
Kureishi, Hanif, 137
Kurosawa, Akira, 214

Laat me nooit alleen (*Never Let Me Go*) (Ishiguro), 106f
Landow, George, 226, 228
language dominance, 254n58
languages: association of with birthplace, 166; books appearing in multiple languages, 1–2; first language. *See* first language: homes as not reducible to, 177; mediating languages, 139; national languages. *See* national languages: native languages, 163, 164, 166, 167, 199; natural language acquisition, 278n15; novels that address readers competent in multiple languages, 170; second-language use, 11; source languages. *See* source languages: target languages. *See* target languages
largeness, 95, 116, 117, 118, 119, 120. *See also* unimaginable largeness
Lawrence, D. H., 55, 264n147
layout, 51, 70, 85
Leaving the Atocha Station (Lerner), 1, 40–41, 43

Lee, Chang-Rae, 137
Legault, Paul, 236, 237, 238, 244
Lennon, Brian, 32
Lennon, John, 141
Lerner, Ben, 1, 40, 41–42, 43, 243
Les mille automnes de Jacob de Zoet (Mitchell), 150
L'été de la vie (Coetzee), 76, 79f
Levine, Caroline, 31, 170
limited belonging, 129, 136
limited participation, 127–137
linguistic diversity, books as contributing to, 100
literary belonging, 25, 44, 129
literary history: Alexander as opening up, 164–165; balance of as tipping, 23–24; born-translated novel as paradigm for, 47; as folded into plot, 273n1; and logic of unique origin, 61; "Multiples" as template for, 48; national literary histories. *See* national literary histories: none without translation, 45; organization of, 23, 44; relationship of with political belonging, 55; translation as condition of, 216; translation as engine of, 5; translation as operating/functioning within as well as between, 19, 173, 212; translation as source of, 122; translation's effects on, 28; translation's role within, 172
literary modernism, 34, 229
literary ownership, 29
literary sequencing, 31, 259n102
literary traditions: as designed by Dimock, Puchner, and Ramazani, 44; as drawing from different sources, 124; as inaugurated in late eighteenth century, 12; Ishiguro's novels as part of several, 97; as regularly interrupted, transformed and initiated by circulation, 174; renovation of, 209

Liu, Lydia, 255n67
local references, contemporary novels use of, 62
Lolita (Nabokov), 12, 66, 221
Losing North (Huston), 14
Lukács, Georg, 262–263n121

Magarshack, David, 98
Magritte, 200
"Manifesto of the New Translation"(Cohen and Legault), 235, 236, 244
Manrique, Jaime, 12
A Map of Love (Soueif), 122, 123, 125–126
Maps (Farah), 168
Marcus, Sharon, 88, 118
Márquez, Gabriel García, 178
Mason, Theodore, 131
mastery, 49, 62, 85, 87, 165, 216
McDonald, Peter, 84, 99
McInerney, Jay, 168
McSweeney's, 235, 236, 237, 240
McSweeney's Quarterly, 235, 241
mechanical translation, 208
mediated editions, 144
metaphor, 19, 58, 59, 85, 116, 133, 171, 189
Midnight's Children (Rushdie), 35, 200
Miéville, China, 6, 7, 10, 14, 22, 30, 40
migration, 2, 5, 25, 28, 47, 61, 65, 70, 75, 122, 127, 128, 129, 130, 131, 133, 137, 208, 216, 228
Mill, John Stuart, 168
Miller, Joshua, 37, 119
minority groups, 125
minority rights, 125, 274n8
minority self-expression, 32
minor literature, 260–261n111
minor-to-major translation, 245
"The Misery and the Splendor of Translation" (Ortega y Gasset), 174
Mitchell, David, 21, 22, 40, 121, 122, 123, 126, 137–155, 156, 244

modernist fiction, 34, 264n147
Modern Language Association, 245
monolingual, testing definition of, 47
monolingual collectivity, 46
monolingualism, 32, 42, 75, 191, 200, 202, 245, 289n24
monolingual literacy, 171
monolingual paradigm, 277n1, 278n11
monolingual readers, 33, 139
Moore, Lorrie, 168
Moretti, Franco, 41, 86, 87, 120
MORNING OF THE MONGOLOIDS (Young-Hae Chang Heavy Industries), 214, 215f, 226, 229
Mosley, Walter, 6, 8f, 9f, 10, 14, 31
mother tongue, 54, 166, 199, 278n11
Moth Smoke (Hamid), 190
MP3s, 1
Mr. Potter (Kincaid), 163, 178, 179–189, 201
Mrs. Dalloway (Woolf), 5, 121, 250–251n26, 264n147, 273n1
multiculturalism, 28, 125, 159, 261n117
multicultural novel, 157, 161
Multilingual Anthology of American Literature, 239
multilingual collectives, 203–210
multilingual conversations, 139
multilingual idiolect, 200
multilingualism, 7, 15, 17, 21, 23, 24, 25, 35, 37, 40, 41, 44, 45, 53, 64, 85, 119, 140, 142, 152, 153, 163, 165, 178, 179, 194, 201, 202, 216, 222, 224, 229
multinational publishing, 31, 235
multiple instance or type artworks, 100
multiple national editions, 20
"Multiples" (Thirlwell), 31, 241, 244
multistranded fiction/multistranded novels, 121, 123, 127, 128, 273n1
Murakami, Haruki, 14–16
My Brother (Kincaid), 180

Nabokov, Vladimir, 12, 73, 209, 221, 228, 232, 252n38

"Narrate or Describe?" (Lukács), 262–263n121

narrating languages, 40–44

narrative apostrophe, 168

narrative structure, 4, 28, 85, 169

national languages, 2, 12, 21, 24, 25, 29, 31, 32, 54, 55, 62, 128, 163, 174, 220, 251–252n34, 283n5

national literary histories, 26, 29, 61, 86, 87

national literature, 5, 22, 30, 101, 153, 155, 177, 258n89

national traditions, 54, 211

nationhood, relationship of to authorship, 26

native competency, 22, 166

native languages, 163, 164, 166, 167, 199

native reader, 6, 47, 162, 163, 172, 181

native voice, 200

natural language acquisition, 278n15

The Nature of Blood (Phillips), 132, 133, 136

negative affect, 187

negative affiliation, 129

negative character, 179–189

negative knowledge, 187

negative representativeness, 170

Neruda, Pablo, 178

Never Let Me Go (Ishiguro), 95, 99, 101–112, 102*f*, 104*f*, 106*f*, 120

"Never Let Me Go" (song), 101, 107, 109, 111, 116

New Criticism, 172, 173, 269n28

A New World Order (Phillips), 128, 130, 131

The New Yorker, 37, 187

New York Review of Books (*NYRB*), 66–67

Ngũgĩ wa Thiong'o, 13

19 Ways of Looking at Wang Wei, 240

NIPPON (Young-Hae Chang Heavy Industries), 283n2, 283n6

Nocturnes (Ishiguro), 95

nonaggregate community, readers as, 165

noncomprehension, 166

nonprofit digital publishing, 240

non-translation studies, 31–39

not reading, 88, 265n3

novel-anthologies, 136–137

novels: as bounded containers and as contained, 94; as genre of many genres, 30; history of, 249n15; as most international genre, 2; as written for translation from the start, 3

Number9Dream (Mitchell), 140–142

Nunca me abandones (*Never Let Me Go*) (Ishiguro), 108*f*

Observations (Smellie), 150, 152

Ole luonani aina (*Never Let Me Go*) (Ishiguro), 110*f*

Ondaatje, Michael, 273n1

1Q84 (Murakami), 15

One Thousand and One Nights, 150, 174, 175, 199

open-ended series, 265n1

openness, 128, 238, 279n18

original editions, 53

Ortega y Gasset, José, 174

Orwell, George, 129

Oyono, Ferdinand, 13

PACIFIC LIMN (video), 287n49

Pacifico, Francesco, 241, 244

Pale Fire (Nabokov), 73

The Palm Wine Drinkard (Tutuola), 57, 280–281n41

Pamuk, Orhan, 16–17

paratext, 48, 49, 89, 138, 147, 152, 177, 197, 232, 244

parity, 121, 122, 125, 152

Parks, Tim, 31, 176

partial fluency, 30, 42, 43, 44, 62

particularist works, 32–33

Paz, Octavio, 240

Peace, David, 137

The People of Paper (Plascencia), 231, 235

Phillips, Caryl, 21, 122, 126, 127–137, 138, 156, 275n20

"Pierre Menard, Author of the *Quixote*" (Borges), 5

Pilgrim's Progress (Bunyan), 2, 5

Plainsong (Huston), 253n48

Plascencia, Salvador, 231, 233, 235, 286–287n45

plural selves, 275n21

Poe, Edgar Allan, 57

poet-translators, 237

political homogenization, 93, 113

Porter, Catherine, 244–245

Portobello Books, 241

Portrait of the Artist as a Young Man (Joyce), 35, 146, 167

possessive collectivism, 25–26, 27, 30, 55, 60, 61

postcolonial literature/fiction/novels, 34, 54, 169, 181, 184–185, 200, 201, 279–280n27

post-digital artworks, 231

post-digital fiction/works, 47, 202, 231, 233, 235, 287n46

Poster, Mark, 226

postmonolingual condition, 251n27

post-multicultural, 125

Pound, Ezra, 209, 220, 228, 229

preemptive translation, 11, 12, 13, 14

Premchand, 12

Pressman, Jessica, 208, 209, 230

production: aesthetic production, 61, 95; Bolaño's strategies of, 17; building of circulation into, 80, 82; circulation as incorporated within, 231; circulation as instantiating, 129; circulation as internal to, 224; circulation as preceding and shaping, 123; circulation as shaping, 51, 57, 61, 126, 179; circulation as source of, 64, 155; circulation as trailing of in dominant model of literature, 31; collaboration between writers and translators as extension of, 98; contemporary novels as incorporating translation into, 45; desequencing of, 127; in dominant models of literary sequencing, 31; effects of circulation on, 6; as integral to translation, 229; Ishiguro's novels as emphasizing influence of global circulation on, 95; reception activities as within, 127; role of audiences in, 66, 83, 122, 202; role of readers and translators in, 162; sources of, 30; thinking of largeness as prompting acts of, 119; translation as condition of, 4; translation as part of, 174; translation as source of, 233, 238; translation as species of, 14; translators as arguing for more robust account of, 178

proleptic translation, 145

Proust, Marcel, 78, 98–99, 250–251n26

Puchner, Martin, 44, 259n98, 259n99, 272n23

"The Pura Principle" (Díaz), 37

Pym, Anthony, 255n70

Pym, Barbara, 31

Queneau, Raymond, 288n12

Rainey, Lawrence, 265n3

Ram, Harsha, 119–120

Ramazani, Jahan, 44, 155, 156, 263–264n137

Rashomon (film), 214

reading: close reading. *See* close reading: close reading at a distance. *See* close reading at a distance:

in detail, 89; distant reading, 86, 87, 120; distant reading up close, 87; enlarged reading, 119; with the grain, 88; intrinsic reading, 170, 172, 189; strategies, 86, 90, 210, 287n49; surface reading, 88; suspicious reading, 88; symptomatic reading, 88, 118; in translation, 171–179, 188, 198, 216

reception: activities associated with, 127; as altering work, 24; approaching translation from perspective of, 42; books in print as indebted to, 230; of *Childhood of Jesus*, 5; of Coetzee's book compared to Rowling's book, 3; collaborative reception, 242; content of works as including, 136; as contributing to imagination of communities to which book belongs, 28; as distinguishing social itinerary of one version from another, 98; effects of global reception on meanings of national location, 128; effects of on citizenship of art, 161; Hack's interest in dynamics of, 87; histories of as adding dimension to question of character, 158; as producing citizenship of authors, 156; strategies for recovering histories of, 45; translation as augmenting work of art by assessment of, 244

Reid, Alastair, 178

relative fluency, 163–171, 179, 180, 189, 202

reluctant character, 189–199

The Reluctant Fundamentalist (Hamid), 178, 189–197, 199, 201

The Remains of the Day (Ishiguro), 95–96, 112–119

replication, 112

"Report to an Academy" (Kafka), 57

resident writer, 164

ridiculous, 115

Rings of Saturn (Sebald), 122

RIVIERA (Young-Hae Chang Heavy Industries), 221

Robinson Crusoe (Defoe), 2, 3, 248n8

Rogers, Gayle, 255n67, 258n95

Roth, Henry, 37

Rowling, J. K., 100, 249n13

Rushdie, Salman, 35, 200

sadness, commodification of, 286–287n45

Sakai, Naoki, 165, 166

sampling, as device crucial to development of multistranded fiction, 123, 124, 127, 132

SAMSUNG (Young-Hae Chang Heavy Industries), 207, 208, 221

Samsung Heavy Industries, 210

Sancho, Ignatius, 129

Saro-Wiwa, Ken, 35

Satrapi, Marjane, 252n38

Savage, Steve, 237

The Savage Detectives (Bolaño), 17–20, 18f, 19f

Schleiermacher, Friedrich, 12

Schor, Naomi, 89

Schulz, Bruno, 232, 233

Sebald, W. G., 122, 124, 126, 133

second-language use, 11

second-person fiction, 168

second-person narration/voice, 40, 47, 165, 167, 168–169, 171, 180, 186, 190, 194, 196, 198, 199, 200, 279n18, 279n19

Self Help (Moore), 168

self-translation, 15, 22, 45, 205, 228, 258n95

semi-belonging, 129

serial collective, 272n30

serial translation, 31, 139, 143, 245

Shafak, Elif, 12, 177

Shakespeare, William, 5, 69

Shell, Marc, 119
The Silent House (Pamuk), 16
simile, 189
simultaneous community, 55
singular artworks, 100
Sinha, Indra, 169
Siskind, Mariano, 273n2, 274n6, 274n10
slang, 19, 37, 62, 145, 147, 200
Slow Man (Coetzee), 55, 61–65, 82
small details, 89, 90
A Small Place (Kincaid), 188
Smellie, William, 150
Smith, Adam, 151
Smith, Zadie, 35, 137, 241, 273n1
Snow (Pamuk), 16
social categories, 158
Sollors, Werner, 119
Sommer, Doris, 32–33
The Sonnets: Translating and Rewriting Shakespeare (Legault and Cohen), 237, 241
Souief, Adhaf, 122, 126
sourced manuscripts, 144
source languages, 98, 139, 140, 146, 149, 151, 209
Sozaboy: A Novel in Rotten English (Saro-Wiwa), 35
speed, as characterizing contemporary novels' entrance into new markets, 2
Spitzer, Leo, 254n59
Srivastava, Dhanpat Rai, 13
Stein, Gertrude, 220
Stowe, Harriet Beecher, 57
The Street of Crocodiles (Schulz), 232
The Submission (Waldman), 122, 123, 156, 157–162
Summertime (Coetzee), 49, 55, 66, 72–82, 77f, 85, 90
surface reading, 88
suspicious reading, 88
symptomatic reading, 88, 118
synecdoche, 230, 280n29

Tan, Amy, 137
Tanner Lectures (Princeton University), 59
target: Americans imagining selves as, 201; art as, 161; born-translated novels as generating histories of literary production rooted in, 122; language as source sometimes, target sometimes, 139; in translation studies, 258–259n97; world literature as privileging, 30
target languages, 30, 98, 128, 139, 140, 141, 146, 148, 149, 152, 173, 178, 229, 239, 240
TEASER (Young-Hae Chang Heavy Industries), 285n23
Telephone (journal), 237, 238, 239, 240, 241
Telephone Books, 236, 237, 240
The Tempest (Shakespeare), 273n1
Thackeray, William Makepeace, 129
Their Eyes Were Watching God (Hurston), 264n147
Things Fall Apart (Achebe), 13
"The Thing Around Your Neck" (Adichie), 168
Thirlwell, Adam, 22, 31, 137, 231, 232, 233, 235, 241–244
This Is How You Lose Her (Díaz), 35, 38
Thornber, Karen, 258n95
The Thousand Autumns of Jacob de Zoet (Mitchell), 121, 147–155
tokens, 99, 105, 109, 111
Toker, Emily Brown Coolidge, 278n13
Tolstoy, Leo, 71, 98
translatability, 94, 101, 208, 209, 218, 221, 226, 238, 272n31
translatese, 175, 176, 178, 280–281n41
translation: according to Coetzee, 53, 76; ban on, 261n117; Benjamin's sense of, 113; Coetzee as emphasizing translation as source, structure, and outcome, 75; as

condition of literary history, 216; contemporary novels as having incorporated translation into production, 45; effects of on literary history, 28; *Elizabeth Costello*'s approach to, 61, 66; as engine rather than caboose of literary history, 5; as functioning within as well as between literary histories, 173, 212; as index of dominance, 259–260n106; as integral to production, 229; as leading to cultural and political homogenization, 93; Murakami's use of as method of composition, 14–16; no literary history without, 45; as often built into form of novels, 14; as operating inside and not only between languages, 166; as operating within as well as between, 19; paradox of, 6; as part of literature's second act, 29; of poetry, 238; preemptive translation, 11, 12, 13, 14; reading in, 171–179, 198; role of literary history within, 172; as seeding production, 45; as shaping narrative structure of contemporary novel, 4; *Slow Man*'s approach to, 61, 66; as source of literary history, 122; as source of production, 233, 238; unforgetting translation, 23; untranslated, 140. *See also* untranslatable/untranslatability: visual and aural culture of, 209; writers as mitigating need for by writing in dominant language, 11
Translation (Cayley), 283n6
translationese, 175, 280–281n41
translation studies, 83, 164
The Translation Zone (Apter), 29
translatorese, 175, 280–281n41
translators, power of, 97
The Translator's Invisibility (Venuti), 172

translingual writing, 12
transnational activities, 122
transnational book history, 86
transnational circulation, 28, 83, 95
transnational collectivities, 80
transnational communities, 28, 72
transnational literary marketplace, 58
transnational literary movements, 17
transnational literary studies, 86, 87
transnational novels, 72, 257n87
transnational origins: of national literatures, 155; of world literature, 61
transnational poetics, 155
traveling characters, 122, 143
TRAVELING TO UTOPIA: WITH A BRIEF HISTORY OF TECHNOLOGY (Young-Hae Chang Heavy Industries), 205, 206*f*, 216, 217, 218, 219, 226, 229, 233
Tree of Codes (Foer), 231, 232, 233, 235, 241
Triumph of the Will (movie), 126
Truong, Monique, 37, 137
Turner, Henry, 211
Tutuola, Amos, 280–281n41
types, 99
typography, 10, 49, 84, 85, 123, 140, 205, 240, 262n120, 287n46

Ulysses (Joyce), 35, 57, 66, 81, 157, 159, 160, 264n147
The Unconsoled (Ishiguro), 95
Une vie de boy (Oyono), 13
unforgetting translation, 23
unimaginable largeness, 95–96, 112–113, 115
uniqueness, in Ishiguro's novels, 112, 120
untranslatable/untranslatability, 31, 32, 33, 34, 42, 44, 62, 218, 261n117, 261n118, 262n120, 267–268n18
U.S.A. (Dos Passos), 121

Venuti, Lawrence, 172–173, 175, 176, 178

Vila-Matas, Enrique, 243
visual culture, 204, 209, 214, 221, 230
Visual Editions, 235, 240
visual media, 10, 128
visuals, 17, 19, 48, 49, 51, 140, 146, 147, 213, 217, 218, 224, 229, 235, 236, 238, 240, 287n49
visual writing, 6
Vlies, Andrew van der, 54
Vocabulaire européen des philosophies (Cassin), 33
vocabularies, new, 44–45
Voge, Marc, 203, 205, 208–211, 213–216, 219, 220, 222, 226–230, 233
voices: as artifacts (embedded), 142–155; native voice, 200; restriction of, 124; second-person voice. *See* second-person narration/voice
Voltaire, 174

Waiting for the Barbarians (Coetzee), 97
Waldman, Amy, 21, 22, 122, 123, 126, 156, 158, 159, 160, 161
Warhol, Andy, 212
Watashi o hanasanaide (*Never Let Me Go*) (Ishiguro), 102f
Waters, Sarah, 137
The Wealth of Nations (A. Smith), 151, 152
Wei, Wang, 240
Weinberger, Eliot, 240
The Welsh Girl (Davies), 122, 125, 126
White Teeth (Z. Smith), 35, 273n1
White Tiger (Adiga), 169

White Writing (Coetzee), 53
Wieniewska, Celina, 232
Williams, Bert, 130, 132
"Wingless" (Kincaid), 181
Winterson, Jeannette, 137
Wolf, Uljana, 237
Woolf, Virginia, 121, 250–251n26, 264n147
Words Without Borders (periodical), 239, 240
world literature: collaboration and, 98; *Elizabeth Costello* as classic example of, 57–58; Ishiguro's novels as functioning as, 97; making of, 49–55; as referring to network/system/republic/problem, 29; *The Reluctant Fundamentalist* as mimetic of, 194; studies of as requiring comparison of close readings, 120
world-shaped novels, 47, 121–127, 162
writing technologies, 69
written as translations, 4
written for translation, 3, 4, 93
written from translation, 4
written languages, as diverging from spoken languages, 11, 12

Yildiz, Yasemin, 40, 251n27, 278n11
Young, Robert, 169, 184
Young-Hae Chang Heavy Industries, 22, 31, 40, 203–233, 207f, 235, 240
Youth (Coetzee), 72

Zambra, Alejandro, 243

CPSIA information can be obtained
at www.ICGtesting.com
Printed in the USA
LVOW12s1139030717

540185LV00003B/20/P